Wolde-Selassie Abbute

Gumuz and Highland Resettlers

D1618243

Göttinger Studien zur Ethnologie

Herausgeber:
Institut für Ethnologie
der Universität Göttingen

Redaktion:
Ulrich Braukämper und
Brigitta Hauser-Schäublin

Band 12

LIT

Wolde-Selassie Abbute

Gumuz and Highland Resettlers

Differing strategies of livelihood and ethnic relations
in Metekel, Northwestern Ethiopia

LIT

Gedruckt auf alterungsbeständigem Werkdruckpapier entsprechend
ANSI Z3948   DIN ISO 9706

Cover Picture: Gumuz and resettlers in a Metekel market
Photo: Wolde-Selassie Abbute

Bibliographic information published by Die Deutsche Bibliothek
Die Deutsche Bibliothek lists this publication in the Deutsche
Nationalbibliografie; detailed bibliographic data are available in the
Internet at http://dnb.ddb.de.

ISBN 3-8258-7819-8
Zugl.: Göttingen, Univ., Diss., 2002

© LIT VERLAG Münster   2004
Grevener Str./Fresnostr. 2   48159 Münster
Tel. 0251-23 50 91   Fax 0251-23 19 72
e-Mail: lit@lit-verlag.de   http://www.lit-verlag.de

Distributed in North America by:

Transaction Publishers
New Brunswick (U.S.A.) and London (U.K.)

Transaction Publishers
Rutgers University
35 Berrue Circle
Piscataway, NJ 08854

Tel.: (732) 445 - 2280
Fax: (732) 445 - 3138
for orders (U. S. only):
toll free (888) 999 - 6778

CONTENTS

VI

VII

List of Maps

List of Figures

List of Tables

Acronyms and Abbreviations

AAU	Addis Ababa University
ARTF	Agricultural Research Task Force
BEAI	Burcz-Endalama Agro-Industry
BGNRS	Benishangul-Gumuz National Regional State
BRAI	Bengez River Agro-Industry
CISP	Comitato Internazionale per lo Sviluppo dei Popoli (International Committee for the Development of Peoples)
CPAR	Canadian Physicians for Aid and Relief
CSA	Central Statistical Authority
DA	Development Agent
DFID	Department for International Development
DPPD	Disaster Prevention and Preparedness Department
EARO-PRC	Ethiopian Agricultural Organisation, Pawe Research Centre
E.C.	Ethiopian Calendar
EDSSO	Economic Development and Social Services Office
EPA	Environmental Protection Authority
EPRDF	Ethiopian Peoples' Revolutionary Democratic Front
EPRP	Ethiopian Peoples' Revolutionary Party
FAO	Food and Agricultural Organisation
FDRE	Federal Democratic Republic of Ethiopia
IDR	Institute of Development Research
IDS	Institute of Development Studies
L	Left Side of Beles River
LUPT	Land Use Planning Team
m.a.s.l.	Meters Above Sea Level
MoA	Ministry of Agriculture
MOAD	Mandura Organic Agricultural Development
MPO	Metekel Planning Office
MZAD	Metekel Zonal Agricultural Department
MZCA	Metekel Zonal Council Archive
n.d.	No Date
NGO	Non-Governmental Organisation
n.s.	Not Stated
NSCRP	National Study Committee of Receiving Provinces
PHCC	Population and Housing Census Commission
ONCCP	Office of the National Committee for Central Planning
PA	Peasant Association

PDPU	Population and Development Planning Unit
PHCC	Population and Housing Census Commission
PHCE	Population and Housing Census of Ethiopia
R	Right Side of Beles River
RDS	Right Down-Side of Beles River
RRC	Relief and Rehabilitation Commission
RUS	Right Up-Side of Beles River
SAERP	Sustainable Agriculture and Environmental Rehabilitation Program
TBP	Tana Beles Project
UNECA	United Nations Economic Commission for Africa
WARDIS	Woreda Agriculture and Rural Development Integrated Services
NWZADO	North-Western Zonal Agricultural Development Office
WPE	Workers' Party of Ethiopia
ZAI	Zimbeha Agro-Industry

Glossary of Local Terms[1]

Amicha	Affinal kinship. It also refers to festive labour mobilised among affinal kin (mainly a labour support called from the son-in-law by his father-in-law).
Angiya (Gum.)	Sister-exchange marriage
Araqe	Locally distilled alcoholic drink
Ato	Mr.
Awraja	Provincial administrative structure (formerly bridging the *woreda* and the Regional administrations)
Balambaras	'Commander of the citadel', honorary title originally equivalent to a Lieutenant-Colonel military rank
Balinjeera	A close friend. It also refers to a festive labour mobilised based on intimate friendship
Bega (Gum.)	An emic ethnic reference to the members of Gumuz
Birr	Ethiopian currency unit
Borde	Local brew (slightly thicker)
Bu'illa (Kam.)	Best quality food prepared from *enset* plant
Daabbo	Normal locally prepared bread
Dabo/Jigi	Festive labour mobilised preparing abundant food and drinks
Dega	Cold to very cold climatic area usually at a high altitude above 2400 m.
Derg	Military Committee that ruled Ethiopia from 1975 to 1991
Elfinna-qaso	Festive labour mobilised based on intimate friendship
Enset	Banana-like plant, staple food of many south-western Ethiopians (*Ensete ventricosum*)
Ettimissgideya (Gum.)	A spirit-medium person solely responsible for ritual performance of *miss-gideya,* spirit believed to have influence in the overall daily lives of the village community
Fitawirari	'Commander of the vanguard', honorary title originally equivalent to a major-general military rank
Fuga (Kam.)	marginalised traditional pottery handicraftsmen

---

[1] In the list, terms in local languages other than Amharic are indicated in respective languages abbreviated and placed inside brackets. In the abbreviations, (*Gum.*) refers to Gumuz, (*Kam.*) refers to Kambaata, (*Had.*) refers to Hadiyya, and (*Oro.*) refers to Oromo languages. Amharic terms are transcribed according to their local pronunciation.

XIII

Iddir/Qire	Multi-purpose community institution mainly meant for burial and mourning of the dead
Iddir-dagna	Leader of an *iddir*
Inga (Gum.)	Stiff porridge usually prepared from sorghum, finger millet, and maize
Injera	A round pancake-type staple food of many Ethiopians
Iquub	Local money pooling institution, rotating the sum among the members weekly, bi-weekly, and monthly
Ittemoqqota (Gum.)	Traditional practitioner of bodily scars (*moqqota*)
Gabare	A farmer
Gafia (Gum.)	A magico-religious and traditional medicine person who plays a multiple role as a medium between the *missa* and the community
Ganza (Gum.)	Elders
Gola (Gum.)	A higher level spirit-medium person above the *gafia*
Kancha (Gum.)	Cutting and clearing stage activities in the temporal successive phases of shifting cultivation
Kebele	A basic unit of local administrative structure bridging the people at the grassroots level and the higher *woreda* administrative organ
Keya (Gum.)	Local brew
Kirstinna	Baptism. It also refers to the feast organised on the occasion of baptism of babies especially among the followers of Orthodox Christianity.
Kirstinna abbaat	God-parenthood
Kuta-gatam sefera	Planned conventional resettlement covering an entire area
Limmaano	Supportive full-time labour extended to the weaker members in the village based on the latter's dire request (begging)
Mahber	Religious festive association formed in the name of a selected Saint organised monthly rotating among members (mainly by followers of Orthodox religion)
Mangima (Gum.)	Traditional institution of conflict resolution
Mareet maagaazaat	Tenancy Arrangement (sharecropping and renting land)
Matte	Newcomer (connoting alien)
Mehe	Harvest of main season
Meqennet	Cloth waist-band (belt) worn by women

Michu (Oro.)	An institution through which friendship bonds are established mainly by performing traditionally prescribed rituals (the term is said to have etymological roots in Oromo/Oromiffa – the language)
Mihantsuquma	Gathering wild forest foods
Missa (Gum.)	Multi-spirits believed in the traditional belief system
Mittiha (Gum.)	A pejorative generic term used by the Gumuz to refer the highlanders for the latter's alleged cruelty and brutality, signalling mistrust and hatred
Moqqota (Gum.)	Bodily scarification
Moqqota'ea (Gum.)	Scars on the lower arms
Moqqotaiila (Gum.)	Scars on the abdomen
Moqqotbongua (Gum.)	Scars on the back
Moqqotlissa (Gum.)	Scars on the cheeks
Moqqotqo'ea (Gum.)	Scars on the upper arms
Qaadi	Religious leader responsible for the affairs of Muslims in the villages
Qaareza	Stretcher
Qoomate-dabo	A *dabo* type that do not last full day and have no evening feast
Qolla	Hot to warm climatic area usually at a low altitude below 1600 m
Qollegna	Lowlander
Qotcho	Standard food prepared from *enset* plant and staple diet for many south-west Ethiopian population
Safaari	State-sponsored resettlers
Seelo (Kam.)	Slightly thicker local brew (equivalent to *borde* in Amharic)
Seera (Kam. & Had.)	An equivalent of *iddir* among the Kambaata and Hadiyya as well as the legal framework and insurance of local community
Senbete	Religious association formed by the followers of Orthodox religion where *daabbo* and *tella* are prepared rotating among members and consumed inside a compound of the church together with the weak and destitute
Shanqilla	A derogative generic term used by the highlanders to refer the Gumuz for their darker pigmentation, signalling contempt and inferior status
Shifta	Bandits

Shuwa (Gum.)	An ascription used by the Gumuz as a categorical reference to their neighbouring highlanders
Sigsega sefera	Integrated resettlement filling into spaces inside an already existing settlements
Tella	Local brew
Tazkar	Memorial feast organised as a remembrance for the dead
Tuut Abbat	Fictive parenthood
Waari/Maarfeja	Supportive labour extended to weaker members of the village at early hours in the morning before going to the regular daily tasks in the fields
Weizerit (W/t)	Miss
Weizero (W/ro)	Mrs.
Wodaajinet	Mutual bond-friendship
Woina-daga	Tepid to cool climatic area usually at a mid altitude between below 1600m to 2400 m
Wonfel/Qaanja	Pooled reciprocal labour formed among voluntary group members
Woreda	District administrative structure (between *kebele* and *zone*)
Wot	Spiced stew or sauce usually served with *injera*
Yamba (Gum.)	A supreme deity traditionally believed to be above *missa*
Yelimat qan	A day of development activities in the villages
Yetsidat qan	A day of sanitation activities
Yeafer iddir	*Iddir* for burial and mourning
Yebalinjeera iddir	*Iddir* formed among close friends
Yebeetsira iddir	*Iddir* for house construction
Yekebt iddir	*Iddir* meant for mutual support upon death of members' cattle
Yeqaareeza iddir	Stretcher *iddir* for transporting the sick to health centres
Yetesfa-sira qan	'Hope work day' where voluntary free labour is extended to weaker members in the villages mostly by followers of Protestant and Catholic Christianity
Yezemed iddir	*Iddir* formed among close relatives (kinship members)

Zeka (Zakat)	*Zakat* (the alms-tax, one of the principal obligations of Islam prescribed for Muslims to pay certain percentage of one's possession to support their weak members)
Zellan	Any nomadic cattle-keeping people
Zone	An administrative structure below a Federal State and above a *woreda*

Acknowledgements

Many people, more than can be mentioned, contributed in various ways to the completion of this study to all of whom I am most grateful. I apologise if anyone feels that his/her name should have been mentioned. I express my sincere gratitude to Prof. Dr. Ulrich Braukämper, my main advisor, for his guidance and insightful comments extended throughout my research, including his visit to my field research site; Prof. Dr. Brigitta Benzing for her guidance and determined facilitation throughout my research; Prof. Dr. Hans Meliczek for his advice and comments extended primarily on the socio-economic aspects of my research, in particular on population resettlement; Dr. Taddese Berisso for his advice and facilitation during my field research; *Ato* Dessalegn Rahmato for his critical comments; Mr. Paolo Dieci for his long-time encouragement and support; and Mr. Kim Dammers (native English speaker and doctoral candidate in Ethnology) for his generous support in proof-reading my thesis and the stimulating arguments during our subsequent discussions.

I am very grateful to Prof. Wendy James (University of Oxford) for her comments and keen interest in my research on the Gumuz, sending me a number of her publications including her unpublished original manuscript from the days of her fieldwork in the 1970s among the Gumuz to the south of Abbay River; Prof. Dr. Thayer Scudder (California Institute of Technology) for his comments and guidance, reading my early research reports and sending me his recent publications; Prof. Dr. Günther Schlee (Max Planck Institute for Social Anthropology) for his comments especially on ethnic identity, conflicts and integration (part four); Prof. Christopher McDowell (University of Wollongong), Prof. Antonio Palmisano (University of Trieste), and Mr. Luca Russo (Development Researchers` Network, Rome) for their comments and guidance at the initial stage of my research; Dr. Regina Birner for her comments on my early report on the indigenous knowledge and resource management systems of the Gumuz; and my friend Dereje Feyissa, for his comments, stimulating discussions, and exchanging relevant literature. Additionally, I thank Prof. Dr. Michael M. Cernea, (The World Bank), Prof. Dr. James C. McCann (Boston University), and Prof. Eisei Kurimoto (Osaka University) for providing literature and their keen interest in my research. I also thank my friend Dr. Solomon Assefa for his encouragement and moral support, motivating my study feelings.

I owe my gratitude to all the Gumuz and resettler informants, without whose patience, hospitality, and cooperation this study would not have been made possible; all CISP staff for their constant support and facilitation towards the realisation of this study; the local expert staff and administrators in the Metekel Zone and Pawe Special *Woreda*, including the "development agents" in all *Kebele* of the latter; and my research assistants Wubalta Enno, Belete Gawo, *W/t* Asham Mohammed, and Sebsibe Alamirew for their facilitation, patience, and contribution at different stages of my fieldwork – the first three assisted my research on the Gumuz and the latter on the resettlers.

My deepest gratitude goes to my parents *W/ro* Eraaye Anniito, *Ato* Lambiye Deboch, and my brothers and sister for their encouragement and support throughout my studies. It is to my parents that I dedicate this study.

I express my thanks to DAAD (*Deutscher Akademischer Austauschdienst*/German Academic Exchange Service) for the financial support for my Ph.D study both in Ethiopia and Germany. I also thank all the staff of the Institute of Ethnology, in particular the librarians and the secretary, for facilitating a pleasant research environment; my fellow students, in particular those who participated in my presentations in the weekly colloquia, for their insightful feedback; and to all my personal friends for creating a pleasant living and study atmosphere during my stay in Germany.

Wolde-Selassie Abbute

Preface

My first encounter with the state-sponsored resettlers of the 1980s and the autochthonous Gumuz in the Beles Valley and its environs goes back to June 1988 – a time when I was employed as a "social researcher" in an international NGO called CISP engaged in the rehabilitation of the resettlers. I lived and worked there until the EPRDF forces controlled the area on March 2, 1991 (*Yekatit* 23, 1983 E.C.). In 1988, the total resettler population of the resettlement scheme reached its highest level of 82,106 and was relocated in 48 villages. The whole Pawe resettlement program area was further divided into six *woreda* administrations under the direct authority of the head of the Workers' Party of Ethiopia (WPE) in Addis Ababa.

In the project, my main task was to conduct a socio-economic and cultural survey of all the villages concerning the resettlers' adaptations to life in a new social and physical setting. The results of the regular assessments were intended for planning as well as monitoring and evaluation of the project activities. In order to freely travel inside the scheme area and conduct interviews with the resettlers and the village authorities, I was granted special written permission from the local party office. These early days were a time when I was given a chance to come into contact with the resettlers. Then, from my own direct observation and the personal accounts of the informants during the interviews, I began learning and understanding their indescribable sufferings in adapting to the new social and physical environments of the malaria-infested lowlands of the Beles Valley. Similarly, I also came into contact for the first time with the autochthonous Gumuz who were pushed out of the resettlement scheme area, residing along its environs. In fact, my early encounters with the resettlers and Gumuz paved the genesis for of this study and triggered my interest that has been progressively strengthened through my subsequent research activities in the area. Throughout my extended stay in the field since 1988, I encountered several striking instances and experiences, some of which are recounted below.

Except on Sundays, which is a local market day, resettlers' village-to-village travel was possible only with pass letters obtained from village authorities. A Hadiyya woman from village L10 who came to a local market in L14 heard of the death of her nephew in village L21 and suddenly went there in mourning without a pass letter. The next morning, returning to her village she was stopped at the checkpoint at village L14 and asked to show her pass letter. Apart from her lack of the pass letter, she was not able to communicate with the guards because they spoke Amharic and had been recruited from the resettlers of North Shoa. She was detained and was weeping, uttering repeatedly *"I-wa'a!"* "My god!" By coincidence, I was also stopped at the same checkpoint and saw the woman. The guards were not able to understand what she was uttering. Since I speak her language, I translated and explained to the guards all about her case, and she was released. Then, I gave her a lift and brought her back to her village. Her reaction to my assistance, speaking to her in Haddiyya language, was full of blessings.

Two of my late resettler informants who were in ill health at the time of interview in 1988 (and later died) explained their painful experiences. The first informant was a resident of village L6 and explained that he was severely beaten by the village militia under the orders of the tyrant party cadres and left in an open prison overnight, which, he complained, had caused his partial paralysis. The allegations for his punishment, he stated, were related to an epidemic that occurred in the village and claimed twenty-nine lives in a single day. Bewildered by the shocking incidents, all the village government employees, including the party cadres, ran away to the administrative centre at Pawe (around 15 kilometres away). In such a situation when the village resettlers were shaken by the epidemic, foreigners said to be data assessors for project formulation visited the disturbed population. Then, this young resettler explained to them about the situation. After a few days, the village cadres returned and accused him of giving sensitive secrets to foreigners and ruthlessly punished him as a result. The second informant was a resident of village R4 who stated that he was severely beaten by the village militia under the orders of the tyrant party cadres and left in custody outside overnight. He explained that this had caused him to be partially paralysed. His punishment followed the visit to the area by a higher party official from Gojjam. In a public meeting of the resettlers on the occasion of the visit of the party official, he spoke in public and said "neglecting the excessive death of many resettlers daily due to malaria and other epidemics, the resettlement authorities have rather given better concern and attention to the livestock (oxen brought to the area) by taking them out of the area after being affected by trypanosomiasis." Later, the same evening, he sustained the stated punishment for openly expressing the facts, which, according to the cadres, constituted severe sabotage on the tireless care and concern of the state and its resettlement program.

Orphanages were established in some villages at central locations for the children who had lost their parents. It was quite common to hear stories of entire families having died; a lonely mother who lost all her family members; a lonely father who lost all his family members; a lonely family whose members do not know the whereabouts of their other family members dispersed during the recruitment and transportation process of the program. In their weakened state, the death of resettlers was very common. The dead were buried without a proper ritual meant for the salvation of the soul and without attendant mourners. The cadres allowed only four members from the agricultural cooperative group to dig a grave and bury the dead. For instance, I personally observed and witnessed a similar burial in village L1. After digging a grave in the nearby graveyard, the four men came to the house of a deceased husband and took out the corpse attended only by his very weak wife. I observed her attempting to weep but with no tears due to her weakened state, following the four men carrying the corpse on a bamboo stretcher to the graveyard. These already weakened group members usually could not dig graves of proper depth, and cases of corpses being eaten by wild animals were reported. Moreover, it was stated that after digging a grave, the diggers usually checked the entire village to find out other dead persons so as to bury them together in the same grave. Informants stressed that burial of a person alone in a single proper grave was even considered a privilege. The cadres forbade proper mourning for the dead. Resettlers were observed wearing sewn sacks as skirts and shorts. However, especially later the Tana-Beles Project and the RRC provided a significant amount of relief aid of food, clothing, utensils, and farm tools to the resettlers. Still, it was quite common to observe most of this being sold despite the efforts of the authorities monitoring.

In 1996 and 1997, I conducted one year of fieldwork in Pawe for my M.A. thesis in three rounds. Here, I noted myself being under strong observation by the resettlers – "the observer observed." During the introductory meetings, I explained, stressing that I came to learn from them. However, in almost all the study sites, my initial introductions with the communities were full of suspicions and certain expectations. Some of the resettlers were highly disillusioned and felt suspicious of my presence among them. They were sceptical and doubtful of the true reason of my study. At the end, some of these doubting resettlers stated (in Amharic): *"Atinan, ignaam innaate-nahaallen!"* – which literally means, "let you study us, we do also study you!" The same was true when I was introduced to the resettlers belonging to the Kambaata and Hadiyya ethnic groups. Here, one Kambaata elder stated (in *Kambaatissa*): *"Iilleenne hawwigama laaganne tahaateent yin ka keesii amma'ininaam yiteentindo, birita lanqima tuundaanke!"* – which literally means, "due to the excessive suffering we have been encountering, we can not trust you immediately just because you speak our language; we will study you and develop trust as you proceed staying with us."

XXIII

Coloured group photographs facilitated a lot in establishing rapport with many of my informants, clearing their last doubts of my presence both among the resettlers and the autochthonous Gumuz. It is one of the strong lessons I learned in the field that, at least in my research context, almost everybody liked to see his/her photo. In order to avoid personal requests, I explained about the costs and took mainly group photos. However, I did also take family photos in certain cases when some resettlers asked me to take their photos together with their possessions such as granaries, livestock, and houses, mostly meant to be sent to relatives in home areas. I carefully made a number of prints of these photos and gave them during my repeated returns to my research villages. Apart from offering me openly expressed valuable rapport as someone so faithful, it also enabled me to make insightful notes penetrating and sharing their deeper feelings. Once I give out the group photos, everyone almost regardless of gender and age difference, likes to look at his/her image and that of others, mostly commenting humorously and joyously and smiling at the postures of others in the photo. Since I cannot distribute to everyone, they select someone to keep their group photo. Of course, there were certain occasions when they and I were deeply saddened by the photos, particularly when one of the group members in the photo alive at the time of photographing had passed away before my next visit.

In the eyes of many of my resettler study communities, I was considered as a recorder of their history in the dislocation and relocation process of the resettlement scheme, focusing on the suffering they encountered. So, many informants either voluntarily came to me or called me to their home and mostly told me their painful heart-rending accounts of suffering due to the resettlement scheme, requesting me to record them. Among other things, resettlers repeatedly explained the enormous climatic difference between their original areas and the new context as, "*Agaraachin balten inniwozallen, sawunnetaachin muuz yimaslaall; izzih, balten anniwozam, sawunnetaachinim kasal yimaslaal.*" This expression (in Amharic) literally means, "in our home areas, with what we ate, we were used to having a lively and bright complexion, looking like a banana fruit; whereas here, we rather look like charcoal." After explaining the accounts, they usually felt gratified and usually expressed their feelings by stating: "Now, we do not worry much about death, having observed alive while all our suffering being recorded." Furthermore, clearing their initial suspicions and doubts, they felt happy with my presence and expressed their appreciation of my work, stating: "It is our prayer that brought you to us to investigate and record our experiences in this new location!;" "we have never been queried in such minute details and intensity for such an extended period by anybody, like you have been doing!"; and "since you are ours, please, channel all our problems to the authorities at different levels!"

The Gumuz have strong grievances towards the resettlement scheme that has taken their traditional land resources pushing them away to the peripheries. In 1988, a very old Gumuz informant (who was estimated to be 90 years old and later died) at Aypapa village in Dangur Woreda proximate to R101 village expressed his reaction to the scheme as part of the age-old marginalisation and segregation process of the Gumuz by the neighbouring highlanders under all the different political regimes. He explained and argued by citing a case of a certain highland feudal chief who had been granted rule over the Gumuz of Metekel by the old imperial regime. Disappointed by his appointment, he explained, this feudal chief appealed to the monarch by stating: "Your excellency, what grave fault have I committed to your governance that you are punishing me by assigning me to rule an area where there exist no humans but only baboons and monkeys?" The cited case by the old man clearly depicts the marginal status of the autochthonous Gumuz, strongly affecting their relations with the neighbouring highlanders even today.

The mistrust and suspicions deep-rooted between the Gumuz and highlanders are reflected in many contexts and expressed through several stereotypes. For instance, according to the explanation of my Gumuz research assistant, Wubalta Enno, during the fieldwork some Gumuz members in Mandura were sceptical of the effectiveness of the 1999 and 2000 polio vaccinations offered free of charge. Their suspicion, in their perception, was of the unusual behaviour of the highlanders, whom the Gumuz designate as *Shuwa,* to offer something of real value free of charge. So, some members of the Gumuz were sceptical of getting their children vaccinated, considering that "had the medicine really had the stated true preventive value, the *Shuwa* would not have given it free of charge."

My late key Gumuz informant in Maataaba explained their marginal status in their traditional land, expressing his comparative views on the special care and excessive support extended to the resettlers by the state, totally neglecting the autochthonous population. It was in December 1996 that I was introduced to the Maataaba informants, living around ten kilometres away from the nearby resettlement villages of L132 and L134. After my interview with the village elders, this particular key informant took me to his home and invited me to drink *keya*. He was very much pleased with my visit to the village and had showed strong interest about the issues discussed during the interview. He explained that as part of the age-old prejudices and bias of the highlanders that undermined the Gumuz, their village had never been visited by people from outside. While we were drinking the *keya*, he expressed once again his happiness at my visit, promising that he would offer me a chicken (a most valuable and symbolically meaningful gift) on the occasion of my next visit to his village in the future. He further expressed his strong grievances towards a number of regimes that had marginalised them to remain inside a forest, completely denying them access to a number of social and economic services such as schools, health centres, grain mills, rural roads, pipe water, and all other relief and rehabilitation supports, comparing it with what he had observed being provided only to the resettlers. He went on, explaining that the government even used to equip the resettlers with automatic weapons and ammunition to shoot and kill the Gumuz whenever they express their grievances in their ancestral land. He compared the resettlers' weapons with that of their mostly old guns and serious shortage of ammunition even to defend their rights in the absence of any legal protection. He pointed out how the Gumuz are discriminated against by the highlanders in various contexts. After returning to the zonal administrative centre of Metekel, I discussed my visit to Maataaba with the Gumuz elite administrators. They showed strong interest in my visit and appreciated, explaining how vital such visits would be in bringing the two communities nearer and facilitating grounds for understanding each other. They stressed that such visits could clear all allegations and stereotyping attributed to the Gumuz, considering them as "unfriendly savages." Thus, they encouraged me to continue my visits, sharing my information to others and affirmed that they would extend their unreserved support to my research endeavours.

I made my second phase visit to Maataaba in July 1999 as part of my dissertation research and unfortunately found my former key informant inside the nearby forest next to the village, having been ordered there by the *gafia* in order to heal his illness. It took no time for both of us to recognise each other. The *gafia*, after repeated attempts to heal his sickness, told him that he was afflicted by the anger of his deceased father's spirit for not organising a proper *tazkar*. In order to appease his father's angered spirit, the *gafia* ordered him to leave the village and stay inside the nearby forest and make the necessary prayers to the spirits. In his weakened state of health, he was frequently visited and attended by one of his neighbours, who built a shade for him and provided firewood. His wife brought him *keya* daily. The next day, after obtaining permission from the elders, I took him to Pawe hospital and his sickness was found to be tuberculosis. He began taking the medicine and his health showed improvement. However, deceived by the immediate improvement, he stopped taking the medication. After a while, his health again began deteriorating. This time both the *gafia* and the village elders felt convinced that the angered spirit wanted to take away his life. Hearing of his deteriorating health condition, I went to visit him in early October 1999. I found him in his house, lying on the floor on a woven palm mat but without any attendant. All the family members had gone to the neighbouring Sunday market at Kuyissa. He expressed his strong desire for me to take him once again to hospital. I went to the market, got his wife and asked her if it would be possible to take him to hospital. She told me to discuss the issue with his brother, who is the prospective inheritor after her husband's death. Finally, I managed to see the brother. However, he rejected the idea of taking the sickman to hospital, explaining the very idea as a futile attempt because the spirits had already decided his fate so that he cannot be healed at all. In spite of my repeated attempts, they refused to take him to the hospital. Since I could do nothing without the permission of the village community, especially the elders, the *gafia*, and the brothers, I left the sick key informant feeling deeply saddened. He died a month later in November 1999.

Although still more striking instances and experiences encountered and observed in the field can be recounted, I would like to conclude this preface with the following condensed metaphorical saying in Amharic, noted by one of my immigrant resettlers' informants in village R104.

Bizuum dess alaalegn;	Neither great my pleasure;
Ijjigim alkeffagn:	Nor great is my sorrow:
Inde telba sifir,	My feelings barely heaped,
Bedirbibu negn.	Like a linseed measure.

The above saying was a reply from the stated informant to my question "How are your relations with the neighbouring Gumuz?" It is a very condensed poetic answer reflecting the entire relations and uneasy coexistence prevailing between them. The immigrant resettlers in R104, whose detailed case is described and discussed in the main text, belong to the early immigrants of Wollo to Metekel in the 1950s. Due to the ethnic conflict with Gumuz in areas around Dibati and Guangua *Woreda*, they were displaced and immigrated once again to the Beles Valley and settled in their present village abandoned by the state-sponsored resettlers. This village is located at the western periphery of the resettlement area bordering the Dangur Gumuz. Thus, the informant compared the interactions and relations between them, taking the analogy of "a linseed measure." On the one hand, considering the denotative poetic explicit meaning, the informant used a *simile* in the saying to compare their relations, which have a lot to do with abstract feelings, with much simplified and physically observable concrete "linseed measure which barely heaps in a 'cup'." Since the seed of linseed is very smooth, it simply slides from the top of a measuring cup and does not heap up like other, rougher grains. On the other hand, considering the connotative, poetic, and deeper meaning, the informant used a highly condensed *metaphor* to explain their entire interactions and relations with the Gumuz. Moreover, what he stated in the singular first person point of view in the saying applies fully to all his immigrant resettler group members and even beyond to the entire non-Gumuz. They are not quite happy about their interactions with the Gumuz since their relations are not mutually harmonious, being rather based on mistrust and suspicion. In the meantime, they were not too sad because (at least at the time of my interview) there were no reported cases of severe ethnic conflicts in the area that commonly used to evoke an atmosphere of tensions and hostilities. Therefore, the above "linseed measure" metaphor truly depicts important attributes concerning the prevalent troubled relations, uncomfortable interactions, and uneasy coexistence of the autochthonous Gumuz and highland resettlers in Metekel, particularly in the Beles Valley resettlement area and its environs.

Wolde-Selassie Abbute

PART ONE: RESEARCH METHODOLOGY AND THEORETICAL APPROACHES

Chapter 1. Introduction: Research Setting, Objective, and Methodology

1.1 Profile of the Study Setting

Metekel Zone, the main focal area of this study, is located in north-western Ethiopia, and its recent capital Gilgel Beles (formerly Pawe up to the end of 2000) is located around 555 km from Addis Ababa. It is one of the three zones of the Benishangul-Gumuz National Regional State (BGNRS) located in the far western part of Ethiopia-Sudan borderlands. It stretches from north-west to south-west bordered by the Amhara National Regional State in the north and north-east, Oromia National Regional State in the east and south-east, Gambella National Regional State in the south, and the Republic of Sudan in the west as shown in *map one*. The Metekel Zone occupies an estimated total area of 22,028 km². Its altitude ranges from 600 m.a.s.l. along the Sudan border to 2731 m.a.s.l. at Belaya Mt. and 2488 m.a.s.l. at Dangur Mt. According to a study conducted by the Metekel Zonal Agricultural Department (MZAD 1999), low-lying topography dominates most of the zone with 74% flat plains, 16% hilly and plateaus, 6% valley bottoms and 4% mountainous land. The same study classifies the climatic conditions of the zone as: 82% *qolla,* 10% *woina-dega,* and 8% *dega*[1]. The population distribution in the three climatic zones is estimated to be 34% in the *dega*, 28% in the *woina-dega*, and 38% in the *qolla*. In addition, the land use pattern is estimated in the stated study as 79% forestland, 7% cultivated land, 7% cultivable land, and 7% non-utilisable land. Based on a ten years' (1989-1999 [1981-1991 E.C.[2]]) meteorological data of the areas around Beles Valley resettlement area, the annual average temperature ranges from 16.2 - 32.5⁰C with annual mean rainfall of 1,607.8mm, where the annual rainfall months ranging from May to October (EARO-PRC, 2000). The total population of the regional state, according to the 1994 population and housing census of Ethiopia, is estimated to be 440,459, out of which members of the

---

[1] *Qolla, woina-dega*, and *dega* are terms (Amh.) for classifying low, mid, and high altitudinal ranges.

[2] The Ethiopian calendar is seven years and eight months behind the Gregorian calendar. The calendar is made up of 12 months of 30 days and a 13th month of five or six days, depending on whether or not it is a leap year.

Gumuz[3] ethnic group in the region numbered 107,495 (CSA 1996:10). The autochthonous[4] Gumuz settlements are spread thinly across wide areas extending from Metemma southwards through Gondar, Gojjam, Metekel and cross the Abbay River up to the Diddesa valley in Wollega. In the present administrative context, most of the Gumuz inhabit Metekel Zone to the north and Kamashi Zone to the south of the Abbay River.

Map 1. Ethiopia: Regions and Zones after 1991 (Unofficial Map)

Source: Adapted from EU-Food Security Unit-WFP (Ethiopia)

---

[3] In the written sources, the people are referred to by different ethnic and generic names such as *Bega, Gumis, Gumus, Gunza, Gumz, Gumuz, Saysay, Say, Sese*, and *Shanqilla*. The local people call themselves Gumz while referring to their ethnic group. However, in this study the ethnic term *Gumuz* is used because it is a widely used term referring to the group both in the written sources and by the regional administration.

[4] The terms 'autochthonous', 'native' and '*indigenous*' are used in this study with relatively similar meaning implying birth or origin in the region ('aboriginal' inhabitants of the region); not having been introduced from another region.

The total population of Metekel Zone is estimated to be 201,521 (male being 101,134 and female 100,387, of which 181,914 are rural inhabitants and 19,607 are urban dwellers) and the number of major ethnic groups is described as 66,965 Gumuz, 47,900 Amhara, 32,037 Shinasha, 27,050 Oromo, 17,155 Agaw, 2875 Kambaata, 2179 Hadiyya, 725 Tigraway[5], and the rest composed of others (CSA 1996:41). The average family size is estimated to be 4.4. The population density is around nine persons/km^2. The main religions of the population include: Christian, Muslim, and traditional belief systems.

The zone is further divided into seven *woreda* (districts); namely, Dangur, Guba, Mandura, Dibate, Bulen, Wombera and Pawe Special *Woreda* as indicated in *map two*. The last named of these is exclusively occupied by the state sponsored resettler population of the 1980s and recent highland voluntary immigrants, while the remaining six *woreda* are inhabited by relatively mixed ethnic groups of Gumuz, Amhara (including spontaneous Wollo migrant settlers), Shinasha, Agaw, Oromo, and Kumfel (*Qollegna* Agaw (lowlanders) known for their traditional apiculture – mainly in Dangur Woreda). The Gumuz, who constitute the most numerous ethnic group of the area, mostly inhabit the lowlands in all the six *woreda*, while the others mainly inhabit the middle and high altitudes of the area. On the other hand, the former state sponsored resettlers in Pawe Special *Woreda* fully inhabit a lowland area at an altitudinal range of 1000 m.a.s.l. to 1200 m.a.s.l.

Before the arrival of resettlers, the area was inhabited by an estimated autochthonous Gumuz population of 18,312[6], who as a result of the resettlers' arrival were displaced and pushed to the peripheries, being stripped of their land resources that had served them as an extricable livelihood source. Other documented accounts made similar estimates. In the Master Plan no. 2B of the Tana-eles Project, the number of Gumuz displaced from the project area is estimated around 18,000 (LUPT-NWZADO-MoA 1987; cited in Studio Pietrangeli 1988:29).

In addition, Agneta and Tommasoli (1992:343) estimated the number of autochthonous Gumuz inhabitants of the area to be within a range of 15,000 to 20,000 before the implementation of the resettlement scheme.

---

[5] The ethnic group name "Tigraway" is used following the same ethnic reference made in the statistical report of the 1994 Population and Housing Census of Ethiopia results for the Benishangul-Gumuz Regional State, in particular Pawe Special *Woreda* (CSA 1996:43).

[6] These data are obtained from Metekel Zonal archive document numbered 01.02.029 (page 4) based on a socio-economic study conducted in 1978 E.C. (1985/86 G.C) (no year of the report indicated).

Map 2. Benishangul-Gumuz National Regional State (after 1991)

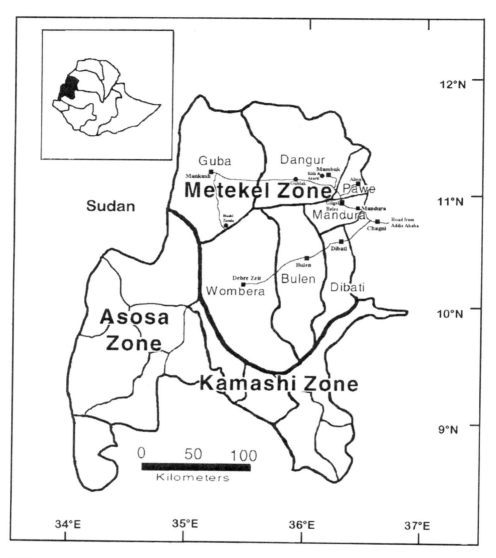

All borders are unofficial and approximate

Source: Adapted from Benishangul-Gumuz Regional State (no date)

Today, an estimated 35,858 state-sponsored resettlers of the 1980s inhabit the resettlement area. They are ethnically differentiated into 26,900 Amhara (from Wollo, North Shoa, Gojjam, and Gondar), 2,868 Kambaata (south-western Shoa), 2,178 Hadiyya (south-western Shoa), 1,286 Oromo (southern Wollo and northern Shoa), 1,110 Agaw (Wollo-Tigray (Seqota)), 502 Tigraway, and the rest others (CSA 1996:43).

The multi-ethnic composition in Metekel can be divided into four sub-categories just to facilitate contextual explanation. The first includes the autochthonous Gumuz, who claim to be the original inhabitants of the area. The second includes those ethnic groups who lived neighbouring each other for centuries, such as Shinasha, Amhara (Gojjam/Gondar), Agaw (Gojjam), and Oromo. The third includes those spontaneous immigrant resettlers of the 1950s from Wollo (Amhara). Finally, the fourth includes those state-sponsored resettlers of the 1980s, which in turn are further differentiated into diverse ethnic groups as stated above. Since dealing with all these categories is beyond the scope of this study, the special focus of my investigation will be on the first and fourth categories. However, the second and third categories are also examined significantly in the study whenever deemed necessary.

1.2 Objective and Significance of the Study

Objective of the Study
The general objective of the study is to examine the differing strategies of livelihood, encroachment on resources, and ethnic relations of the autochthonous Gumuz and highland resettlers in Metekel, principally focusing on the impact of the state-sponsored resettlement scheme in the Beles Valley and its environs. In order to realise the stated objective, the study aims to:

- Examine the indigenous ecological knowledge and natural resource management systems of the Gumuz as blended in their traditional belief systems;
- Investigate the human and environmental impacts of encroachment across regimes on the land resources of the Gumuz;
- Examine the impact of the state-sponsored resettlement of the 1980s on the host, resettlers, and the environment.
- Inquire the role of local social institutions in the livelihood adaptations and interactions of Gumuz and resettlers;

- Investigate the ethnic relations of the Gumuz and highland resettlers; and
- Examine the social change and continuity prevailing in the study area.

Significance of the Study

The significance of this research is manifold and attempts to contribute to the advancement of anthropological approaches to resettlement, of which the major ones include:

- Contributing to the anthropological literature on resettlement in general and to the ethnographic studies of north-eastern Africa, in particular to the study of peoples and cultures of Ethiopian-Sudanese borderlands in western Ethiopia;
- Enabling to understand the multiple impacts of resettlement on the *host* and *resettlers* as well as on the *ecology;*
- Attempting to offer insights into the centrality of local institutional dynamics and processes in the adaptations and interactions of autochthonous populations and immigrant settlers;
- Contributing to the anthropological literature gap on the host population in studies of resettlement, which is rather a neglected aspect because all major resettlement theories and studies have narrowly focused only on the resettlers;
- Enabling to realise the importance of indigenous ecological knowledge in natural resource management systems;
- Enabling to understand the social change prevailing in the study area; and
- Contributing to the formulation of possible future research questions.

1.3 Research Methodology

Site Selection

Three main and two supplementary locales of research were selected for the ethnological fieldwork of the study based on accessibility, representativeness and proximity as well as my own prior familiarity and knowledge of the study area. I lived and worked in the area as a "Social Researcher" from 1988 to 1991 as an employee of an international European non-governmental organisation (NGO) known as CISP engaged in the rehabilitation and development of the resettlers. Between 1992 and 1995, I had intermittently conducted consultancy research assignments both in the resettler and neighbouring Gumuz communities with special emphasis on the changes that occurred inside the scheme area and its environs after the 1991 political change. Then, from 1996 to 1997, I conducted one year of fieldwork for my *Master of Arts* in *Social Anthropology* (Addis Ababa University. Based on my long-term experience in the area, I conducted the fieldwork for this study in two phases. The first phase of fieldwork was conducted from July 1999 to April 2000. Then, I returned to the university and presented my early findings at the Institute of Ethnology colloquia. Consolidating the feedback with further literature inquiry, I went back to the research site and conducted the second phase fieldwork from October 2000 to April 2001. Towards the end of this phase in February-March, 2001, my advisor visited and supervised me in the field for about three weeks. Altogether, the fieldwork was conducted for about fifteen months.

Of the seven *woreda* in Metekel Zone, three of them, namely Mandura, Dangur, and Pawe Special *Woreda*, were selected as my main site-specific research setting and fairly represent the cultural, socio-economic and agroecological conditions of the study area. These are also areas in which encroachment pressure on the land resources of the Gumuz has persisted across regimes. For instance, Mandura *Woreda*, the most dominantly inhabited stronghold of the autochthonous Gumuz and located fully in a *qolla* climatic zone, is an area where inter-ethnic interactions has been occurring between the Gumuz and their neighbouring highlanders. Here, the latter have been spilling over into the lowlands, descending from *Kar* mountain ranges all along the eastern parts that is said to have served as a buffer for many years. On the other hand, it borders with Pawe Special *Woreda* to the north, which is an area exclusively inhabited by the state-sponsored resettlers of the 1980s and located fully in a *qolla* climatic zone. Dangur *Woreda* is also predominantly inhabited by the Gumuz with a moderate mix of Agaw, Shinasha, Kumfel (*Qollegna* Agaw) and former spontaneous settler Amhara ethnic groups and located at climatic zones of 5% *dega* (high altitude at near Belaya and Dangur Mountains), 19% *woina-dega* and 76% *qolla*. In addition, it is an area of the former state farm as well as the present most dominant rain-fed agricultural investment sites in addition to being an area of long established encroachment by the highlanders. It also borders with Pawe Special *Woreda* to the east which is exclusively a site of an involuntary resettlement scheme inhabited by state-sponsored resettlers of the 1980s.

These three *woreda* are also areas of both slow or gradual and rapid encroachment. Meanwhile, they are proximate to each other and relatively better accessible due to the main Chagni - Guba highway that crosses them. These are also areas of high population pressure with diverse ethnic composition and complex inter-ethnic relations. These are areas most overwhelmingly encroached by different groups such as neighbouring highlanders, a state farm, state-sponsored resettlers of the 1980s, voluntary and displaced immigrant peasants of the 1990s, and the present private investors mainly in rain-fed agriculture (cf. section1.1 in this chapter).

In addition, two relatively short duration supplementary sites were selected in Dibati and Guba *Woreda* as part of the broader exploratory aspect of the research in order to strengthen the findings. The two depict the major features of the entire area that are not fully represented in the main research sites. In addition to a majority Gumuz population, mixed ethnic groups of Shinasha, Agaw, Amhara, and Oromo inhabit Dibati *Woreda*, which is slightly distant from the other three *woreda*. It is located at a climatic zone of 15% *woina-dega* (mid-altitude) and 85% *qolla*. It is a major location of the spontaneous resettlers from Wollo since the 1950s up to the present. It is an area of repeated ethnic conflicts between the hosts and immigrants. Finally, Guba *Woreda* is located at the very far peripheries near the Ethio-Sudanese border in a fully lowland *qolla* climate. Guba is considered to be the most important location in the study of the Gumuz in the entire Metekel for its historically and ethnologically significant travel accounts, documented by Juan Maria Schuver (1882) as well its *Funj* aristocratic rulers. The Gumuz of Guba are predominantly influenced by the Muslim traditions from the Sudan. Further exploratory assessment was conducted in Bulen *Woreda* by collecting secondary data from the Woreda Council and EDSSO as well as discussion being held and interviews conducted with the local staff about the overall socio-cultural and economic features of the area. Additionally, a brief visit was made to the difficult of access area of Wombera *Woreda* (up to its capital Debre-Zeit) so as to grasp an overview by direct personal observation.

Both site-specific ethnographic fieldwork and exploratory assessments were conducted in those main and supplementary research sites. Regarding the autochthonous Gumuz, specific ethnographic fieldwork was conducted in five main research sites in the villages of Manjeeri, Wondbil, Maataaba, Kitli-Azarti, and Gublak. The first two sites are considered as part of the Mandura *Woreda*[7] and the latter two in Dangur *Woreda*. The detailed loca-

---

[7]This information is based on personal communication with Mr. Mitt Mihe, a Gumuz from Mandura and a representative of the Metekel Gumuz in the Ethiopian Parliament. He suggested that I consider Maataaba, Manjeeri and Wondbil under the Mandura Woreda in my ethnological research, because they are fully part of the larger Gumuz ethnic group in all socio-cultural and economic aspects. He explained that discussions are underway between Agauawi Zone (in Amhara Regional State) and Metekel Zone to solve their confusing locations at this excessively en-

tions of both site-specific and exploratory assessment research sites among the autochthonous Gumuz are shown in *map three*. In addition, *Baabi-Zanda* village in Guba *Woreda* and the suburbs of Dibati town in Dibati *Woreda* served as supplementary research sites. The detailed features of each one of these sites is described below.

Manjeeri: This is a village inhabited by the *Dimtsatse* clan and most severely affected Gumuz community of all by the resettlement scheme convened at the centre of their land. Apart from depriving them from their entire livelihood resources, the scheme has divided them apart, displacing them into two corners. The remaining section of the clan members is located to the far north-western periphery of the resettlement near Mambuk town in Dangur *Woreda*.

Wondbil: This village is mainly inhabited by the *Dunawa* clan and located at the south-eastern part of the resettlement scheme between Manjeeri and Maataaba villages bordering the L134[8] resettler village. Despite their suffering from the adverse effects of the scheme and uneasy coexistence, there is a noticeable emerging mutual interaction between them and the neighbouring resettlers.

Maataaba: It is inhabited by the *Maataaba* clan and located along the eastern part of the resettlement scheme bordering resettler villages of L134, L132, L131, L28, and L29. Their relationship with the neighbouring resettlers is predominantly conflicting due to the scheme's consequences. In the views of the resettlers, the Maataaba Gumuz are characterised as the most aggressive, depicting their hostile relations.

---

croached frontier area bordering Dangila *Woreda* (in Agauawi Zone), Pawe Special *Woreda* and Mandura *Woreda* so as to incorporate them with their ethnic group in the latter. However, the consideration of these sites in Mandura *Woreda* in this study by no means whatsoever determine or prejudge the legal status and the results of the ongoing discussions.

[8] The prefixed letter 'L' represents those resettlement villages located at the left side of Beles River. The government authorities numbered rather than named villages in the resettlement scheme.

Map 3. Part of Metekel in Northwestern Ethiopia

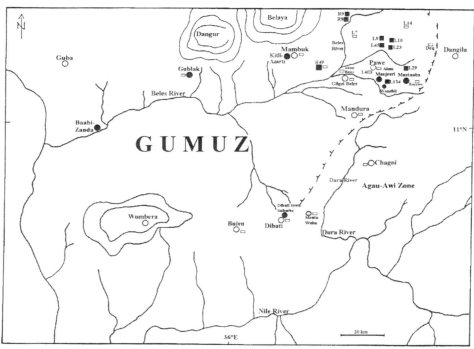

Legend:

○ — Woreda Capitals Served as Centers of Exploratory Assessment and Observation on Market Days and Sources of Secondary Data
● — Native Gumuz Research Sites
■ — Highland Resettlers Research Sites

𝒇 — Kar Mountain Range
L — Resettlement Villages on the Left Side of Beles River
R — Resettlement Villages on the Right Side of Beles River
⊙ — Main Centre of Spontaneous Migrant Resettler Peasants from Wello
⊡ — Local Bi-Weekly and Weekly Market Places

Source: Adapted from Kuls (1962:45)

10

Kitli-Azarti: This *kebele*[9] was formed by merging the former independent peasant associations of Kitli and Azarti named after the clans inhabiting the two respectively. It is located at the north-western part of the resettlement scheme behind the former state farm to the west of *Mambuk* town (administrative centre of Dangur *Woreda*) proximate to Belaya Mountain. The Gumuz of Kitli-Azarti is not directly affected by the resettlement scheme. However, they have been under heavy pressure of encroaching highland plow cultivators. A considerable portion of the Kitli sub-section of the *kebele,* especially from the parts to the east bordering the Mambuk town, is fully inhabited by the highland plow cultivators. Due to their being adjacent to Belaya Mountain, the Gumuz of the area (according to the fresh memory of the informants), had been under the ruthless rule of an Agaw chief called *Fitawirari* Zeleke during the imperial regime. The latter's headquarters was located at the top of Belaya Mountain. Despite the predominant uneasy coexistence, there are significant existing and emerging mutual interactions between the Gumuz and settlers in the area

Gublak: This is a very large *kebele* located at a central position of the Dangur *Woreda* around sixty kilometers away from the Beles Valley resettlement scheme area: It is exclusively inhabited by Gumuz, belonging to *Dachichaha, Dapura, Dubahiya,* and *Dibate* clans. The local market centre of Gublak, established at the former campsite of Ethiopian Road Construction Authority while the Chagni-Guba road was being built, an important meeting point for the entire communities at the bi-weekly market days on Wednesdays and Saturdays. It also serves as the *woreda* police sub-post due to the location of Mambuk at the far eastern frontier. As part of the grand resettlement scheme in Metekel[10], Gublak was selected as the second resettlement site where resettlers from Wollo were resettled in eight villages at the initial stage in 1985/86. However, immediately after the first two years, they were re-relocated and incorporated into the larger resettler population

---

[9] A *kebele* is a basic unit of local administrative structure bridging the people at the grassroots level and the higher *woreda* administrative organ. In the present post-1991 federal state administrative structure, *kebele* Administration constitutes ideally one thousand households with autonomous elected council and executive committee. Mostly, a *Kebele* was formed as a replacement by merging two or more former Peasant Associations.

[10] In addition to Pawe, the government had selected Gublak and Aisik (farther to the direction of Guba, in Guba *Woreda*) as resettlement scheme areas. Although shelters were built by the university students and staff in a campaign, resettlers were not relocated in the latter.

11

in Beles Valley (Pawe) as a result of severe causalities from frequent ethnic conflicts with the autochthonous Gumuz and other logistical constraints. Gublak represents a typical Gumuz socio-cultural and economic context which has not as such been influenced by any form of external encroachment and is used for comparative study.

Baabi-Zanda: This is a village mainly inhabited by *Damtaya* clan and located around thirty kilometres away from Mankush (*woreda* administrative centre) to the south along the right bank on the lower course of Beles river in Guba *Woreda* (along the part bordering the Wombera *Woreda*).

Dibati Town and Its Environs: This small district town of Dibati and its environs served as favourable settings for investigation especially with the informants of Amhara (Gojjam) Shinasha, Agaw, and Oromo ethnic group members who have been long-time neighbours of the Gumuz. As already stated earlier, it is also an area excessively encroached by the immigrant resettlers from Wollo since the 1950s.

Additionally, the local bi-weekly and weekly market places such as Mandura, Gilgel-Beles, Kuyyisa, Mambuk, Gublak, Chagni, Menta-Wuha, and Dibati have served as broad comprehensive and exploratory centres of assessment for data collection through direct observation and discussion, especially with informants coming from far away and inaccessible Gumuz villages as can be seen on *map three.*

On the other hand, concerning the state-sponsored resettlers of the 1980s in the Pawe Special *Woreda,* site-specific research was conducted in one main and five sub-sites alongside broader assessment in the entire scheme area. The locations of specific research sites among the resettlers are already shown in *map three* within the broader context of Metekel. Nevertheless, the detailed locations of the entire Beles Valley resettlement scheme area, including those specific research sites, are shown in *map four.* The main research site selected in the resettlement area is the L23 *kebele* Administration that was formed merging the former resettlement villages[11] of L9, L10, L45, and L23. This *kebele* represents a prime example of the predominant socio-cultural, economic and environmental backgrounds of the setting. These diverse features represented include ethnic composition, religious back-

---

[11]A 'resettlement village' was constructed based on a 'villagisation model' of the *Derg* regime with a similar administrative structure and status of a Peasant Association.

ground, origins of resettlers, category and density of population, soil type, resource ownership, and its strategic position between two important local markets – *L7* main resettlement area market on the one hand and the nearby local *Deq* market located outside the scheme area in the neighbouring communities on the other. In addition, these four merged villages under the new *kebele* are located at a place relatively central to the entire area and proximate to each other. Description of the representative features in each village is stated as follows:

> *L9* - Inhabited mainly by Kambaata, some Hadiyya, Amhara (Gojjam), and a few Wolaita ethnic group members. The main religions of the village are Protestantism (*Kale-Hiwot* or Baptist Congregation and Seventh Day Adventist) and Catholicism, with significant followers of Orthodox Christianity and Islam.

> *L10* - Inhabited mainly by Hadiyya, some Amhara (Gojjam), Kambaata, and a few Wolaita ethnic group members. The main religions of the village are Protestantism (*Kale-Hiwot* or Baptist Congregation and Seventh Day Adventist) and Catholicism with significant followers of Orthodox Christianity and Islam.

> *L23* - Inhabited mainly by Oromo (North Shoa and South Wollo) and a significant number of Amhara (Wollo, Gojjam and Shoa). Islam is the main religion of the village with significant followers of Orthodox Christianity.

> *L45* - Inhabited exclusively by Amhara (mainly from Wollo and few from Gojjam), with around 60% followers of Orthodox Christianity and 40% being followers of Islam (cf. chapter 6, sub-section Religious Background).

Due to the complexity of the socio-cultural and economic features in the resettlement scheme setting, five additional sub-sites were selected to strengthen the study and fill the gap of some important aspects of the predominant features of the area, which are not fully represented in the main research site. These research sub-sites include *L29, L134, R8*[12], *R9 and R49*,

---

[12] The prefixed letter "R" represents resettlement villages located on the right side of Beles River.

Map 4. Sketch Map of the State-Sponsored Resettlement Scheme Villages in Beles Valley

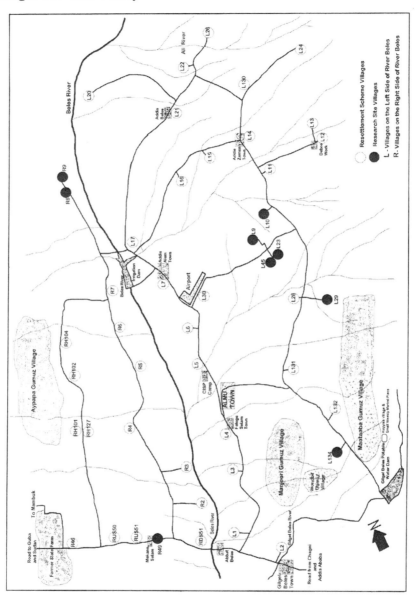

which are former resettlement villages forming the sub-sections of the present *kebele* and located at different places in the scheme area. The representative features of each one of the sub-sites is described in map 4.

L 29 -Located at the central-eastern far left side of Beles River bordering with the neighbouring Agaw (Gojjam) ethnic group. The village is inhabited by resettlers belonging to the Amhara (mainly from Wollo and substantial number from Gojjam), Agaw (Wollo-Tigray (Seqota)), and Tigraway ethnic groups with 68% followers of Orthodox Christianity and 32% Islam. Although there occur conflicts due to cultivable land dispute at their border, the resettlers and neighbouring Agaw (Gojjam) interact and co-exist harmoniously. It is also the only village where land was redistributed after the 1991 political change entitling ideally every household to 1.5 hectares, whereas the formal landholding of households in the entire scheme villages is 0.75 hectares.

L134 - Located at the south-eastern far left side of Beles River closely bordering (enclosed in a semi-circle) the stronghold of the Gumuz. The village is inhabited by resettlers belonging to the Amhara (Wollo) ethnic group with 69% followers of Orthodox Christianity and 31% of Islam. Their relationships with the neighbouring Gumuz, which were displaced to those peripheral areas by the scheme, has been characterised by frequent cases of serious hostilities. However, there are interesting cases reported and observed of emerging mutual interactions especially through institutional arrangements such as renting land.

R49 - Located along the east-west Chagni-Guba main highway on the right side of Beles River and inhabited exclusively by the Amhara (Wollo) ethnic group with 77% followers of Islam and 23% Orthodox Christianity. The village borders with Gumuz in its southern frontier where there occurred fierce conflicts of shocking scale. This village is affected by the controversial rain-fed agricultural investment that claimed their land resources – particularly by its indiscriminate deforestation. In addition to its opportunistic location along the main highway, the village enjoys a weekly Saturday market as an important centre of interaction and exchange, increasing the pursuit of livelihood adaptation. The village also enjoys its proximate location to the Mambuk town's local big bi-weekly market outside the resettlement area. To a substantial extent, it also has business exchange links to the

Chagni market around 55 km away to the east. According to the local standards, it is one of the rich and well-adapted villages and also known for its rice production.

R8 and R9 - Located at the far north-west on the right side of river Beles bordering with the Kumfel (*Qollegna* Agaw) ethnic group along the frontiers of Dangur *Woreda* and Gondar (Amhara Regional State). Kambaata ethnic group members, who are mainly followers of Protestantism and Catholicism with only few followers of Orthodox Christianity and Islam, inhabit these two neighbouring villages. Most of the resettlers from these villages have deserted them, returning to the areas of origin after the 1991 political change. In the present context, the resettlers have established complex networks of mutual relations with the neighbouring Kumfel communities of *Jawe* in Gondar. Besides, due to the desertion of many of the state-sponsored resettlers for origins and its location at the peripheries with substantial farming and grazing land potential, the two villages at the moment are predominantly inhabited by the *voluntary* and *displaced* immigrants of the 1990s. The latter have immigrated mainly from Gojjam and Gondar (voluntary) as well as a few from Dibati *Woreda* within Metekel (displaced due to ethnic conflict). For instance, in R8 village out of the estimated total population of 550, 270 (49%) are resettlers and 280 (51%) are immigrant farmers. Whereas in R9 village out of the estimated total population of 675, 360 (53%) are resettlers and 315 (47%) are immigrant farmers. However, formal administrative jurisdiction is fully in the hands of the state-sponsored resettlers till the latter's legal status is formally recognised by the *woreda* and regional authorities. Despite certain implicit scepticism by both parties on issues concerning land resource rights in the future, at the moment the immigrants and resettlers are living in harmony, interacting through several local social institutional arrangements.

Additionally, the weekly market places at L4, L7, L14, R49, Abbat Beles, and Almu have served as broader exploratory centres of assessment for data collection through direct observation and discussion especially with the different categories of highland resettlers of the 1980s and the immigrants of the 1990s (see *maps three* and *four*). In the Beles Valley resettlement context, a village is located at one place where residential houses are built in planned rows with a 0.1 hectare homestead plots for each household, it is easier to have access to many households in a shortest time possible. Almost all villages are near to each other in the same area and are accessible by gravelled all-weather road.

Data Collection
Throughout the research investigation period, a combination of different data-collection methods was applied, including secondary literature review, participant observation, semi-structured interview with key informants, focus group discussion, questionnaire, and extended case study. Field data collection tools such as field note-taking, tape cassette recording, photographs, slide-films, video-films and sketch-maps were made so as to record various important discussions, events, occasions, issues, and ecological settings. Most important of all, tape-cassette recordings were used to a very good effect during interviews with key informants and group discussions throughout the fieldwork period in addition to the intensive note-taking.

Secondary Data Collection
Secondary source materials both on the concepts and practices relevant to the research subject were reviewed. Data were collected from different government, non-government and private institutions. The government institutions include Metekel Zone (Social and Economic Affairs Division of the Metekel Zonal Administrative Council, Planning and Programming Service, Department of Agriculture, and Department of Education and Culture); Dibati *Woreda* (*Woreda* Council, *Woreda* Economic Development and Social Services Office (EDSSO)); Mandura *Woreda* (*Woreda* Council, EDSSO); Dangur *Woreda* (*Woreda* Council, EDSSO); Pawe Special *Woreda* (*Woreda* Council, EDSSO); and the Tana-Beles Project (TBP) at Pawe. The non-governmental institutions include CPAR (Canadian Physicians for Aid and Relief) at Dibati and CISP (International Committee for the Development of Peoples) at Pawe. Finally, the private institutions or investment schemes include Mandura Organic Agricultural Development, Burcz-Endalama Agro-Industry, Bengez Agricultural Development, Zimbeha Agricultural development, and Abbat-Beles Agricultural Development.

Participant Observation
Systematic and purposeful observation of the diverse socio-cultural and economic practices of the population living in the study villages was conducted (observing the visible and discussing what was seen). In addition, several social practices and physical sites that have special relevance to the study were directly observed.

Semi-Structured Interview with Key Informants[13]

An in-depth interview was conducted with numerous key informants. They include local Gumuz informants in Mandura, Dangur Dibati and Guba *Woreda*; Amhara, Shinasha and Agaw informants in Dibati and Dangur *Woreda;* state-sponsored resettler informants in Pawe Special *Woreda,* and immigrant settlers of the 1990s in Pawe Special *Woreda.* In addition, key informants from the local residents and immigrant farmers were interviewed at their respective *kebele* as well as at the local market places. Informants from government, non-government, and private institutions were also inter-viewed at their respective offices.

Focus-Group Discussion

Focus-group discussions were held in order to obtain qualitative data as well as to validate and probe crucial points of already obtained data. Several in-formants with multiple backgrounds have participated during group discus-sions held in different contexts, especially at local market places.

Questionnaire

In order to receive the basic features of the study villages and support the qualitative data obtained by observation and discussion with quantitative statements, a village-level census questionnaire was administered, particu-larly in all the villages of the Pawe Special *Woreda.* It was also intended to obtain up-to-date empirical data on the demographic composition of the different categories of peoples residing in the Beles Valley as well as to un-derstand a few of the predominant local institutions. It was further intended to identify disaggregated data on the number of voluntary/forced immigrant farmers who immigrated into the area after the 1991 political change, who are alleged to be in "illegal" settlements in the peripheral forestlands of the main fields of state-sponsored resettlers. The immigrants of the 1990s are accused of indiscriminately cutting and drying trees by peeling their bark and clearing the forest for village settlement, crop fields, and pasture, caus-ing severe adverse impact on the environment, which is mainly attributed to the temporary nature of their settlement and tenure insecurity.

---

[13] Out of the numerous informants, only 126 are identified as key informants based on the dura-tion of interview during the fieldwork usually for not less than a half-day. The number of women key informants is only 12 because mostly they do not stay longer hours during the interview. In order to protect the privacy of all the names and personal data of informants, their list is omitted in this publication, which was included in the original thesis submitted for defence.

Case Studies

Case-history data on encroachment pressure issues were collected. For instance, the case history of Beles State Farm from its inception up to its collapse was recorded and documented, paying particular attention to its impact on the natural resources. Similar cases were documented concerning the immigrant resettlers of the 1950s at Dibati, state-sponsored resettlers of the 1980s, latter immigrant resettlers of the 1990s at Pawe, and Tana-Beles Project, as well as recent investment schemes in rain-fed agriculture such as Mandura Organic Agricultural Development, Abbat-Beles Agricultural Development, Bengez agricultural Development, Zimbaha Agricultural Development, and Burcz-Endalama Agro-Industry.

1.4 Organisation of the Study

This study is organised into five parts, consisting of fourteen chapters. *Part one* consists of two chapters. Chapter 1 introduces the study setting, objective and significance of the study and the research methodology. In chapter two, the conceptual review and the theoretical approaches applied in the study are presented.

Part two consists of three chapters mainly dealing with the ethnography of the autochthonous Gumuz. Chapter 3 describes the socio-cultural institutions and modes of livelihood. The indigenous ecological knowledge and systems of natural resource management are explained in chapter 4. Chapter 5 describes and discusses the impact of encroachment on the Gumuz's land resources and management systems.

Part three consists of four chapters, focusing on the ethnography of highland resettlers. An overview of the state-sponsored resettlement of the 1980s in the Beles Valley is described in chapter 6. Chapter 7 explains and discusses the human and environmental impacts of the resettlement. The resettlers' socio-cultural rearticulation as well as livelihood recovery and adaptations in the new setting are explained in chapter 8. Chapter 9 explains and argues, highlighting new insights into the central role of local institutions in the resettlers' interactions and livelihood adaptations.

Part four consists of three chapters dealing with the interactions of the Gumuz and the resettlers. The ethnic identifications of the two categories of populations are discussed in chapter 10. Chapter 11 describes the predominance of ethnic conflicts and conflict resolution mechanisms, with a particular emphasis on the traditional *mangima* institution. The existing and emerging patterns of coexistence, despite the frequent conflicts are presented in chapter 12.

Part five consists of two chapters dealing with the analysis, synthesis, and conclusion of the study. Chapter 13 analyses the major findings of the study, synthesising the arguments with the theoretical approaches applied. Additionally, in this chapter, new insights are made into the centrality of local institutional dynamics and processes in the interactions and adaptations of autochthonous populations and immigrant settlers. The study is summarised and concluding remarks are made in chapter 14.

Finally, after the bibliography, selected illustrations are presented, aimed at providing additional visual highlights on some of the important ethnographic issues described and discussed in the main text. Then, important additional detailed data and related information are enclosed in a number of appendices.

Chapter 2. Conceptual Review and Theoretical Approaches

2.1 Theoretical Considerations for Examining the Research Subject

In order to come up with theoretical premises for examining the research subject, an attempt is made to review important theories and practices relevant to examine the research subject. The focal areas of the conceptual review are in the domains of ethnicity and ethnic relations; indigenous knowledge and natural resource management; involuntary resettlement; and rural livelihood strategies and local social institutions. Owing to their relevance, these theoretical approaches in the stated four thematically important topics are considered in the study of the differing strategies of livelihood and resource management, encroachment on resources, and ethnic relations between the autochthonous Gumuz and highland resettlers in Metekel.

In a complex context of the Beles Valley in Metekel where both people from different parts of the country with diverse backgrounds as well as the autochthonous host people inhabit the area, these theoretical stances are applied accordingly as guiding analytical frameworks either singly or in combination based on the contextual demands of the study. For instance, in this ethnically complex and multiple research context, the conceptual approaches of *ethnicity* and *ethnic relations* enable us to understand the differing socio-cultural factors that underpin the dynamics of existing and emerging inter-ethnic relations and interactions of the different categories of population inhabiting the area at large and most particularly the Gumuz and highland resettlers. The *analytical framework of indigenous ecological knowledge and resource management* that considers "traditional ecological

20

knowledge as knowledge-practice-belief complex" enables us to better understand the Gumuz's indigenous knowledge, environmental thought, ethical values, and natural resource management systems as blended in their traditional belief systems. The *theoretical approaches to involuntary resettlement* enable us to recognize the multiple impact of resettlement upon the resettlers, hosts and the environment at large, especially emphasising the trauma and stresses of the relocatees and the alienation and deprivation of the autochthonous Gumuz from their vital livelihood resources. Finally, the *analytical framework of rural livelihood strategies and local social institutions* enables us to realise the invisible and often neglected aspect by resettlement planners but most indispensable role of local social institutions in the pursuit of livelihood adaptation, which channel access to livelihood resources, and fix the web of social relationships within and across groups. Above all, at the crux of this study, principal importance is attached to the investigation of the crucial significance of local social institutions.

2.2 Theoretical Approaches to Ethnicity and Ethnic Relations

There are two broadly predominant but competing approaches to the understanding of ethnicity, ethnic identity, ethnic groups and ethnic relations. These are usually characterised as *primordialism* and *constructivism*. Some scholars do also categorise the paradigms of understanding ethnicity into three approaches: *Primordialism, instrumentalism, and constructivism* (Sokolovski and Tishkov 1996; Kaufman 2000). Nevertheless, many of the theoretical accounts of ethnicity are clustered under the former two categories, combining the arguments of instrumentalism and constructivism under one category and labelling it by either of the terms or several related others such as circumstantialism, situationalism, interactionalism, and subjectivism (Thompson 1989; Jenkins 1996; Banks 1996; Llobera 1999). On the other hand, primordialism is also labelled by several other related variant terms such as essentialism, naturalism, objectivism, and socio-biology. In order to simplify the excessive terminological overcrowding, the researcher preferred *primordialism* and *constructivism* as main terms while reviewing the respective conceptual literature. The other variant terms of the two concepts may also be used whenever found necessary.

Primordialist Approach

Primordialists view ethnicity as an objective given that is bound to be natural and innate to human identity based on fixed deep primordial attachments to a group or culture. They believe and contend that ethnic identity is a primordial feature of humanity existing deeply rooted in the historical experiences of all societies with inherent characteristics of irrational attachments based on blood, race, language, religion, territory, and a common mentality of recognisable membership (Shils 1957; Geertz 1973; Isaacs 1975; van den Berghe 1981, 1986, 1996; Grosby 1996). The primordialists attempt to describe the objectivity of ethnicity by asserting the existence of some real and tangible foundation to ethnic identification. However, within the broader category of primordialists, they are subdivided into those who view ethnicity as a predominantly natural and biological phenomenon and those who view ethnicity as a construed product of culture and history (Sokoloviski and Tishkov 1996:190). For the extremist socio-biological primordialists, ethnicity is conceived as based on biology and determined by genetic and geographical factors in which group identification is genetically coded as a product of early human evolution when the ability to recognise members of families and primary groups was essential for survival.

The central concept of socio-biological primordialists is "inclusive fitness" and they define ethnicity as "a comprehensive form of natural selection and kinship connections, a primordial instinctive impulse, which 'continues to be present even in the most industrialised mass societies of today'" (Van den Berghe 1981:35 cited in Sokoloviski and Tishkov 1996:191). Thus, according to the naturalist, positivist, essentialist, or evolutionary extreme form of the primordialist conceptual approach, ethnic identity is genetically or ethno-biologically predetermined, based on species' features of "group-based endogamy and descent-based membership" in which ethnic groups are considered "natural kinds" like "species." This extreme primordialist position holds ethnicity as an innately given aspect of human identity – something deeply embedded in the psychological cognition of its members – which can only be described rather than explained. However, the cultural and historical moderate primordialists view ethnicity as extended groups or collective identities deeply rooted in historical ties and based on assumed kinship or descent, custom, language, and race (Thompson 1989).

The strength and major contribution of the primordialist approach to ethnicity is its strong stress on the emotional power of ethnic attachment. Group identity, the approach notes, is frequently marked on "*the body*, either naturally as racial characteristics or carved on by scarification, circumcision or other artificial means"; "*native language*, the conceptual lens by which one understands the world"; and "*religion*, that explicitly and intentionally shapes values and identity" (Kaufman 2000:4, emphasis added). Kaufman further considers the mutually reinforcing bonds of the stated markers' significance in providing ethnicity its power in the primordialist view and describes "ethnic loyalty" as "some fundamental biological drives, such as defence of kin and territoriality, in addition to such ubiquitous social derives as the desire to honour one's ancestors."

Constructivist Approach

Constructivists view ethnicity as not objectively "given," but rather fluid, situationally defined, and strategically manipulated subjective and rational socio-cultural constructions (Barth 1969, 1994, 1998; Ronald Cohen 1978; Eller and Coughlan1993, 1996; Jenkins 1994, 1996, 1997). For constructivists, ethnic identity is conceived as dynamic, flexible and variable in which both the contents and boundaries of an ethnic group change based on circumstances. For them, ethnic groups are subjectively constructed collective entities without fixed boundaries based on economic, social or political processes. They consider ethnicity as a complex and highly adaptable social construction created by individuals and groups to bring together members for a common purpose. In this conceptual discourse, ethnicity is conceived as an affiliation and a repertoire rationally chosen or indoctrinated by individuals or groups to promote and achieve certain interests and goals. Here, ethnicity is seen as a representation constructed and manipulated by ethnic entrepreneurs and political elites or leaders to pursue their own multiple interests. This approach sees individuals to be ready to change group membership if necessary since they are not assigned permanent membership to an ethnic group. Under this paradigm, ethnicity is something to be explained, rather than described.

Ethnicity, explains Ronald Cohen (1978:397), is "a series of nesting dichotomizations of inclusiveness and exclusiveness" where "the process of assigning persons to groups is both subjective and objective, carried out by self and others, and depends on what diacritics are used to define membership". Ethnic groups, Cohen (1978:385) considers, "are those widest scaled subjectively utilised modes of identification used in interactions among and between groups". Ethnic identity is considered to "refer to a process by which individuals are assigned to one ethnic group or another', which 'implies boundaries, their creation, maintenance and change" (Kunstadter1978 cited in Cohen 1978:386).

The most influential and seminal *constructivist approach* is that of Fredrik Barth (1969), which explains the situational and contextual nature of ethnicity. Barth's (1969) constructivist approach to ethnicity, writes Anthony P. Cohen (1994:59), is an "intellectually liberating paradigm shift" accredited for taking "ethnicity out of its social structural closet, and locating it firmly in the realms of the interactional, the transactional and the symbolic." The primary focus of investigation, Barth (1969:15) argues, should be on "the ethnic boundary that defines the group, not the cultural stuff that it encloses." This statement highlights the central tenets of his ethnic groups and boundaries. Barth's constructivist conception of ethnicity, explained as a summarised account in his "preface to 1998 reissue," of the seminal collection *Ethnic Groups and Boundaries*, is further elaborated to emphasise:

- That ethnicity is a matter of social organisation above and beyond questions of empirical cultural differences: it is about "the social organisation of culture difference";
- That ethnic identity is a matter of self-ascription and ascription by others in interaction, not the analyst's construct on the basis of his or construction of a group's "culture";
- That the cultural features of great import are boundary-connected: the diacritica by which membership is signalled and the cultural standards that actors themselves use to evaluate and judge the actions of ethnic co-members, implying that they see themselves as "playing the same game" (Barth 1998:6).

Ethnic identities in Barth's approach are not necessarily fixed. They are situational. What counts are boundaries rather than their content. Ethnicity is first and foremost a form of organising social life rather than an inborn characteristic (Verdery 1994:54). Barth's and his followers' approach to ethnicity is considered as fresh and innovative where their perspective emphasised an understanding of "the development and maintenance of ethnic group boundaries, social distance between ethnic groups, and the processes of social interaction" (Salamone and Swanson 1979:167). They elaborated further that the consciousness of separateness, which is the hallmark of ethnicity, is generated through sharing a common social field with other ethnic groups where, in the process of contact and interaction with others, that ethnic group finds the need to reaffirm or redefine itself maintaining boundaries and asserting differences. They explain that "very small differences will be magnified by a group wishing to remain unique from another group while major differences will be ignored by that same group should it wish to emphasise its solidarity with another groups" (Salamone and Swanson 1979:169f.). While recognising the freshness of Barth's approach to ethnicity, they have also expressed their critique in terms of certain limitations of the approach: "While Barth's observations shed valuable light on how groups maintain boundaries and manipulate identities, he does not account adequately for why a person presents a different self when engaged in interactions with members of different ethnic groups, nor does he deal fully with changes in ethnic group allegiances" (Salamone and Swanson 1979:170).

The constructivists stress the relational feature and situational character of ethnicity in the contexts and at different levels, which includes within groups, between groups, within the nation-state, and the transnational contextual horizons. Barth (1994:22-29) distinguished *micro, median,* and *macro* levels of ethnicity. Micro level ethnicity looks into how individuals form and experience ethnic identity in the interactional context with other individuals. Median level ethnicity looks into the formation and mobilisation of groups "whereby people sort themselves out by locality, neighbourhood, niche, and access to public goods in the story of ethnic mobilisation." Macro level ethnicity looks into how ethnic identity is affected both by nation-states as well as global and international organisations of various kinds. Nation-states affect ethnicity through legal frameworks and policies including use of force or threat as well as ideologically manipulating and controlling information through media, schools, and the like, imprinting particular ethnic or national world views. Meanwhile, international organisations influence ethnicity through global discourse on human rights and the role of United Nations in peace keeping and peace enforcing including extended roles of other specialised non-governmental organisations.

Inter-ethnic interactions are patterned on an ethnic boundary dichotomization of an in-group/out-group of "we" and "they" basis (Barth 1969). Ethnic identities are manipulated in the situations of inter-ethnic relationships. Ethnicity has no existence apart from inter-ethnic relations (Cohen 1978:389). The ethnic identities of marginal groups are considered as "essentially political products of specific situations, socially defined and historically determined" (Fukui and Markakis 1994:6).

The immediate generation of ethnological studies of ethnicity, following his joint volume on *Ethnic Groups and Boundaries*, states Barth (1994:18), "gave much attention to the linkage of ethnicity to the concept of *niche*, and to the theme of resource competition." By emphasising the divergent adaptations, he explains, "particular cultural traits may be useful as adaptations to particular environments and modes of subsistence" where "resource competition between populations with distinguishing cultural features may provide a special impetus to their mobilisation in collective action on the basis of shared ethnicity." Hence, the divergent ecological adaptations perspective, according to Barth (1969, 1994), provides a necessary component in the study of plural situations and the analysis of competitive ethnic relations. In other words, identity politics usually entails competition over resources (including economic, social, and political) in which collective identities are mobilised on the basis of unequal and divergent distribution of resources.

"Oppositional Model of Ethnic Solidarity": Combination of the Primordialist and Constructivist Approaches

Could the two conceptual approaches to ethnicity be re-synthesised in combination? The two approaches seem to conceptualise ethnicity rather in a mutually exclusive manner as if they are irreconcilable. Ethnicity seems both *primordial* and *circumstantial,* which needs further verification through cross-cultural research. Since both the *primordialist* and *constructivist* approaches seem to hold important elements of convincing arguments of varying degrees in their respective positions, they could possibly be re-synthesised in combination because neither of them alone provides sufficient and complete explanation and description of ethnicity.

An important conceptual point of view that could be reconsidered in differing contexts for a possible re-synthesis of the two approaches is Spicer's (1971:797) concept of "the oppositional process" that attempts to explain ethnicity, linking the primordial sentiments to circumstances in his arguments of "persistent identity systems." In an attempt to resynthesise *primordialist* and *constructivist* approaches to ethnicity, Scott (1990:164) reformulated "an explanatory model" by applying the concepts of Spicer's "oppositional process" as indicated in *figure one* below.

Figure 1: Oppositional Model of Ethnic Solidarity

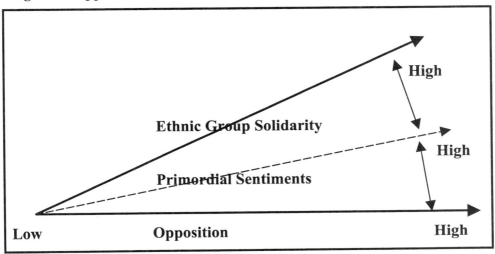

Source: Scott (1990: 164.)

As depicted in the above figure, Scott (1990:164) termed his reformulated explanatory model as "oppositional model of ethnic solidarity" and proposes its operational explanations as: *"The greater the opposition – economic, political, social, religious, or some combination thereof – perceived by an ethnic group, the greater the degree to which its historical sense of distinctiveness will be aroused, and hence the greater its solidarity or the more intense its movement towards redress"* (emphasis in the original).

The plausible argument in the above model lies in Spicer's and latter Scott's conscious stress that the approach cannot be applied in "every interethnic situation" except to those "persistent identity systems." Emphasising the explanatory power of the oppositional model as flexible and responsive to the "physical and socio-cultural" environment, Scott (1990:162f.) comparatively criticises the interactional approach as "more general" and the primordial approach as "monolithic." The approach does not intend to dichotomise persistent and fluctuating ethnic identities; rather it "places them along a continuum of *degrees of ethnic solidarity,"* a dimension considered in the model as a "dependent variable." While the degree of opposition is considered as an "independent variable" to explain the "dependent variable." So, explaining Spicer's theory, Scott (1990:163) notes that "the degree of an ethnic group's identity will vary in direct proportion to the amount of oppo-

27

sition encountered by the group, the greater the opposition, the greater the degree of identity, and conversely, the lesser the amount of opposition, the lesser the degree of identity." The model places primordial sentiments as an "intervening variable" between the "dependent and independent variables" explaining that "the greater the degree of opposition, the greater the primordial sentiments engendered, and the greater the degree of ethnic solidarity expressed by the group."

In other words, opposition "does not lead directly to ethnic solidarity, but operates indirectly through the psychological mechanism of primordial sentiments." Opposition may take "economic, political, social, religious or some combination of these forms, depending on which rights the group perceives it is being denied." Scott (1990:165) further notes the persistence of ethnic identities by subjugated groups against all odds of the dominant conquerors as: "most subjugated populations after the ancient period were in fact large, dispersed, and resilient enough to have survived even the harshest treatment from their conquerors, with their separate ethnic identities remaining intact."

In this attempt of resynthesising primordial and circumstantial approaches to ethnicity, Scott (1990:167) argues, "primordial sentiments have to be tied to the circumstances under which they are aroused or maintained." He notes that the primordial ties to circumstances often occur "when the members of an ethnic group face opposition from another group on the basis of their ethnic, or ethno-religious, distinctiveness." Scott uses Spicer's "persistent identity systems" as an account of "continuing opposition across different environments;" though "opposition can also explain fluctuating ethnicity." Thus, Scott's explanatory model based on Spicer's concept of "opposition" attempts to combine and resynthesise both the primordialist and circumstantialist or constructivist approaches "to account for the ebb and flow of ethnic group solidarity."

Therefore, instead of conceptualising ethnicity from the extreme positions of purely *primordialist (objectivist)* versus *constructivist (subjectivist)* dichotomization of discourses, a possibility of reconciling the two paradigms seems more plausible like the above one argued by Spicer (1971) and later by his follower Scott (1990). Although the focus on either approach differs, a combination of both subjective and objective conceptual positions of understanding ethnicity yields credible and important representation of ethnicity on differing complex and dynamic circumstances.

2.3 Conceptual Approaches to Indigenous Ecological Knowledge, Thought and Natural Resource Management Systems

Review of Concepts and Definitions

Indigenous Peoples
Indigenous peoples are categorised as communities having relatively small populations with ancestral cultures of their own typically accompanying the status of minority groups within a nation-state controlled by others and remaining largely invisible to members of the world's dominant societies (Greaves, 1996:635f.). The defining characteristic features of indigenous people is considered to be their original inhabitation of the land they have lived in from time immemorial (Alfredsson 1993; cited in Plant 1994:7). Based on international criteria, Berkes (2001:115) identifies four characteristics that distinguish indigenous peoples from others: "They are descendants of groups inhabiting an area prior to the arrival of other populations; they are politically not dominant; they are culturally different from the dominant population; and they identify themselves as indigenous."

It is estimated that there are roughly 200 million indigenous people (about 4% of the total population) in the world mostly living in harsh, remote and varied environments practising a mode of subsistence based on cultivation, hunting, gathering, fishing, pastoral nomadism or a range of these in combination (Beauclerk et al. 1988:3). The indigenous peoples' special relationships with their lands, territories and the surrounding environment make them different from the rest of the national population. These relationships are extremely important and encompass and incorporate economic, social and cultural aspects of life in which the people are spiritually attached to their invisible world that guarantees ownership, mediates resource allocation, and endows meaning of identity on both a collective and an individual basis. The indigenous peoples reveal a high degree of knowledge about their natural resources based on observation and practice due to their close relation to the land they own and use, thus maintaining the underlying stability of the environment. Their values and priorities are rational responses to the environment.

Indigenous Knowledge
Indigenous knowledge is a local knowledge unique to a local setting of a given culture (Warren et al. 1995:xv). Brush (1996:4) considers the existence of two definitions of indigenous knowledge – one broad and the other narrow. According to Brush, a broader approach contrasts the popular or

29

folk culture-specific knowledge preserved in unwritten oral traditions with "decultured" formal and specialised knowledge preserved in written text, whereas the narrower definition, which is more common in current usage, refers to the knowledge systems of indigenous people and minority cultures. Seeland (1997:102) explains the term indigenous knowledge to mean something that originates locally, emerging as peoples' perceptions and experiences in a specific environment as a continuous process of observation and interpretation in relation to the locally acknowledged everyday rationalities and transcendental powers. Indigenous knowledge is considered to represent the best fits under marginal circumstances having been tried and tested over generations. It is believed to comprehend processes and continuities in diverse environmental contexts and play a central importance in the indigenous people's systems of local level natural resource management. As a user-derived information base of a society, it provides a foundation for indigenous innovation. Since indigenous knowledge is derived from accumulated experiences continually influenced by internal creativity, it offers much to the construction of scientifically sound and humanistically oriented concepts and strategies for action, especially within a changing environment where the threat to the loss of bio-diversity is ever increasing.

Indigenous Ecological Knowledge, Thought and Belief System/Worldview
Indigenous ecological knowledge is considered as a subset of indigenous knowledge and limited, more explicitly, to ecological knowledge. More specifically, indigenous ecological knowledge is considered as a body of intimate and detailed knowledge of the environment built up by local people through generations of living in close contact with nature (Appiah-Opoku and Mulamoottil 1997:167).

The ecological knowledge of indigenous people, Seeland (1997:102) states, is based on their local world where human, plant, and animal lives constitute interconnections of nature and culture. What indigenous people know, notes Seeland (1997:103), "is drawn from their experience of appropriating nature as culture." He explains, in the stated context, culture to mean "the amalgamation of both local natural resources and their mobilisation through social cognition and institutions at distinct local levels." He further tries to reveal the amalgamation and interconnection of nature and culture, considering the appropriation of nature to constitute a local culture according to a distinct indigenous pattern. Interestingly enough, what local people know about nature is also a reflection of their culture, which asserts the interconnection of nature and culture. Seeland considers the aggregate complex of mankind, plants, and wildlife to constitute a natural world that has evolved as culture where knowledge results from the processes of appropriating nature as culture.

In a study that explores the nature of ecological thinking concerning the meaning of the earth and human being's rightful place within it, Peter Marshall (1994) considers humans to be an integral part of nature, stressing that the politics of ecology are the interaction between human species and the environment. Marshall (1994:138) describes the empirical account of the North American Indians' native ecological thinking concerning the very web of nature, which sustained their life in the face of encroaching western civilisation as follows:

> Despite the rude intrusion of Europeans, the Indians still kept their circles complete, holding the earth together in their travels along its sacred ways. They lived in comparative harmony with the natural world, following the cycles of nature and developing a subtle and profound understanding of their surroundings. They were true conservationists, realizing that life depended on the well-being of the earth. The earth was considered as a goddess and was worshipped for her fertility and abundance. Strongly animistic, they lived in close contact with other creatures and believed that all nature is an interconnected living organism: 'In the circle of life every being is no more, or less, than any other. We are all sisters and brothers. Life is shared with the bird, bear, insect, plants, mountains, clouds, stars, and sun. To be in harmony with the natural world, one must live within the cycles of life' [Steiner, 1987]. The art, music, stories and spirituality of these tribal peoples were intimately connected with their environment.

Marshall's account above considers every part of the mother earth that sustains all life as sacred where all things are perceived as interconnected. The native people are closely identified with nature and its creatures, where the natural and cultural being harmoniously bonded. So, in the native's ecological thinking, nothing is insignificant in nature, in which plants, rocks, animals, humans, the living and the dead all have a share in the maintenance of the universal natural order.

The worldview or traditional belief systems of many indigenous peoples are viewed as incorporating the idea and thought that humans are part of the natural environment. Lovelace (1984:198) explains the ecological significance and impact of traditional belief systems as: "Beliefs and the ideas, emotions, and motivations that beliefs frequently generate often serve as important stimuli for a wide range of human behaviour that directly or indirectly affects the environment. Beliefs affect how humans position and organise themselves within, and with respect to, the landscape. Beliefs also affect human decisions about which environments to occupy, which resources to exploit, and how, when, and to what degrees these should be occupied or exploited." Beliefs, considers Lovelace, often provide interpretations, explanations, understanding, security, and the basis for social solidarity and action taken as adaptive and sometimes even critical for the survival and continued well-being of the society and its members. Stressing the cultural belief aspect of human ecology, Lovelace stresses that traditional belief systems are often highly integrated into the patterns and processes by which humans relate to and adapt to their environments.

Analytical Framework of Indigenous Ecological Knowledge and Adaptive Resource Management

Traditional Ecological Knowledge as "Knowledge-Practice-Belief Complex": A framework of Analysis (Fikret Berkes)
Traditional ecological knowledge, defines Berkes (1999:8), "is a cumulative body of knowledge, practice, and belief, and evolving by adaptive processes and handed down through generations by cultural transmission, about the relationship of living beings (including humans) with one another and with their environment." Berkes (1999:13f.) further explains traditional ecological knowledge as a *knowledge-practice-belief complex* considered at four interrelated analytical levels: (a) the local knowledge of animals, plants, soils, and landscape based on empirical observations; (b) the natural resource management system that includes an appropriate set of practices, tools and techniques using local environmental knowledge; (c) the traditional social institutions that include sets of rules-in-use and codes of social relationships; and (d) the worldview or belief system that shapes environmental perception and gives meaning to observations of the environment, a level within which the other three levels are embedded as indicated in *figure two* below.

Berkes' (1999:14) *knowledge-practice-belief complex*, depicted in *figure two*, "shows four levels of analysis as concentric ellipses, with the management system including local knowledge, the institutional level enveloping the management system, and all three levels embedded within a worldview." However, he emphasises that the four levels are not always distinct, with particularly the management system and the social institutions that govern them often being closely coupled. Berkes (1999:14) explains that "there are feedbacks among the levels, and the linkages are dynamic relationships.

Local knowledge may grow; both management systems and institutions may adapt, change, and fall apart and may be renewed. Worldviews shape observations and social institutions but may themselves be affected by changes occurring at the other levels, such as the collapse of management systems."

Figure 2: Levels of Analysis in Traditional Knowledge and Management Systems

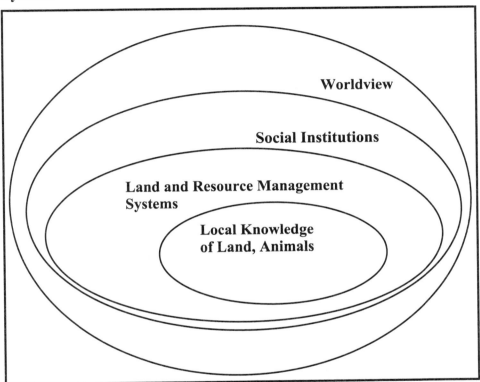

Source: Berkes (1999: 13)

By treating traditional ecological knowledge as an interrelated *knowledge-practice-belief complex*, he states, "it is possible to examine ecological practices and worldviews, and their dynamics together." He further states "the knowledge-practice-belief complex of many indigenous traditions incorporates wisdom that has implicitly or explicitly inspired the centrality and beauty of the larger whole and the place of humans in it." In his analytical framework of the *knowledge-practice-belief complex*, traditional worldview and belief system matter most as a fundamental lesson of indigenous eco-logical knowledge crucial to its analysis. As part of the belief system and worldview component of indigenous ecological knowledge, states Berkes (1999:163), one encounters an ethic of non-dominant, respectful human-nature relationship, a sacred ecology. He stresses that traditional worldviews are diverse, but many share the belief in a sacred, personal relationship be-tween humans and other living beings. Additionally, Berkes (2001:109) points out that, "world-views limit and inspire human behaviour, shape ob-servations, and perceptions." Meanwhile, he considers worldview as the larger conceptual complex in which ethics is embedded. He further defines ethics to be "codes that exert a palpable influence on human behaviour," which "provide models to emulate, goals to strive for, and norms by which to evaluate actual behaviour."

Adaptive Natural Resource Management
As earlier explained, indigenous ecological knowledge plays a central role in the indigenous people's system of natural resource management, which is also considered "adaptive management." Indigenous natural resource man-agement systems, argues Berkes, are adaptive responses to the uncertainties and surprises of diverse environments that have evolved over time and should not be recognised as mere traditions. Adaptive management, he ex-plains, "is fundamentally interdisciplinary and combines historical, com-parative, and experiential approaches." He argues that indigenous ecological knowledge represents the summation of millennia of ecological adaptations of human groups to their diverse environments and explains "adaptive man-agement" as:

> Adaptive management is an integrated method for natural resource man-agement. It is adaptive because it acknowledges that environmental conditions will always change, thus requiring management institutions to respond to feedback's by adjusting and evolving. Adaptive management, like traditional knowledge systems, takes a dynamic view of ecosystems, emphasizes processes (including resource use) that are part of ecological cycles of renewal, and stresses the importance of resilience, that is, the buffering ability of the system to absorb change without breaking down or going into another state of equilibrium (Berkes 1999:60).

Meanwhile, according to Berkes et al. (1998:412), traditional ecological knowledge is akin to adaptive management because it is based on detailed observation of the dynamics of the natural environment, feedback learning, social-system ecological-system linkages, and resilience enhancing mechanisms.

The indigenous institutions of resource management enshrined within the indigenous people's knowledge systems ensure smooth functioning of the system in the local context enabling the members to manage their natural resources in an environmentally friendly and ecologically stable manner. These indigenous institutions include a complex system of community norms, values, ethics, customs and taboos that have been institutionalised as customary laws and conventions for regulating resource use and management. These institutions, mostly manifested in the traditional belief system, act as powerful moral sanctions against wanton destruction of natural resources. In addition, among other actions, the wrongdoers are usually socially sanctioned through the local institutions by shaming them publicly and using the example to remind everyone else of the rules of proper resource use and management.

Integral Shifting Cultivation as Natural Resource Management System
Integral shifting cultivation (also known as "swidden farming" or "slash-and-burn cultivation") is considered as not only an agricultural system but also a "most important natural resource management system" (Permpangsacharoen 1999:3; Warner 1991:9). It is practised as a mode of subsistence by an estimated 5% of the world's total population (200 to 250 million) on 30% of the world's exploitable soils in the humid tropics (Warner 1991). There are two forms of shifting cultivation: "integral swidden" and "pioneer swidden". According to Conklin (1957), integral swiddeners practice a land-use system based on "a more traditional, year-round, community-wide, self-contained, and ritually sanctioned way of life" (Conklin 1957:2 cited in Warner 1991:10). Integral swiddeners are considered as stable communities, which reside and have strong cultural and historical ties to the area for generations and possess a deep knowledge of the local natural environment. They practice swidden farming as a way of life.

The pioneer swiddeners, on the other hand, are peasants with strong socio-cultural ties outside the immediate swidden area, practising partial swidden predominantly based on economic interests and using the swidden to supplement the permanent field (Conklin 1957:3 cited in Warner 1991:10). The distinction between these two forms of swidden farming is very important, because the two systems have different impacts on the natural environment. The pioneer swiddeners cause a destruction of the forest ecosystem because they mainly belong to the land-hungry migrants who do not have enough knowledge of the forest ecosystem and use agricultural

35

methods from the area of origin rather than those suited to the area of resettlement (Moran 1987:227 cited in Warner 1991:10). In contrast, integral swiddeners practice an established and self-contained way of life skilfully maintaining the underlying stability of the forest ecosystem or the local natural environment. Integral swiddeners intervene temporarily in the forest ecosystem without destroying it forever. Their practices allow the forest to be replaced with a successional series of regrowth that is more productive than the original forest for the swiddener (FAO 1978 cited in Warner 1991:12). Usually, the distinction between these two forms of swidden farming systems is not precisely differentiated and critically considered. Hence, integral shifting cultivation is defined as a complex agricultural system that is well adapted to the environmental limitations and ecological realities of the tropical forest which requires an in-depth knowledge of the tropical environment and a high degree of managerial skill (Warner, 1991:2). It is regarded as a most important natural resource management strategy because the fields are shifted in order to consciously use the rich nutrients of the natural vegetation-soil complex (McGrath 1987 cited in Warner 1991:9).

The indigenous ecological knowledge is the foundation for integral shifting cultivation, which is found to be a dynamic and flexible system of cultivation where forest is traditionally cut and burnt on a long-term rotational basis so as to transfer nutrients into food crops by eliminating other competitor species and consciously maintaining the underlying ecological stability by conserving the forest eco-system. However, based on bias and misconception of the "experts" or "central authorities" due to lack of properly understanding the ways of the lives of the integral shifting cultivators, there is an increasing trend of promoting permanent agriculture by eradicating shifting cultivation (Permpongsacharoen 1999:17).

A Critique of Indigenous and 'Western' Environmental Thinking
Berkes (1999:163) states, "the globalization of western culture has meant the globalization of western resource management." The indigenous worldviews are considered to be diverse and different from the dominant western worldviews. The western environmental thinking that displaces indigenous ecological knowledge and excludes people from nature asserting that "the users of resources cannot be managers at the same time" by insisting "professionals know best" is termed, according to Berkes (1999:176), a "positivist-reductionist paradigm," which in turn is challenged by indigenous ecological knowledge. Berkes (1999:178) considers western conventional science as reductionistic, too mechanistic, and detached from people and politics based on a search for universal truths assuming the existence of a reality driven by

immutable laws. According to this positivist-reductionist simplistic approach that dominates conventional resource management, he explains, the role of science is to discover universal truths with an ultimate aim of predicting and controlling nature. He criticises that the scientists themselves for being detached from the real world and operating in a value-free environment using reductionism by breaking a system into discrete components, analysing the components and making predictions on the basis of the analysis of the parts in which knowledge about the world is then synthesised into generalisations and principles independent of context, space and time.

The western ecologist is viewed as a scientist who treats "nature as essentially non-living, a machine to be dissected, interpreted and manipulated" (Evernden 1993:20 cited in Berkes 1999:54). The western cosmology is perceived as far too heavily dependent on "empiricism and scientism and is too mechanistic and analytic; it is insufficiently based on humanistic notions and morality toward nature" (Skolimowski 1981 cited in Berkes 1999:54). As a result, in the place of indigenous resource management systems, explains Berkes, the "western scientists [whom Berkes refers to as 'high priests'] enforced a system characterised by disembeddedness; universalism; supremacy of individualism; nature/culture and subject/object dichotomy; mobility; and an instrumental, utilitarian attitude toward nature" (Banuri and Apffel Marglin 1993 cited in Berkes 1999:177). In other words, the "western scientists" reject traditional knowledge and management systems due to the following characteristics, which do not fit their new paradigm due to such characteristics as "embeddedness of knowledge in the local culture; boundedness of local knowledge in space and time; the importance of community; lack of separation between nature and culture, and between subject and object; attachment to local environment; and a non-instrumental approach to nature" (Banuri and Apffel Marglin 1993 cited in Berkes 1999:176f.). Thus, Berkes points out that a secularised and utilitarian-dominant western worldview of depersonalised nature is not shared by the indigenous worldviews. Instead, indigenous worldviews of nature are diverse, which according to Berkes, "share the belief in a sacred and personalised relationship between humans and other living beings." Thus, indigenous peoples are often considered having mutual relationships with their environment and co-evolving with it.

On the other hand, critically considering the obvious challenges affecting the indigenous ecological knowledge systems of native peoples in the face of market economy, Berkes (1999:151f.) argues, "...perhaps the overzealous attempts to portray all indigenous peoples as natural conservationists places unrealistic expectation on native groups to preserve land ceded to them in the same state as they received it. This is happening at a time when many indigenous groups are linked to the market economy and may be compelled to engage in activities that differ in type and intensity from traditional patterns of resource use." Explaining the causes of the challenge, he states that due to loss of control of resources, breakdown of land use and knowledge systems, population growth, commercialisation, and technology change, many of the indigenous peoples of the world cannot be considered conservationists. However, irrespective of the challenges faced by the indigenous knowledge systems, he emphasises that many of the indigenous peoples do still retain elements of natural resource use and management practices that are consistent with the protection of biodiversity.

Rooted in different worldviews and unequal in power, states Berkes (1999:179), Western and indigenous ecological knowledge are not easy to combine. The most useful way to think of it is to consider indigenous knowledge as complementary to Western scientific knowledge and not a replacement for it. Since each is legitimate in its own rights, contexts and its strengths the two knowledge systems and thoughts could be pursued separately but in parallel, with opportunities to enrich one another because the two can be brought together and used on common grounds such as sustainability. Moreover, indigenous ecological knowledge, thought and management systems have the potential to contribute to the current understanding and use of a wide variety of ecosystems. Thus, according to Berkes (1999:182), the indigenous ecological knowledge, thought and management systems of diverse native peoples provide an alternative "view of an ecosystem pulsating with life and spirit," incorporating people belonging to the land and having special "relationships of peaceful co-existence with other beings."

2.4 Theoretical Approaches to Involuntary Resettlement

Review of Definitions and Concepts

Resettlement refers to a variety of migration and settlement types and can be broadly categorised into two: *spontaneous*, which leaves full scope for individual initiatives; and *involuntary* or *forced*, which refers to a planned and controlled transfer of people from one area to another. Involuntary resettlement schemes are conducted in the entire world as a response to diverse factors, out of which the major ones include: the need for power production such as dams (Colson 1958, 1960, 1963, 1964, 1971; Scudder 1962, 1968, 1973, 1991, 1993, 1996; Scudder and Colson 1982; Chambers 1970; Cernea

1991 1993, 1996; Cernea and Guggenheim 1993; McDowell 1996; Cernea and McDowell 2000); infrastructural construction such as highways, urban growth and ports, (Cernea 1993); open-pit mining and construction of thermal energy plants (Cernea 1996); the establishment of biosphere reserves and parks (Brandon and Wells 1992; West and Brechin 1991); population pressure and natural catastrophes (Hansen and Oliver Smith 1982); man-made adversities, poverty, unemployment, and structural adjustment reforms (Cernea 1996); and "politically mandated mass relocations" (Clay 1988; Dessalegn 1988, 1989; De Wet 1993; Dieci and Viezolli 1992; A. Pankhurst 1992; Wolde-Selassie 1998, 2000). Cernea (1993:379) consolidates the major causal agents which lead to forced population displacement and relocation into four broad categories. These are (1) natural disasters: droughts, floods, and earthquakes; (2) wars/political turmoil; (3) persecution: ethnic/racial/religious; and (4) development programs causing major changes in land/water use.

Success and failure in resettlement schemes depend on a combination of factors. Proper planning based on adequate pre-investment surveys of the physical and human resources and the social setting is a key element in implementing resettlement schemes, whereas inadequate planning and implementation of resettlement schemes creates serious difficulties and costly re-adjustments. According to Scudder (1996a:34), several rural resettlement studies have documented high failure rates, demonstrating that resettlement is a distinctive and complex type of development. Based on his research experience of over forty years among Zambia's Gwembe Tonga, he emphasises the importance of longitudinal research for studying resettlement as a dynamic process (Scudder 1993:123, 1996a:35).

In emergency situations, resettlement schemes are not well planned in advance, and at the same time the resettlers are not selected carefully. The three main victims of inadequately designed and poorly planned rural resettlement schemes are *the resettlers, the host population, and the environment*. Involuntary resettlement severely impoverishes or disintegrates the livelihood resources of the resettlers. Relocation of resettlers often destroys their previous way of life and involves adaptation to a new land and communities where their once-effective local knowledge often no longer functions appropriately. Governments and executing agencies take control of people's lives, property and economic resources, which are alienated from family and community control. The community's social, political, and religious leaders are impotent to prevent the disruption and disorder – in which case everyone is affected. Mathur (1995) considers resettlement as an unmitigated disaster when viewed from the perspectives of the resettlers; and states an observer's account as: "No trauma can be more painful for a family than to get up-rooted from a place where it has lived for generations and to move to a place where it may be a total stranger" (Varma 1985 cited in Mathur 1995:17). Mathur is critical of the lack of sound policy and legal frameworks in many countries world-wide to fully protect the rights of resettlers and hosts affected by the state-sponsored resettlement schemes.

Involuntary resettlement is full of stress for the people being relocated. Colson and Scudder (1982:269-270) synergistically categorise these stresses into three types: physiological, psychological, and socio-cultural. Physiological stress is measured by increased morbidity and mortality rates; psychological stress is due to trauma, grieving for lost home and anxiety about the uncertain future; and socio-cultural stress is associated with the economic, political, and other cultural effects of relocation. Moreover, socio-cultural stress is inferred from the way in which people react to the implementation of resettlement. In responding to the stress, the resettlers attempt to cling to the familiar through what Scudder (1973:53) called "a process of cultural involution". Thus, Scudder expressed that the stress of resettlement reduces the resettlers' capacity for innovation during the transition period; and he suggested that the resettlement authorities have to keep their plans simple, emphasise the familiar, and encourage the people to get back on their own feet at the earliest possible moment. According to his views, the lesson for developers and social engineers of the resettlement scheme is that resettlement is a dramatic step, inevitably accompanied by a transitional period of suffering; and should be used as a development strategy only after an intelligent and extensive examination of alternatives has been completed (Scudder 1973:55). For example, Scudder (1973:51) explains stress experienced by the communities by the Kariba dam on the Zambezi as:

> At Kariba women bemoaned the fact that they would have to leave the gardens, and especially the garden shelters, that had passed through the female line over generations. Shrine custodians feared that sickness would follow them if they left the area with which their ancestors' authority was associated. Adults did not wish to leave the graves of their ancestors and complained that they were being thrown away by government into an unfamiliar and hostile hinterland far from their beloved Zambezi river.

Meanwhile, Downing (1996:34) explains the fact of social disintegration, which affects the social fabric of resettlers in a resettlement context, in this way:

"[I]nvoluntary resettlement unravels the underlying social fabric [...]. Vital social networks and life-support mechanisms for families are weakened or dismantled. Authority systems are debilitated or collapse. Groups lose their capacity to self-manage. The society suffers a demonstrable reduction in its capacity to cope with uncertainty. It becomes qualitatively less than its previous self. The people may physically persist but the community that was is no more.

Cernea (1993:393), meanwhile, argues that relocation caused by *planned* programs does not make the disruptions any less or the hardship any lighter, for those uprooted. He believes that the magnitude of adverse effects of resettlement schemes can be reduced, provided that political commitment, fair legal frameworks and adequate resources are put in place. However, most research results demonstrate the fact that involuntary relocation causes countless adverse effects on local communities destroying economies, disrupting production systems, disintegrating socio-cultural life and causing multiple stresses giving rise to multidimensional impoverishment (Gray 1996:99).

Involuntary resettlement imposes adverse effects on the host population by alienating them from their vital livelihood resources (land, forest, water, pasture, and so on). In many cases, areas endowed with agricultural potentials and selected by planners for resettlement being considered as "unutilised" are frequently found to be already under use at least in a very expansive way by populations practising shifting cultivation in tropical rain-forests or by nomadic people in arid areas (Meliczek 2000:29). According to Meliczek, hostilities between the host and resettlers develop not only because the indigenous population loses part of its resources, but the hosts also become marginalised and will not receive the support extended to the resettlers by the state. The violation of the rights of the host population frequently creates difficulties and hostilities towards the newcomers. Moreover, in most cases, the socio-economic and cultural differences between the two categories of people threaten to create conflicts between the host and the new comers (Dessalegn 1989:721). Hence, the adverse effects of resettlement on host (indigenous) population in relocation sites have been seriously criticised in rhetoric. However, in practice, the effects of resettlement upon the livelihoods of the host populations have received little consideration; and there is generally a tendency showing reluctance to investigate further into the welfare of the host communities (Salem-Murdock 1993:307).

Resettlement changes the natural and social environments in the relocation sites. In poorly planned resettlement, land clearance and deforestation accelerates soil and water erosion, extinguishes the flora and fauna, and creates an imbalance in the eco-system of the relocation areas (Dessalegn 1989:722; Wolde-Selassie 1998:30). Resettlement, states De Wet (1988:182), involves the movement of communities from one environment to the other and changes or modifies the physical and social environment in which the resettlers find themselves and adapt. He further elaborates that the magnitude of stress resettlers face can be better understood by the kind and degree of environmental modifications they undergo since some moves will involve greater modification and adaptation and greater stress than others. According to De Wet (1988:182), "the greater the physical and social environment modifications, the greater will be the stress." De Wet (1988:183) describes, the physical and social environments resettlers undergo:

> The new physical environment will provide the broad context to which re-locatees will have to adapt, and within which new social patterns will develop. Of relevance here will be factors such as whether relocatees are close enough to their old home area to be able to keep up contact, or if the old area has been transformed, whether they are in an area which is topographically, agriculturally and climatically similar or different, whether they will have to adopt new means of making a livelihood, and what new economic opportunities are available in the area....The social component of the environment aspect of relocation relates to matters such as demography, organisation of the new residential areas, layout of the resettlement area as a whole, and the administrative structure under which the relocated community falls.

De Wet (1993:323) argues that the nature of spatial changes in the resettlers' physical and social environments determines, to a large extent, their socio-economic and cultural behaviour patterns that develop as they respond to the new circumstances. He emphasises that resettlers will be affected differently, both across and within communities, and will accordingly respond differently to their physical and socio-economic spatial circumstances.

Thus, the wide range of involuntary resettlement research shows the fact that relocation results in multiple impacts of differing magnitude upon rural livelihood resources as well as causing enormous human and environmental consequences affecting the resettlers, host communities, and the environment at large.

"Impoverishment Risk and Reconstruction Model" (*Michael M. Cernea*)
Cernea (1991:196, 1993:388, 1996:21, 2000:20) identifies impoverishment
as a main variable in the resettlement process and formulates eight most
important sub-processes in which resettlement makes for impoverishment.
He argues that focusing on these eight sub-processes will enable planners
and implementers to turn the impoverishing tendency "on its head," into
initiatives to transform the resettlement experience from "stress-based" to
one of potential "reconstruction," and development. Cernea's eight most
important sub-processes that converge in impoverishment, which occur in
different locations with variable intensity are:

Landlessness: Expropriation of land removes the main foundation upon
which a people's productive systems, commercial activities, and livelihoods
are constructed. This is the principal form of de-capitalisation and pauperisa-
tion of displaced people, as loss of both natural and man-made capital.

a) *Joblessness*: The risk of losing wage employment is very high both in
   urban and rural displacements for those employed in enterprises, services, or agriculture. Unemployment or underemployment among resettlers often endures long after physical relocation has been completed.
b) *Homelessness*: Loss of shelter tends to be only temporary for many resettlers; but, for some, homelessness or a worsening in their housing
   standards remains a lingering condition. In a broader cultural sense, loss
   of a family's individual home and the loss of a group's cultural space
   tend to result in alienation and status deprivation.
c) *Marginalisation*: Marginalisation occurs when families lose economic
   power and spiral on a "downward mobility" path. Middle-income farm
   households do not become landless, they become small landholders;
   small shopkeepers and craftsmen downsize and slip below poverty
   thresholds. Many individuals cannot use their earlier acquired skills at
   the new location; human capital is lost or rendered inactive or obsolete.
   Economic marginalisation is often accompanied by social and psychological marginalisation expressed as a drop in social status, in resettlers'
   loss of confidence in society and in themselves, a feeling of injustice,
   and deepened vulnerability. The coerciveness of displacement and the
   victimisation of resettlers tend to depreciate resettlers' self-image, and
   they are often perceived by host communities as a socially degrading
   stigma.
d) *Increased Morbidity and Mortality*: Massive population displacement
   threatens to cause serious declines in health levels. Displacement-
   induced social stress and psychological trauma are sometimes accompa-

nied by the outbreak of relocation related illnesses, particularly parasitic and vector-born diseases such as malaria and *schistosomiasis*. Unsafe water supply and improvised sewage systems increase vulnerability to epidemics and chronic diarrhoea, dysentery, and so on. The weakest segments of the demographic spectrum – infants, children, and the elderly – are affected most strongly.

e) *Food Insecurity*: Forced uprooting increases the risk that people will fall into temporary or chronic undernourishment, defined as calorie-protein intake levels below the minimum necessary for normal growth and work.

f) *Loss of Access to Common Property and Services*: For poor people, particularly for the landless and assetless, loss of access to common property assets that belonged to relocated communities (pastures, forested lands, water bodies, burial grounds, quarries, and so on) results in significant deterioration in income and livelihood levels. Typically, losses of common property assets are not compensated for by governments. These losses are compounded by loss of access to some public services, such as school that can be grouped within this category of risks.

g) *Social Disarticulation*: Forced displacement tears apart the existing social fabric. It disperses and fragments communities, dismantles patterns of social organisation and interpersonal ties; kinship groups become scattered as well. Life-sustaining informal networks of reciprocal help, local voluntary associations, and self-organised mutual service are disrupted. This is a net loss of valuable "social capital" that compounds the loss of natural, physical, and human capital. The social capital lost through social disarticulation is typically unperceived and uncompensated for by the programs causing it, and this real loss has long-term consequences. (Cernea and McDowell 2000:23-30).

Cernea (1996a:22) explains that his "conceptual construct of the impoverishment process has not only *cognitive value*, but *operational* usefulness as well" (emphasis in the original). "The basic policy message embodied in the impoverishment/reconstruction model is that the intrinsic socio-economic risks must be brought under control through an *encompassing strategy* and cannot be tamed through *piecemeal* random measures based solely on financial compensation for condemned assets" (Cernea 1996a:23, emphasis in the original). Scudder (1996a:21) characterises the impoverishment model as "more a policy-oriented than a theoretical analysis of resettler and institutional behaviour during the resettlement process, with the identification of each risk directing attention to the needs for corrective action." He considers

44

the model to be compatible with the more descriptive analysis of impacts during the initial years of resettlement; and welcomes it as a way to more systematically assess the reasons why living standards for the majority are apt to decline, and then remain lower than before removal, during what Scudder and Colson have called the transition stage (Scudder, 1996a:21). De Wet (1996:21) comments on Cernea's concept of impoverishment, considering its importance in refining understanding of impoverishment risk and reconstruction dynamic in resettlement. He further elaborates Cernea's concept to have the potential to contribute towards a much more detailed analysis and understanding of what happens in various stages of the resettlement process, and thus to lead to a refining of processual approaches, such as that of Scudder and Colson (1982).

"Processual Analysis of Resettlement as a Sequence of Stages"
(*Thayer Scudder and Elizabeth Colson*)
Scudder and Colson (1982) have formulated a four-stage resettlement conceptual framework dividing the relocation process into successive stages, namely, 1) the recruitment stage, 2) the transition stage 3) the stage of potential development, and 4) the handing over/incorporation stage (1982:274f.). This is the most developed theoretical approach, based on very long time longitudinal research on resettlement for over forty years.

a) *The recruitment stage* deals with the decision-making of the government and executing agencies to move a given population and about where they shall go and how the move shall take place. This stage does not directly involve the community. It is a stage in which the initiators of relocation think about the socio-cultural characteristics of the population to be moved and how these will affect their response to relocation and to the new environment. Decisions taken at this stage will influence the length and stressfulness of the transition stage (Scudder and Colson 1982:274; Scudder 1991:161, 1993:130, 1996a:8, 1996b:1112).

b) *The transition stage* is characterised by the struggle to adjust to loss of homeland and to new surroundings. This stage is characterised by multi-dimensional stress, with *physiological, psychological* and *socio-cultural* components interrelated synergistically. The stress reveals itself through higher morbidity and mortality rates, anxiety about loss of home and what the future may bring, and temporary or permanent loss of cultural inventory, including indigenous knowledge, customs, and institutions. This stage commences when the communities to be moved discover that they are to be moved, and involves the move, and the period immedi-

45

ately after it. During this stage, resettlers are risk-averse coping with the stress and uncertainty. In responding to the stress, the resettlers attempt to cling to the familiar through what is called "cultural involution." Stage two adjustment and coping usually continues for a minimum of two years following removal (Scudder and Colson 1982:274; Scudder 1991:163, 1993:131, 1996a:8f., 1996b:1112f.).

c) *The stage of potential economic and social development* is characterised by a more open-ended stance where previously risk-averse resettlers begin to be ready to take risks. Economic development is fostered as households increasingly pursue dynamic investment strategies. Initially, they begin shifting from a reliance on consumption crops to higher value cash crops. Production systems at the household level also begin to diversify, not so much as risk-avoidance strategy but as a means of reallocating family labour into more lucrative enterprises including livestock management and small-scale non-farm enterprises. A number of indicators characterise the transition between stages two and three which includes naming of physical features, increased emphasis on community as opposed to household development as reflected in the establishment of funeral and other social welfare associations and places of worship. Institutional developments continue throughout stage three which is characterised by a resurgence of cultural symbols, becoming almost a renaissance, as community members reaffirm control over their lives. According to Scudder, stage three development must be sustainable into the next generation for a resettlement project to be considered successful. Sustainability here refers to institutional sustainability as well as to environmental and economic sustainability. However, Scudder notes, relatively few resettlement projects reach stage three. The majority of people in many resettlement areas never arrive at stage three, which must be reached if the potential of the resettlement process is to be realised (Scudder and Colson 1982:275; Scudder 1991:264, 1993:133, 1996a:12, 1996b:1113f.).

d) *The stage of handing over and incorporation* commences when a second generation of resettlers that is able to compete successfully for national resources takes over from the pioneers. It is also characterised by the devolution of management responsibilities from specialised settlement agencies to the community of settlers and various line ministries. This stage is usually reached when a second generation has grown up in the new area and has assumed command (Scudder and Colson 1982:275; Scudder 1991:167; 1993:134, 1996a:13, 1996b:1114).

Scudder and Colson's resettlement theory has been criticised for its being a "stress centred model" (Cernea 1996) and for its high level of generalisation which obscures the importance of societal and environmental variation that influences significantly how people behave during the various stages (De Wet 1988, 1993, 1996). De Wet is critical of the model's fairly high level of generality, which lessens its explanatory power. He comments that the limitation of the model is in its formulation to explain the similarities rather than the differences in peoples' reactions to involuntary relocation (De Wet 1993:322). However, De Wet (1988:186) confirms the importance of the Scudder and Colson model at the recruitment and transition stage, which are the most stressful stages of relocation.

"Physical-Social Spatial Approach" (*Chris de Wet*)

De Wet's (1988, 1993) environmentally based physical-social spatial approach explains that relocation modifies a community's spatial setting in specific ways, and people respond to those particular modifications and change their behaviour accordingly. The spatial approach, as a conceptual framework to the analysis of relocation, explains in greater detail the nature of people's reactions to involuntary relocation, both in its more stressful stages and in the longer term. According to the *spatial approach*: "Inasmuch as relocation involves the movement of people from one place to another, it brings about a change in the spatial setting or context in which people find themselves, and to which they have to adapt. This change in spatial setting has both physical as well as socio-economic aspects, since as relocation involves people in new sets of social, economic, and political relationships" (De Wet 1993:322). Thus, De Wet suggests that a focus on elements of spatial change provide a means of accounting in greater detail for the similarities and differences in people's responses to relocation. According to De Wet (1993:323), "changes in the people's physical and social settings will to a large extent determine their new economic, demographic, and social circumstances, and the behaviour patterns that develop as they respond to these new circumstances. People will be affected differently, both across and within communities, and will accordingly respond differently to their new circumstances." In his *spatial approach* De Wet (1993:322) further explains:

> The kind and degree of spatial change that people undergo will vary from case to case. Some moves will involve a greater change in a people's physical setting and correspondingly greater degree of stress than will others. People may have to move to a new area with different agricultural, climatic, and economic conditions and opportunities [...]. Or people may

remain within their area of origin, moving only a few kilometers... Some moves will involve a greater change in people's social setting, placing them in much larger settlements than they were used to, and resulting in the breaking up of old social groupings and the ecological patterns on which they were predicated.

According to De Wet (1988:186), an environmentally-based physical-social spatial analysis of community relocation provides insights into the behaviour of relocatees. It is an approach which is able to cast light on why some relocation experiences are likely to be more stressful than others, by suggesting that the greater the environmental modification involved, the greater will be the corresponding stress.

"Social Spatial-Temporal Approach"/"Social Geometry Model" (*Theodore E. Downing*)

Downing (1996:42) explains social impoverishment caused by population relocation from his perspective of social geometry and argues "social dislocations accompanying involuntary resettlement may change some of the spatial-temporal dimensions which define a people's identity, threaten intangible spaces and moral order, modify behavioural orders, set new priorities and have a differential impact on people depending on their age, sex and rank". He notes that "space and time are socially defined and ordered in many ways" (Downing 1996:37). His social geometry approach shows properties of inclusion both temporally (e.g., second, minute, hour, day, year) and spatially (e.g., yard, neighbourhood, town, country). He explains that orders may be temporally sequential (baby, child, teenage, adult, old) and spatially sequential (gate, courtyard, entrance, house); and further complex orderings may involve a sequential intersection of time, space and personages (baptism, confirmation, first communion, and marriage). Downing also argues that social impoverishment occurs when the displaced are unable to answer the primary cultural question – "where are we?" For many, he states, the answer to this question also defines "who are we?" Downing (1996:48) promotes a theory of "social geometry," finding that "the answers to primary questions are encoded in the linkage of socially constructed places, socially constructed time and socially constructed personages; in which case, this linkage provides a framework for routine and ritual activities."

Downing's conceptual model can be taken as a deeper advancement of the socio-cultural impoverishment aspect of the sub-processes of Cernea's model, which Scudder commends as a major advantage of Cernea's model.

Scudder appreciates Downing's conceptual framework to be very important since it explores more systematically than others how involuntary resettlement adversely affects a society's working capacity by overloading it with "uncertainty and disorder" (Scudder 1996a:23). Here, Scudder states Downing's expression of how people "navigate in socially constructed time, socially constructed space, and among socially constructed personages" in which Downing emphasises that economic rehabilitation in a relocation context is a necessary but insufficient means for restoring order within a wider cultural domain.

2.5 Conceptual Approaches to Local Institutions and Livelihood Strategies

Local Social Institutions[14]

Local social institutions are structures that have been serving rural communities for longer periods passing from one generation to the other and through which local peoples' indigenous knowledge is manifested. The loyalty and accountability of local institutions are to the members of a given local community. Local social institutions are a stable part of a web of long established customs, values, norms, conventions, ethics and traditions that entail fundamental behavioural patterns of a community which are proven to sustain local needs having been tried and filtered for generations.

Institutions are defined as a humanly devised set of rules or constraints that structure social, economic, and political interactions that determine both what people are prohibited from doing, and under what conditions people are permitted to undertake certain activities (North 1991:97). North (1990:3) further elaborates that institutions have been devised by societies throughout history in order to guide human interaction, to create order, to reduce uncertainty, and to provide structure to everyday life as a dynamic framework within which human interaction takes place. Institutions are also considered as regularised practices or patterns of behaviour structured by rules and

---

[14]Local social institutions are also known by several related expressions such as local organisations, community organisations, social institutions, indigenous (social) institutions, voluntary associations, mutual self-help, informal civil societies, customary institutions, traditional institutions, social capital, informal institutions, and many other terms in combination. In this study, the term 'local social institutions' is simply selected as a convenient term to connote particularly those rural, local, informal, community social institutions/organisations. Once differentiated, the terms 'institutions' and 'organisations', are nevertheless used more-or-less interchangeably with similar meanings in order to avoid a complex meaning confusion that might result from distinguishing these closely related terms.

norms of society, which have widespread use (Giddens 1979 cited in Scoones 1998:12). Although the interplay of both institutions and organisations provides a structure to human interaction, North (1990:5) tries to make distinctions between institutions and organisations by taking the analogy of rules of a game (institutions) and the players (organisation) in a competitive team sport in which the purpose of the rules is to define the way the game is played. However, a strict division between *institutions* and *organisations* is often hardly possible, as *organisations* are created to operationalise institutions in specific situations. Nevertheless, Nuijten (1999:3) points out attempts to distinguish organisations and institutions on the basis that former stresses structural aspects while the latter stresses normative aspects. Hence, institutions are considered as complexes of norms and behaviour (Uphoff 1986:8, cited in Nuijten 1999:3). Additionally, institutions, Scott (1995:33, cited in Nuijten 1999:3) explains, "consist of cognitive, normative, and regulative structures and activities that provide stability and meaning to social behaviour. Institutions are transported by various carriers – cultures, structures, and routines – and they operate at multiple levels of jurisdiction."

In the context of power differences, Nuijten (1999:4) notes, mechanisms of inclusion and exclusion are part and parcel of any organisation and institution. In the natural resource management context, Berkes and Folke (1997:7, cited in Nuijten 1999:4) state that "institutions have to deal with the two fundamental management problems that arise from the two basic characteristics of all such resources: how to control access to the resource (the exclusion problem), and how to institute rules among users to solve the potential divergence between individual and collective rationality."

A distinction can often be drawn between "institutional environment" and "institutional arrangement." These two often related concepts are defined as: "The institutional environment is the set of fundamental political, social and legal ground rules that establishes the basis for production, exchange and distribution [...]. An institutional arrangement is an arrangement between economic units that govern the ways in which these units can cooperate and/or compete. The institutional arrangement is probably the closest counterpart of the most popular use of the term 'institution'" (Davis and North 1971:6f. cited in Birner 1997:3).

Institutions can be either formal (written rules, constitutions, laws, and contracts), or informal (customs, sanctions, taboos, traditions, and unwritten codes of conduct) and regulate access to resources. Since formal and informal institutions mediate access to livelihood resources, an understanding of institutional environment and arrangements is therefore indispensable in designing interventions that improve rural livelihood security. According to

50

Davies (1997:24 cited in Scoones 1998:12) *institutions* are "the social cement which link stakeholders to access to capital of different kinds to the means of exercising power and so define gateways through which they pass on the route to positive or negative livelihood adaptation."

Local social institutions can serve as a vital ingredient in the process of creating community development. Tirfe (1999:209f.) explains the most indispensable but rather neglected role of the social institutions among the rural communities in Ethiopia:

> [R]ural families have local institutions to serve them in times of need. The local institutions, in turn, are rich in ideas of solidarity and mutual understanding and well rooted in public lives. For many centuries peasants in many regions and communities of Ethiopia were interwoven in social networks provided by these institutions. ... However, none of these were given serious consideration in the efforts to transform Ethiopian society – be it during the regime of Haile Selassie or the *derg*. This was because both had erroneously conceived modernisation as the graveyard of old traditions and a field in which to sow modern ideas.

Local institutions are regarded as the web of social networks, fixing human interactions. Social networks are viewed as systems of relations formed in a state of flux, considering people as interacting with others, some of whom in their turn interact with each other and yet others (Boissevain and Mitchell 1973:viii). The social networks approach views individuals as embedded in a web of networks through their social relations. Schweizer (1997:739), acknowledging the importance of social networks approach to the study of embeddedness and linkages of social actors, notes that "people at the local level are increasingly being drawn into larger circuits through economic linkages, demographic processes, social interaction, political control, and flows of information that transcend local and even national boundaries." The social networks perspective sheds important insights into the understanding of the central role of local institutions in the interactions and adaptations of populations in the present study context. The basic postulate of social networks perspective is that society is viewed as a network of choice-making and self-interested entrepreneurial individuals, interacting beings capable of manipulating others and being manipulated by others. Its predominant emphasis is on individuals rather than groups. Although the social networks approach is equally important, I primarily applied in the study the other four approaches due to the multiplicity and complexity of issues in the research context.

Sustainable Rural Livelihoods

A livelihood is defined as comprising the capabilities (what people can do or be with their entitlements), assets (including both material and social resources) and activities required for a means of living (Carswell 1997; Scoones 1998). Ellis (1998:4) elaborates a livelihood to be more than just income and explains as: "A livelihood encompasses income, both cash and in kind, as well as the social institutions (kin, family, compound, village and so on); gender relations: and property rights required to support and to sustain a given standard of living." A livelihood is considered to be sustainable if it can cope with, and recover from, stresses and shocks, maintain or enhance its capabilities and assets both now and in the future without undermining the natural resource base (Carswell 1997:3, Scoones 1998:6, Hussein and Nelson 1998:3).

Scoones (1998:9) explains three broad clusters of rural livelihood strategies as agricultural intensification/extensification, livelihood diversification, and migration, which are often heavily reliant on livelihood resources, such as natural, economic/financial, human, social and other capital. Scoones (1998:9) further notes, rural livelihood strategies to cover broad range of options open to rural people to pursue: livelihood either from agriculture through the processes of intensification or extensification; or diversify to a range of off-farm income earning activities; or move away and seek a livelihood, either temporarily or permanently, elsewhere; or more commonly, pursue a combination of the strategies together or in sequence. Livelihood adaptation can be either positive, if it is by choice, reversible, and increases security; or negative, if of necessity, irreversible, and fails to contribute reducing vulnerability (Davies and Hossain 1997:5).

The concept of "sustainable rural livelihoods" has become increasingly important in the recent rural development debates. According to Scoones (1998:1), sustainable livelihoods are achieved in different contexts through access to a range of livelihood resources, which are combined in the pursuit of different livelihood strategies (agricultural intensification or extensification, livelihood diversification and migration). Scoones (1998:3) elaborates that the key question to be asked in the analysis of sustainable rural livelihoods as: "Given a particular *context* (of policy setting, politics, history, agroecology and socio-economic conditions), what combination of *livelihood resources* (different types of 'capital') result in the ability to follow what combination of *livelihood strategies* (agricultural intensification/extensification, livelihood diversification and migration) with what *outcomes*? Of particular interest in this framework are the *institutional processes* (embedded in a matrix of formal and informal *institutions* and *organi-*

sations) which mediate the ability to carry out such strategies and achieve (or not) such outcomes" (emphasis in the original). The central focus in Scoones' elaboration of sustainable rural livelihoods is the analysis of a range of formal and informal organisational and institutional factors that influence livelihood outcomes. In a given context, Scoones (1998:4) explains, the ability to perform the multiple *rural livelihood strategies* based on the combination of *livelihood resources* so as to achieve an outcome of *livelihood adaptation* is mediated by *institutional processes* embedded in a matrix of *formal* and *informal institutions* and *organisations* as outlined in *figure three* (emphasis added). Scoones' analytical framework of sustainable rural livelihoods emphasises the crucial importance of local institutional and organisational contexts as central to the model that influence sustainable livelihood outcomes.

Figure 3: *Sustainable Rural Livelihoods: A Framework for Analysis*

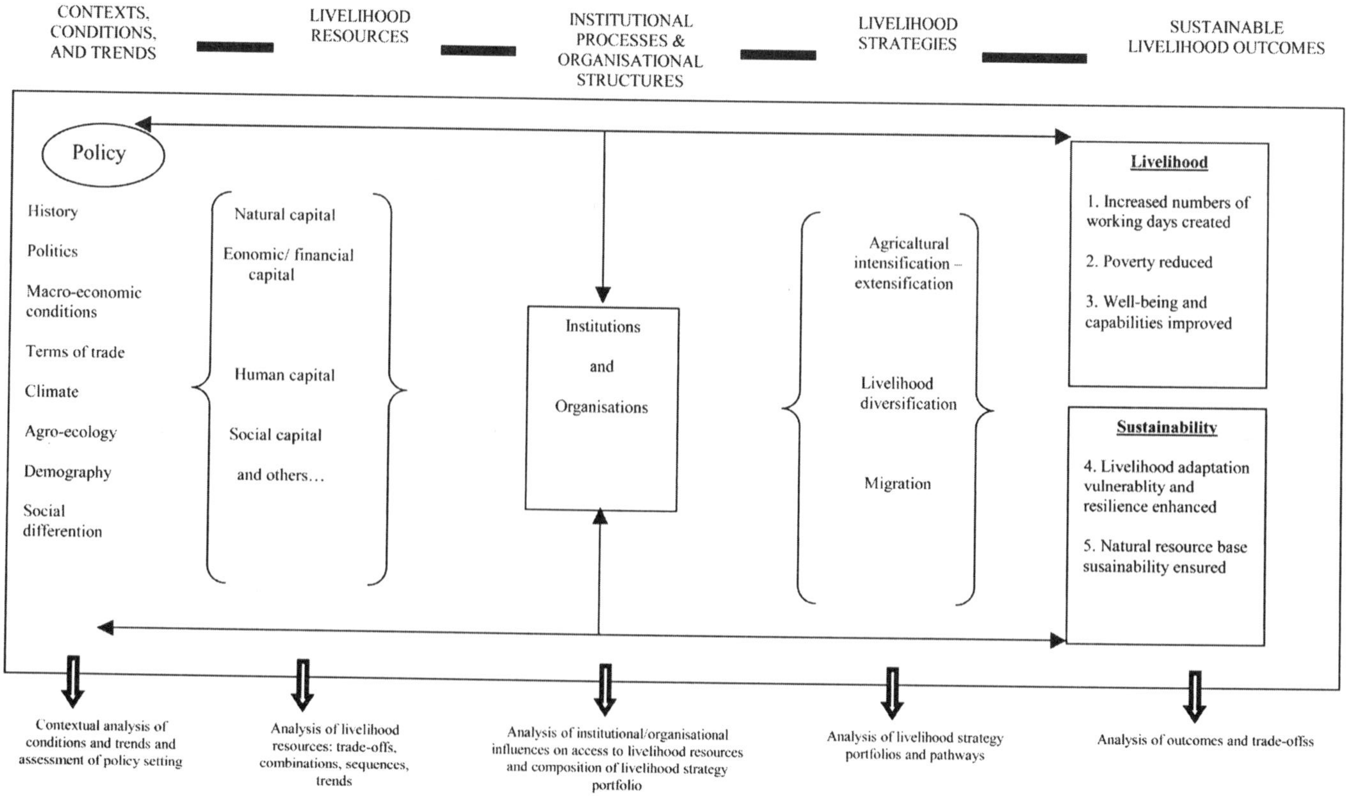

| CONTEXTS, CONDITIONS, AND TRENDS | LIVELIHOOD RESOURCES | INSTITUTIONAL PROCESSES & ORGANISATIONAL STRUCTURES | LIVELIHOOD STRATEGIES | SUSTAINABLE LIVELIHOOD OUTCOMES |

Policy

History
Politics
Macro-economic conditions
Terms of trade
Climate
Agro-ecology
Demography
Social differention

Natural capital
Economic/ financial capital
Human capital
Social capital
and others…

Institutions
and
Organisations

Agricultural intensification – extensification

Livelihood diversification

Migration

Livelihood

1. Increased numbers of working days created
2. Poverty reduced
3. Well-being and capabilities improved

Sustainability

4. Livelihood adaptation vulnerability and resilience enhanced
5. Natural resource base susanability ensured

Contextual analysis of conditions and trends and assessment of policy setting

Analysis of livelihood resources: trade-offs, combinations, sequences, trends

Analysis of institutional/organisational influences on access to livelihood resources and composition of livelihood strategy portfolio

Analysis of livelihood strategy portfolios and pathways

Analysis of outcomes and trade-offss

Source: Scoones (1998:4)

54

PART TWO: THE AUTOCHTHONOUS GUMUZ – SHIFTING CULTIVATORS

Chapter 3. Socio-Cultural Institutions and Modes of Livelihood

3.1 Sketch of Gumuz Ethno-History

In the present Ethiopian regional administrative context, the Gumuz are a relatively populous but powerless minority inhabiting Metekel Zone to the north and Kamashi Zone to the south of the Abbay (Blue Nile) River in the Benishangul-Gumuz National Regional State as shown in *map five*. Based on mainly secondary literature review, Haberland and Straube (1979:139) note the various ethnic designations used to refer to the different Gumuz groups in the Nile Valley. Their descriptive account of Gumuz in German is stated as follows:

> *Gumuz:* Nennen sich auch Gunza (= Menschen); haben widersprüchliche Traditionen, die sowohl von einer Vertreibung aus dem äthiopischen Hochland wie auch von einer westlichen Herkunft sprechen; letztere beziehen sich entweder auf die Herkunft der in Gubba ansässigen Funj-Aristokratie oder einiger aus dem Berta-Gebiet stammender Gumuz-Gruppen im Nil-Tal. Die Gumuz sind in mehrere isolierte Gruppen aufgesplittert: im Didessa-Tal zwischen Lekemti und Gimbi die Mao, Gobato und Sai; im Tal des Blauen Nils zwischen der Einmündung des Didessa und des Dabus die Naga (nach Weld Blundell), die Dukunz und die Saysay oder Sese (nach Lee Irwin), deren Eigenbezeichnung Baga (=Männer) lauten soll (nach Klausberger) und bei denen es sich sehr wahrscheinlich um einstige Berta-Einwanderer handelt; im Balas-Tal die Dizzela (nach Salt), die Gizi, Dugisa, Dabo, Mambuk und Fakaya (nach Kuls). Weitere Gumuz-Gruppen siedeln in Wombera (von den Shinasha abhängig), in Gubba und in dem Tieflandstreifen zwischen dem Dinder und Metemma; unter den Gumuz nördl. des Dinder lebt eine abhängige Gruppe namens Dac; die Kadalo auf den Inselbergen nordwestlich von Gubba sind in das Nil-Tal abgewandert.

According to the above description, the local designations of the Gumuz in Diddesa Valley include the Mao, Gabato, and Sai; in the Blue Nile Valley from the confluence of Deddesa River with the former to that of Dabus River with the same include Naga, Dukunz, Saysay or Sese, and Baga; and in Beles Valley include Dizzela, Gizi, Dugisa, Dabo, Mambuk, and Fakaya.

Map 5. Gumuz Inhabited Zones in Benishangul-Gumuz Regional State

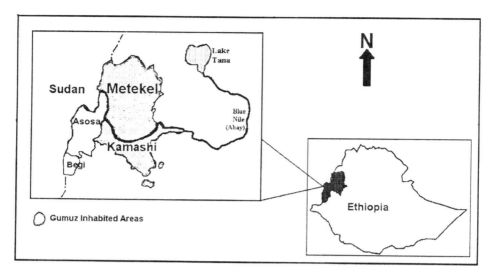

Source: Wolde-Selassie Abbute's own adopted sketch

They state that the Gumuz also inhabit areas closer to Wombera, Guba, and lowland areas between Dinder River and Metemma. They mentioned a Gumuz group called Dac that used to live to the north of Dinder River. Finally, they name the Kadalo Gumuz group who were said to have immigrated from north-west of Guba to their present location along Nile Valley. However, based on my ethnographic accounts in Metekel, except *Baga* (an emic ethnic designation) many of the above different group references are rather reported to be clan names and do not designate variant ethnic terms.

The Gumuz mostly inhabit the lowland (*qolla*) climatic areas. The approximate area where the Gumuz live is pointed out in *map six*. James (1976:28) describes the basic features of the Blue Nile Valley inhabited by the Gumuz to be "a narrow corridor of low, undulating country penetrating the heart of Ethiopia and sandwiched between the high plateaus of Wallega and Gojjam." She further characterises the contrasting climatic conditions of the two areas, the highlands being cooler with fresh air as opposed to the hotter valley with low hills and plains covered with woodland and savanna vegetation of tall grass (in wet season) which is burnt off in the dry season, making the landscape scorched. Their scattered settlements and the less hospitable physical ecological feature of the valley, according to James

(1976:35), are seen in some ways as an advantage by the Gumuz as a natural shield protecting them against potential domination from the highlanders, and notes the following:

> Easy retreat, mobility and inaccessibility through dispersion and bad communications have been the means of self-preservation of communities in living memory, and quite possibly the bases of survival in the past. The amorphous settlement pattern is an indicator of the fact that the society of the Gumuz has never been successfully controlled, either from outside or from within; and also that it is remarkably well designed to resist control in the future.

In other words, she explains that the patterns of scattered and shifting settlements of the Gumuz in the valley, in contrast to the fixed settlement patterns of the highlanders, is intimately interconnected with the geographical, economic, political and historical circumstances, the details of which are discussed in the following parts of this study.

Linguistically the Gumuz belong to the Koman group of Central-Sudanic branch in the Nilo-Saharan language family (Blench 2000, James n.d., p. 40) whose approximate locations are shown in *map seven*. Gumuz, according to Unseth (1989:630f., 1985:92) is "a Nilo-Saharan language of western Ethiopia and eastern Sudan, found along Blue Nile and further north." Bender (1983:3 cited in Unseth 1985:929) classified Gumuz together with the Koman languages into 'Komuz'.

According to the origin myth documented from Manjeeri informants, once upon a time, twin sons were born from a mother. One of the sons was darker black (Gumuz) and the other was fair-coloured (non-Gumuz highlander). As they grew up and matured, they contested for power in the presence of a local assembly. First, they were given a horse for galloping where the Gumuz fell down while the latter galloped well. Then, they were offered to choose from bow and arrow on the one hand and spear and shield on the other, the Gumuz taking the former and the non-Gumuz the latter. Again, they were made to choose from *inga* (porridge) and *injera* (pancake like unleavened bread), with the Gumuz favouring porridge while the non-Gumuz favoured *injera*. Later, they were asked to settle either to the "right" (in the central highlands) or to the "left" side (towards the lowlands and the periphery). The non-Gumuz chose to settle to the right in the central highlands and the Gumuz chose to settle to the left towards the lowlands and the periphery. So, the Gumuz claim genealogically to have originated from a

Map 6. The Gumuz in the Blue Nile Basin

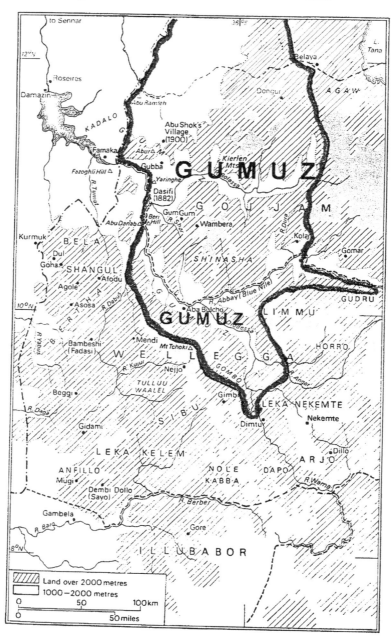

Source: Adapted from Donham and James (1986:53)

Map 7. The Gumuz: Geographic Location and Language Family

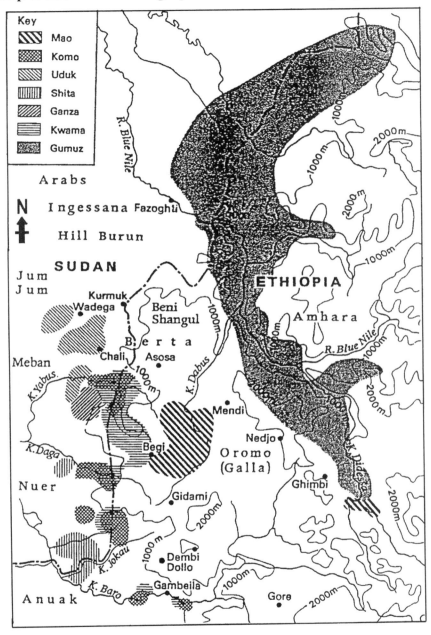

The Koman-Speaking Peoples. Source: James (1979: 6)

59

common ancestor who was born as a twin from the same mother as their neighbouring highlanders.

According to an Agaw tradition recorded by Charles Beke (1945 cited in R. Pankhurst 1997:91) in the nineteenth century, it is asserted that the Gumuz were the previous occupiers of Agaumidir, but had been displaced by the Agaw. Additionally, reviewing documentary sources, Ernesta Cerulli (1956:15) explains the pressure and subjugation exerted on the Gumuz, forcing them to be driven out of their former inhabited areas as:

> [A]ccording to traditions of the Awiya Agaw, collected by Beke in Agaumidir, the first inhabitants were Shankala, perhaps the Gunza, who were driven out by the Agaw when they came from Lasta. The Gumuz also had trouble with the Sidama people called Gonga or Shinasha to the south of their territory, and it is recorded that in the area of the Dura River the Shinasha compelled the Gumuz to pay tribute in cereals, meat, and honey, under threat of causing drought or excessive rain. Pressure caused by the Galla invasion in the 16th century, which drove many of the inhabitants of the land north of the Gibe across the Abay, and the expansion of the Fung in the west, had serious results for the Gumuz, and their territory became much contracted. In 1587 Sarsa Dengel went to Balya and subdued a tribe of Shanqella who may be the Gumuz […].

Additionally, James (1986:121) considers the documentary accounts of early scholars such as James Bruce, Henry Salt, and Charles T. Beke who had witnessed the fact that the Gumuz lived in the highlands of the present central and southern parts of Gojjam in the eighteenth and early nineteenth centuries. These accounts try to point out that, in the process of the exploitative predatory expansion of the highlanders, the Gumuz were exposed to intermittent slave raids and retreated moving down to the lowlands in the far western periphery of the country looking for greater safety. The raiding of the Gumuz for slaves both by the neighbouring Agaw and Amhara of Damot/Gojjam was personally observed by Beke (1844:9) and described in his account as: "These Negroes form the slave population of Agawmidir, where they are in great numbers, and many are also to be met with in Damot and Gojjam. They are captured in the expeditions into their country of Dejach Barea and his chiefs." Dejach Barea was the chief ruler of that part of the country when Beke visited the area.

Abdussamad (1988:238) further explains the Gumuz to be the worst loser minority in the struggle to keep the most fertile and well-watered highland areas of Metekel, being driven to the hot valleys in the lowland periphery, to struggle against malaria and other diseases. Abdussamad notes the accounts of the central highland Ethiopian fame hunters' experience and its impacts on the defenceless Gumuz. He explains that a chief called *Zeleqa*, who was assigned by the then governor of Gojjam, monitored all hunting activities in Metekel. *Zeleqa* was stationed at around Belaya Mountain and charged with giving permission for hunting, collecting tax from the booty and awarding honour to the hunters on their return based on their performances. According to Abdussamad (1988:241), in addition to hunting wild animals, the hunters used to frequently raid the defenceless Gumuz on their way back from hunting for their livestock and slaves. Based on historical documentation, after the 16th century and with the centre of state in Gondar, the Gumuz of Metekel were close to it. According to Taddese (1988:12-14), in order to bring the land, its resources and the people under control, kings such as Sarsa-Dengel (1563-1597), Susenyos (1607-1632), Fasiledes (1632-1667), Yohanes (1667-1683), and Iyasu the Great (1683-1706) had successively conducted devastating and destructive campaigns on the Gumuz, achieving a final breakthrough and attaching them through the ancient system of indirect rule by appointing neighbouring Agaw chiefs (under patron-client relationship) over them. This relationship lasted up to the overthrow of the imperial regime by the *Derg* in 1974.

During the fieldwork of the present study, the Gumuz informants distressfully recounted the vivid memory of the horrible experiences of slave raiding by the highlanders practised during the time of some of the informants themselves. According to their explanation, the worst of all is the frequent cutting of the strong muscle of the legs of the enslaved making them partially lame, completely preventing them from escaping. More than the plunder and forceful expropriation of the land and human resources of the Gumuz, the highland expansionists had been considering them as a Negro tribe of racially lower status, heathen and an inferior race, referring to them categorically by a generic and pejorative term *Shanqilla* for their dark-coloured skin. The first-hand accounts documented in 1882 by a traveller Juan Maria Schuver explains the overall power relations and its associated stigma as follows:

> The Abyssinians in these parts have a most excellent system of keeping the conquered negro-tribes in subjection. No garrisons, eating up the produce of the country, are dreamt of, but each time a strip of land is annexed, a certain number of families are told off out of overpopulated Gojjam to settle as colonists in the new territory. These are judiciously not allowed to herd together in separate villages, but distributed all over the country, so that even the most insignificant negro hamlet shall have its

own one or two Abyssinian houses. These colonists are liable to be levied 'en masse' at any moment and the system extends so far to have established beforehand centres of concentration for each well-defined district. Not much persuasion is needed to induce these people to leave their native country, where every inch of land is private property for the half-desert negro-lands where any amount of as good as virgin soil can be had for the taking. They interfere little with the blacks, most seldom intermarry with what they consider a heathen and inferior race, and feel no necessity of propagating Christianity (James et al. 1996:200).

James (1986:124) further explains that, apart from the highland Ethiopian expansion, the Gumuz had also been facing pressures from the then Turco-Egyptian government of the Sudan on the other side, which sanctioned slave raids into their hills. Similarly, Simoons (1960:55) notes the remarkable survival of the Gumuz culture "against the pressures of Islam from the Sudan and against Amharization from Ethiopia." Strengthening the same point, Abdussamad (1995:66) notes the persistent existence of Gumuz on the margins of Ethiopia and Sudan where they survived the long pressure and threats of the competing overlords from both sides by retreating into the less accessible open lowlands. He also points out that the slave raiding was conducted alongside with elephant hunting in those Gumuz inhabited areas mostly by the aristocrats from Gojjam and Begemidir (Gondar).

According to the oral accounts I documented from Mandura and Dangur informants, in the past the Gumuz had lived in the highlands, occupying extensive territory to the east from Zage at Lake Tana and Bahir-Dar in the northeast to southwards through Dangila, Enjibara, Koso-Berr, Bure, Debre Marcos up to the Abbay River basin bordering Gojjam with Shoa and Wollega to the south and southeast as pointed out in *map eight*. This map, based on the participatory sketch maps of my Gumuz informants, attempts to indicate those approximate areas of Gojjam traditionally claimed to have been inhabited by the Gumuz in the past. Additionally, these accounts are supported by written records (Taddese 1988:10) where areas such as Fudi or *Gimbeha* (which in Gumuz is said to mean "see black or Gumuz") Mountains to the west of Koso-Berr up to Chagni were inhabited in the recent past by the Gumuz. It is because of the ceaseless encroachment pressure of the highlanders that the Gumuz were pushed and forced to retreat down to the less accessible remoter lowlands of the western periphery, and a section of them were said to have crossed the Abbay River to Wollega in the south (the present Kamashi Zone). The experience of the escape and retreat of the Gumuz into the Blue Nile valley in the face of the overwhelming pressure of the "Abyssinian taxation and servitude" is described and discussed in the ethnographic accounts of James (1986:139) among the Gumuz of *Aba Bulcho* village to the south of Abbay River. Documenting their flight to Wollega, she states that the Gumuz of *Aba Bulcho* claim their forebears arrived from across the river in Gojjam like the majority of Gumuz on the southern bank of the Blue Nile.

Map 8. Traditionally Claimed Gumuz Inhabited Areas in Gojjam

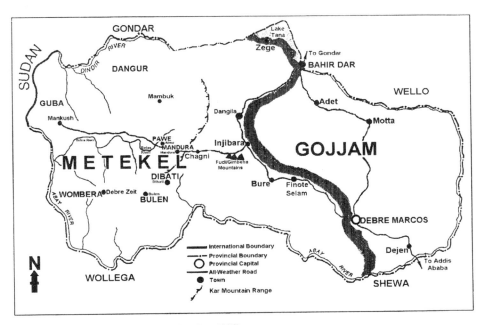

Gojjam Administrative Region (Pre-1987)

 Approximate Area of Gojjam traditionally claimed to have been inhabited by Gumuz in the past based on participatory sketch maps of informants (in 1996/97, 199, 2001)

Source: Adapted from a map of traditional Ethiopian administrative regions until 1987, commonly reprinted

3.2 Population and Family Profile of Gumuz in the Research Sites

The detailed basic features of those specific research sites as well as the entire research setting are described in chapter 1 (sections 1.1 and 1.3). In the table below, the population profile of the Gumuz inhabiting those specific research sites selected is described to its relevance to the discussions in this part of the study.

Table 1: Gumuz Population in the Research Sites

| Research Sites | Gumuz Population | | | | | | Total |
| | Heads of Households | | | Family Members | | | |
	Male	Female	Total	Male	Female	Total	
1 Manjeeri	89	11	100	168	273	441	**541**
2 Wondbil	24	3	27	34	63	97	**124**
3 Maataaba	61	2	63	139	183	322	**385**
4 Kitli-Azarti	112	3	115	186	276	462	**577**
5 Gublak	172	6	178	520	726	1246	**1424**
6 Baabi-Zanda	68	2	70	147	203	350	**420**
Total	**526**	**27**	**553**	**1194**	**1724**	**2918**	**3471**

Source: Wolde-Selassie Abbute survey (October - November 1999)

As indicated in the table, a total Gumuz population of 3,471 (553 heads of households, 2,918 family members) inhabits the six selected research sites. The average number of family members in the study sites is around six. The Gumuz family system is significantly polygynous as pointed out in the table below.

64

Table 2: Polygyny among the Gumuz Heads of Families in the Study Sites

Research Sites		Polygyny among the Male Heads of Families				Total
		Four Wives	Three Wives	Two Wives	One Wife	
1	Manjeeri	–	2	32	55	89
2	Wondbil	–	2	3	19	24
3	Maataaba	2	3	14	42	61
4	Kitli-Azarti	–	6	13	93	112
5	Gublak	3	11	37	121	172
6	Baabi-Zanda	1	2	30	35	68
Total		6	26	129	365	526
%		1.2	4.9	24.5	69.4	100%

Source: Wolde-Selassie Abbute survey (October - November 1999)

Out of the 526 male-headed households in the study sites, 161 (31%) of them are polygynous, where 6 heads of household (1.2%) have four wives, 26 (4.9%) have three wives, and 129 (24.5%) have two wives. On the other hand, 365 (69%) heads of household have only one wife each. Moreover, in the case of the polygynous families, two and more wives frequently share the same residential house. For instance, out of the six 'four wives' polygynous families, two of the families share the same house, another two families live in eight separate houses, while in the case of the remaining two families, the eight wives share four houses for two each. Out of the twenty-six 'three wives' polygynous families, fifteen share the same house, six live in separate houses; and in the case of the remaining five, two in each share the same house while one in each lives in a separate house. Out of the one hundred twenty-nine 'two wives' polygynous families, eighty-seven of them share the same house, while forty-two live in a separate house. A polygynous Gumuz family is considered as a single unit based on the contextual socio-cultural and economic patterns of the study community.

3.3 Socio-Political and Religious Institutions

Socio-Political Organisation

Family, Neighbourhood/Commune and Clan
A family is the most important basic social institution among the Gumuz. The husband, wife/wives, and children form a Gumuz family. Usually, grandparents and grandchildren form part of the extended family. The head of the family is the husband. Infants and small children are taken care closely by the mothers. Polygyny is quite common. At an early stage, after the marriage of a junior wife, co-wives usually share the same house. The husband usually builds a separate house for the junior wife/wives after the latter have a number of children. In the absence of the husband, the senior wife will be in charge, supervising the junior wife/wives. Customarily, Gumuz senior wives encourage and push their husbands to marry junior wife/wives, taking charge of organising and facilitating the wedding. This is because the new wives are considered to be instrumental in strengthening the family labour and sharing the care of the husband. Additionally, children begotten from polygynous marriage increase the number of members of the family, which is considered as an important status symbol and security. Budge (1928:629) notes the experience of polygyny among the group generically referred to *Shanqilla* as: "The polygamy of the Shankalla is not the result of lust on the part of the man, but of the woman, who wish their husbands to have large families for the sake of the protection which many children give."

Inside a family, girls learn the chores of their mothers; whereas boys learn the activities of their fathers. A family, usually including co-wives, shares food from the same dish and dines together. In the case of a polygynous family, the co-wives either cook together or pull their food in one of their homes and eat together. However, the husband prepares separate crop fields for each. The harvest will also be stored in the respective wife's separate granary. The husband fairly shares his working time in each wife's field in order to prevent any conflict that might arise among them. In most cases, all the extended members of a family share the same nearby compound forming a hamlet. Mostly, a grandfather, father, co-wives, sons and daughter in-laws live in a hamlet. Very close kin members of living parents form the closest neighbourhood. The neighbourhood distance increases with the growing distance of blood relations. Several hamlets form a neighbourhood or village commune.

A commune is a very important social unit among the Gumuz. Members of the same neighbourhood seem to be ideally egalitarian in nature. They perform all field cultivation activities together, facilitated by elders. They share closely in all aspects of the village life. They also drink together *keya* (local brew), prepared on rotating basis. Most of the time, they pool their labour. The neighbourhood wives gather and fish together. When the distance of the village increases far from the shifting cultivation fields, the whole neighbourhood moves to a new site. Through time, a neighbourhood grows and splits into more neighbourhoods.

A Gumuz clan is mostly composed of its different neighbourhood members related by descent along patrilineal lines. The clan is a symbol of identity for its members. The clan territory is strongly defended by the members against outsiders. Inter-clan relations are held with mutual recognition according to customs. Violation of such recognition results in inter-clan feuds. Members of closer kin groups live in villages inside the clan territory. Appropriate village locations are selected by elders on the basis of the suitability of the site both in vegetation and soil types, according to the local criteria. They accordingly shift their village sites on the basis of the distance and locations of their cultivation fields as well as other causes related to their traditional belief system (e.g. announcement of pollution by spirit-medium person). In addition, a number of clans of the respective territories form larger broader territorial groups such as the Gumuz of Mandura, Dangur, Gublak, Guba, Dibati, Wombera, etc. In turn, the different Gumuz groups form a much larger territorial category such as the Gumuz of Metekel. At a higher level, wider categories such as Gumuz of Metekel, Gumuz of Kamashi, and Gumuz of Metemma form the entire Gumuz ethnic group as a whole.

Marriage and Kinship System
Four forms of marriage are practised. These are sister exchange, elopement, abduction, and marriage through bride-price payment. Marriage is exogamous from outside one's own clan. Hard work and pleasant behaviour are qualities expected from a bride.

Sister exchange (*angiya*) is the most dominant and standard form of marriage. A groom gives his sister or a daughter of his close relatives in exchange. In the process, parents select the would-be bride as well as the girl to be given in exchange in consultation with their sons and send elders to the girl's family. When both parties agree, they fix a date of wedding in the two families at the same time. Except for the wedding feast, no form of bride price is paid or exchanged. On the wedding day, the parties that go to bring the respective brides fix a central place where they can meet on their return. On their way back, they meet at this central place and exchange greetings making the two brides kiss each other with a facilitation of elders and then take them to the respective families. In case of divorce, either the wife given in exchange is returned upon demand or a replacement is requested and given. Exchange marriage among the Gumuz, James (1986:133) explains, "is a long-standing contractual relationship which should last a full generation and is fulfilled by the plentiful birth and survival of children on either side."

Elopement is another form of marriage practised to a significant extent. Here, a boy and a girl love and agree to marry each other. However, the boy may not have a sister or a daughter of close relative readily available to be given in exchange. In such a case, the boy persuades the girl and elopes with her. Then, he totally disappears and hides himself to avoid the dangerous consequences that result from the furious girl's family and close relatives. Respected and neutral elders will be sent as soon as possible for intervention. Through the facilitation of elders, according to the custom, the issue will be settled either by immediately giving a girl from the boy's group or with an understanding of the boy's family being indebted to give a girl sometime later. In a few cases, the couple will give their first-born daughter in exchange for her mother. Unless handled carefully, such acts are quite delicate and dangerous, resulting in bloodshed because the kin's girls are highly valued, enabling their clan boys to get wives in exchange. The boy and his close kin group members pay fines in a form of livestock for taking the girl without the consent of her clan, which violates and hurts their dignity.

Abduction is a form of marriage in which the girl is taken by force. This is the most dangerous form of marriage, and it is frequently a cause of inter-clan feuds that costs lives from both parties and lasts long period due to a common practice of revengeful killings. Except for the high risk of causing severe conflicts, the method of handling its effect by neutral elders is similar to elopement apart from the higher intensity exerted in handling the matter.

Marriage with a payment of bride price (biicza) is the most rare and least practised form of marriage. According to informants, it was practised in exceptional cases only in Mandura Woreda. Informants explained the amount of a typical bride price paid in such case is said to be: 10 cattle, 10 goats or sheep, 2 guns and 50 bullets, 100 Ethiopian birr, 10 spears, 10 salt blocs (amoole chew) in former days, and a meqennet (a strip of cloth to be tied around the waist of a bride's mother). However, in case of divorce, initiated by either partner, the bride price paid is reclaimed. This form of marriage is considered quite disgraceful.

Residence after marriage is virilocal. Women leave their natal village after marriage and join their husband's kin. Gumuz women are the most ingenious and hardest working members of the community. They perform innumerable livelihood activities. In addition to performing several gender-specific home chores, they are also fully involved at all levels in the field production as well as construction and exchange activities.

Traditionally, women do not stay at home during menstruation and at child delivery. It is believed that dropping menstruation and delivery blood at home is polluting, and the anger of *missa* (spirit) will cause serious consequences and retribution. So, women are secluded in a separate hut (constructed specifically for the menstruation period) during their menstruation. They stay day and night in this hut until their period has ended. They refrain from touching any object of their home. During this period, both the menstruating women and their families are attended and given food by neighbouring women or co-wives. The first menstruation of a young girl is celebrated with a joyful feast full of chanting and singing. It marks her maturity to become a woman (rite of passage). When the girl completes her first period, her father and brother slaughter chickens commemorating the occasion. Irwin (1968:132) describes such practices of Gumuz young girls as: "Girls are not circumcised. Their coming of age is marked only by the onset of menstruation. On this occasion, the girl's friends will celebrate by singing. A month later, all the villagers will come visiting for a feast, each bringing a chicken. Here the girls and women will sing special songs."

During child delivery, women leave their home and stay a certain distance away. At night the husbands guard them from wild animals at a distance. The labouring women deliver without anyone's assistance, except those women at their first delivery who need help. Tolerating the pain of delivery alone is considered to be a mark of socially accepted good value of the village women. Those who fail to bear the pains are ridiculed and ashamed. After childbirth, the mother washes herself and the infant. Then, after proper cleaning, she returns home accompanied by warm rejoicing and chants. Before she enters her home, the husband slaughters a chicken at the main gate and puts the blood on both the mother and the infant. The skin from the chicken's neck is removed and inserted under the right arm of the infant said to be an offering to the *missa* for the newborn's well being.

Newborn babies are named according to custom, mostly reflecting contextual meaning or happenings that occurred at a time of birth meaningful to the family. Usually, they are also named after a guest or stranger who first appeared in the village at a time of the birth. Ernesta Cerulli (1956:22) notes the naming of newborn child being dependent on the circumstances of birth. Infants of both sexes are equally desired because girls bring wives to their men and boys strengthen the capacity of their group in defending them from attack of others.

Married women occasionally visit their natal village and play a very important role in bridging the two clans. Clans that have exchanged women in marriage seldom quarrel with each other since they established affinal kinship and blood relations through their children. The in-law families respect each other. In case of any conflict that arises within these clans, the exchanged women and their children play an important role in preventing the two sides from attacking each other. Both consanguinal and affinal kinship forms are strongly valued.

The Gumuz are patrilineal. A member of the Gumuz belongs to any one of the clans, claiming to have descended from the same ancestor. All clan members claim to have blood relations. Each clan has its respective territory. Members of the same clan live in several villages within their clan territory. Affinal kinship with other clan groups also has a very important significance where they share a lot in common in their daily life. Although the two kinship forms are important in respective contexts, consanguinity is more preferred to affinity due to the Gumuz being patrilineal. The patrilineal kin groups are the true owners of all the resources inside the clan territory. However, based on their consent, a member of an affinal kin group can come and share the resources of his mother's clan.

Death of a younger member in the estimated age span of four to forty is seen as very sad. Within this age span, the extent of mournfulness is greater for younger ones. Deaths of children under age four are felt less and limited to a family level. The death of an older member is not as sad. It is, rather, full of feasts, songs, chants, and firing guns because of his/her successful completion of the worldly life. This is one of the singing and chanting occasions where young boys attract and select their future wives. Direct descendants of a deceased person inherit his home property, cleared farmland and field products. Children inherit their parents' property. Unmarried young girls inherit their parents' property, but they pass it to their brothers or closer kin members upon their marriage. Levirate and sororate are commonly practised among the Gumuz.

Elders and Patterns of Authority

The Gumuz tend to be egalitarian. No hierarchy of recognised strata is noticeable. There is no group despised or marginalised on the basis of its occupation such as farming, trading, crafts, gathering, and hunting. There is a strong sense of sharing resources at all levels within the village community. Hard work and production of large amounts of crops are values highly appreciated. Laziness and weaker production are condemned, laughed at and despised. More production and raising livestock have important social significance as better status markers. More production means more *keya* (local brew). In other words, a large harvest enables one to brew a large amount of *keya* for the communal labour of the next harvest. Less production means less *keya* will be available for communal labour in the next season. Those who are not capable of brewing the necessary *keya* for this purpose in their fields feel ashamed and ridiculed, especially by their wives (in the case of those married) and other village women who joined them through marriage. Although, the gap is not so wide (due at most to the rare individualist interest in wealth accumulation), noticeable wealth differentiation exists contextually among families. Gumuz informants in Mandura explained it in terms of strong and medium categories identified for land-tax payments by district authorities. The stated grouping is explained as based on local swidden farm sizes cultivated, where members of the first paid forty *birr* and the latter twenty-five *birr*. The same informants stressed that most of the community members wanted to pay in the first category so as not to be considered economically weaker, which has a scorned negative value.

The role of community elders (*ganza*) based on wisdom is very decisive in all aspects of the day-to-day life of Gumuz. On the basis of the accepted values, norms, ethics and customary laws of the community, elders exercise unlimited administrative and judiciary responsibilities. They are responsible for the administration of the overall affairs of the community at all levels including the family, neighbourhood, commune, intra-clan, inter-clan, and the entire community at large. Elders are in most cases also leaders of their respective clans at the same time.

In the patterns of authority, members of the community commonly consult elders. Elders guide, supervise and give advice on every aspect of village life. They care for the young and weak; motivate to work hard and discourage laziness; condemn theft, lying, adultery, and crime; settle both ordinary and serious conflicts at all levels; facilitate marriages; organise burial and mourning ceremonies; teach use and management of natural resources based on their accumulated wisdom. They are considered the pillars who are tirelessly concerned about the well-being of their community. Without elders, many informants said, life would be meaningless for the Gumuz. Elders care about and work hard to prevent and solve every problem their community encounters. All members unanimously reject anything that is rejected by elders. Similarly, all members accept anything that is accepted by elders.

The government's local unit of administration is the *kebele*. It is a formal administration that functions with a close support of the elders. In many cases, the formal *kebele* administrators come from among the elders. Almost all issues from within the Gumuz are taken care of by the elders irrespective of the presence of formal administration. The majority of the members are less aware of the very presence of formal administration than the elders. The elders manage all aspects of the community. The administrators, both at Mandura and Dangur *Woreda* councils, confirmed the indispensable fact that they work in close collaboration with the respected elders. Had it not been for the close support and guidance of elders, the *woreda* council would have not fulfilled its tasks properly. The *woreda* council delegates and refers back most of the cases to be managed by respected elders according to their accepted customary values and norms. The problem-solving capacity of elders is so high that issues settled by their intervention are more binding. Mostly, elders take preventive measures on those actions that would instigate conflict. Once conflict occurs, they resolve it in a compromising way such that neither of the conflicting parties will be a total winner or total looser. Their conflict-resolving mechanism is a process of mediating the parties through a customarily acceptable binding manner. The administrative role of the elders in all aspects of the community life is unrivalled.

Traditional Belief System and Spirit Mediums

Belief System
The Gumuz are primarily followers of traditional beliefs, with a noticeable influence of Orthodox Christianity from the Ethiopian highlands along the East and Islam from the Sudan along the West of their territory. They believe in *missa* (poly-spirits). There are multiple *missa* believed in diverse contexts for different issues important in their day-to-day life. These multiple spirits include: *Miss-aya* (river spirit), *miss-kuancha* (sorghum spirit), *miss-gumba* (stick spirit), *miss-siila* (hunt spirit), *miss-gitsiya* (possession spirit), *miss-taanqa* (finger-millet spirit), *miss-gaariya* (song spirit) *miss-jaa* (tree spirit), *miss-indeya* (earth spirit), *miss-gokuna* (sky spirit), *miss-paatua* (pumpkin spirit), *miss-bahiga* (gourd spirit), *miss-gaaba* (cotton spirit), *miss-zaara* (dog spirit), *miss-teha* (delivery spirit), *miss-dema* (rain spirit),

miss-kiyna (hail spirit), *miss-giziya* (grass spirit), and *miss-maanja* (fire spirit). The supreme *missa* above all of them is known as *yamba* (*supreme deity*). The different *missa* are respected and believed in their respective specific venues; whereas *yamba* is believed as an omnipotent and versatile supreme spirit above all others who created all living creatures and the nature as well as who gave the knowledge to human being in the use and management of natural resources. *Yamba* safeguards and controls the functioning of all his living creatures and the natural world at large. Thus, the earth and its land resources are believed to be sacred. Under *yamba*, all other spirits function. Furthermore, belief in ancestor spirits is equally important.

The *evil eye* is one of the dominant forms of evil-spirit belief practised, which is mostly a cause of frequent conflict and bloodshed among the entire community. If someone is seen three times in the dream of another Gumuz, he will be suspected of evil eye and called to confess the truth. The person who dreamt about the other will be given local medicine so as to make him utter the name of the suspected person. Then, the suspected is requested to spit saliva on the affected person. If the affected person does not heal after the spit of saliva, the suspect is believed not to be an evil-eye person any more. However, if the affected heals after the spit of saliva, the suspect is proven to be an evil-eye person. Then, the evil-eye person is either given traditional medicine that frees him/her from the possession of evil eye; or that person is exiled from the community to an isolated area. Alternatively, those who are identified as evil-eye possessors, move of their own accord and disappear forever to unidentifiable distant areas away from their community. In former days, a person proven of possessing an evil eye was usually sold out as a slave to the highlanders.

In the case of a death where the cause is believed to have been an evil-eye attack, serious conflict will emerge that results in bloodshed unless intervened immediately by respected elders from neutral clans. In such a case, the possessor of the evil eye will compensate the deceased family by giving a girl. However, if this girl on her maturity fails to give birth inside the family of the deceased, it is believed that the evil-eye allegation will be considered false and she returns to her own family. Then, the alleged evil-eye possessor claims compensation in return. The whole practice of evil eye requires complicated ritual performance in the Gumuz day-to-day life. As already stated, it is also a widely believed practice, which is mostly a cause of frequent conflict and bloodshed among the entire Gumuz community.

Spirit Mediums

The spirit-mediums who play a decisive role in the traditional belief system of Gumuz are *ettimissgideya, gafia,* and *gola. Ettimissgideya* is a spirit-medium person who is solely responsible for a ritual performance of *miss-gideya* (*gideya* spirit). *Miss-gideya* is a spirit prayed to and ritually cele-brated annually in July by organising a big feast that is believed to have a very important significance in the overall daily lives and land resources of the whole village community. The *ettimissgideya,* as the *gideya* spirit-medium, tells the community to prepare the feast and announces the date of its celebration. Every member of the village prepares the local brew (*keya*) and chickens to be slaughtered. On the date of celebration, the community will gather outside the village, and the *ettimissgideya* performs the ritual. After laying two small trees across a path, he cuts leaves of *gideya* tree and prays to the spirit for the well-being of the community and for a prosperous harvest. In the ritual performance of the prayer, the *ettimissgideya* empha-sises strongly the sacred earth believed to be the source of life and livelihood as well as the final home of all living things where all return. After the ritual, every member returns home and touches household utensils and furniture with dry sticks and inserts them into the roof straw of the main gate together with *gideya* tree leaves. Then, they slaughter a chicken and feast on it. After performing the ritual, the community feels secure in their well-being in that they believe that their children will grow safely, their crop harvests and live-stock production will be prosperous, and their hunt and gatherings will be abundant. Similar ritual performances will be repeated every year. In addi-tion, especially when children get sick, *ettimisgideya* performs curing ritual using leaves of the *gideya* plant. Upon death or incapacity of *ettimissgideya,* the spirit medium-ship is inherited and succeeded by one of his sons or close relatives.

The *gafia* is a very crucial magico-religious and traditional medicine-person who plays a multiple role as a medium between the poly-spirits and the community. Every village has a *gafia* who performs a multiple ritual in diverse contexts. When a member of the community feels sick, a *gafia* is most often consulted. He visits the sick, identifies the respective spirit that attacked and performs the necessary magical ritual by sorting out and reliev-ing the illness. In the ritual processing, the *gafia* mostly picks up a chicken and moves around the sick. He kisses the earth and prays to the particular spirit for its benevolence and honour. In the name of the earth, he prays to the respective spirits for the health and prosperity of the village community at large. He prays the earth-spirit not to kill the villagers before their age and to take them back only after they are old enough at the proper time. He prays

74

to the earth to provide abundant source of livelihood. Moreover, he gives traditional herbal medicine to the sick. As a medical specialist of the community, his knowledge of medicinal plant species is quite enormous. When a sick person gets cured, he/she gives chicken and/or goats as a gift to the *gafia*.

In day-to-day life, the orders of *gafia* are fully respected and fulfilled without hesitation such as changing the entire settlement area due to spiritual pollution, outbreak of inter-clan conflicts, ritual purification sacrifices, and other related spiritual orders to be practised. Those *gafia* with a proven curing knowledge are highly respected and frequently consulted even by members of other clans; whereas the ones with poor curing capacity are not respected with the same esteem. In the usual daily life of the community, the *gafia* leads an ordinary life as any member of the village without enjoying any extraordinary privilege. The descendants or close relatives inherit the spirit-medium possession power of the *gafia*.

Gola is a higher spirit-medium person above the *gafia*. He acts as a witchdoctor and plays the role of local "prophet." He is consulted frequently on heavy issues beyond the capacity of *gafia*. Like a *gafia*, he will not travel to the homes of community members; rather, he performs his spiritual task in his village compound. His power of communicating with the different poly-spirits (*missa*) as well as the supreme deity (*yamba*) is very high. Due to his closer communication with the spirits, he is believed to know and understand the cases and solutions of clients even without being told. At times, he will refer some of the clients with less serious cases back to the village *gafia*. Unlike the *gafia*, *gola* are not available in every village. They are found in one out of several villages. The kind of case in which a *gola* most frequently consulted is to identify a cause of the death of a member of a community.

The *gola*, with his spiritual power, is believed to identify immediately the cause of a death. When the cause of death is identified as having been an evil eye, he calls the suspect and asks for his confession. If the suspect fails to confess the truth, the *gola* puts the head of a poisonous snake, a splint from a lightning-struck tree and an herbal medicine (specific to such occasion) on the earth and makes the suspect swear in the name of the earth. If the suspect swears to having committed the act, it is believed that he will immediately die on his way back home either by lightning attack (during the rainy season) or snakebite. The death, as a consequence of swearing, is marked as revelation of the truth of having committed the "crime." Then, the matter is delegated to elders to solve the matter according to custom mostly by giving out a girl to the deceased's family. In rare cases, if this girl fails to bear child in the deceased's family, which is believed to mark the false allegation of the *gola*, she returns to her natal family. Then, the *gola* is charged to pay compensation mostly in livestock to the vindicated individual and the family, as facilitated by elders. Moreover, a *gola* is frequently consulted for many cases such as destruction of crops, theft of livestock, complicated illness and several other related serious issues. In his daily life, a *gola* leads a common life as any member of his community. The descendants or close relatives inherit the spirit-medium possession power of the *gola*.

In addition to their spirit mediumship, *gola* and *gafia* provide traditional medicine and enjoy the respect of their community. They possess a thorough knowledge of medicinal plants used for treating human and animal diseases, which needs further investigation since it is beyond the scope of this study. For instance, a medicine prepared from pounding leaves of a plant locally called *yibrah* is used to treat wounds of domestic animals as an effective cure. On the other hand, *akiwa* is a human medicine prepared from pounded seeds of a plant dissolved in water and drunk by labouring women in order to quicken delayed child labour. *Tihiya* is a human medicine prepared from pounded roots of a plant dissolved in water and drunk for pneumonia and dysentery. Moreover, *giyamandiyata* and *giyamangola* are medicines prepared from pounded roots of plants used for treating swells in human beings.

3.4 Modes of Livelihood

The basic livelihood system of Gumuz depends upon several sources of subsistence. Integral shifting cultivation forms a major source of livelihood. It is the indigenous farming system of Gumuz. In addition, several other important components of activities are undertaken as a supplementary means of sustaining livelihood. These include gathering wild forest foods, livestock raising (mainly goats and chicken), hunting, fishing, honey collection, handicrafts, traditional alluvial gold mining, and local market exchange. In addition, sharecropping and wage labour employment are noted getting significant introduction, especially in those encroachment pressure areas and emerging administrative town centres respectively.

Integral Shifting Cultivation: Indigenous Farming System

Temporal Successive Phases of Integral Shifting Cultivation
The temporal successive phases of integral shifting cultivation cycle practices are site selection, cutting/clearing, burning, cropping, and fallowing/succession.

Site selection: A suitable site for cultivation is assessed and selected either individually or in groups. The selected site is marked either by cutting a branch of a tree or tying grass onto a branch of a tree so as to communicate with other assessors the site's being already selected. In the process of selection, those sites on well-drained soils along valley bottoms or gentle slopes are most preferred. The fertility of the selected site can be locally recognised by the type and amount of tree and other vegetation species.

Cutting/Clearing (*kancha*): After preparing the necessary food and drink (*keya*), a neighbourhood communal labour party will be mobilised first for clearing the grass and the underneath shrubs; then, all the minor trees are cut at a proper height so that they can sprout shoots and vegetate easily. While cutting the trees, all major trees are maintained in the field, since cutting big trees would cause the anger of tree spirits (*miss-jaa*), which is believed to punish by hail, insects, or drought.

Burning: Once the cut and felled forest vegetation has properly dried, it is burnt into ashes to make use of the energy or nutrients for food crop production. Moreover, burning clears the field and eliminates competitor weeds and concentrates the transfer of fertile nutrients into food crops.

Cropping: Planting and cultivation of crops is done using simple hand tools. A newly prepared plot will be used mostly for three successive harvesting seasons. In the cropping pattern, a new field is cultivated in a successive temporal sequence of finger-millet (*taanqa*) → sorghum (*kuancha*) → sorghum (ratoon). The first year finger-millet field is intensively intercropped with a number of other plants such as pumpkin (*patuha*), *oppa* (a climbing leguminous plant on remaining trees in the field), sesame (*giziqua*), maize (*gisraaba*), ochre (*endaha),* and *kimaa.* Gumuz harvest all these multiple varieties of crops from the same field in one harvest. The second season harvest is mainly sorghum (*kuancha*) of local varieties. The third season sorghum harvest is ratoon (*bukaancha* (Gum.) and *gaabo* (Amh.))[1], i.e., sorghum that sprouts from the earlier season's shoots. Then,

---

[1] The abbreviations (Gum.) represent for local names or terms in "Gumuz" and (Amh.) in "Amharic."

77

the land will be left fallow. Maize (*gisraaba*), yam (*awuna*), haricot-beans (*aranguhe*), pumpkin (*patuha*), and gourd (*bahga/kebuhe*) are predominantly cultivated in the backyards. Ginger (*aczbilha)* is mainly cultivated near riverbanks and valleys. Cotton (*baaga*) is usually planted mixed with sorghum in the fields. Pumpkin (*patuha*) is planted in the swidden fields, backyards and in smaller scattered places inside the forest. Tender pumpkin leaves (*tsepatuha*) are one of the important vegetable foods of the Gumuz. The list of major crops cultivated in the swidden fields is stated in the table below:

Table 3: Major Crops and Plant Varieties Cultivated in the Swidden Fields

Vernacular Names			Botanical Name[2]
Gumuz	**Amharic**	**English**	
Taanqa	*Dagusa*	Finger-millet	*Eleusine coracana (L.) Gaertner*
Kuancha	*Mashilla*	Sorghum	*Sorghum bicolor (L.) Moench*
Gisraaba	*Boqollo*	Maize	*Zea mays L.*
Awuna	*Boena/-Boye*	Yam	*Dioscorea abyssinica*
Aranguhe	*Adan-guare*	Haricot beans	*Phaseolus vulgaris L.*
Biliza	*Nug*	Niger-seed	*Guizotia abyssinica (L.) Cass.*
Taambeqa	*Timbaho*	Tobacco	*Nicotiana tabacum L.*
Aczbilha	*Jinjebel*	Ginger	*Zingiber officinale Rosc.*
Gaaba	*Tit*	Cotton	*Gossypium spp.*
Chenta	*Talba*	Linseed	*Linum usitatissimum L.*
Giziqua	*Saliit*	Sesame	*Sesamum orientale L.*
Bahga/-Kabuhe	*Qil*	Gourd	*Lagenaria siceraria (Mol.) Standley*
Fikancza/-Yawuqaandia	*Berbere*	Hot pepper	*Capsicum frutescens L.*
Endaha	–	Ochre	–
Patuha	*Dubba*	Pumpkin	*Cucurbita maxima Duch.*
Qosha	*Gulo*	Castor bean	*Ricinus communis L.*
Midanjala	*Tematem*	Tomatoes	*Lycopersicon esculentum Mill.*

---

[2] The main sources of botanical names are from Rehm and Espig (1991), Westphal (1975).

Vernacular Names			Botanical Name
Gumuz	Amharic	English	
Baaga	*Goman*	Cabbage	*Var. viridis L.*
Oppa*	–	–	–
Kimaa*	–	–	–
Anqarpap*	–	–	–
Omasea*	–	–	–
Maante*	–	–	–
Siineda*	–	–	–
Eppitsa*	–	–	–
Chachoha*	–	–	–
Dahka*	–	–	–

*Vernacular names of the asterisked plants are documented only in Gumuz because I was not able to identify their equivalents in Amharic and English nor the scientific botanical names.

Fallowing: Mostly after the third harvest, when the fertility of the field declines, it will be left fallow for a number of years to regenerate through re-growth and vegetation. The decline in the fertility of the land is recognised with an increased weed infestation and insufficient yield of crops. The fallow period varies according to natural and socio-economic factors. For instance, the fallow period on red (poor in nutrient) soils is longer than black (rich in nutrient) soils. Moreover, the fallow period along the cooler higher altitude areas is shorter than in areas located at a flat lower altitude. Also, a fallow period in areas of high population pressure and encroachment is shorter than in those with low population pressure with no encroachment. Informants stressed the fact that the fallow period varies according to the stated contextual differences. At the same time, they confirmed that the fallow period duration in the past was much longer (ten to fifteen years) than the present (three to six years). The trend in fallowing is far continuously decreasing periods due to encroachment and population pressure.

James (1976, 1986) and Wallmark (1976a, 1981) have also highlighted similar practices of integral shifting cultivation among the Gumuz to the south of Abbay River. Additionally, Simoons (1960) stated the practice of shifting cultivation among the Gumuz of Gondar (inhabiting lowland areas from Metemma southwards up to Metekel), contrary to the sedentary plow-cultivation practice of the highlanders. Outside the experiences of the Gumuz, Stauder (1971) described and discussed related practices of shifting cultivation among the Majangir of southwestern Ethiopia.

79

Local Farming Tools and Technology
Local simple hand tools and implements are used at all levels of field cultivation. These are *gawud* (for cutting and clearing), *ghaa* (cutting and chopping), *chagia* (for clearing, harvesting and gathering vegetables), *teba* (for
digging and cultivating soil), and *gomba* (for digging soil and edible roots).
There also exist several food preparation and carrying equipment and containers such as *endenga* (carrying stick), *sii'aya* (suspended nets at both ends
of a carrying stick), basketry and gourd containers of different size used for
carrying and transporting harvest and several other movable products.
Members of the Gumuz, who have learnt the skills, produce these tools (cf.
sub-section "Handicrafts" in this chapter). Harvested crops are mostly either
piled on wooden-platforms or stored in different forms of local granaries. In
most cases, threshed and processed grain is stored in big pottery containers.

Subsidiary Means of Livelihood
As already pointed out, the other important subsidiary means of livelihood
activities undertaken alongside and supplementary to shifting cultivation
farming include gathering wild forest foods, livestock raising (mainly goats
and chickens), hunting, fishing, honey collection, handicrafts, traditional
alluvial gold mining, and local market exchange.

Gathering Forest Foods
Forest foods gathered in the form of tender leaves, fruits, and roots are main
supplementary sources of subsistence. Additionally, *waaga* (mushrooms or
fungi) are gathered as the most favourite type of the forest food. The availability of forest foods varies seasonally, being abundant during the rainy
season and slightly scarce during the dry season. Wendy James (1976:32)
noted the same among the Gumuz south of Abbay River, stating that wild
vegetable foods are a vital part of the daily diet of Gumuz. Women are the
main actors here and are experts of the wild forest foods gathered especially
for preparing sauce and served with the main dish *inga* (stiff porridge prepared mainly from sorghum, finger-millet, and maize).
Some of the major forest foods gathered are indicated in the table below.

Table 4: Gathered Forest Foods in the Form of Fruits, Leaves, and Roots.

Gathered Wild Forest Foods[3]		
Fruits	Leaves	Roots
Boha	Kaakima	Echa
Gohaanga	Bada	Yaaga
Diiwa	Obosea	Ampaapaasiiha
Baanczeha	Oppiraasia	
Qota	Osqaanda	
Baancza	Obidaambira	
Feya	Otseyaanta	
Suhka	Paapita	
Deqomsa	Edaakusa	
Duguha	Ubulaanda	
Goha	Dahoka	
Agumaanza	Shiinya	
Ansiisa		
Andada		
Konguha		
Andargaaguha		
Antsijina		
Huya		

Apart from its being an important component of the basic livelihood, gather-ing is also considered as one of the best coping strategies practised by the community. Whenever, crop failure or food shortage occurs due to any of the several reasons, gathering wild foods becomes a major coping strategy. Mostly, those households, which cultivate meagre production engage in intensive gathering.

Hunting
Hunting constitutes one of the most important subsidiary sources of subsis-tence and is practised throughout the year with varying magnitude and only by men. The meat from the hunt is a substantial source of protein. James

---

[3] Vernacular names of the gathered forest foods are documented only in Gumuz because I was not able to identify their equivalents in Amharic and English nor the scientific botanical names.

81

(1976:32) explains that the Gumuz get more protein from hunting than from domestic animals. Hunting is done either individually or in groups. March is considered to be the best time for peak group hunting after the forest is cleared by fire in January and February. Guns and bows-and-arrows are the main hunting tools. During the hunt, the group surrounds the forest site chosen and part of the group enters into the forest accompanied by their dogs and chases the animals, locating their direction by shouting and whistling. Upon approaching the hunt animal, they shoot it with arrows at a low distance or with guns at a greater distance. Dogs are of a great support in the hunt, chasing and tiring the game until it is finally exhausted. On the other hand, in big game hunt such as hunting elephants, Beke (1844:9) noted what he had been informed during his visit to Metekel on the frontier of Agaumidir and described the following: "I am informed that they dig pits for the elephant in its path to the watering-places, which they cover over with branches of trees, grass, etc. and when the animal has fallen into one of these, they dispatch him with their spears."

Today, the Gumuz possess automatic guns and much of the big game is hunted using these weapons. However, my Gumuz informants at Gublak informed me about their experience of hunting crocodiles. In order to hunt a crocodile, they prepare a strong longer cord. At one end of the cord, an iron hook is tied hiding inside a dead rat attached to it. On the other end of the cord, a piece of light dry wood is tied. Then, the cord is placed near a river putting its hooked end into the water and the hunters leave the area. After a while, they return in a team of not less than two men. If the crocodile has been hooked, its location is traced following the lightwood that remains floating in the water. Finally, one or more of the men carefully pull the cord towards the bank of the river, while other spear at the crocodile.

In the subsistence hunting, ideally precaution is taken not to kill female animals in their reproductive age. The organisational pattern of hunting varies from one place to the other. Usually the hunting expeditions take a number of days. In the subsistence hunting, the meat will be brought to the house of the village elder and consumed together by the members of the village community. The extra leftover meat will be distributed among the village inhabitants.

In addition to supporting their subsistence, hunting among the Gumuz men is practised for status as well. Those animals hunted for fame include lion, leopard, wildcat, jackal, hyena, buffalo, and giraffe. In the fame hunt, the hunter wins prestige and increased status not only for himself but also for his wife and the whole family and lineage. The women of a village respect a hunter's wife. She is given priority while fetching water and also receives a wide range of gifts from the community. She puts bracelets on her arm and feet prepared from the skin of the hunted animals. The hunter himself is ritually cleansed of the harmful effects of the spirits of the game. The ritual is done in the name of *miss-siila* (hunt spirit). It takes place by organising a special festive occasion for rejoicing and bragging. In the ritual process, the hunter's face and head are anointed with ash. Singing, chanting and bragging are performed in his name. On the occasion, every hunter shows his bravery by bragging and chanting in public. During any social occasion and public feasts, hunters and their family members are given high respect and provided honourable seats.

The major hunting tools are bow and arrow (*dugaa*, a name for both). However, a local name for a bow is *jieduga,* and an arrow is called *cheduga.* In addition, tools such as gun (*libinda*), spear (*muha*), and *ankaasse* are used for hunting. Wild animals hunted for fame reported in the order of importance are *gumba* (lion), *omenza* (leopard), *sagila* (jackal), *gniwa* (hyena), *beguso/buga* (wild cat), *tirign* (civet), and *wagliya* (fox). On the other hand, the major wild animals including birds hunted as supplementary sources of food are described in tables 5 and 6 below.

During hunting, ritual prayer to *miss-siila* (hunt-spirit) is very important for being successful in getting the animal to be hunted at a short distance. Usually, traditional herbal medicine from leaves, fruits and stems of plants are ritually processed and then either held in the pocket or smeared or tied to the hunting tools and weapons. For instance, hunting medicines processed from leaves, stem, roots and fruits are known as *ogishaya* (held in the pocket and/or smeared on weapon), *gaaguha* (smeared on weapons), and *dita* (smeared or attached to weapons) widely applied by hunters, are believed to enable easy access to the desired game.

Table 5: Wild Animals Hunted for Food (Mammals and Amphibians)

Wild Animals Hunted for Food (Mammals and Amphibians)			
Vernacular Names			Zoological Name[4]
Gumuz	Amharic	English	
Ambugeha	Dikkula	Bushbuck	Tragelaphus scriptus
Guanja	Midaqua	Duiker	Cephalophus monticola
Medena	Kerkerro	Warthog	Phacochoerus aethiopicus
Koh/Kugna	Agaazen	Nyala	Tragelaphus strepsiceros
Mospa	Dafassa	Waterbuck	Kodus defassa
Zaraafa	Qachine	Giraffe	Giraffa camelopardalis
Gemuga	Goosh	Buffalo	Syncerus. caffer
Jaana	Zihoon	Elephant	Loxodonta africana
Edguara	Awuraris	Rhinoceros	Ceratotherium simum
Jiraantsa/ Kajo	Jaart	Porcupine	Hystrix sp.
Ogina	Toota	Long-tailed monkey	Cercopithecus aethiops
Daaya	Zinjeero	Baboon	Papio anubis
Goteha	Tinchel	Rabbit	Poelagus marjorita
Kokoba	Eeli	Tortoise	Geochelone sulcata
Kalaalah/Keses	Zando	Python	Python regius
Kohajiya	Ibaab	Snake	Aspidelaps scutatus
Buya	Ayit	Rat	Liphiomys imhausi
Inchiya	Gumaarre	Hippopotamus	Hippopotamus amphibius
Qiha/Qigna	Azzo	Crocodile	Crocodylus cataphractus
Pabatuwa	Gureeza	Colobus	Colobus abyssinicus
Yawuya	Yeduur Asaama	Bush pig	Potamochoerus porcus
Banga	Arjaano	Nile lizard	–
Baata*	–	–	–
Ogulaambeha*	–	–	–
Weesa*	–	–	–
Baguza*	–	–	–
Yappida'a*	–	–	–
Saambisa*	–	–	–
Waanyaha*	–	–	–
Enza*	–	–	–
Ekakata*	–	–	–

* Vernacular names of the asterisked animals are documented only in Gumuz because I was not able to identify their equivalents in Amharic and English nor the scientific zoological name.

---

[4] Many of the zoological names for the mammals are obtained from Dorst and Dandelot (1970).

Table 6: Birds Hunted for Food

Birds Hunted for Food			
Vernacular Names			Zoological Name[5]
Gumuz	Amharic	English	
Ejiya	Irjib	Dove	Streptopelia capicola
Biyanguha	Chilfiit	Eagle	Aquila rapax
Kanza	Jigra	Guinea fowl	Numida meleagris
Meho	Qooq	Partridge	Ptilopachus petrosus
Embawuga	Daakiye	Duck	Anas sparsa
Chikohay*	–	–	–
Chiya*	–	–	–
Cheeya*	–	–	–
Okuha*	–	–	–
Ogaafiya*	–	–	–
Yagriga*	–	–	–
Ee'eyya *	–	–	–
Eyagewa*	–	–	–
Odeya*	–	–	–
Daduba*	–	–	–
Odankuwa*	–	–	–
Oqulitiya*	–	–	–
Ozunka*	–	–	–
Ochuwaaya*	–	–	–
Gaaga*	–	–	–
Erkuanda*	–	–	–

* Vernacular names of the asterisked animals are documented only in Gumuz because I was not able to identify their equivalents in Amharic and English nor the scientific zoological names.

Fishing

Fishing is an equally important supplementary subsistence activity, serving as an additional source of protein. Locally, fish are collectively called *gosha*. The rivers and streams that form the perennial water sources of the area serve as a best source of fishing. The widely used local fishing tools are known as *iiha* (circular flat and hollow net with wooden edge) and *gambiida* (a hive-like basketry work with an inwardly bent and hooked opening on only from one side that lets in fish and traps avoiding exit). In the calm and clear waters, mainly in the dry season, bows and arrows are also used for fishing simply by shooting. As a recent introduction, fish-hooks (*jibaad*) and nets are also applied to a very limited extent in areas of encroachment pres-

---

[5] The stated zoological names for the birds are obtained from Williams and Arlott (1980).

sure. Dazing fish using traditional medicine is also widely used. In order to daze fish, the medicines applied include *asisuha* (inner bark of tree), *yawula* (roots and bark of a tree), and *eduqawa* (leaves and fruits). In the process of application, the medicine is put in upstream, and fishing immediately below enables the Gumuz to catch big harvest of dazed, using *iiha*. However, it is stressed that applying medicine has a risk of destroying the fish resource, because more than dazing, it also kills the fish. Fishing is practised through-out the year; but done mostly in the dry season months of October to February. Both sexes are involved in fishing. However, dry season fishing from streams is part of the frequent practices of women, whereas the rainy season fishing is particularly done by men because of the increase in the volumes of river waters. Men also fish from big rivers in the dry season.

Honey Collection

The collection of honey from hollow trunks of big trees and caves along banks of rivers and streams is an important additional source of subsistence. Similar to hunting, honey collection is done mostly in groups. Men mainly do it. Usually, a honey collecting expedition takes a number of days or weeks in the forest during the peak wild honey-harvesting period. In the process of harvesting honey from big trees, members of the group climb up the tree and use smoke to subdue the bees, while the remaining group members stay on the ground and receive the honey sent down suspended in a container tied to a rope. After completing the honey collection, the group returns back to its village and shares the harvested honey among themselves. The extra honey is sold and the income is used to buy salt (which at times is also locally extracted from ash by women) and other spices. Recently bee-hives have also been introduced to a substantial extent in areas of increased encroachment.

Livestock

The livestock owned by the Gumuz are cattle (*koissa*), goats (*me'a*), sheep (*jaja*), chickens (*metta*), and donkeys (*nanuha*). At the moment, the Gumuz in Metekel own very few cattle. The informants' explanation for a limited – or even in many cases lack of – cattle ownership is to an outbreak of epi-demic (probably rinder-pest) sometimes in the past, which needs further investigation. They explained that in earlier days, they used to own many cattle, which were lost due to the stated outbreak of cattle epidemic. Even now cattle are rarely owned. Even if certain members own a few head of cattle, they do not use oxen for plowing, and the cows are not milked, milk products being rarely known. The few cattle raised are used either for meat during festivals or sold to generate income and buy defence weapons (mostly guns of various types) because these weapons are the most valued in order to defend their community and territory against external encroachment and attacks as well as defend one's clan from clan feuds.

The most important livestock among the Gumuz are goats raised both for meat and sale. They rear an indigenous goat species well adapted to their agro-ecological context. Goats are not milked. Apart from using them for food and sale, the community raises many goats as a status marker. Chickens are another very important domestic animal, raised for meat, egg and sale. Chickens and goats in particular find important ritual sacrificial use, mostly by the *gafia*.

Although not in equal magnitude, the Gumuz also raise sheep both for meat and sale. Additionally, they keep donkeys for packing agricultural products from the field as well as for transporting things to distant areas such as local markets. Dogs are the other most important domestic animals raised by the Gumuz for multiple purposes. Dogs are useful for guarding the home and village. They are indispensable partners in both subsistence and fame hunting.

As pointed out above, the Gumuz informants strongly complained about the prevalence of different livestock diseases and explained the features some of them. For instance, *lulluwa* (probably *trypanosomiasis*) kills cattle by weakening; and *otate'a* (probably rinder-pest) kills livestock by producing wounds on its body. Specially, these two were considered as the worst cattle diseases. It was stressed that *otate'a* can be even transmitted to human beings. Both *lullawa* and *otate'a* affect goats, sheep, and donkeys as well. Mostly a disease called *tirissa* (*fengil* (Amh.)) affects chicken. Dogs are mainly affected by a disease known as *zaara* (probably *rabies*). *Zaara* is explained as transmittable to human beings.

Handicrafts

Those handicrafts which are widely performed both for generating income as well as for home and field use include bamboo works (basketry), woodworks, iron works, pottery, skin works and gourds/calabashes. Most of the household utensils and furniture as well as simple hand farm tools, gathering tools and hunting/defence weapons are mostly the handicraft products of the community members. Apart from home utilisation, handicrafts are produced for generating substantial income for the households. Many of the handicraft products are exchanged in the local markets. Handicraft products are observed in local markets being sold for generating income. The products include pottery items of different sizes, basketry (e.g., *mankuban – injera* cooking pan lid) and *keya* filter (*dingha*), carrying-net cords (*sii'aya*), wood works (e.g., *legeda* for serving food, mortar and pestle for coffee pounding, chairs made of a wooden frame), woven-skin (*angirib)*, iron works (e.g., *gawud* for cutting and clearing bush and small vegetation), and gourds and calabashes.

Other handicraft furniture and utensils used at home include: *Tega* (wooden chair), *duqufa* (round hollow basket container*), kaake'a* (round flat basket container), *ankudida* (door), *tichkiya* (*keya* brewing big jar), *antarsa* (small cooking pot), *tichanga* (porridge cooking pot with wide opening), *tichangiza* (flat pottery container for mixing and frying flour for *keya*), *jinga* (porridge mixing stick), *bahiga* (water and *keya* serving gourd calabash), *mandinah* (storage pot for brewed *keya), gishgeresh* (local grain grinding stone), *nuka'aya* (small calabash for serving drinking water*), wancha* (small calabash for serving *keya*), *tanga* (wooden bed*),* and *inta* (mattress). As earlier stated, handicraft products are produced by members of the community, who learnt the skills. Unlike the widespread practice in many parts of Ethiopia, the handicraftsmen do not belong to any specialised occupational groups. They are not marginalised at all and no form of stigma is attached to the producers. Instead, the handicraftsmen enjoy increased respect from the community for their additional skills of the crafts. Unlike among the highlanders, similar non-discriminatory social status of handicraftsmen was observed among the Gumuz in the western lowlands of Begemder/Gondar (north of Metekel) by Simoons (1960:54). He noted that the Gumuz "do not look down on craft work, or discriminate against craftsmen or place them in separate classes."

Local Market Exchange
Exchange of products in the local markets is an important component of the very existence of the community. Except trading for subsistence, no basic trading for surplus accumulation is observed. In order to generate supplementary income for the households, the Gumuz sell several items in the markets of Mandura, Mambuk, L4, and Gilgel Beles. For instance, I observed them selling crops such as finger-millet, sorghum, ginger, niger-seed, hot pepper, pumpkin, maize (green), smoking root plant, *kakima* (wild leaves), *kuya* (wild fruit); domestic animals such as goats, chickens, and sheep; as well as handicraft products of different types. The local market

places are areas where both Gumuz and non-Gumuz interact. The market exchange and trading take place both within Gumuz and between Gumuz and non-Gumuz community members. Most of the Gumuz are first-order sellers who make use of the area market network.

Renting Land

The land renting arrangement between Gumuz and non-Gumuz highland immigrant settlers is a practice being established in recent years. This practice is introduced in those Gumuz areas under the pressure of external encroachment. Here it is to be recalled that the encroachment pressure has shortened the fallow period due to limitations in land resources. This has introduced among the shifting cultivators a claim of ownership to an earlier cleared field left fallow. Therefore, most land rental arrangements are made on these fallow fields, which are rented-out by the Gumuz claimant to immigrant plow cultivators from the highlands. The usual terms of renting land arrangement is in an exchange for grain where an estimated one hectare of farmland is rented out for 300-500 kg of grain (mainly finger-millet or sorghum) depending on the fertility potential and location of the land.

In the renting land arrangement, the Gumuz and the immigrant highlander agree first on the details of the terms of exchange. Then, the final decision is made in the presence of Gumuz elders. After harvest, the two partners exchange on the basis of the terms fixed in their earlier agreement. However, there exists a predominant stereotype on the part of the Gumuz condemning the highlanders as being liars and deceptive. The former repeatedly complain about the immigrants' frequent failure in fulfilling their agreements manifested mostly in lack of giving the proper exchange. In addition, complete clearance of all trees from the cultivation fields is stated as sources of conflicts. Despite the shortcomings, the attitudes of those Gumuz members who practice renting land seem positive towards the arrangement. However, in those areas where there is no encroachment, renting land arrangements are rarely known.

Traditional Alluvial Gold Mining

Traditional panning for gold mainly along the major rivers such as Abbay and Beles is an important sideline income-generating activity of the Gumuz in Metekel. It is practised in almost all the *woreda* of the zone (except Pawe) mostly in the lower course of the rivers named. Both men and women, using traditional hand tools, perform it mainly during the dry season. The gold recovered is sold to local merchants who in turn channel it to others in the central parts of the country. The Gumuz informants stressed that panning for gold is most lucrative, the income being used to buy guns and several other important items.

Wage Labour Employment
During peak weeding season, I observed young members of Gumuz working as daily labourers in private and public organisations engaged in large farm activities such as the Tana-Beles project and many private investment schemes in rain-fed agriculture in the area (cf. chapter 5, sub-section "Rain-Fed Agricultural Investment Schemes"). A number of Gumuz members from a *Manjeeri* village have been employed by CISP on a contractual basis as guards and gardeners. Similarly, members of Gumuz were observed employed as guards, messengers, gardeners, and clerks in most administrative *woreda* of Metekel Zone. Except those political appointees holding the highest administrative positions of the *woreda* and the zone, most employed Gumuz held only lower level auxiliary positions. They rarely held professional positions due to lack of the necessary educational background, which in most cases are held by non-Gumuz. It seems that wage labour is recently getting introduced to the community with the increased encroachment by various interest groups. However, this is an area which calls for further investigation.

Seasonal Calendar of Livelihood Activities
The seasonal calendar of livelihood activities practised by the Gumuz disaggregated by month and gender is described in the following table.

Table 7: Gender Disaggregated Seasonal Calendar of Livelihood Activities

Months (in Gu-muz)	Gender-Disaggregated Seasonal Calendar of Livelihood Activities	
	Men (*Gunza*)	Women (*Gaafa*)
Metta (July)	• First weeding of most main field crops such as finger-millet, sorghum, maize, and others; • Planting sesame and cotton; • Preparing field for niger-seed (*nug*) and tobacco.	• Participating in field crops weeding and planting; • Preparing *keya* (local brew); • Undertaking *mihantsuquma* (gathering forest foods); • Performing the usual home chores.
Dhibija (August)	• Second weeding of main field crops; • Planting sesame and tobacco; • Harvesting pumpkin.	• Participating in weeding and planting; • Harvesting pumpkin; • Preparing *keya*; • Undertaking *mihantsuquma*; • Performing home chores.
Miczgidi-bija (September)	• Undertaking heavy tasks of *kancha* (clearing bush and cutting trees to prepare new swidden plots); • Harvesting pumpkin and maize.	• Preparing *keya*; • Participating in the harvest; • Undertaking *mihantsuquma*; • Performing home chores.
Iibija (October)	• Harvesting finger-millet (short maturing variety), sesame, and niger seed; • Collecting honey; • Fishing from rivers.	• Preparing *keya*; • Participating in harvesting; • Undertaking *mihantsuquma*; • Performing home chores.
Baanduha (November)	• Harvesting same crops as October including ginger; • Harvesting cotton; • Collecting honey; • Fishing from rivers.	• Preparing *keya*; • Participating in harvest; • Fishing from streams; • Undertaking *mihantsuquma*; • Performing home chores.
Bibba (December)	• Harvesting sorghum and finger millet; • Piling harvest on wooden platforms; • Fencing around crop piles.	• Preparing *keya*; • Participating in harvest; • Transporting harvest to piling areas; • Fishing from streams and rivers; • Undertaking *mihantsuquma*; • Performing home chores.

Months (in Gumuz)	Gender-Disaggregated Seasonal Calendar of Livelihood Activities	
	Men (*Gunza*)	Women (*Gaafa*)
Eebagunda (January)	• Cutting roof thatching grass; • Building residential houses; • Fencing around crop piles; • Constructing granary; • Hunting (individual).	• Transporting building materials (wood/bamboo and thatching grass); • Preparing *keya*; • Fishing from stream and rivers; • Undertaking *mihantsuquma*; • Performing home chores.
Eebit-kaagicha (February)	• Threshing finger-millet; • Constructing granary; • Building residential houses; • Hunting game (both singly and in groups).	• Preparing *keya*; • Preparing threshing ground; • Participating in the construction of residential houses and granary; • Fishing from rivers and streams; • Undertaking *mihantsuquma*; • Performing home chores.
Dooka (March)	• Collecting, piling and burning *kancha;* • Hunting mainly in groups including big games; • Constructing residential houses and granary.	• Preparing *keya*; • Participating in house and granary construction; • Intensive fishing from streams and rivers; • Undertaking *mihantsuquma*; • Performing home chores.
Duufazika (April)	• Preparing main field plots; • Planting main crops such as sorghum, finger millet (red), maize, pumpkin, sesame (white), ginger, *oppa*, etc.	• Participating in field preparation and planting of the main crops; • Preparing *keya*; • Fishing from streams and rivers; • Undertaking *mihantsuquma*; • Performing home chores.
Dugu-chaka (May)	• Preparing main field plots; • Planting main crops such as sorghum, finger millet (red), maize, pumpkin, sesame (white), ginger, *oppa*, etc.	• Participating in field preparation and planting of the main crops; • Preparing *keya*; • Fishing from streams and rivers; • Undertaking *mihantsuquma*; • Performing home chores.
Quada (June)	• Planting main crops; • Re-planting those field plot parts destroyed by wild animals; • Begin first weeding.	• Participating in planting and early weeding; • Preparing *keya;* • Undertaking *mihantsuquma*; • Performing home chores.

Social Organisation of Production and Labour Arrangements

Work Pattern and Labour Arrangements
The overall work pattern of performing activities basic to their livelihood is mostly undertaken both at neighbourhood communally and individually at family levels. The swidden cultivation activities at all levels, gathering forest foods, hunting and honey collection are mostly performed in groups. The successive shifting cultivation activities such as clearing/cutting the swidden vegetation; burning the dried swidden; and cropping tasks at all levels of planting/cultivating, weeding, harvesting and threshing are basically performed in pooled labour groups. The communal labour is mobilised by a closer facilitation and supervision of village elders who are responsible for smooth and fair distribution of the pooled labour among the village inhabitants. Traditionally, a member who needs to pool communal labour prepares the local brew (*keya*) to be feasted by the work party. Those families who prepare and serve more *keya* can mobilise more labour that in turn enables them to harvest more production. The number of communal labour participants depends upon the demand and amount of work. The Gumuz measure their field farm size by the frequency of *keya* brewed and number of communal labour mobilised. Moreover, men go for both hunting and wild honey collection in groups. Although the catch as well as forest foods are individually possessed for family diet, village women go for both fishing and gathering in groups. Moreover, women are also observed going to local markets in groups.

Although most of the major tasks are performed by communal labour, members of the community could also perform multiple tasks of daily importance at a household level limited to family labour. The head of the household is the father, who is responsible for the overall administration of the household. The mother is the most important partner of the household, providing the true meaning to it and performing multiple tasks including taking care of the household members. Members of the household perform several tasks. In a family where a father is weak, the mother supports and encourages him to work hard. On the other hand, in a household where the mother is weaker, the husband supports and encourages her to work hard. If the weaker party does not improve, it might result in a divorce. However, in a family where both are hard working, they perform their respective tasks smoothly. Household members under the parents perform the tasks of parents of the respective sex. As already stated, the recruitment of additional labour is mobilised by organising a feast (preparing *keya*) for those activities beyond the labour capacity of the family.

Gender Division of Labour

There exists a clear division of labour along gender lines. Gumuz women are observed as the most ingenious and hardest working members of the community. They perform innumerable livelihood activities tirelessly. Apart from performing several gender-specific home chores and many others, they are also fully involved at all levels in the field production as well as construction and exchange activities already described earlier. In the daily performance, there are activities undertaken either by men or by women alone or by both where the details being stated in the table below.

Table 8: Gender Division of Labour

Gender Division of Labour		
Men (*Gunza*)	**Women (*Gaafa*)**	**Both**
• Constructing residential houses; • Working on handicrafts such as wood work; basketry, and iron work, • Cutting and clearing swidden; • Collecting honey from the forest or bee-hives; • Sowing crops; • Cutting roof thatching grass; • Splitting bamboo and fencing the compound; • Piling harvested crops; • Hunting wild animals; • Protecting field crops from wild animals; and • Constructing granary.	• Performing home chores; • Gathering forest foods; • Transporting products to local markets, harvest to piling places, and do most manual transportation; • Fishing mainly during the dry season; • Fetching fuel wood and drinking water; • Preparing mud and plastering it on granary; • Preparing *keya* for communal labour during field clearing, planting/sowing, weeding, harvesting, threshing, house construction as well during all other socially important festive occasions and every day use.	• Planting crops; • Weeding/culti-vating crops; • Harvesting crops; • Transporting roof thatching grass; • Preparing and transporting fencing bamboo and barks for tying; • Preparing live-stock barn; • Raising livestock; • Fishing (mostly men in the rainy season and women in the dry season); and • Working on handicraft products particularly pottery.

Seasonal Distribution of Labour Requirements

The distribution of labour requirements varies according to the demand of the seasonal calendar of activities. The labour demand can be broadly grouped into two categories of dry season and rainy season requirements. In the dry season months of October to March, agricultural activities such as protecting field crops, harvesting, piling, fencing and house construction, threshing, cutting/clearing and burning swidden are undertaken. In the rainy season months of April to September, agricultural activities such as sowing/planting crops, repeated weeding at different levels are performed. The rainy season activities are considered demanding much, heavy labour, which is aggravated by a usual food deficit that in turn adds a burden on women who engage in intensive gathering of forest foods as a coping strategy. On the other hand, the dry season activities are considered to be equally demanding of labour due to the pressure of forest fires, which destroy crops in the field. However, the stress of dry season activities is felt less because of their larger festive nature and the availability food in abundance. The availability of harvested food in turn reduces women's burden of intensive gathering, which increases field labour (women work longer hours in the harvesting field). Moreover, the dry season diet is also augmented by harvests from hunting and honey collection by men. Furthermore, the dry season is a time full of traditional feasts among which the memorial feast for the dead (*tazkar*) is a major one.

Chapter 4. Indigenous Ecological Knowledge and Systems of Natural Resource Management

4.1 Ecological Thought and Knowledge

Perceptions of Territory
The Gumuz possess a clear notion and contextually well-defined perception of their territory. They view their territory as a symbol of identity. The perception of territory starts with neighbourhood/village → clan (*e.g., Dimtsa-atse, Maataaba, Azaarti, Kitli*) → sub-regional group (e.g., Gumuz of Mandura, Dangur, Guba) → regional group (e.g., Gumuz of Metekel, Kamashi, and Metemma) → and the entire Gumuz territory (cf. chapter 3, sub-section "Family, Neighbourhood/Commune and Clan"). An important area unit in the Gumuz perceptions of territoriality is the clan territory. As stated earlier, a Gumuz identity is marked by his membership in a clan, which has ideally a clearly marked territory. Members of the group belonging to the same clan are the common owners of the territory and its resources. The clan territory is strongly defended and preserved by its members. Rivers and streams, hills and mountains, big old trees (marked by cuts on the branches), big stones, roads and footpaths, etc. mark the boundary of a clan territory.

The Gumuz possess detailed knowledge of the natural resources existing in their respective territories. They recognise soils of different quality for cultivation in backyards and in swidden fields. Their knowledge of primary and secondary forests and the products is immense. They have accumulated knowledge of both terrestrial and aquatic wildlife consisting of mammals, reptiles and birds. Their land-use practices are composed of areas for swidden fields, village residential settlement, fallow fields, and forests. They prefer waters from springs for household use although they depend on rivers and streams in the absence of springs. The waters of rivers and streams are used for fishing and hunting other aquatic animals. They know clearly the web of footpaths in the forest and savannah territories, which lead them to multiple destinations.

Ecological Thought and Knowledge Blended in Belief System
The Gumuz have special relationships with their lands, territories, and the surrounding environment. As a defining characteristic of their close attachment to the natural environment, they view natural resources as substances endowed with sacred meanings. They possess a thorough knowledge about their natural resources based on observation and practice that offers an immense understanding of the natural environment. The knowledge plays a central role in their systems of natural resource management. Their knowledge of the natural environment are intimately interwoven and blended with their belief systems. They believe that natural resources are the ingenuous gift, blessing, and creation of *yamba* (the supreme deity), who is the source of life and livelihood to the past, present, and future generations. As stated earlier, *yamba* is believed to be an omnipotent supreme deity under whom all *missa* (poly-spirits) function. *Yamba* is believed to have provided them with the knowledge of proper use and management of natural resources. They perceive that the responsibility of passing the natural resources to the next generations after proper usage is a commandment from *yamba*.

The different natural resources have their respective *missa* (spirits) that ensure safe and proper use and management of each resource. Violations result in severe retribution from the respective *missa*. Their indigenous environmental knowledge meshed with the belief system is explained as follows:

Indigenous Environmental Thought Blended in the Belief System
Miss-jaa (tree-spirit) is responsible for trees and the forest at large in which cutting big trees without proper ritually justified reason (such as for construction and household use (furniture)) results in a curse that will be manifested in rain failure and drying up of waters in springs, streams and

rivers. Additionally, *miss-indeya* (earth-spirit) is responsible for the soils and the entire land resources at large in which clearing its clothing (forest and vegetation) and exploiting too much the earth's resources without rest/pause (fallowing) results in a retribution by eroding the soil, decreasing fertility and yield, turning the waters muddy, and finally warming and drying them up, creating an imbalance upon the climate by raising the temperature and increasing the intensity of wind blowing. *Miss-Siila* (hunt-spirit) is in charge of hunting wildlife and mismanagement such as killing female animals in their reproductive age would cause severe punishment by extinguishing the animal species in the future.

Source: Manjeeri Gumuz Informants (August 1999)

The Gumuz community views land as sacred because they believe it to be the source and destination of life. They consider that life on earth is sustained by the products of land. In their perception, vital natural resources cannot be privately possessed except its fruits such as harvested crops. Since natural resources do not belong to only one generation, they should not be disposed of. They view their natural resources as symbols of their identity because the natural habitat proves their rightful traditional ownership. It also stands for their ethnic identity because without their resource, the clan or the whole ethnic group would be lost. Their natural environment is perceived as a place where their ancestors have lived and were buried. Thus, as earlier stated, they view their vital natural resources as properties of *yamba, missa,* and the *ancestors*, which should be properly used and managed by the present community preserving for the future generations.

Traditional Ecological Knowledge
The practical knowledge of natural resources meshed with their belief system is explained based on experience and observation. Their knowledge of the natural and human environment, including humans, forests, soils, water and wildlife is holistic and dynamically interconnected. In their holistic interconnected ecological view, the Gumuz consider themselves as part of the web of life on earth, harmoniously bonded with nature and its creatures. Under this broad perception, the forest resource is viewed as the *basis* for the whole complex inter-linkages of all the other resources. It is because they consider the forest to be one that preserves the underlying stability of the entire natural environment. The description of their knowledge the forest resource in the entire agro-ecology of the area include the following functions:

- Serve as windbreak and protect our field crops and houses (specially the thatched roofs) from destruction;
- Prevent soil erosion;
- Increase soil fertility with litter and ashes;
- Maintain environmental stability;
- Keep the climate hospitable (big trees suck water and cool the air);
- Serve as a home of wildlife;
- Serve as a home for us to which our lives and livelihood are inextricably tied;
- Reduce weed infestation;
- Keep the soil soft and easy for hoe cultivation;
- Serve as a clothing to the land protecting it from heat and heavy rain (misery);
- Provide proper rain;
- Provide shade. During the dry season it serves as a naturally cool place where adults rest and drink *keya* during field labour; travellers sit and take rest; mothers sit and breastfeed their babies; their nude children rest and play comfortably. During rainy season, shade trees protect from heavy rain;
- Serve as a source of multiple gathered wild forest foods;
- Serve as a home for honey bees;
- Serve as a source of clean and cold water for drinking;
- Regulate proper flow of river and stream waters by keeping clean and cooler where fish and other aquatic animals grow well and are harvested easily;
- Enable us to identify the seasons of the year by the changing colours of the leaves of big trees; and the number of years by the different growth stages of young trees underneath from the dropped seeds of the mother tree; and
- Serve as a source of special roof thatching grass (locally known as *gizimp'a*).

As previously stated, the Gumuz explained their practical knowledge of the forest resource when it is carefully preserved based on their ecological thinking and ethical values. On the other hand, they also possess a knowledge of the consequences of the loss of forest resource on the natural environment that include:

- Loss of the "land's dressings", making it naked and exposing it to misery;
- Depletion of fertile soils, creating soil compaction, increasing weed infestation and reducing yield;
- Reduction of water flows initially, warming it by direct sun heat (increased evaporation), turning it muddy, and finally drying up the waters completely;
- Severe health problems due to lack of clean water, dietary deficiency and loss of medicinal plants;
- Destruction of the habitat of wildlife, causing them to disappear;
- Extinction of fish and other aquatic animals by drying up the waters;
- Loss of honey bees;
- Loss of water-sucking big trees that make and attract rain to fall; and as a consequence cause loss of proper rainfall;
- Loss of trees for construction, household use and roof-thatching grass;
- Loss of shade trees during dry and rainy seasons; and
- Creation of an imbalance in the entire agro-ecology and the natural environment by raising the temperature, intensifying wind blow, increasing soil and water erosion, and spoiling the climate.

4.2 Systems of Resource Management

Natural Resource Base

Metekel is well known for its relatively ample but fragile natural resource potential such as rich and fertile soils; diverse flora and fauna composed of natural vegetation with different arboreal tree species and bamboo, shrubs, and grasses that also serve as a habitat for several types of wildlife; and ample perennial water resources with many rivers, streams, and springs. However, an emphasis on rich and abundant natural resources in Metekel should not obscure the fragile ecological characteristics of the area maintained mainly by the adaptive management system of the Gumuz. Climatically, the area is dominantly hot humid tropical. Most of the area is infested with malaria (a common cause of human death) and trypanosomiasis (a common cause of livestock death).

Based on my former assessment (Wolde-Selassie 1996b:10), major perennial rivers that flow in the area include: Abbay (Blue Nile), Dim, Tiksi, Dabila, Timbil, Bishan Adi, Chembi, Dawi, Beles, Gilgel Beles, Dindir, Dura, Shar, Ardi, Bilq, Dabila, Kiwil, and Bichkis. In addition, there are several tributary streams, which either considerably decrease their flow or dry completely in the dry season. Some of these streams include: Aduraja, Chewatam, Shentella, Mar-Zenneb, Menta-Wuha, Sahi, Aleltu, Azib, Bunka, Aybanka, Goncha, Aysika, Keker, and Gublak. Furthermore, there are many perennial springs in the area such as: Worgra, Sigade, Filklik, Semania, Tis, Addis-Zemen, Banogn, Gich-Bedel, Yeabeshahu, Gumsa, Kubs, Dangczri, Menta-Wuha, Mambuk, Mambuk Qutir Hulett, and Yesirar-Wuha. There also exist many other springs that usually dry up in the dry months.

The three major soil types that exist in the area are red, black, and brown soils. Depending on the topographical difference, there also exist other different types of soils. A study carried out in Metekel (MPO 1993) describes the different types and characteristics of the soils of the area depending on the different topographical features. According to this study, the soils found in flat or almost flat topography of 0-2% slope are black or black-brown in colour with a high clay content and deep profile that crack severely in the dry season and become elastic and water-logged in the wet season, making them difficult for agricultural purposes. Soils of the undulating topography of 2-8% slope show different characteristics depending on the vegetation types. Compared with the flat slope, the soils of undulating slopes are better-drained and mostly red in colour and are covered with a forest of various arboreal tree species and bamboo. The profile of soils under this category varies, ranging from poor-shallow to rich-deep, the latter being very much preferred by farmers and useful for agriculture. Soils of the rolling topography of 8-16% slope are shallow in depth and stony, being often unsuitable for agriculture. Soils of the hilly topography of 16-30% slope are mostly located along the gorges of big rivers with a minimum depth, which can be easily eroded if vegetation is absent. Soils in the greater than 30% slope topography are stony and rocky with least soil depth and more useful for afforestation than cultivation. In addition, there exists an abundant red and black clay soil suitable for the production of diverse pottery products by the traditional handicraftsmen.

The areas inhabited by Gumuz are endowed with vegetation types composed of a variety of tree species, shrubs, grasses, and herbs, which have long been adapted to the different topographical features of the slope classes, soil types, altitude, and agro-ecology of the entire area. The forests and vegetation resources provide a wide range of livelihood sources. Forests serve as a home and habitat for several types of wild animals and provide a direct source of food products for human beings as well as feed and browse for livestock. Parts of plants that serve as a source of food for the indigenous peoples include buds, young-tender leaves, fruits, roots, inner-parts of the bark, and stems. Forests and vegetation are sources of traditional medicine; sources of honey collection; and serve as sources of necessary materials for construction and roof thatching, fencing, farm implements, furniture and utensils making, fuel wood, etc. as well as sources of incense collection in the lowlands. Above all, as pointed out earlier, forests and vegetation keep the resource balance of the eco-system of the entire area preserving and conserving water, protecting the land from wind and water erosion, preventing desertification, and modulating the climate. However, at the moment, the forests and vegetation resources are seriously threatened by unwise human intervention. Due to its endowment with natural forests and vegetation and water resources, the Metekel area hosts many types of wild animals (cf. chapter 3, sub-section "Hunting"). However, due to the human intervention upon their habitat, the wildlife is endangered.

Land Resource Tenure
The natural resources in the area have been used a source of basic livelihood to the Gumuz. Land is the most valuable resource. Land resources among the Gumuz are ideally communal property. In their customary communal tenure, rights to natural resources are derived from the community. The community as a group rather than individuals decides the overall use and management of natural resources. Since the community (ideally the clan in its defined territory) is the true owner of natural resources, individual members are accorded only usufruct rights. A similar land tenure system is observed by Wallmark (1981:83-84) among the Gumuz on the southern bank of the Abbay River, and he notes: "In the entire Bega land, all land is owned by the clans, even if idle at the moment." Land among the Gumuz, he stresses, "is not sold under any circumstances, either inside or outside the clan." In the mean time, he states, land is not inherited because members of a clan can freely farm as much land as they can on any uncultivated land inside their clan territory. He further states that, "each clan strongly prefers that other clans stay out." Individual members of the clan can cultivate as much as they are able to do so providing the necessary feast for mobilising communal field labour. Although members have unrestricted access, the full control over natural resources is in the hands of the community.

In the shifting cultivation system, ideally, any other member from within the same group can use land left fallow by a previous user later. Those communal resources can be further grouped into two sub-categories. The first category is land resources under a shifting cultivation system, which is exclusively owned by the clan. The other category is natural resources under large forests and vegetation cover and river waters, which can be widely shared by all other neighbouring clans of the area for common hunting, fishing, and honey collection.

Shifting Cultivation and Multi-Niche Management Strategy

The traditional farming system of Gumuz, shifting cultivation, is a useful strategy of natural resource management. James (1976:30-31) notes its appropriateness to the fragile eco-systems in the valley and explains "in the long term, the system of shifting cultivation using hand labour actually conserves the soil and forest resources of a region in a manner impossible under mechanical or plough cultivation. The periodic recovery of the land and vegetation cover enables the natural fertility of the soil to be renewed, and the dangers of soil erosion are much reduced."

In the successive phases of the shifting cultivation cycle, the cropping field plot is considered as the first stage in the transition back to forest because it is skilfully managed to re-establish the forest. In their strategy of managing the natural resources, the Gumuz shift their settlements within the clan territory. Regular settlement shifting reduces the stress that would occur upon the resources of the village and its surrounding microsite due to the pressure of over-utilisation. They establish village settlement at sites on well-drained soils selected mostly on hilltops and along gentle slopes. Such sites are selected on the basis of their suitability for home gardening as well as to reduce mosquito infestation, which is common in flat waterlogged areas. In the swidden cycle, the sites for field plots are carefully selected on gentle slopes and well-drained valley bottoms suitable for crop cultivation. The Gumuz easily recognise the fertility of the selected plots by the type and amount of tree and vegetation species as well as the texture of the soils. Field sites are not selected along steep slopes in order not to expose the sites to easy erosion. At the same time, field sites are not selected on flat waterlogged vertisols, which are difficult to cultivate.

James (1976:47) made a similar observation concerning the traditional ecological knowledge and natural resource management practices of the Gumuz to the south of Abbay River. She considers the shifting cultivation and intercropping patterns in the swidden fields with multiple crops as part of the "traditional fund of knowledge" of the Gumuz in the Blue Nile Valley. She also notes that the Gumuz have generations of experience in the cultivation of indigene crops familiar with the climate and soils of the valley, but which are foreign to highland farmers. Hence, she suggests that "it would be wise for any agricultural development to take into account the value of this experience and knowledge in such a way as to widen the opportunities of the local population to cultivate the area they are familiar with, rather than encourage an invasion either of peasant farmers or agricultural labourers on big schemes devoted to the production of one or two crops familiar to the highlanders."

Since the shifting cultivation field is small in size and already skilfully cleared, the fallow field regenerates rapidly. The longer the fallow period, the better will be the soil recovery. For the Gumuz, the re-established dense succession secondary forest is relatively more productive in terms of abundant gathered wild forest foods than the primary forest with its higher carrying capacity of wildlife for hunting. The swidden fields are cultivated with several crop and plant varieties. Ginger, for instance, is cultivated along riverbanks without even clearing the forest as the most sustainable resource management strategy. Pumpkin is also planted in any suitable site inside the forest. Preserving the forest resources, foods are gathered in the form of leaves, fruits and roots as an important component part of the livelihood of Gumuz (cf. chapter 3, sub-section "Gathering Forest Foods"). These forest foods are gathered from the wild by maintaining the forest as a main strategy of managing the resource. As part of collecting wild honey, the Gumuz also make careful maintenance of holes/caves of the hollow trunks of trees by widening the openings to attract honeybees and facilitate later honey harvesting. In subsistence hunting, ideally precaution is taken not to kill female animals at their reproductive age. The water logging flat vertisol savannah grassland areas are mainly used for hunting. Trees and vegetation along riverbanks are consciously maintained and used as important sites of hunting. By consciously maintaining the natural forest ecosystem, they practice a multi-niche strategy of sustainable management of natural resources and view beyond the immediate use towards future sustainability.

"Fire" as Resource Management Strategy

Apart from its use in the burning stage of the shifting cultivation cycle, fire is considered to be part of the eco-system of the entire area and skilfully utilised by the Gumuz in their indigenous natural resource management systems. According to the Gumuz informants, the importance of fire is strongly stressed as part of the eco-system management. In their indigenous natural resource management systems, wild bush fire emerges annually and clears the dried tall savannah grasses and undergrowth bushes in the forests. The

Gumuz explain that after the annual burnings, the vegetation easily rejuvenates, responding swiftly to the effects of the fire. Most of the local tree and vegetation species and especially acacia seem to endure the annual burning by the fire.

As part of their local resource management, the Gumuz possess a thorough knowledge of when to set fires by observing the moisture contents of trees and grasses. They usually begin setting fire in January when the savannah grass has moderately dried without loosing its moisture totally. According to the local explanation, this is the proper stage when fire can manageably clear the bush and grass without damaging its easy rejuvenation and re-vegetation. Due to the existence of a certain amount of moisture, the burning power of the fire will be manageable since it spreads more slowly. Moreover, since the roots of the burning bush and grasses are not completely dried, they can swiftly re-vegetate immediately after the burning. In addition, due to the pattern in which they set fires while moisture is still left in the woods and grasses, the Gumuz are capable of clearing the savannah areas and yet leaving the trees essentially undamaged by the fires. Furthermore, the moisture maintains the presence of wildlife, which does not have to migrate to water sites along rivers and streams. Thus, the Gumuz conduct their major sideline livelihood activities of hunting at this time of burning and immediately afterwards, when the wild animals are feeding on the rejuvenated fresh grasses and vegetation in the cleared meadows and forests with high visibility. In addition, the existence of moisture also keeps particularly snakes inside the bush and grass, where some will be burnt by the fire reducing the consequences of bites by poisonous snakes.

For instance, during the second phase field work period of the present study, the Gumuz were very critical of the adverse effects of bushfire, which claimed the life of people by the unmanageable spread of fire and snake bites due to local state institutions' intervention forbidding the unavoidable annual bush fire, assuming it as destructive. The actions of the formal local state institutions seem to be due to insufficient understanding of the indigenous knowledge. As a result, the local authorities (mainly in Mandura and Dangur *Woreda* in those *kebele* neighbouring the administration centres) forbid the setting of bush fires at the proper time when the Gumuz used to do so, observing the moisture contents of trees and grasses. However, the unavoidable annual bush fire emerged late at the wrong time in February and March, which is considered a difficult period to manage the fast spreading fire with high-speed flames burning completely the dried bush and grasses.

The adverse effect of fire at that time is that it completely burned the bush and grass including its roots so that it cannot rejuvenate. Due to lack of moisture, snakes migrated to water points along rivers and streams. These numerous snakes attacked people and animals who go to these water points. As a result of the combined effects, ten persons died. Six of the victims died of snakebites (three of them were Gumuz and the other three were Agaw). The remaining four victims died due to the sudden and uncontrollable huge fire. These uncontrollable damages were threatening even the environs of the *woreda* and zonal administrations themselves. For instance, the fire that emerged around the new zonal centre at Gilgel Beles was brought under control only by the huge mobilisation and collaboration of the inhabitants of the town. According to my latest information, the *woreda* administrations themselves passed orders to clear the dried savannah grasses by setting fire, taking the necessary precautionary measures through the participation of the community.

Although it demands further thorough investigation, some of the experts in plant agronomy working as *woreda* staff have supported and agreed significantly with the indigenous knowledge of the Gumuz concerning their fire management. These experts confirmed the facts of fire, considering it as part of the very eco-system where the Gumuz uses it for pruning the bush and bamboo in their forest management so that it will rejuvenate even better, responding positively to the effects of fire.

However, the Gumuz are critical of the damaging effects of misused fire by immigrant highland farmers who do not have the necessary deeper knowledge that they themselves possess. Their misuse of fire is manifested in setting fire at the wrong time without taking necessary precautions, including at times of harvesting honey. As a result, it was the immigrant farmers and their families who were easy victims of fire burning. For instance, all the four victims who died of fire burning that year were all highland immigrants. Among them, one was burnt from the fire set by himself to clear the area around his harvested crop pile. Although it needs thorough multidisciplinary research, the preliminary findings of the present investigation reveal the fact that fire can be considered as an integral part of the entire eco-system of the area, which is skilfully utilised by the Gumuz in their indigenous systems of natural resource management in Metekel.

Institutions for Natural Resource Management

Institutions govern and regulate access, control and management of natural resources. Informal institutional arrangement is a basic feature of communally owned resources. The customary (informal) institutions of natural resource management enshrined within the Gumuz knowledge systems ensure smooth use and management of the resources in an environmentally friendly and ecologically stable way. In the indigenous context, as earlier stated, these institutions are a complex system of norms, values, ethics, customs, and taboos that have been institutionalised as customary laws and conventions for regulating resource use and management.

Respected Gumuz elders are primarily responsible for enforcing clusters of institutional arrangements. According to traditional institutional arrangements, elders make all natural resource conservation, regulation, and allocation decisions. Within the community, all forms of conflicts in general and conflicts related to natural resource in particular are customarily resolved with the intervention and arbitration of elders. Moreover, the spiritual mediators such as *gola* and *gafia* play equally important roles of enforcing strong institutional arrangements through their traditional belief system. Therefore, the customary institutional arrangements of the Gumuz to the land resources are found to be very strong and effective at the community level. These informal institutions of the community have proven to be effective and stable customary rules of natural resource use and management.

Critique of the Gumuz Natural Resource Management System
It is equally important to be cautious not to over-idealise the Gumuz natural resource management systems based on their indigenous knowledge systems. Of course, the Gumuz resource use should be considered as an adaptive management process evolving flexibly to changes along spatial and temporal terms and contexts. Hence, their management system should not be regarded as static. Their system of resource management is part of the broader internal and external complex dynamics of interaction and change. In spite of its integral ecological appropriateness particularly with lower population density, the effects of the successive stages such as forest cutting and burning practices of shifting cultivation seem to have had serious adverse ecological consequences with an ever-increasing population pressure (due to ceaseless encroachment and internal demographic growth) alongside with the decreasing duration of succession, fallow, and regeneration period.

In addition, the classic role of the indigenous institutions in the management of natural resources seems to have been decreasing, most particularly along encroached areas mostly under the competing external pressures of formal state structures and neighbouring societal interactions. In the present context, especially in most areas where they are bordered by their neighbouring highland settlers, some Gumuz are even observed selling fuel and construction wood in the local town centres as a sideline means of generating income. These emerging practices are undoubtedly causing critical and severe environmental and livelihood consequences explained in more detail in the next chapter.

Chapter 5. Impact of Encroachment on Land Resources and Management Systems

The Gumuz have been facing severe stress in trying to maintain their land resources and system of natural resource management based on their indigenous knowledge systems. Basically, this stress results from reductions of their traditional territories. The development policies of the state are among the serious factors adversely affecting their indigenous resource management systems. These policy plans are based on constriction of their land resources and complete neglect of their way of life. The widespread encroachment pressure has adverse effects on the indigenous management systems. Technological change and internal demographic growth have also contributed a significant effect. Due to these combined factors, competition over their land resources have increased by several interest groups, causing stress on the indigenous knowledge and customary institutional arrangements for natural resource management.

5.1 State Policies, Land Resource Rights, and the Environment in Metekel

Land Resource Rights
Even though it is rarely possible to find a place in today's world where natural resources are not used by peoples, modern economic development alters the patterns of the use of resources. As a result, large numbers of autochthonous minority peoples find themselves suddenly deprived of their resource base. Many of the autochthonous peoples practice distinctive ways of socio-cultural and economic life and inhabit marginal lands that formerly had no value for the dominant groups. In the power relations between the dominant and subjugated, the central states were increasingly reluctant to recognise the autochthonous people's rights to their land resources. Resources previously considered as marginal and uneconomic are now claimed by the states to be exploited due to material aspiration and technological advancement. Hence, the autochthonous peoples have been facing pressures of deprivation from their resources.

Land resource rights and tenure issues are the most critical problem faced by the autochthonous peoples. They are the most vulnerable groups, having been threatened and dispossessed of land resource rights. Plant (1994:33) explains the political and economic circumstances, which undermine the security of the land rights of the autochthonous peoples as:

> They may have lost their lands through foreign occupation, when the laws and institutions of the occupying power have discriminated against them in law and practice; through nationalisation, either the outright nationalisation of all lands, or the nationalisation of forests that have provided the traditional source of livelihood for many minority peoples; through colonisation and resettlement programmes; or through mineral, hydroelectric and logging programmes that have led to their displacement; or they may have been the victims of wider economic forces, which have encouraged land commoditisation without effective protection for economically weaker sectors of society.

Concrete evidence shows the fact of states' obsession with the idea of expansion into the lands of autochthonous peoples relocating landless and unemployed people from densely populated or disaster-prone areas to the wrongly perceived "un- or under-utilised empty and virgin lands without people." Such colonisation of unplanned expansion has been causing grave damage to the land and environment, resulting in an ecological imbalance beyond depriving the autochthonous peoples' rights to their resources. Large-scale resettlement schemes have had devastating impacts on the land security of the autochthonous peoples.

Similarly, although the Gumuz have effective ways of indigenous resource management system, they are totally marginalised as one of the most vulnerable indigenous minority peoples of Ethiopia. Land resource rights are the most critical problem they face. They have been facing pressures of deprivation from their resources. Across political regimes, the Ethiopian central states were reluctant to recognise the Gumuz's rights. Their land resource rights are not protected with special legal provisions entitling them to attain greater tenure security.

State Policies and the Human and Natural Environment

Throughout the regime of Emperor Haile Selassie I and most parts of the *Derg* rule, Metekel had been given an *awraja* status (Chagni being its administrative capital) on the western part of the former Gojjam province, bordering the Republic of Sudan. However, during the latter period of the *Derg* regime, Metekel was restructured as an Administrative Region (Pawe being

108

its administrative capital). As already mentioned, in the present post-1991 federal administrative restructuring, Metekel has been reorganised as one of the three zones of the Benishangul-Gumuz National Regional State (Gilgel Beles being its recent administrative capital since 2000).

As pointed out earlier, Metekel is better endowed with rich but fragile natural resources compared with the central parts of the country. The development policies of the successive regimes have neglected Metekel and left it marginal along with other peripheral parts of the country. What has been quite common in Metekel has been a continuous effort of colonising the natural resources of the area by different interest groups. For instance, the three successive five years' development plans of the Haile Selassie regime (first five year 1957-61, second five year 1963-67, and third five year 1968-73), which aimed at accelerating the utilisation of natural resources to modernise and bring rapid economic development, were rarely accomplished in Metekel. In terms of development endeavours, Metekel seems to remain one of the "darkest" areas of the country. This area remained under the tight grips of the central highlanders through the indirect rule of the neighbouring Agaw chiefs. Apart from exploiting the Gumuz, the highlanders frequently used the area for big-game fame hunting, which caused a serious impact on the ecological balance of the area. Moreover, throughout the imperial regime, the exploitative expansion of the highlanders continued unabated on the land resources of the Gumuz, pushing them farther toward the western peripheries.

The *Derg* regime, which took power by overthrowing the imperial regime, on the other hand, intensified the pressure on the environment through its rapid encroachment schemes such as state farm and resettlement. The development policy plans of the *Derg* regime focused more on the exploitation of the misperceived "un- or under-utilised, virgin" natural resources of the area in the interests of the central government, thus completely neglecting the interests of the autochthonous Gumuz. Both the state farm and resettlement schemes implemented in Metekel have adversely affected the natural environment, displacing the Gumuz from their traditional land resources.

The present regime, which took power by overthrowing the *Derg* regime, seems to have opened an extra chance for an ecological imbalance and environmental degradation through unchecked excessive highland immigration to Metekel and investment schemes particularly through rain-fed agriculture without thorough multi-disciplinary study and proper planning.

The successive state policies have further aggravated tenure insecurity of the autochthonous Gumuz. They have been facing stresses while trying to maintain their land resources in the fact of encroachment. Due to inadequate policies, different interest groups are over-exploiting the natural resources of the area depleting the environment and depriving the livelihood of the Gumuz.

The present Ethiopian government has restructured the formerly centralised institutional administrative structures into decentralised federal state structures by devolving certain aspects of government powers to the regions. Among other things, it has restructured "The Environmental Protection Authority (EPA)" to be directly responsible to the Council of Ministers. Through the EPA, the federal government has formulated a new policy for the environmental management of the country. The overall goal of the new policy is: "to improve and enhance the health and quality of life of the Ethiopians and to promote sustainable social and economic development through the sound management and use of natural, human-made and cultural resources and the environment as a whole so as to meet the needs of the present generation without compromising the ability of future generations to meet their own needs" (EPA, 1997:3).

Meanwhile, the environmental protection objectives of the Benishangul-Gumuz National Regional State are expressed in Proclamation No.2/1996 of the Regional Council that formulates the Benishangul-Gumuz National Regional State Constitution. According to article 97, no. 1-4, of the Proclamation, the objectives of the regional environmental protection are stated as: "(1) The Regional State has the responsibility to make an effort in which all the inhabitants of the Region may live in clean and a healthy environment; (2) Any step taken for the economic development must not disturb the ecological balance of the environment; (3) When the State designs the policy about the environmental protection and when it implements the policy, the concerned people must give the proposals of their own; and (4) The State and the inhabitants of the Region have the obligation to protect and care for their environmental conservation" (BGNRS 1996a:26). Additionally, article 40, no.3 of the same proclamation stipulates the property ownership rights in the region as: "The rural and urban land and natural resources ownership belongs to the state and the public only. Land is the common property of the people of the region that shall be neither sold nor changed as commodity of trade" (BGNRS 1996a:11).

Concerning the realisation of the regional constitutional provisions of article 97 stated above, the practice in Metekel reveals the facts to be quite incompatible to the environmental protection provisions in the highest legal document of the Regional State. The incompatibility of the provision with reality can be observed from the widespread practices of investment schemes operated in the rain-fed agriculture in the area. Additionally, the regional government has offered extra incentives of an eight-years land-tax exemption both on pioneer and promoted agricultural investments in order to attract investors to the region (BGNRS, 1999:15). However, the facts directly observed in the field completely contradict the overall spirit of the provisions of environmental protection in general and most particularly that of Article 97, no.2. Ideally, article 97, no.2 states: "Any step taken for the economic development must not disturb the ecological balance of the environment" (BGNRS 1996a:26). Contrary to the above statement, the ethnographic evidence demonstrates that the investment schemes aimed at attaining economic development have been causing severe environmental consequences through the indiscriminate deforestation of the forest.

The Benishangul-Gumuz National Regional State has planned to resettle the Gumuz by regrouping them in accessible villages with the aim of providing necessary social and extension services including the introduction of ox-plow cultivation aimed at replacing their shifting cultivation. According to the explanation of the regional authorities, the scattered settlement pattern of the Gumuz in inaccessible locations is considered as a constraint for extending agricultural extension and other services to the communities. However, the attitude of the Gumuz toward these planned schemes seemed rather sceptical. They felt insecure due to its envisaged risks and threats explained according to Gumuz informants in Mandura and Dangur *Woreda* as:

- Destruction of indigenous knowledge and the strategies of natural resource management system;
- Damage of autochthonous land tenure system;
- Depletion of soil fertility;
- Marginalisation of distant field plots and related resources;
- Intensification of inter-clan conflicts and enmity by destroying clan territoriality;
- Destruction of communal self-help social organisation and social structure;
- Intensification of intra-Gumuz conflicts and enmity due to evil-eye and adultery;
- Threat to the community's security, lives and livelihoods; and
- Threat to the entire socio-cultural and economic set-up of the community.

Concerning the introduction of the ox-plow farming system, the Gumuz were also sceptical of its realisation due to the prevalence of livestock disease as well as lack of the knowledge of plowing skills and handling the oxen. The Gumuz stressed the importance of detailed and well-thought-out educative approaches in which the two envisaged schemes should not risk their lives and livelihoods. The envisaged schemes were reported to be part of age-old neglect and lack of positive attitude towards the indigenous knowledge and resource management systems of Gumuz by policy planners even today.

5.2 Encroachment on Land Resources

The forms of encroachments occurring on the land resources in Metekel across political regimes can be broadly categorised into two – *gradual* and *rapid*. The gradual encroachment has been happening in the area for centuries, slowly claiming the natural resources of the Gumuz. The gradual encroachment has been manifested through the continuous push of the neighbouring highland plow cultivators and spontaneous settlers who immigrate to the area mostly in search of cultivable and grazing land. The Gumuz are critical of the encroachment. Both the oral traditions and written accounts reveal that the Gumuz used to live in parts of the central highlands of the present Gojjam (cf. chapter 3, section 3.1).

The rapid encroachments are manifested in the fast and sudden occurrence of programs such as state farm, state-sponsored resettlement, and rainfed agricultural investment schemes. These schemes are government-sponsored programs that have been claiming large expanses of the land resources of the area.

A case of the effects of both forms of encroachment pressure is indicated in the sketch social and resource map of Kitli-Azarti *Kebele* in Dangur *Woreda* (see *map nine*). This sketch map attempts to depict the basic theme of this study. It tries to show pictorially a representative case of the differing strategies of livelihood, resource management, encroachment on resources and ethnic relations between the autochthonous Gumuz and highland resettlers in the study area. It represents both the spatial and social contexts of the area, delineating the different category of the present inhabitants. For instance, the Gumuz of Kitli-Azarti *Kebele,* under encroachment pressure, are shown practising their traditional shifting cultivation along with gathering wild foods, hunting, fishing, and honey collection. In those areas inhabited by Gumuz, the forest resources are better preserved based on their indigenous knowledge systems. Their farming system is shown integral to their fragile ecology. The second category of people includes their long-time neighbours of Agaw and Shinasha, who predominantly inhabit those cooler

112

Map 9. Sketch Social and Resource Map of Kitli-Azarti Kebele (Dangur Woreda). Gradual and Rapid Encroachment on Resources

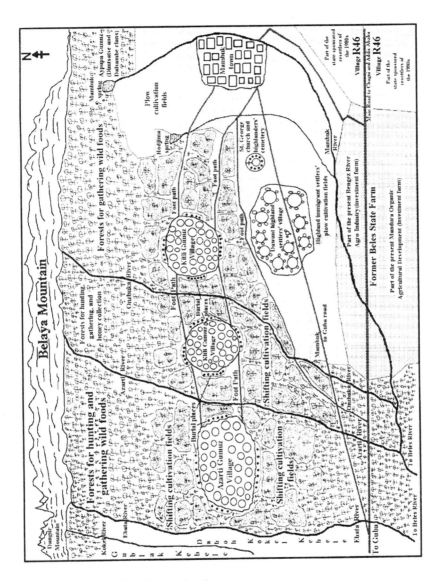

Source: Wolde-Selassie Abbute's own sketch

Legend: Symbols and places explained by associated texts in map

113

areas around Belaya and Dangur Mountains respectively to the north, northeast, and northwest. Additionally, the Amhara dwell interspersed in both areas as well as in areas around Mambuk. The third category of people includes those highland immigrant settlers encroaching large areas in the south and southeast, practising plow cultivation. They are predominantly followers of Orthodox Christianity with significant number of Muslims. The fourth category of people includes those state-sponsored resettlers of the 1980s where only a small portion of the large areas they inhabit nearby are indicated in the southeast. The fifth category includes the dwellers of Mambuk town, many of whom have direct and indirect interest and influence on the land resources of Kitli-Azarti *Kebele*. Finally, a different category from all the others includes those investors shown allocated large expanse of land resources, including the previous Beles state farm. Thus, the sketch map represents a summarised account of both gradual and rapid encroachment on the resources of the study area. Additionally, based on the map, one can understand the dynamics of ethnic relations among the different categorical groups at different levels.

Pre-1974 Encroachment
In the past, as stated earlier, the Gumuz were exposed to sporadic slave raids by the highlanders. During the imperial regime of pre-1974, they were then subjected to encroachment pressure. In the process of the expansion of the highlanders, they moved gradually down to the lowlands in the western periphery looking for greater safety.

The gradual encroachment of highlanders expanded throughout the imperial regime moving down beyond the *Kar* mountain ranges that served as a frontier for a long period between the two groups in areas neighbouring the Beles Valley as pointed out in *map ten* (see also *map eight* in chapter 4). While reading *maps eight* and *ten,* one has to bear in mind that I attempted to indicate the general trend of encroachment pressure based on participatory sketch maps drawn together with several Gumuz informants at Mandura and Dangur *Woreda.* Except attempting to show the trends, it is not easy to indicate the exact areas with accurate details. Indicating the trends of lower scale individual or fewer group members' encroachment usually in interspersed settlement with the Gumuz is more difficult in the sketches. The low scale interspersed settlement trend inside the Gumuz forms the initial step in the process of encroachment. The encroachment pressure increases with the arrival of more and more highland plow cultivators in which the Gumuz abandon these areas, being forced to shift and opt for the remaining peripheral forests.

Map 10. Pre-1974 Encroachment on Claimed Traditionally Gumuz Inhabited Area in Gojjam

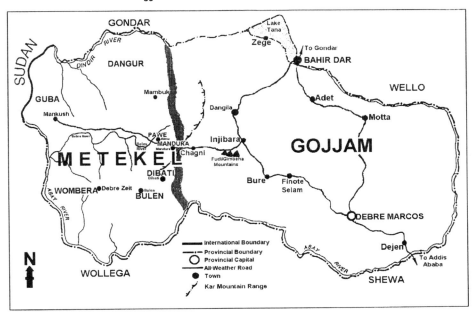

Gojjam Administrative Region (Pre-1987)

Approximate traditionally Gumuz inhabited areas claimed to have
been encroached during the different Imperial regimes till 1974
(Based on participatory sketch maps of informants in 1996/97,
1999, 2001)

Source: Adapted from a map of traditional Ethiopian
administrative regions until 1987, commonly reprinted

On the other hand, the Gumuz informants cited the case of overwhelming pressure from the Wollo immigrants since the 1950s. The obvious cause of the immigrants was environmental degradation in their original areas. These immigrants initially made agreements with the local Agaw chiefs at Chagni, who are also charged with the affairs of the Gumuz, in order to get access to settlement and cultivation field locations in areas around Chagni, Dibati and Bulen. It was emphasised that the agreement included levying an annual land tribute from the immigrants to the Agaw chiefs.

Since the 1950s the number of these immigrants has increased with a continuous influx of fellow members from Wollo. Today, large expanses of land formerly claimed to have been owned by Gumuz all around Chagni, Dibati, Bulen, and the environs are inhabited by Wollo immigrants. As a result of competition over resources and particularly due to the immigrants' intensive ox-plow farming system that demands smooth field plots, severe pressure and ecological imbalance was reported. These immigrants are alleged by the Gumuz to be utter destroyers of the forest resources based on their alleged insatiable demand for wood, such as for constructing compounds, houses, granaries, kraals, fuel wood and at times storing for future use. They are even accused of cutting wood logs indiscriminately with their axes always carried on their shoulders. In the local stereotype, they were accused of even "cutting and felling any tree nearby under which they sit while defecating." The practice of these immigrants has been cited one of the main causes of frequent ethnic conflicts with the autochthonous Gumuz.

Encroachment during the *Derg* Regime (1974-1991)

The gradual encroachment upon the land resources of the Gumuz by the neighbouring highlanders and immigrant resettlers continued throughout the *Derg* regime as well. As stated earlier, two forms of rapid encroachment also occurred during this period. The first is the "the Beles state farm" established in 1978/79. The second is the 1980s massive state-sponsored resettlement scheme. The approximate Gumuz inhabited area claimed to have been rapidly encroached during the Derg regime is indicated in *map eleven* (see also *maps eight* and *ten*).

The Beles State Farm

The Beles State Farm was established in 1978/79 as part of the expansion scheme of state farms under the *Birr-Humera Agricultural Development*. The farm is located in the *Dangur Woreda* of the zone. At its initial stage, the farm cleared 500 hectares of land and latter managed to clear 1161 hectares in 1986/87 and had a plan of clearing an additional 1000 hectares in 1987/88 (MZCA 1992:11). However, the farm ceased its operation after the 1991 political change.

According to one of the former employees of the farm, the farm began its operation near the Gilgel Beles by clearing four hectares before shifting to its later location. At Gilgel Beles, the farm operated only for one cropping season and then immediately shifted to its later main location because of water logging problems. Based on the document cited above, the soil types of the main farm area are 75% red, 15% black, and 10% brown.

In its history, the farm faced repeated instability due to insurgency movements of the Ethiopian Peoples' Revolutionary Party (EPRP) in the area. Its properties had been repeatedly plundered until its collapse at around the 1991 political change. In 1991, the area including the farm was put under the control of the EPRP liberated section of the country. Almost all the properties of the farm were said to have been looted. After the political change, the farm ceased its operation for two consecutive years. Small portions of the farmland were distributed the former employees of the farm in order to rehabilitate them, leading new life as smallholder farmers.

Map 11. Encroachment during the Derg Regime (1974-1991)

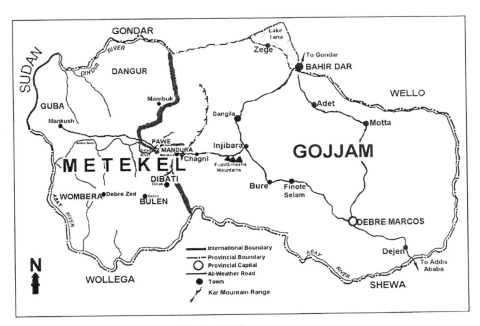

Gojjam Administrative Region (Pre-1987)

) Approximate traditionally Gumuz inhabited areas claimed to have
   been encroached during the Derg regime (1974-1991)
   (based on participatory sketch maps of informants in 1996/97,
   1999, 2001)

Source: Adapted from a map of traditional Ethiopian
administrative regions until 1987, commonly reprinted

The area had been inhabited by Gumuz before the establishment of the farm. They were then displaced to the farm's peripheries. According to informants in Dangur *Woreda*, there were two Gumuz community villages located in the farm site. One of them was located in the northern part of the farm near

117

Mambuk town and named after a prominent Gumuz called *Grazmach Yismaw Shaabur*. After the establishment of the farm, he crossed the Mambuk River together with his community and settled on the other side of the river. The other Gumuz community was located in the southern part of the farm site near a small hill located to the left of the main highway from Chagni to Guba and called *Woregnaw* village, named after their prominent community elder.

As pointed out above, the farm ceased its operation after 1991. Later, an investment firm in rain-fed agriculture named *Pop Agricultural Development,* used part of the farmland for only two cropping seasons from 1994/95-1996/97. However, it abandoned the farm after the next year due to destruction of their crops ready for harvest by fire, which was suspected to be deliberately set.

In 1996/97, the southern part of the farm to the left of Chagni - Guba highway was given to an investment firm called *Mandura Organic Agricultural Development* as a replacement, transferring it from its former farm location at *Gilgel Beles*. The farm's former location was selected as a new zonal administrative capital. In 1997/98, the northern part of the farm to the right of Chagni-Guba highway was given to an investment firm called *Bengez River Agricultural Development* as a replacement to its former investment farm located near the Bengez river on the direction to Gublak along the road to Guba. These two investment firms have almost fully occupied the former state farm area as part of the large forestland allocated to them. At the moment, the two schemes are operating in an already cleared former state farm area. However, when they begin expanding their farm areas, it is quite inevitable that the autochthonous Gumuz communities will once again be displaced from the area. Apart from adversely affecting the livelihood of the Gumuz, the environmental consequences of the farm are self-evident. Since the area has been completely cleared by bulldozers, it is rarely possible to observe even a few shade trees in the entire farm. Hence, the farm with its human and environmental impact represents the inadequate policies of the regime.

State-Sponsored Resettlement of the 1980s
The Beles Valley resettlement scheme in Metekel is one of the biggest programs implemented in the country in order to overcome the emergency needs of the population affected by the 1984/85 drought and famine (cf. chapter 6, section 6.2). The Beles Valley resettlement scheme is situated in the basin of the Beles River and covers an area of around 250,000 hectares (Salini Costruttori 1989:8). It is also considered to be the most important

water source base, which offers a considerable amount of untapped perennial water resources both from the main Beles River and a number of its tributaries that flow throughout the year.

The Ethiopian authorities considered the Beles Valley area to be previously "unoccupied/uninhabited virgin" lands with agricultural potential while planning the resettlement scheme. However, as earlier described (cf. chapter 1, section 1.1), before the arrival of the resettlers, the present Beles Valley resettlement area was inhabited by an estimated 18,312 autochthonous Gumuz (MZCA 1992:4). As a consequence, these Gumuz were pushed farther to the peripheries. The operation of the scheme has taken away their traditional resources without their knowledge and permission. They were displaced, leaving their former settlement, cultivation fields, hunting and fishing areas as well as their socio-cultural space.

The resettlement scheme and the later aid extended to rehabilitate the resettlers, to build infrastructure, and meant eventually to develop the economy of the area, has neglected the Gumuz. No form of support to compensate them for their losses was extended. No effort was made to integrate them into the social development processes. They are simply deprived of their traditional resources. Additionally, following the program, the influx of people coming to the area looking for opportunities has enormously increased. Due to its combined impact, there has been an indiscriminate deforestation, accelerating the destruction of the flora and fauna of the area.

As a result, the Gumuz have shown hostile attitudes towards the scheme. Their relationships with the resettlers increasingly deteriorated as more and more land resources were claimed by the scheme. The detailed account of this resettlement scheme is discussed in part three of this study.

Post-1991 Encroachment

Both gradual and rapid encroachment pressure on the land resources of the Gumuz has still continued unabated even today by several interest groups of neighbouring highlanders, investors, immigrant farmers, and others searching for opportunities. Since this is an on-going fresh encroachment process, it is difficult to sketch the incomplete account in participatory maps in a manner similar to that attempted for the past political regimes. In this section, special emphasise is given to the practices of rain-fed agricultural investment schemes in the area.

Rain-Fed Agricultural Investment Schemes

At present, land resources in Metekel are leased to investors without a genuine participation of the community as well as without detailed socio-cultural, economic, agronomic, and environmental studies. This allocation of land and forest resources to investors without thorough investigation has been causing serious consequences on the environment and the livelihood of the Gumuz.

Land in Metekel is granted lease-rights to investors at Assosa, the Regional capital located very far from the zonal capital, Gilgel Beles (formerly Pawe). In addition, the *Ethiopian Investment Incentives Regulations No. 7/1996* granted investors (in this relatively "underdeveloped" area) engaged in "pioneer" investment activities an exemption from "custom duty tax" on imported machinery and accessories as well as exemption from "income tax" for five years. These pioneer investment activities include irrigated agriculture, agro-industry, and manufacturing. Additionally, the same regulation grants exemption from "custom duty tax" on imported machinery and exemption from "income tax" for four years those investors engaged in "promoted" investment activities (including rain-fed agriculture, livestock farming, manufacturing, hotels and tourism, and transport and storage service). Moreover, the region in turn has offered an exemption of "land use tax" for eight years, a fact that was also verified from the field offices of some of the investment schemes. Although the above regulation provides incentives for encouraging investment in the peripheral parts of the country, its implementation without adequate monitoring of its adverse effects has serious implications on the human and natural environment. The details of the investment schemes are stated in table 9. As indicated in the table, a total of eleven investors are engaged in rain-fed agriculture on 38,250 hectares of land allocated to their schemes. Except their titles, those investment schemes under "agro-industry," have not yet begun agro-industrial processing. Almost all the investors indiscriminately cleared natural forests for preparing farming fields. Some of them were even alleged to have produced timber and charcoal. In the local colloquial accusations, those alleged of such actions were termed "investors in charcoal." Some of the investors have even ceased their operations after clearing the natural forest.

Table 9: Rain-fed Agricultural Investment Schemes in Metekel

No.	Name of the Enterprise	Woreda	Area (Ha)	Farm Status
1	Bengez River Agro-Industry	Dangur	2000	Operational
2	Mandura Organic Agricultural Development	Dangur	3500	Operational
3	Burcz-Endalama Agro-Industry	Dangur	5000	Operational
4	Zimbeha Agro-Industry	Dangur	5000	Operational
5	Diiza Agricultural Development	Dangur	3000	Ceased Operation
6	Pawe Agricultural Development	Pawe	1000	Ceased Operation
7	Abbat-Beles Agricultural Development	Pawe	5000	Operational
8	Abi-Egzi Agricultural Development	Guba	1000	Operational
9	Benishangul-Gumuz Agro-Industry	Guba	10,000	Under Preparation
10	Tesfa Mekonnen Agricultural Development	Guba	2000	Under Preparation
11	Baaruda-Gebriel Agricultural Development	Bulen	750	Under Preparation
	Total Hectares		**38,250**	

Source: Social and Economic Sector of Metekel Zonal Council, and consolidated with data obtained from some of the farm field offices, February-March 2001

By whatever standards, the natural forest resources destroyed in being cleared simply for rain-fed agricultural investment farms cannot at all be compensated by the intended crop production from the farms. The ecological consequences of the forest destruction are very severe and in turn affect gravely the life and livelihood of the local population. According to the experts in the zonal council, such natural resource depletion is occurring unabated because, on the one hand, the investment regulation of the regional state itself has not yet formulated operational directives to guide, monitor, and evaluate its implementation and impact. On the other hand, the administrative and technical management of the investment schemes are structured separately, opening up a gap that constrained the local authorities from taking immediate corrective measures on those adverse effects of the schemes.

In the operations of the schemes, the local authorities (especially at the *woreda* levels) are charged to deal with only the administrative aspects of the schemes, whereas the technical aspects of each investment scheme are directly charged to and dealt with by the investment head office at Assosa. Thus, the *woreda* and zonal authorities have no real say on the technical aspects of investment schemes under their administrative *woreda* and *kebele*.

One can imagine the effectiveness of the schemes where the technical management is located at *Assosa* around 1,000 km away from schemes in Metekel. This makes to raise a question: 'Why are local authorities at the grassroots charged only with the partial aspects of the schemes that have been affecting the livelihood of their people and its microenvironment?' Specifically, the relevant administrative and technical staff of the present study *woreda* are seriously critical of this situation that opened a room for the misappropriation of the natural resources. Therefore, the inadequate policy of investment, which focused much on attracting investors at the damaging costs of the natural environment and the livelihood of the Gumuz is reported to be responsible for the destruction of the forest by short-term profit oriented investors.

Cases of Rain-Fed Agricultural Investment Schemes
Four cases of investment firms engaged in rain-fed agriculture are presented below based on my own personal observation. Of the four cases, one of the schemes is located in Pawe Special *Woreda,* and the other three are located in Dangur *Woreda.*

Case One: Abbat-Beles Agricultural Development
This investment scheme is located in Pawe Special *Woreda* just below the bridge on the main Beles River to the left side in the direction to Guba. It was established in 1987 E.C. (1994/95) on a 5,000 hectare plot of dense forested land. Out of the 5,000 hectares, the farm managed to clear around 150 hectares for farmland at a time of interview. In order to clear the dense forest, the farm management hired daily labourers from the resettlers for five *birr* a day. In the process of clearing, first smaller trees and bushes are cut and cleared while the bottom barks of the bigger trees are peeled leaving them to dry. Once the cut bushes and smaller trees have dried, they will be piled surrounding the bigger trees the bottom bark of which has already been peeled. Then,

fire is set to the pile, burning all and clearing away the forest. So far, the farm has been producing crops such as sesame, sorghum, maize, soya bean, and groundnuts.

Since this farm is located very near the resettlement villages of RDS51, RUS51, R49, RUS50, and R46 with resettlers who originally came from Wollo, there have been frequent complaints against the farm for claiming the land resources. In addition, the forestland allocated to the scheme is the most densely forested area, which has a record of more than thirty indigenous tree species by the previous Tana-Beles Project. It was said that even during the huge clearing operations of the Tana Beles Project period, this thick forestland was exempted from being cleared thanks to an effort of one forestry expert who fought in favour of its preservation. Due to its proximity to both the zonal and *woreda* administrations, the forest destruction by the farm had been repeatedly felt, and the two local administrations intervened to halt the indiscriminate destruction by temporarily stopping the forest clearance. Then, the two administrations reported the case to the investment office in the regional capital, Assosa. However, the experts from the region visited the farm and decided in favour of the investor to proceed with the clearing as long as the investor takes the necessary precaution not to clear the mother tree. The effect of such a decision is noticed in the devastating destruction of even the mother trees. This happens because once every tree around the said mother tree has been cleared, that mother tree remains exposed to the wind and falls down easily. Both the administrative and expert staff of the Pawe Special *Woreda* and Metekel Zone have furiously reacted to this devastating destruction of the natural environment to the extent of stopping it with the local police for. According to key resettler informants in nearby villages, this farm is continuing its destruction of the forest of indigenous non-replaceable tree species just to produce the above stated crops.

Case Two: Burcz-Endalama Agro-Industry

The *Burcz-Endalama* investment scheme took its name from two local geographical features of the farm site. These are the *Burcz* River and *Endalama* hill, and by merging the two the name of the farm is coined. This farm has not yet been engaged in agro-industrial processing as the name designates. At the moment, it has simply engaged in rain-fed agriculture. It was established in 1989 E.C. (1996/7) and located in Dangur *Woreda,* occupying 5,000 hectares of forestland. So far, it has managed to clear around 406 hectares of farmland using bulldozers for clearing the forest.

Since its establishment, the farm has produced crop varieties such as maize, sorghum, soya bean, rice, sesame, groundnuts, and chickpea. The clearance of the natural forest by the farm has evidently put pressure on the natural environment. The farm has no reforestation program as a component for substituting at least part of what has been cleared. Moreover, this farm is located in an area well known for its honey production by the neighbouring local lowland Agaw ethnic group known as *Kumfel* as noted earlier. More than the loss of the forest resources, the application of agro-chemicals has also adversely affected the bee resources of the local inhabitants, which resulted in reduced production of the local people's traditional honey harvesting. The reported impact of the farm on the honey harvest is confirmed by the farm's field office itself. Additionally, the field office has seriously complained about the lack of a proper feasibility before the establishment of the investment scheme. As a result, the farm is currently facing problems of a water-logged black soil farm field difficult to manage, infestation of the area by malaria, presence of numerous crop-destroying wild animals, lack of necessary labour required, and inaccessibility of the farm itself to basic services. There are hardly any compensation schemes devised for the local peoples' loss of their traditional resources.

Case Three: Mandura Organic Agricultural Development
As the name indicates, this farm is intended to produce agricultural products without applying agro-chemicals. Initially, the farm was established in 1988 E.C. (1995/96) at Gilgel Beles on 1000 hectares of forestland in Mandura *Woreda* (from which it took its name to date). Out of the 1,000 hectares of forestland allocated for the scheme, the farm managed to clear 40 hectares of it using bulldozers and produced sesame for two cropping seasons. After the second season's harvest, the authorities claimed the farm at Gilgel Beles for establishing a new Metekel Zonal administrative capital. However, there were already serious reactions from the local people against the expansion of the farm in its clearance of the dense forest of the area. As earlier noted, the farm was later transferred to the left part of the former Beles state farm on the highway to the direction to Guba with an estimated new allocation of 3,500 hectares. Out of the new allocation, around 300

hectares of land was part of the former Beles State farm, while the remaining 3,200 hectares is an extension on the surrounding forest land, which is already under use by the local people.

Since the local people are already aware of the consequences of the former state farm, they reacted furiously against the scheme disapproving the new allocations. As a result, the farm presently is limited to the already-cleared plots. The local people inhabit the remaining allocations of forestlands where they have even established new settlements in order to counteract and react vigorously against the claims of the investor. So, the situation seems tense with the increasing settlements of Gumuz and other highland immigrant farmers on the allocated land area in which the investor has not yet begun clearing the forest for expanding its new farm area.

The farm management at the field office has strong resentment over the loss of the better fertile and newly cleared farm location at Gilgel Beles. After the transfer to the new location, the farm produced groundnuts, sesame, and niger-seed without applying agro-chemicals. Nevertheless, it seems very ideal to proceed with the production of only organic products of a profitable quantity in such a fragile and disturbed agro-ecology without applying agro-chemicals. Based on my observation, it is hardly possible to find a shade tree in the entire cleared farm area.

Case Four: Bengez River Agro-Industry

The name of this farm is taken from a river called Bengez alongside which the farm had formerly been located. The farm was established in 1988 E.C. (1995/96) in Dangur *Woreda* on 2,000 hectares of forestland. Out of the allocated 2,000 hectares, the farm managed to clear around 200 hectares in its two years operation in the area. Due to certain difficulties (most seriously due to lack of water during the dry season and farm labour) in this location, the farm was transferred to its present location of the former Beles state farm area on the right side of the main road to the direction of Guba. The transfer was done at the request of the investment scheme management. Then it was given equivalent land including part of the former state farm area.

This farm is also facing a similar problem with the local people as the neighbouring *Mandura Organic Agricultural Development Farm* on the left side of the main road. Similarly, the scheme, at the moment is limited to the previously cleared state farm area. It was intending to expand the farm area, clearing farther the allocated forestlands. It seems evident that conflict might emerge with the local inhabitants. Unlike its name, the farm has not yet been engaged in agro-industrial processing, instead operating only in rain-fed agriculture. The major crops produced from the farm are cotton, sesame, maize, groundnuts, red pepper, sorghum, soya bean, and niger-seed.

The farm management complained of the lack of a serious feasibility study concerning its farm location. The farm is facing a serious shortage of daily labourers. The problem of labourers is very serious because most of the neighbouring farmers are busy with their own farm activities. Even the highland seasonal immigrant labourers prefer to be temporarily employed in the farmers' fields rather than in the investment farms. This is because working in the farmers' fields is worth more in terms of payments, food, and residential services, than working in the investment farm for 4-6 *birr* daily without other services. The same problem is also stressed by other investment schemes.

Moreover, the farm management itself stressed the problem of ever increasing heat intensity due to the loss of forest cover in the farm area. The farm management explained their resentment over the farm area where its fertility has already declined. They also stressed the evident conflict that might arise with the local population inhabiting the area allocated for their farm when they begin clearing for expanding their farm. The field manager has critically stressed a complete lack or an inadequate multi-disciplinary feasibility studies before the establishment of the farm, which was reported to be true of almost all the investment schemes in the area.

5.3 Impact of Encroachment and Perceptions of the Gumuz

Impact on the Livelihood, Resource Management, and the Environment
As earlier discussed, encroachment across political regimes has been causing adverse effects by increasing the pressure on land resources of the Gumuz. The encroaching highlanders have a different farming and tenure systems. They are plow cultivators and need clear field plots suitable for the plowing with oxen. Their field plots are prepared clean by cutting and uprooting the tree stumps for smooth plowing. On the other hand, the farming and tenure systems of the Gumuz are different from that of the highlanders (cf. chapter 3, sub-section "Integral Shifting Cultivation: Indigenous Farmng System"). In addition, the influx of encroaching immigrants increased the

number of livestock in the area. The increased livestock grazing and browsing inside the forests causes soil compaction and destruction of bamboo sprouts that serve as a source of food to the Gumuz.

The state-sponsored resettlement scheme has also divided the Gumuz belonging to the same clan. For instance, the Gumuz clans of *Dimtsatse* and *Dalsambe* were separated by the scheme to two corners in the eastern and western peripheries. The increased population density decreased the size of land owned by the Gumuz. The reduction in the land holding caused a decrease in fallow period. Since a short fallow field cannot rejuvenate well, weed infestation increased, decreasing crop yields. The pressure on the land resources intensified forest destruction, causing adverse effects such as:

- Scarcity of construction wood and grass;
- Decrease in the water flow of rivers and streams;
- Lose or disappearance of wild hunt animals;
- Scarcity in fish resources of rivers and streams;
- Shortage of gathered forest foods;
- Loss of wild honey collection and bee resources;
- Scarcity of shade trees and windbreaks in villages and fields;
- Change in the intensity and distribution of rainfall;
- Increased intensity of soil and water erosion;
- Increased intensity of heat and wind;
- Increased soil depletion due to over-utilisation;
- Overall noticeable changes on the micro-climate of the natural environment; and
- Increased suppression and eventual loss of indigenous knowledge of natural resource management.

So, the destruction of forest resources has serious consequences. The wildlife, honey-bees and the gathered foods have been severely affected and became inaccessible resulting in reported dietary deficiency. The pressure on the forest also caused shortage of wood for construction (houses, fences, and granary) and household use as well as inaccessibility of medicinal and ritual plants. This in turn has affected the cultural inventory of the Gumuz. Encroachment has affected the role of local informal institutions enshrined within the indigenous knowledge system to ensure a sustainable management of the natural. The pressure and competition over the land resources is the single prime factor of severe ethnic conflicts – especially among the encroaching highland neighbours, spontaneous immigrants, state-sponsored resettlers and the autochthonous Gumuz (cf. part 4).

In areas of encroachment pressure, the soils are exposed to crusting and compaction, being naked in the absence of vegetation. Severe decline in soil fertility is observed in the increased weed infestation and lower productivity. Some of the affected areas are even abandoned due to fertility decline, increasing pressure on the remaining forests for preparing new farm plots. The subsequent loss of forest caused reduction in the availability and flow of water. The decreased flow and at times even complete drying up of waters in rivers, streams and springs has been causing problems of clean water and lack of fish and other aquatic resources. The Gumuz emphasised a sharp decline in their traditional fish catches from rivers due to alteration of aquatic environment.

Intensified heat as well as lack shade trees and windbreaks for field crops and residential settlements have been reported. I observed a substantial part of the area being bare and vulnerable. The demand of wood for multiple uses such as charcoal production, fuel-wood, construction, and infrastructure buildings has dramatically increased. On the whole, encroachment pressure created an imbalance on the stability of the agro-ecology.

On the other hand, the Gumuz informants recognised certain aspects as positive effects of encroachment. They approved the increased local market exchange as the most important positive effect. They stressed that improved local market exchange brought about noticeable change upon their livelihoods. Although most of the services are not primarily targeted to the benefit of the Gumuz, they considered recent improvements in infrastructure and services such as transportation, potable water, education, health services, and grain mills. In addition, those Gumuz informants who practised the institutional arrangements considered the renting land with immigrants as positive. However, most Gumuz were sceptical of the renting land arrangements on sustainability grounds. The stated limited positive effects, according to the informants, cannot be at all compared on with the adverse effects of encroachment on their lives and livelihood.

Perceptions and Reactions of the Gumuz

The Gumuz have been critically aware of the consequences of both the gradual and rapid encroachments upon their land resources. Interviews with the Gumuz informants of Mandura revealed that in spite of their being pushed, raided, and enslaved as defenceless victims in the struggle under the past regimes, they used to take frequent defensive and revengeful attacks upon the encroaching highlanders, at the same time retreating. It is usually after a heavy revengeful attack against the encroachers (usually in the night), that they retreat farther into the inaccessible forests in fear of more organised and better equipped plundering from the highlanders. Due to their long time mistrust, the Gumuz have developed a deep-rooted hatred and suspicion towards the encroaching highlanders. Their relation with the highland neighbours is characterised by uneasy coexistence perturbed by recurrent conflicts.

As discussed earlier, during the *Derg* regime, the Gumuz faced the bitterest experience of the adverse effects of the resettlement and showed hostile attitudes towards the scheme. Their relationships with the resettlers increasingly deteriorated as more and more land resources were claimed by the scheme. They disapproved the scheme and began expressing their grievances by attacking resettlers located in those frontier villages. Conflicts and mistrusts continued slowly throughout the period up to the fall of *Derg* in 1991, at which time where the entire scheme area bordering the Gumuz were guarded by armed militia recruited from the resettlers. Low-scaled frequent causalities have been occurring since the resettlers' first arrival. Based on information obtained from informants in Pawe Special *Woreda* and my own long experience in the area, the already volatile relations between the two groups burst out into an open ethnic conflict that claimed considerable loss of life on both sides immediately after the 1991 political change in the country (cf. chapter 11, sub-section "Conflicts between the Gumuz and the Resettlers of the 1980s").

Similar ethnic conflicts have also occurred with the slowly encroaching spontaneous settlers and the Gumuz in the neighbouring central parts of Metekel that resulted in severe causalities on both parts and caused a displacement of around 10,490 former spontaneous immigrant peasant settlers from Wollo (Wolde-Selassie 1996a:11). These displaced Wollo immigrants of the 1950s from Metekel (mostly from areas around Dibati and Chagni) re-immigrated to the Beles Valley, seeking better security near the zonal administrative centre (by then Pawe), as well as looking for adequate farm and grazing land. Most of these displaced have resettled in areas abandoned by state-sponsored resettlers of the 1980s (mostly at peripheral locations), who either returned to their origins or were reintegrated into the already existing villages at the centre of the scheme, seeking more safety. They have also settled at the peripheries of the state-sponsored resettler villages, clearing forests. Some of them also settled inside already established state-sponsored resettler villages, appropriating land through several local institutional arrangements.

On the other hand, despite the dominant conflicting relations, there are also elements of mutual interactions emerging between the Gumuz and highlanders in certain contexts such as local market places, bond friendship, renting land arrangements, elementary schools and similar other networks of relationships (cf. chapter 12).

5.4 Emerging Change in Livelihood and Resource Management

At present, changes emerging in the livelihood and resource management strategies of the Gumuz can be considered in two contexts. On the one hand, there are changes that affect Gumuz residing all along the areas bordering the non-Gumuz plow-cultivators, where external encroachment pressure is noticed as a severe constraint. On the other hand, changes happening on Gumuz residing in areas away from encroachment, which results from the very internal dynamics of the lives and livelihood of the community. The main focus of this section is on the former imposed rapid change emerging on the Gumuz way of life, livelihood and resource management strategies.

Despite influences from highland Orthodox Christianity in the east and Islam from Sudan in the west, the Gumuz remain primarily followers of their traditional belief systems. Even those converts to Christianity and Islam are not strong adherents to the new religious demands in its strict sense. They were observed mixing many of the traditional belief practices into their newly accepted religion. The practice of consulting the *gafia*, a magico-religious person, is said to be most frequent by the "converts" during illness, hardships and related issues daily life.

Integral Shifting Cultivation
Shifting cultivation is still the single most important source of livelihood and resource management strategy of the Gumuz both in encroached-pressure and non-encroached stable areas. In areas experiencing encroachment pressure, a tremendous change has been occurring in the shifting cultivation, which is mainly noticed in the decreasing fallow period. The Gumuz in these contexts are forced to be restricted to the remaining land resources. The restriction has caused limitations in field plot sizes and locations. The average plot sizes are decreasing due to limitations of free areas for expanding the size of field plots. They are forced to utilise fallow fields without proper vegetative substitution. The former long fallow period of 10-15 years or even more has been continuously decreasing to the present 3-5 years. The ever-shortening fallow duration has severe implications on their lives and livelihood.

In order to cope up with the shortening fallow period and the resulting yield decrease, many of the Gumuz bordering the plow-cultivators have begun making renting land arrangements with the latter. In such arrangement, an estimated one-hectare of land is rented-out in kind for one cropping season in exchange for three to five *quintals* (300-500 kg) of grain. However, the terms of arrangement vary from one area to the other. The agreed amount of grain is paid after the harvest, and the type of grain to be exchanged depends on the variety cultivated in the rented plot (mostly either finger-millet or sorghum). The grain generated from the rented-out fallow fields is used as a temporary measure to support the meagre production from the shifting cultivation field. Meanwhile, the renting land arrangements in the bordering areas are also considered by the Gumuz to serve as a buffer zone between the two groups of population meant to restrict and check the encroachment of the plow cultivators.

Except for its temporary strategy of coping with the effects of encroachment, the Gumuz informants were critical of the renting land arrangement since the practice depletes severely the soil fertility and intensifies the destruction of forest resources. This is because plots plowed by oxen cannot easily reconstitute the former vegetation at all. Unless forced by existing circumstances, the Gumuz prefer not to make long-term land rental arrangements with plow-cultivators. They also stressed that in principle their agreements include an understanding that the plow-cultivators should not cut and clear any major mother trees in the field. However, as observed in practice, the plow-cultivators usually violate the understanding by clearing most or all trees while preparing clean and smooth fields. Due to the emerging widespread changes in the shifting cultivation strategy, the indigenous ecological knowledge system has been severely affected.

Multi-Niche Means of Livelihood

The encroachment pressure along areas bordering the non-Gumuz has adversely affected the multi-niche component means of livelihood such as gathering, hunting, fishing, and honey collection. Gumuz informants in Mandura and Dangur explained that due to the human and livestock population pressure, the availability of wild foods to gather became scarce, forcing the Gumuz women to have to travel long distances to the remaining forests in the distant peripheries. Gumuz informants complained seriously about the protein deficiency (expressed in decreased meat consumption) in their diet because most of their favourite game animals hunted have disappeared. As earlier noted, their harvest from fishing has dwindled due to both the reduced flow of streams and rivers as well as the continued human and livestock interference in the waters of the area. Both for hunting and fishing, they have to search a lot and travel to far-away locations. Additionally, harvesting wild honey has become very scarce. Some members of the community have begun using local beehives for honey production, a practice they have learnt from the highlanders.

Considerable numbers of Gumuz men from the adjacent communities are observed being employed (mostly as guards) in different offices of the zonal administration and others in Pawe and Gilgel Beles. These employed members are observed spending part of their income on consumption goods and services as well as investing part of it on livestock (cattle and goats). Their cattle are herded together with the cattle of neighbouring Agaw ethnic group members sharing the neighbourhood as observed in Manjeeri Gumuz village. Although these members of Gumuz own cattle, use of oxen for traction and cows for milking are still rarely practised in the tradition. However, as an introductory element, a few of my informants at Manjeeri expressed their emerging experience of milking cows with the support of their Agaw neighbours. However, none mentioned their experience of oxen traction, instead using them mostly for slaughtering on festive occasions.

Some members of Gumuz have even been observed engaged in selling fuel and construction wood in the local town centres as a sideline means of generating income, which has severe environmental and livelihood consequences. For instance, I frequently observed Gumuz women selling fuel wood to residents at small town centres of Almu, L4 reseller village, Mambuk, Mandura, Menta-Wuha (near Dibati), and Gilgel Beles. I also observed members of Gumuz men and women selling construction wood and bamboo at Gilgel Beles town, which is a new administrative centre of the Metekel Zone.

Land Resource Tenure
The renting land arrangement stated above (5.4.1) as well as the limitation of the land size itself have been strengthening individual possession rights to the fallow field plots by those who cleared it first. The pressure on land resources has introduced changing perceptions in the land tenure system from a type of fully communal to an individually oriented tenure system. Fallow fields are considered an area of major change leading to individual ownership of land. Those plow-cultivators who need to sharecrop-in land first search for Gumuz fallow land inside the forest along the border. Once they find the fallow fields they were looking for, they go to the Gumuz village and ask the claimant if it could be rented-out. If the Gumuz agrees to do so, the two will agree on the details of the rental arrangement in the presence of

elders and witnesses from both sides. Then, usually a letter of agreement will be written (in Amharic) by someone from the non-Gumuz group and signed by both parties including the witnesses. Once the final agreement is reached it is feasted by a local alcoholic drink called *araqe* (spirit distilled of grain) served by the parties involved.

Local Resource Management System

According to informants both in Mandura and Dangur, the classic role of the indigenous institutions in the management of natural resources seems to have been increasingly loosing significance – most particularly all along encroached areas. In those Gumuz villages proximate to the *woreda* administration centres, the formal *kebele* grass-root institutional set-up is gradually getting stronger. In these *kebele*, the role of elected formal *kebele* administrators is gaining significance. These formal leaders from the neighbouring *kebele* were frequently seen at the *woreda* centres (e.g., Mandura and Mambuk) either on request by the *woreda* authorities or on their own initiative. Their villages are also one of the accessible areas frequently visited by the *woreda* administrative and expert staff.

As a result, the functions of these formal *kebele* leaders are considerable in the formal management aspects of the *kebele*. In the management of the land resources, the *kebele* leadership is also getting significant recognition. For instance, in Kitli-Azarti *kebele* near the Dangur *Woreda* administration (Mambuk), both Gumuz and non-Gumuz live together. Here, the *kebele* leadership chaired by a Gumuz has demarcated the boundary defining the share between the two groups. Considering the non-Gumuz's use of plow cultivation, their land share is made to be relatively smaller. Correspondingly, the share of the Gumuz is made to be relatively bigger taking into consideration their traditional shifting cultivation practice, which requires wider area.

In the Gumuz share of the *kebele*, members can voluntarily make renting land arrangements with the plow cultivators. Ideally, the formal leadership is charged with responsibilities to monitor hunting. Encroachment pressure seems to be resisted and checked fiercely both by the formal and local community leaders. They monitor forest destruction by outsiders where the Development Agents (DAs) from the *woreda* were said to be providing expert advice. These experts seem to have shown strong interest in mobilising the community whenever required so as to enable them to get access to the necessary formal social and agronomic services.

Using the formal *kebele* institutional structure, the *woreda* attempted to disarm "illegal" guns and introduced elected *militia*. Going to public centres such as local markets with bows and arrows is strictly forbidden. Accordingly, these actions are said to have contributed to improved security in the area both among Gumuz and with outsiders. Moreover, the same action of disarming has been applied to monitor the unlimited hunting of wild animals by the *woreda* authorities supported by the formal leadership of neighbouring *kebele*. The emerging role of formal *kebele* leadership gets weaker as its location gets ever less accessible from the *woreda* centres with no encroachment pressures. However, in reality, the role of local elders remains indisputably dominant in the entire affairs of their community using the indigenous customary institutional arrangements. In many of the *kebele*, the same community elders and clan leaders also act as elected formal leaders.

Basic services in health, education, and agriculture are in a process of dissemination to reach the grassroots by establishing development centres, elementary schools, and health posts based on data obtained from key informants and discussions with the experts of both Mandura and Dangur *Woreda* Economic Development and Social Services Office (EDSSO) as well as personal observation. Although it is in its infancy, an element of extending agricultural extension to Gumuz farmers has been noticed. Since the Gumuz do not practice plow cultivation, different forms of arrangements were made while introducing the extension package service. Only very few Gumuz farmers were reported to have participated in the extension program in Mandura, Dangur, Dibati, Bulen, and Guba *Woreda*. Some participated in the extension simply by cultivating their plots with hand-tools using communally mobilised labour. Others participated in the program through arrangements made with plow cultivators. In this form of arrangement, the plow cultivator works on the extension plot for the Gumuz, and in return the former gets an equal plot from the latter for one cropping season. The extension plot is prepared in the fields left fallow. However, the *woreda* staff were rather strongly sceptical of the results of the extension service trial. They stated that the initial aim of the extension package is meant just to introduce and attract the attention of Gumuz to "modern" farming.

Changes Emerging from Gumuz and Non-Gumuz Interactions

In areas of frequent contacts with the non-Gumuz, both groups have established several local institutional networks of relationships and interactions through which important experiences were shared and exchanged. The Gumuz and non-Gumuz interaction areas include local market centres, religious occasions, sharecropping arrangements, wedding and mourning festive occasions, friendships, field labour mobilisation, employed job places, and schools (cf. chapter 12).

In their daily interactions, both used to exchange experiences with each other. For instance, the Gumuz shared experiences from the non-Gumuz in practices such as ox-plowing, timber production, milking cows, "wearing clothes," using grain mills, using clinics for health treatment, brewing local beer (*tella*), Christian religion, preparing and eating *injera* and *wot* (sauce), cultivating vegetables in the home-gardens, and several related practices. On the other hand, the non-Gumuz shared experiences from the Gumuz in practices such as gathering forest foods like *endaha, kimaa, Kakima,* and *echa* for sauce preparation; planting and consumption of *oppa*, pumpkin, and bamboo sprouts; field cultivation using simple digging hand tools (e.g., *teba*) to maintain soil fertility; using red finger millet seed variety; brewing local beer (*keya*), and several others.

During the fieldwork, many Gumuz children were observed attending inside Gumuz as well as non-Gumuz village elementary schools. At times, those Gumuz children who attend non-Gumuz village schools were noticed playing important roles of bridging the two communities. For instance, informants in L29 village reported that Gumuz pupils coming from Mataabaa *kebele* and learning in their village elementary school played an important mediation role in settling a conflict that emerged due to Gumuz field crop destruction by the resettlers' cattle. These pupils were also observed being dressed with clothes, rather than practising their usual nudity. Although the practice of consulting the *gafia* during illness remains predominant, members of Gumuz especially proximate to *woreda* administrative centres were also observed visiting health clinics.

As already described earlier, the Gumuz are still predominantly followers of traditional belief systems. However, the Gumuz in Guba are largely followers of Islam due to their long influence from relations with the Sudan. Orthodox Christianity relatively influences those Gumuz in the East bordering the Christian highlanders. These converts to either Christianity or Islam, as noted earlier, do not seem to be strict adherents to the new religions. They are observed mixing many of the traditional beliefs and practices into their newly accepted religion.

Both at the zonal and *woreda* offices, employment opportunities are open to educated Gumuz. However, this opportunity is not yet exploited due to the limited number of the educated Gumuz. Many of the educated are at the administrative leadership positions of the area. The Gumuz experts in the operational offices are very few or even in some cases none at all. However, there are many Gumuz who are employed as guards in different offices. For instance, a considerable number of Manjeeri Gumuz members are employed as guards in Tana Beles project, CISP-Beles project, and in the zonal government offices. They are at the same time engaged in the village farming activities using their family labour as well as making numerous renting land arrangements with the plow cultivators. Compared with their fellow villagers, they are wealthier due to additional income, indicating emerging social differentiation. They began introducing cattle husbandry. Their family members are relatively better dressed. They also possess radios and watches. It was reported that they regularly buy and feed on meat while others are complaining much about the disappearing wild animals. These members of the community have better access to information and are relatively more aware of the working environment of the area and serve as contact persons in their villages for visitors from outside especially searching for land in rental arrangement.

Therefore, the foregoing description and explanation in this sub-section highlight those noticeable socio-cultural, political, and economic changes emerging in the lives, livelihood and resource management systems of the Gumuz. The existing and emerging changes have noticeable effects on the indigenous environmental thought, ethical values, ecological knowledge, and adaptive renewable natural resource management systems. However, in areas not seriously affected by encroachment, significant change is rarely observed, and the people are still strong adherents of traditional belief systems, practising their traditional way of life.

PART THREE: THE HIGHLAND RESETTLERS – SEDENTARY PLOW CULTIVATORS

Chapter 6. State-sponsored resettlement of the 1980s in Metekel

6.1 Overview of Resettlement in Ethiopia

Ethiopia is one of the African countries that realised massive resettlement schemes. In Ethiopia, resettlement has been practised both on an ad-hoc and an organised basis. The former occurred with the individual initiatives without any central co-ordination, whereas the latter tended to be massively implemented through centrally co-ordinated government policy with double pronged motives – the one explicitly development-induced economic and the other implicitly political. A. Pankhurst (1989:319) stresses the pre-1974 Ethiopian resettlement schemes as being largely of an ad-hoc type and summarises his account as:

> Prior to the revolution in 1974, resettlement in Ethiopia occurred largely on an ad hoc basis, through the individual initiative of local governors, without any centrally coordinated policy. By the time of the revolution, 20 settlement sites had been established, including some 7,000 household units, which represented less than 0.2 per cent of rural households [...]. After the revolution, resettlement became far more important. By the end of the first post-revolutionary decade, some 45,000 households, comprising 180,000 people representing 0.68 per cent of total rural households, had been resettled on 88 sites in 11 regions.

However, according to Dessalegn (1989:670), the earliest and pre-1974 Ethiopian resettlement was equally both ad-hoc and organised where the latter is based on rationalising land use on government owned land in order to raise state revenue as well as to provide additional resources to the hard pressed northern peasantry. On the other hand, he further explains that after the collapse of the imperial government in 1974, resettlement schemes were enlarged and increased. The schemes' initial objectives to be a form of long-term rehabilitation of famine victims of 1974-75 were enlarged. Dessalegn (1989:684) explains the enlarged objective of the increased resettlement schemes in the first decade after the collapse of the imperial regime in 1974 as:

The objectives of settlement which at the beginning were designed to be a form of long term rehabilitation of famine victims were enlarged considerably. Resettlement was now to be employed as a means of assisting poor and landless peasants, relieving the employment crisis in the urban areas, accelerating the sedentarization of transient populations, promoting resource conservation and sound agricultural practices in the densely populated areas, bringing under cultivation "under-utilized" lands, establishing a paramilitary defense force on the Ethio-Somali border, and rehabilitating returning Ethiopian refugees and displaced persons.

Considering resettlement as a lasting solution for the affected population, the former military government of Ethiopia launched a massive emergency resettlement program as a result of the 1984-85 drought and famine. According to A. Pankhurst (1990:126) and Dessalegn (1989:696), the government's initial emergency resettlement plan was to resettle 300,000 families consisting of about 1.5 million people in two phases. During the first phase, 50,000 households were planned to be directed to sparsely populated areas of Wollega, Illubabor and Kaffa through an *integrated* (*sigsega*) resettlement approach. In the second phase, it was planned to move 250,000 households to the "under-utilised" peripheral lowland areas in Metekel, Assosa, and Gambella through a *conventional* (*madabagna/kuta-gattam* (Amh.)) resettlement approach. The former approach conveys the idea of insertion or filling empty spaces within already existing traditional subsistence agricultural settlements, whereas the latter approach designates planned large areas of "unoccupied" land to be allocated to the resettlers, which was found to be more challenging. Meanwhile, Kloos and Aynalem (1988:148) explain the results of the government's resettlement performance against its initial plan as:

> Due to the emergency nature of the 1984/85-resettlement program, which put tremendous requirements on resources, the targets were readjusted, and only about 203,000 families comprising nearly 590,000 persons, were sent to resettlement schemes between October 1984 and September 1985, and another 10,000 by January 1986. Subsequently the resettlement program entered into a consolidation phase, brought about by lack of resources, administrative difficulties and international criticism of the resettlement program. Between 1986 and 1988, fewer than 10,000 persons were resettled in spite of the spectre of another famine in 1987 and early 1988.

Around 600,000 people were resettled within a time frame of a year and half. The explicit reason for the resettlement was to ensure the material well-being of the peasants by dislocating them from famine affected and over-populated areas and relocating them in the presumed virgin or under-utilised fertile lands of the south, south-west, and western peripheral parts of Ethiopia.

Meanwhile, Hurni (1990:97f.) discusses the impact of the post-1974 state-sponsored resettlement, considering the operations of the schemes in two differing phases and notes his account in German as follows:

> Die Umsiedlungen begannen unmittelbar nach der Revolution. Zwischen 1975 und 1983 wurden rd. 80.000 Bauern aus Wello, Tigray und Shewa in die westlichen und südwestlichen Regionen Kefa, Illubabor, Wellega und Shewa umgesiedelt. Die Programme waren von der RRC relativ gut geplant und wurden in kleinen schritten durchgeführt. Die umgesiedelten Familien wurden angehalten, in den neuen Ansiedlungen in Kooperativen zusammenzuarbeiten und wurden in ihren Bemühungen, mechanisierte Landwirtschaft zu betreiben, unterstützt.
>
> 1984/85 wurden dann angesichts der vielen Menschen, die wegen der anhaltenden Dürre in riesige Auffanglager flüchteten, innerhalb weniger Monate westlichen mehr Leute umgesiedelt als in den vergangenen 9 Jahren. Allein zwischen Dezember 1984 und Dezember 1985 wurden 600.000 Menschen aus Tigray, Wello und Shewa in die Regionen Gojam, Wellega, Kefa und Illubabor umgesiedelt (siehe Karte[1]). Diese zweite Umsiedlungswelle machte nicht nur die Mobilisierung der gesamten Transportkapazität des Landes erforderlich, sie brachte vielen Menschen – die Schätzungen schwanken zwischen 1.000 und 100.000 – den Tod. Da viele Umsiedler aus Langern kamen und gesundheitlich geschwächt waren, ist anzunehmen, daß sie an Cholera, Typhus oder allgemeiner Schwäche in Verbindung mit Streß gestorben sind. Aufschlußreich ist in diesem Zusammenhang die Differenz zwischen der Anzahl der offiziell umgesiedelten und der in neuen Gebieten angesiedelten Personen (siehe Karte). Während die Gesamtzahl der Umsiedler mit 640.000 angegeben wird, wurden "nur" 526.000 Personen neu angesiedelt (National Atlas of Ethiopia, 1988). Wenn man unterstellt, daß aus Furcht vor den Umsiedlungen rd. 100.000 Menschen in den Sudan geflohen sind, dann sind während der Umsiedlungsaktion 14.000 Menschen gestorben.

---

[1] Hurni refers to his map showing the sending and receiving areas, which is quoted as map 12 in this study.

In the above account, Hurni tries to show a comparative description of the impact of the state-sponsored resettlement program after 1974 revolution. First, in the years between 1975 and 1983 around 80,000 peasants from Wollo, Tigray, and Shewa were resettled in the western and south-western regions of Kefa, Illubabor, Wellega, and Shewa. The operation in this phase, Hurni notes, was relatively better planned and implemented in smaller steps. However, in the second case, around 600,000 people were massively relocated from Wollo, Tigray and Shewa to areas in Gojjam, Wollega, Kefa, and Illubabor within the short time span of a year (from December 1984 to December 1985). Due to lack of proper planning, the resettlers suffered multiple stresses. Out of the total 640,000 resettlers moved, he notes, only 526,000 of them were resettled in the destination areas. He further states that around 100,000 resettlers crossed the border to the Sudan as refugees and another 14,000 died in the process of resettlement. Although Hurni's account offers important details of the impact of resettlement, there exist significant incompatibility in the time-frame (particularly in the second case) and his estimates of the figures of the resettlers, the dissertions, and the deaths in the process of relocation in comparison with that of other accounts (cf. NSCRP 1988; Dessalegn 1989; Kloos and Aynalem 1988; A. Pankhurst 1992; Elias 1992). The details of the areas of origins and destinations of resettlers are pointed out in *map twelve*.

The added objective of environmental issues in the emergency resettlement launched by the party authorities are noted as: "Peasants were to be relocated not only for rehabilitation purposes but also to promote the conservation of resources in the high population areas and the regeneration of the over-utilised lands" Dessalegn (1989:695). The scheme was considered as an opportunity for socialist transformation accelerating the pace of mechanised agricultural collectivisation in the new locations. Moreover, the resettlement scheme has been criticised for its implicit political motives of dislocating peasants, draining them from insurgency areas, and relocating them in areas where they served as a stronghold for the government against insurgency (Taddese 1995:94).

In his volume based on fieldwork in the "Qeto resettlement scheme in Wollega," A. Pankhurst (1992) documented the conditions of resettlers in the early years after the relocation in the new setting, reflecting the village life in the resettlement area during 1987 and 1988. As pointed out above, Dessalegn (1988, 1989) has quite vigorously criticised the implicitly political motives of the successive Ethiopian regimes' resettlement programs.

Map 12. The 1980s Resettlement Program in Ethiopia

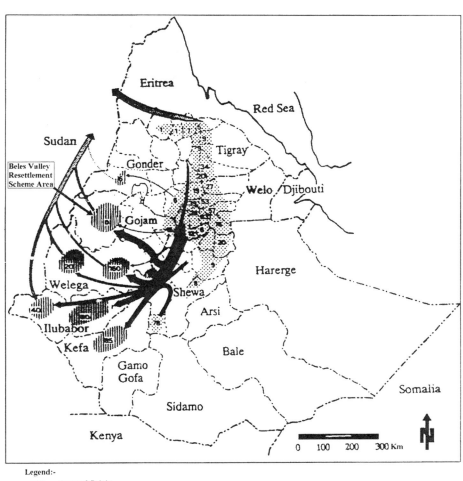

Legend:-

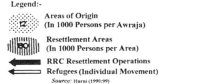

Areas of Origin
(In 1000 Persons per Awraja)

Resettlement Areas
(In 1000 Persons per Area)

RRC Resettlement Operations

Refugees (Individual Movement)

Source: Hurni (1990:99)

————————— Inernational Boundary
— — .— .— Administrative Region Boundary
- - - - - - - Awraja Boundary

141

Unlike Dessalegn, A. Pankhurst (1992:265) considers rather positively the state's rationale of the resettlement program as if it is rooted on genuine grounds such as the impact of famine, the country's independent past and the aspirations of its leaders for bright future by explaining as follows:

> In the encounter between the settlers and the State, the effects of the aid environment placed pressure on people to resettle and resulted in specific adaptations in the village. A combination of political, economic and social forces explains why and how resettlement took place. The failure of peasant survival strategies led many to surrender their autonomy and become dependent on the state. *The rationale of the Government's programme was rooted in the impact of famine, Ethiopia's independent past, and its leaders' aspirations for a brighter future.* The haste with which the programme was implemented left little time for planning, and resulted in much hardship, coercion and family separation [emphasis added].

However, in his later study, A. Pankhurst (1997:540) considered a wider review of cases of the impact of state-sponsored resettlement, for instance, in Assosa (Jemal 1996), Gambella (Kurimoto 1996, Steingraber 1988), Pawe (Gebre 1995, Wolde-Selassie 1997a), Qeto (Meheret 1994, Yimer 1996, A. Pankhurst's own subsequent re-visits) and then strongly criticised the state for imposing its power over the peripheries and appropriating the local peoples' natural resources without compensation or consultation. A. Pankhurst's later reconsideration is a noticeable shift from his earlier position that viewed positively the rationale of the state's resettlement program as one genuinely "rooted in the impact of famine, Ethiopia's independent past, and its leaders' aspirations for a brighter future." Contrary to his earlier approach, he later criticises the program as: "In the ebb and flow of recent centre-periphery relations in Ethiopia, *the 1985 resettlement carried out by the Derg represents an extreme case of state power exercised over multiple peripheries*" (A. Pankhurst 1997:540). The state's rationale he considered earlier as "genuine" was later noticed being condemned in his own terms as the "State Myths to Justify Resettlement." In his later explanation of the "myths" of the state's rationale of resettlement that failed on all counts, A. Pankhurst (1997:542) notes as: "At the roots of the state ideology on resettlement, it may be argued, lie three inter-related myths: the chimera of socialist transformation, delusions of agricultural transformation, and illusions of food self-sufficiency." Thus, A. Pankurst's later reconsideration of the rationale of the program critically reflects the multifaceted impacts (on resettlers, hosts, and the ecology) of the inadequately planned state-sponsored emergency resettlement of the 1980s in Ethiopia.

As a result of the hasty decision-making, the planning of the emergency resettlement was inadequate. It was a disorganised action plagued with confusion and mismanagement. Professional assessment of the environmental, economic and socio-cultural features of resettlement was neglected. The participation of the resettlers in the decision-making was almost non-existent. Affected people were not given the true information about the program. The recruitment timing was conducted in an unethical way during an emergency that did not allow resettlers an opportunity for rational decision-making. As a result, the inadequately planned scheme was accomplished at severe human costs. The resettlers underwent a distressing, painful and traumatic experience, which brought about the breaking-up of long established social structures, dismantling of production systems, and destruction of traditional coping strategies. It can be argued that this violated the basic human rights of those displaced.

The emergency resettlement scheme resulted mostly in long-distance movements of the resettlers. The implications of such movement, Kloos and Aynalem (1988:146) describe as: "The movement of large populations from the northern, sub-humid, overpopulated seed/plow eco-zone to the western, humid, less densely populated mixed (seed/plow/hoe, shifting cultivation, pastoral/nomadic, hunting/gathering) eco-zone of the western highlands and lowlands has far reaching implications for all sectors of the economy, human welfare and the environment." The dislocation brought large number of people into several different physico-biotic and socio-cultural environments. Agneta et al. (1993) note the major drawbacks of the emergency resettlement scheme, stressing the over zealous interpretations of the central Ethiopian authorities' directives that at times led to the use of coercion creating traumatic experiences for the resettlers. Critically considering the foreseeable adverse effects of the inadequately planned emergency resettlement, Sivini (1986:222) points out that "people were moved to areas which for centuries had not been inhabited by highland peasants who regarded these areas as uninhabitable; the productiveness of these areas in unknown; the resettlement will seriously disrupt the traditional way of life of the semi-pastoralist indigenous population."

Resettlement areas frequently posed health problems to populations unaccustomed to the new environments. In the hasty population dislocation process, family break-up has happened. The transportation conditions were problematic. The sites in the new areas were selected without thorough analysis of their development potential. Superficial site selection was made by high-level delegations composed of party officials and local administrators as well as the Relief and Rehabilitation Commission (RRC). Professional assessment of the environmental, economic, and socio-cultural features of resettlement was neglected. At the local level, planned resettlement operation was delegated to the initiative of the political cadres who were assigned responsibility for each new village. Above all, in the haste of carrying out the resettlement scheme, the indigenous populations (especially in the conventional resettlement sites) were totally neglected.

The operational cost of resettlement was extremely high. The emergency resettlement, during its initial period of 1985-87, cost the government around 600 million *birr*, of which the Metekel scheme alone cost 242 million *birr* (Dessalegn 1989:712). On the other hand, Agneta et al. (1993:276) explained funds already allocated and committed to the Metekel resettlement scheme from the "Italian Aid Fund" through the "Tana-Beles Project" as of July 1989 were US$290 million (approximately 2.5 billion Ethiopian *birr*). Other costs such as environmental damage, the suffering of the resettlers, the agony of separated families, and loss of family members cannot be expressed in material and financial terms. Thus, the hasty site selection, lack of qualified and skilled experts in the planning, lack of infrastructure and settler support systems, management and financial problems, and the resultant incapability of settlers to become self-sufficient, resulted in a failure to achieve the objectives of the program.

Many of the resettlement schemes failed to become self-sufficient and self-reliant. Persistent low production, physical and mental adaptation difficulties of resettlers to the new environment, and high rates of return migration right from arrival indicated the adverse effects caused by haste in planning and implementation. A summarised account of the death and desertion of the resettlers in the receiving areas (without including deaths in transits) in the years 1985 to 1987 was presented by the "National Study Committee of Receiving Provinces (NSCRP)" in 1988 under the auspices of the Council of Ministers of the Military Government. According to the estimate of this study, out of the total 594,190 resettlers involved in both the conventional (planned villages in a presumed "un-occupied" areas) and integrated (filling or insertion in an already existing villages) resettlement schemes, 116,768 of them deserted and/or died – desertions were estimated to be 83,800, and death 32,800 (NSCRP 1988:18). After the 1991 political change in Ethiopia, based on RRC's archival data on the operation of the emergency resettlement scheme, a former Deputy Commissioner of the RRC, Elias Negassa (1992:4) describes the situation as one in which "52,000 households deserted the large-scale farms; of these 7,000 people died and the rest trekked to their areas of origin or crossed international borders to become refugees. From the integrated settlements, 4000 heads of households escaped and

4,000 died." Moreover, he states, approximately 103,000 resettlers returned to northern Ethiopia from different resettlement sites, and another 34,000 resettlers have returned to Southern Shoa regions of Kambaata and Hadiyya. After the political change in 1991, severe ethnic conflicts emerged between the resettlers and hosts, thus adding political insecurity to an already pressing problem of socio-cultural and economic survival.

The adverse effects of resettlement were quite evident. First, the very program failed in alleviating the problems of the sending areas. Second, it had been accomplished at a high cost of human lives (i.e., resettlers unaccustomed to the new environment died in large numbers at the initial stage and were buried in countless horrifying mass graves due to inadequate preparation). Third, it resulted in the agony of split family members due to the prevalence of confusion, disorganisation, mismanagement and coercion during the operation. Fourth, its impacts in the receiving areas were disastrous due to lack of thorough investigation of their development potential. Fifth, the effect on the environment was damaging. Mengistu Wube (1995:100) describes in a summarised account the adverse effects of involuntary resettlement upon livelihood resources of the resettlers and the hosts in Ethiopia as follows:

> [T]he hurriedly designed and executed resettlement schemes are not functioning, owing to improper proper allocation of resources, poor administrative systems, and a lack of understanding of the land resource potential and environmental consequences. People were taken to the planned resettlement areas involuntarily and the government ignored indigenous forms of environmental protection practices. When the resettlers left their cultural landscapes, they left behind their identity, dignity, assets, strengths and know-how. Such negative effects are not only confined to the resettlement sites, but also have spread to the indigenous settlement areas. Government neither introduced environmental protection measures nor given assistance to resettlers and the indigenous population. Since the social geography of the country and the settlement patterns are changed, the physical and social environments are disturbed.

6.2 The Beles Valley (Pawe) Resettlement Scheme

According to Dessalegn (1988), no one knows exactly how Metekel came to be selected as a suitable site for resettlement of highland resettlers. No adequate and thorough socio-economic investigation was carried out before the choice was actually made. He points out the selection was likely to have been the initiative of party and government officials of the area, which was later endorsed by higher authorities around the end of October-November 1984. He points out that in October 1984, a team composed of *awraja* and provincial party members and the head of the regional planning office conducted an assessment of the area; and having found it to be suitable for resettlement, the team transmitted the findings to the authorities. After being briefed by the local authorities during his visit, Lieutenant-Colonel Mengistu Haile Mariam pointed out that the area was endowed with large tracts of 'unused' land, virgin soil, adequate rainfall, numerous rivers, sufficient forest and mineral resources and a good climate (Dessalegn 1988:17f.). During the summer of 1985, university students and professors were sent to the resettlement sites to build huts and other facilities for the people to be resettled before the end of the academic year. Dessalegn (1988:18) describes the initial stage impressions of the implementation of the program as:

> The task of clearing the Pawe area and surveying locations for villages started in mid-November 1984 but the actual work of building huts for the new arrivals did not get underway until late January 1985. Two months later, i.e., at the second week of April, the first group of resettlers arrived in Pawe. To the surprise of officials involved in the program, however, they turned out to be from Kambaata and *Hadiya Awraja* in Southern Shoa province rather than from Wollo or Tigray. The new arrivals were provided temporary accommodations in Pawe until they were assigned to their own villages.

As pointed out earlier, the Beles Valley resettlement scheme was one of the biggest emergency programs that hosted people resettled as a consequence of both the drought and famine of 1984/85 (1977 E.C.) and over-population. The resettlers of the former category were from Wollo, North Shoa and Tigray while those of the latter were from South Shoa and Gojjam. The scheme's explicit aim was attainment of surplus agricultural production through mechanised high-tech agriculture by means of collective organisation of farm labour. The scheme is situated in the basin of the Beles River and covers a planned area of around 250,000 hectares with about 60km length and 30km width (Salini Costruttori 1989:8). The resettlers were relocated along the left and right banks of the Beles River as shown in *map thirteen*.

Once the Beles Valley became a conventional resettlement scheme site, it hosted resettler population of both famine victims from northern Ethiopia and those who suffered overpopulation and cultivable land shortage from south-western Ethiopia. At the peak of the resettlement scheme in 1987/88,

Map 13. Planned and Realized Villages in the Beles Valley Resettlement Area in Metekel

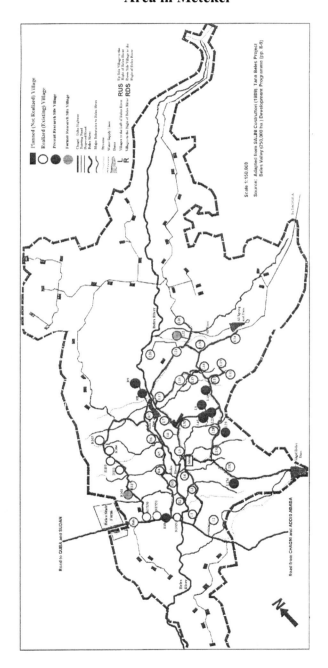

the population involved in the program reached a total of 82,106, heads of households among them being numbered 21,994, family members 60,112 (Wolde-Selassie1998:47). The displaced resettlers are relocated along the left and right banks of the river in a total of 48 villages with an average number of 500 households in each village. Today, the former villages as well as the newly emerging small towns in the area have been merged, forming twenty *kebele* administered under the Pawe Special *Woreda* (cf. chapter 6 "Socio-Political Profile of the Resettlement Area").

In addition to indicating those villages occupied by the resettlers, *map thirteen* shows the entire initially proposed resettlement plan that includes a large expanse of area in the Beles Valley. All the villages to the right of the Beles River are numbered with a pre-fixed "R" letter; and villages to the left of river Beles are numbered with a pre-fixed "L" letter. Except only two built in a circularised hamlet-type settlements, all the other villages are designed on a grid rows and columns where places of community services such as grain mill, potable water, clinic, store, offices, and school were mostly located at the centre of each village.

The ethnic composition of the resettlement population is very heterogeneous, with resettlers originating from different parts of the country. The major ethnic backgrounds of resettlers include: Amhara (from Wollo North Shoa, Gojjam and Gondar), Kambaata, Hadiyya, Oromo (from South Wollo and North Shoa), Wolaita, Tigraway, and Agaw (from Wollo-Tigray/Seqota) (cf. chapter 10, section 10.1). They originated from culturally, linguistically and climatically diverse areas. They have got different backgrounds in their former home areas. For instance, resettlers from north-central parts of the country were intensive cereal cultivators, whereas the south-western resettlers were mainly *enset* (*Ensete ventricosum*) and root crops cultivators with an additional specialisation in income-generating activities. In part of the resettlement villages, resettlers belonging to the same ethnic groups are placed together, whereas in many others resettlers belonging to diverse ethnic backgrounds are settled together. The new location is very far from the original areas of most resettlers. These different ethnic groups with diverse backgrounds in the new location portray a mixture of cultures from larger parts of the country.

6.3 Current Socio-Political Context

Socio-Political Profile of the Resettlement Area

Table 10: Local Administrative Sub-Centres, *Kebele*, and Villages of the Pawe Special *Woreda*

Local Administrative Sub-Centres, *Kebele* and Villages of the Pawe Special *Woreda*			
Administrative Sub-Centres		Post-1991*Kebele* Administration	Pre-1991Villages/Towns under Resettlement Administration
1	*ALMU*	1	*Almu* Town	*Almu* Town
		2	Abbat Beles	Abbat Beles, L1, L2, RDS51
		3	L3	L3, L4
		4	*Felege Selam* Town	*Felege Selam* Town (L4)
		5	L28	L28, **L29***
		6	L134	L131, L132, **L134***
2	*ADDIS ALEM*	7	*Addis Alem* Town	*Addis Alem* Town (L7)
		8	L30	L5, L6, L7, L30
		9	L17	L17, **R8***, **R9***
		10	**L23****	**L9****, **L10****, **L23****, **L45****
		11	R7	R6, R7
3	L14 (*Addis Zemen*)	12	L12 (*Debre Work*)	L11, L12, L13
		13	L14 (*Addis Zemen*)	L14, L15, L16, L130
		14	L21 (*Addis Beles*)	L20, L21, L22
		15	L24	L24
		16	L26	L26
4	LUS51 (*Mekane Selam*)	17	R4	R2, R3, R4, R5
		18	RUS51 (*Mekane Selam*)	R46, **R49***, RUS50, RUS51
		19	R101	R101, R127
		20	R104@	R104@

Source: Pawe Special *Woreda* Administration (February-March 2001)

**The researcher's main study sites
*The researcher's study sub-sites
@Village(s) abandoned by former resettlers and occupied by later immigrant farmers
L - Villages on the left side of Beles River
R – Villages on the right side of Beles River
RUS – Right upside villages
RDS - Right downside villages

Administrative Structure

A total of forty-eight resettlement villages were established at the peak of the scheme in 1987/88. Later, the number of villages had dropped to forty-five. However, the newly emerging three small towns of Almu, Addis Alem and Felege Selam were included under the administration. In the recent Beles Valley context, the former resettlement villages as well as the newly emerging small towns in the area have been merged into twenty *kebele*. These *kebele* are in turn further categorised into four sub-centres administrated under the Pawe Special *Woreda*, which is empowered with special autonomy and directly delegated to the Benishangul-Gumuz Regional State. A detail of the administrative structure is indicated in the table above.

Table 11: Trends in the State-Sponsored Resettler Population

| No. | Years | | Population Trends | | |
	Ethiopian Calendar	Gregorian Calendar	Heads of Households	Family Members	Total Population
1	1977	1984/1985	20078	39293	59371
2	1978	1985/1986	22664	53980	76644
3	1979	1986/1987	21081	53191	74272
4	1980	1987/1988	21994	60112	82106
5	1981	1988/1989	20418	58684	79102
6	1982	1990/1991	18917	53083	72000
7	1983	1991/1992	17638	48453	66091
8	1984	1992/1993	9917	37654	47571
9	1985	1993/1994	9084	20858	29942
10	1986	1994/1995	8092	18568	26660
11	1987	1995/1996	8358	21143	29501
12	1988	1996/1997	8401	22096	30497
13*	*1989*	*1997/1998*	*10423*	*31268*	*41691*
14	1990	1998/1999	No data	No data	No data
15	1991	1999/2000	No data	No data	No data
16	1992	2000/2001	No data	No data	No data
17*	*1993*	*2001/2002*	*11241*	*37121*	*48362*

Sources:
1. Tana-Beles Project for data from 1984/54 – 1996/97 (referring to only state-sponsored resettler population of the 1980s);
2. *Wolde-Selassie Abbute survey for the data of 1997/98 and 2001/2002 (collected in February - March 1997 and February - March 2001 respectively) and includes the different category of population residing in the resettlement area.
3. Data not available for the period from 1998/99 – 2000/2001 because the Tana-Beles Project ceased its previous direct operations with the affairs of resettlers in the resettlement villages.

Trends in Resettler Population
The number of resettlers had reached its peak with a total population of 82,106 in 1987/88, has shown a continuous decline, sharply dropping to a total of only 26,660 in 1994/95. The decline after the 1991 was aggravated by severe ethnic conflicts emerged between the hosts and resettlers as well as the disruption of resettler supporting organisations. The trends in the resettler population involved in the resettlement scheme, since 1984-85 is described in the table above

Table 12: The Different Categories of Population Inhabiting the Beles Valley

Category of Population	Number of Population							
	Household Heads			Family Members			Total	
	Male	Female	Total	Male	Female	Total	Total	%
State-Sponsored Resettlers of the 1980s	5677	1498	7175	10437	12901	23338	30513	**63.1**
Voluntary and Displaced Immigrants Farmers of the 1990s	1235	227	1462	2523	2873	5396	6858	**14.2**
Town Dwellers in the Emerging Small Towns	2134	470	2604	3565	4822	8387	10991	**22.7**
Total Population	**9046**	**2195**	**11241**	**16525**	**20586**	**37121**	**48362**	**100**

Source: Wolde-Selassie Abbute survey (February - March 2001)

Different Categories of Population[2]
The different categories of population presently inhabiting the Beles Valley resettlement scheme area include the state-sponsored resettlers of the 1980s (63.1% of the total population and referred to as resettlers), town dwellers of

---

[2] In this study, the different categories of population inhabiting the resettlement area are mainly referred as *resettlers* (for the state-sponsored resettlers of the 1980s), *town dwellers* (for the residents of the newly emerging small towns), and *immigrant farmers* (for both displaced/voluntary immigrant farmers of the 1990s). Those immigrants residing in the villages and whose livelihood is fully based on farming are referred as 'immigrant farmers' to distinguish them from immigrants residing in small towns. It should also be understood that resettlers in the villages are of course smallholder farmers.

the newly emerging small towns (22.7% of the total population and referred to as town dwellers), and displaced/voluntary immigrant farmers of the 1990s (14.2% of the total population and referred to as immigrant farmers) as stated in the table above.

The town dwellers include those residents of emerging small towns engaging in diverse economic and service sectors as well as those who migrated to the area looking for opportunities. Since the commencement of the resettlement program, small towns initially acting as local market centres, health treatment centres, and project management sites have been emerging at different locations inside the area. At the moment, these small towns have shown a significant increase in the number of dwellers who are engaged in multiple socio-economic and service sectors. These small towns are serving as important centres for undertaking livelihood diversification activities. Moreover, complex networks of interactions have been emerging among the inhabitants of small towns, resettlers, immigrant farmers, and the autochthonous Gumuz based on multiple local social institutional arrangements.

On the other hand, the accounts of my Pawe informants and extended personal observation show an influx of a considerable number of immigrant farmers moving into the area since 1993/94. Following the 1991 political change in Ethiopia and its effects in Metekel in general and the Beles Valley resettlement scheme in particular, the area accommodated a number of immigrant farmers. Part of them were displaced and evicted due to the fierce ethnic conflicts occurred between them and the Gumuz in the neighbouring parts of Metekel around Chagni, Dibati, and Manta-Wuha (the central location of the conflict). Most of the farmers in this category were former spontaneous immigrant settlers of Wollo (cf. Chapter 5 "Pre-1974 Encroachment"). They immigrated down to the Beles Valley together with their livestock, seeking security near the administration and looking for better cultivable and grazing land as noted earlier.

The other immigrant farmers originated from the central parts of Gojjam and Gondar. The majority of the immigrant farmers of Gojjam were from the Qolla-Dega-Damot (former *awraja*) area in West Gojjam, being pushed by land shortage. An equally significant number of immigrant farmers from Gojjam all around Bahir-Dar and its environs immigrated into the valley with their relatively numerous livestock resources (mostly cattle). They are locally known as *zellan* (literally meaning nomads) though their main source of livelihood is crop cultivation. They voluntarily immigrated to the Beles Valley looking for better opportunities of cultivable and grazing land. Many of these voluntary immigrants consciously made prior assessments of the potential of the area by sending selected elders to the area and then began moving step-by-step, bringing family members afterwards. Their immigration strategy steps include, first the adult farmers came; then, grown-up children of working age were brought; and, finally, all the family members moved into the area. Similarly, those displaced immigrant farmers have also made preliminary assessments of the area by sending their elders before immigrating into the valley.

Both the voluntary and displaced immigrant farmers settled at different locations in the entire resettlement area mainly in those places abandoned by those resettlers who went back to their areas of origin. Once they reached the valley, their primary settlement locations were those areas abandoned by former state-sponsored resettlers. However, many of them have also settled in and around different villages, making several institutional arrangements with the resident resettlers and their leaders. Their concentration is mainly in villages where many resettlers deserted, with particular focus on Kambaata-Hadiyya-Wolaita resettler villages. Part of them also settled along the peripheries of main field plots of the resettlers, clearing forests and bush lands. In the process of getting access to the village land resources of the resettlers, they skilfully applied informal institutional approaches such as sharecropping and land rental arrangements. Apart from these dominant groups of immigrant farmers, a significant number of other voluntary immigrants have also moved into the valley from the original areas of state-sponsored resettlers following their fellow relatives or countrymen.

Ethnic Background
The aggregate ethnic background of the different category of population inhabiting the Beles Valley scheme area is diverse, representing the major ethnic and language groups of the country and composed of Amhara (73.1%) (who are in turn disaggregated along different geographic and socio-cultural Amhara groups of Wollo (25.4%), North Shoa (12.5%), Gojjam (30.8%) and Gondar (4.4%)), Kambaata (9.1%), Hadiyya (8.3%), Oromo (3.2%), Wolaita (1.0), Tigraway (1.1%), Agaw (Seqota) (0.7%), Agaw (Gojjam) (3.3%), and others (0.3%). A breakdown of the ethnic composition of the different categories of population is presented in part four, chapter 10 (section 10.1).

Religious Background
The religious background of the people of different categories inhabiting the resettlement scheme area is diverse and composed of Christians (73.6%) and Muslims (26.4%). The Christians are in turn divided into followers of Or-

thodox (57.7%), Protestant (11.3%), and Catholic (4.6%) Christianity. Orthodox Christianity is predominantly followed by more than half of the resettler population mostly belonging to the Amhara, Agaw, and Tigraway ethnic groups. Islam is the second predominant religion in the area and is also mostly followed by the Amhara (mostly from Wollo) as well as almost all of the resettlers belonging to the Oromo ethnic group. Resettlers of the Kambaata-Hadiyya-Wolaita ethnic groups are mainly followers of Protestant and Catholic Christianity. However, some of their members are followers of either Orthodox Christianity or Islam. The Catholic and Protestant religions are not appreciated as such by the followers of the Orthodox because they consider the two as newcomers (*matte*) and a threat to their religion. A breakdown of the religious background of the different categories of population is presented in detail in part four, chapter 10 (section 10.1).

Local Community Institutions
The local social institutions that bind the diverse and complex networks of interactions are usually invisible and difficult to describe in quantitative terms. However, in this study, an attempt is made to assess the number of two of the most important and relatively observable practices of religious and *iddir* institutions in the area. *Iddir* is the Amharic term signifying traditional community institution for multiple purpose. One of its most popular functions is support during death and funeral (cf. Chapter 9 "Neighbourhood")

Nevertheless, except attempting to understand a broad highlight and numerical overview of only those existing, counted, and reported by the local community, the study by no means tries to quantify statistically the multidimensional functions of these institutions. It should also be noted that some of the functions of the *iddir* institutions reported as separate do overlap in different contexts. The investigation was attempted considering the indispensable roles and multiple significance of these two and many other local institutions in the pursuit of the resettlers' livelihood adaptation in a new setting (cf. chapter 9). The existing religious institutions were reported to be around 107, of which 65 are churches and 42 are mosques. The churches are in turn divided into 36 Orthodox, 20 Protestant, and 9 Catholic. On the other hand, existing community *iddir* institutions were reported to be 617, of which 111 are burial, 202 stretcher, 122 oxen, and 182 housing institutions. The details of both institutions are stated in the table below.

Table 13: Local Community Institutions in the Beles Valley Resettlement Area

Local Community Institutions			Number	%	%
Religious Institutions	Churches	*Orthodox*	36	55.4	**33.6**
		Protestant	20	30.8	**18.7**
		Catholic	9	13.8	**8.4**
		Total	*65*	*100*	*60.7*
	Mosques				**39.3**
				42	
Total Religious Institutions			**107**		**100**
Community Iddir Institutions*	*Burial iddir***		111		**18.0**
	Stretcher iddir		202		**32.7**
	Oxen iddir		122		**19.8**
	Housing iddir		182		**29.5**
Total *Iddir* Institutions			*617*		*100*

Source: Wolde-Selassie Abbute survey (February – March 2001)
*The role of the different *iddir* overlap in some contexts
**The burial *iddir* has the highest community membership

Socio-Political Features of Research Sites

The research sites were purposively selected outside the small towns due to the special focus of the study on the highland resettler peasants in the resettlement villages. The socio-political features of the research sites in this section concentrate primarily on the state-sponsored resettlers of the 1980s and later immigrants of the 1990s.

Table 14: State-Sponsored Resettler and Immigrant Farmers' Population in the Research Sites

Specific Research Sites	State-Sponsored Resettlers			Voluntary/Displaced Immigrants			*Total*
	Heads of Households	Family Members	Total	Heads of Households	Family Members	Total	
L9	200	430	**630**	7	33	**40**	*670*
L10	216	413	**629**	27	40	**67**	*696*
L23	294	859	**1153**	12	39	**51**	*1204*
L45	213	617	**830**	7	26	**33**	*863*
L29	294	473	**767**	79	46	**125**	*892*
L134	187	413	**600**	55	10	**65**	*665*
R8	45	225	**270**	35	245	**280**	*550*

Specific Research Sites	State-Sponsored Resettlers			Voluntary/Displaced Immigrants			*Total*
	Heads of Households	Family Members	Total	Heads of Households	Family Members	Total	
R9	60	300	**360**	43	272	**315**	*675*
R49	203	862	**1065**	18	48	**66**	*1131*
Total	1712	4592	**6304**	283	759	1042	7346
Percentage of Resettlers and Immigrants			*85.8*			*14.2*	*100%*

Source: Wolde-Selassie Abbute survey (February – March 2001)
The main research site villages of L9, L10, L23, & L45 are merged into one *kebele* (a basic unit of local administrative structure bridging the people at the grassroots level and higher administrative organs). The sub-site villages of L29, L134, R8, R9, and R49 are parts of other *kebele* located at different places of the scheme.

Population

As indicated in table 14, the total population inhabiting the research sites is 7,346, out of which 6,304 (85.8%) are resettlers and 1,042 (14.2%) are immigrant farmers. In almost all the villages, there are immigrant farmers, but their number varies from one village to the other.

Religious Background

The inhabitants of the research sites are composed of followers from all the major religions of the area as indicated in table15.

Ethnic Background of Resettlers

The ethnic background of the resetter population inhabiting the research site villages is very diverse. Their ethnic background is composed of Amhara (52.2%) (who are in turn divided along different geographic and socio-cultural Amhara groups of Wollo (46.5%), North Shoa (0.8%), and Gojjam (7.9%)), Kambaata (19.2 %), Hadiyya (6.6%), Oromo (15.2%), Wolaita (0.8%), Tigraway (1.0%), and Agaw (Seqota) (2.0%). A breakdown of the ethnic background composition of the resettler population is described in table 16.

Table15: Religious Background of Resettlers and Immigrant Farmers in the Research Sites

Re-search Sites	State-Sponsored Resettlers					Voluntary/Displaced Immigrants				Total
	Christian			Mus.	Total	Christian		Mus.	Total	
	O.	P.	C.			O.	P.			
L9	74	311	140	105	630	9	31	-	40	670
L10	149	312	98	70	629	40	27	-	67	696
L23	220	-	-	933	1153	23	-	28	51	1204
L45	494	-	-	336	830	20	-	13	33	863
L29	521	-	-	246	767	99	-	26	125	892
L134	415	-	-	185	600	40	-	25	65	665
R8	10	189	55	16	270	280	-	-	280	550
R9	15	160	170	15	360	315	-	-	315	675
R49	241	-	-	824	1065	15	-	51	66	1131
Total	2139	972	463	2730	6304	841	58	143	1042	7346
%	33.9	15.4	7.4	43.3	100	80.7	5.6	13.7	100	-

O. = Orthodox; P. = Protestant; C. = Catholic; M. = Muslim
Source: Wolde-Selassie Abbute survey (February – March 2001)

Table 16: Ethnic Background of Resettler Population in the Research Site

R. S.	Ethnic Background of Resettler Population										Total
	Amhara				Kambaata	Hadiyya	Oromo	Wolaita	Tigraway	Agaw (Seqota)	
	Wollo	Shoa	Gojjam	Total							
L9	-	-	65	65	503	42	-	20	-	-	630
L10	-	-	149	149	98	354	-	28	-	-	629
L23	87	51	82	220	-	-	933	-	-	-	1153
L45	787	-	43	830		-	-	-	-	-	830
L29	411	-	150	561	-	-	18	-	63	125	767
L134	600	-	-	600	-	-	-	-	-	-	600
R8	-	-	-	-	270	-	-	-	-	-	270
R9	-	-	-	-	342	18	-	-	-	-	360
R49	1045	-	10	1055	-	-	10	-	-	-	1065
Total	2930	51	499	3480	1213	414	961	48	63	125	6304
%	46.5	0.8	7.9	55.2	19.2	6.6	15.2	0.8	1.0	2.0	100

Source: Wolde-Selassie Abbute survey (February – March 2001)

R. S. = Research Sites

Ethnic Background of Immigrant Farmers
The ethnic background of the immigrant farmers inhabiting the research site villages is composed of mostly members of the Amhara ethnic group (91.6%) {who are in turn divided along different geographic and socio-cultural Amhara groups of Wollo (18.2%), Gojjam (72.3%), and Gondar (0.9%)}. The other ethnic groups in the category together form only 8.4 percent and are composed of Kambaata (3.6 %), Hadiyya (1.9%), Oromo (1.7%), and Tigraway (1.2%). A breakdown of the ethnic background composition of the immigrant farmers in the research villages is stated in the table below.

Table 17: Ethnic Background of Immigrant Farmers in the Research Sites

Research Sites	Ethnic Composition of Voluntary and Displaced Immigrant Population				Kambaata	Hadiyya	Oromo	Tigraway	Total
	Amhara								
	Wollo	Gojjam	Gondar	Total					
L9	-	9	-	9	31	-	-	-	40
L10	-	40	-	40	7	20	-	-	67
L23	13	20	-	33	-	-	18	-	51
L45	26	7	-	33	-	-	-	-	33
L29	87	22	4	113	-	-	-	12	125
L134	48	14	3	65	-	-	-	-	65
R8	-	280	-	280	-	-	-	-	280
R9	-	315	-	315	-	-	-	-	315
R49	18	46	2	66	-	-	-	-	66
Total	*192*	*753*	*9*	*954*	*38*	*20*	*18*	*12*	*1042*
%	*18.4*	*72.3*	*0.9*	*91.6*	*3.6*	*1.9*	*1.7*	*1.2*	*100%*

Source: Wolde-Selassie Abbute survey (February – March 2001)

Local Community Institutions in the Research Sites
A total of sixteen churches and nine mosques exist in the study villages. Of the churches, six are Orthodox, seven are Protestant, and three are Catholic. On the other hand, there are around 204 community *iddir* institutions, out of

which 36 are burial, 83 stretcher, 35 oxen, and 53 housing. Usually, as stated earlier, the functions of the different *iddir* overlap in some contexts. A detailed breakdown of the two institutions is given in the table below.

Table 18: Local Community Institutions in the Research Sites

R. S.	Religious Institutions						Community *Iddir* Institutions*				
	Churches				Mosques	Total	Burial *Iddir***	Stretcher *Iddir*	Oxen Iddir	Housing *Iddir*	Total
	Orthodox	Protestant	Catholic	Total							
L9	-	3	1	4	1	5	5	10	2	4	*21*
L10	1	3	1	5	1	6	3	12	3	6	*24*
L23	-	-	-	-	2	2	4	12	6	7	*29*
L45	1	-	-	1	1	2	5	12	4	11	*32*
L29	1	-	-	1	1	2	7	10	6	9	*32*
L134	1	-	-	1	1	2	2	12	5	5	*24*
R8	-	1	-	1	1	2	1	1	1	1	*4*
R9	1	-	1	2	-	2	4	4	4	4	*16*
R49	1	-	-	1	1	2	2	10	4	6	*22*
Total	6	7	3	16	9	25	33	83	35	53	*204*

Source: Wolde-Selassie Abbute survey (February – March 2001)
R. S. = Research Sites
*The role of the different *iddir* overlap in some contexts
**The burial *iddir* has the highest community membership

As already stated above, the local social institutions are usually invisible especially for an outsider and difficult to describe in quantitative terms. However, in the above table an attempt is made to highlight a quantified numerical overview of these most important and relatively observable practices of religious and *iddir* institutions in the research sites as reported by the local community. It should be noted that the study by no means tries to quantify the socio-cultural functions of these institutions. It simply attempts to highlight an overview as a background to the forthcoming discussion in the later sections concerning the indispensable role of local social institutions in the pursuit of the resettlers' livelihood adaptations and interactions (cf. chapter 9).

Chapter 7. Human and Environmental Impact of Resettlement

The state sponsored emergency resettlement scheme of the 1980s in the Beles Valley has brought about complex changes in the socio-cultural, economic, and environmental conditions in the area. The resettlers from the highlands, the autochthonous Gumuz, and the environment are all affected by the resettlement scheme[3].

7.1 The Human Impact[4]

Impact on the Resettlers: Socio-Cultural Disintegration and Livelihood Impoverishment

The resettlement scheme in the Beles Valley has severely disintegrated the social fabric of the resettlers and impoverished their livelihood resources especially in the immediate aftermath of the relocation. The social impact of the Beles Valley scheme experience discussed in this section profoundly reinforces and confirms what has already been conceptualised, in Cernea's term, as social disarticulation. This phenomenon, Cernea (2000:30) explains as: "Forced displacement tears apart the existing social fabric. It disperses and fragments communities, dismantles patterns of social organisation and interpersonal ties; kinship groups become scattered as well. Life-sustaining informal networks of reciprocal help, local voluntary associations, and self-organised mutual service are disrupted" (cf. chapter 2 "Impoverishment Risk and Reconstruction Model"). Integral to this process is the consideration of how resettlement disrupts what Downing (1996:33f.) conceptualises as "the social geometry of a people," which "consists of socially constructed spaces, socially constructed times and socially constructed personages." According to Downing, "the people may physically persist, but the community that was is no more" because its spatial, temporal, and cultural determinants were gone. Resettlement disintegrates the resettlers' spatial-temporal routines by pulling them out of the spatial context in which those routines are embed-

---

[3] Data on the human and environmental consequences are mainly based on my subsequent observations over a time span from 1988 to 2001 in the Beles Valley.

[4] The planning of Beles Valley resettlement, Agneta et al. (1993:275) explain, "suffered not just from operational mistakes, but also from the absence of clear, adequate planning policies based on already known information about resettlement. In addition to the lack of anthropological research on the resettler and host population, resettlement planning faced serious difficulties overcoming the transition phase. Had deeper and more careful studies been carried out, much of the suffering and hardship would have been avoided."

160

ded. Moreover, the undertakings of the emergency resettlement were full of traumatic experiences for those resettlers undergoing relocation, what Colson and Scudder (1982:269f.) termed "physiological, psychological and socio-cultural stresses."[5]

Reconsidering the adverse effects of the state-sponsored emergency resettlement of the 1980s on the resettlers, A. Pankhurst (1997:554) in his later study, which also reviews wider works of other authors in the relocation sites at the country's western peripheries, noted the following.

> From the viewpoint of the settlers, the process of relocation uprooted them and placed them in unfamiliar physical and social environments in arduous conditions, which forced a change in diet and exposed them to new diseases. Moreover, resettlement made settlers totally dependent on the state in the early stages. In the collectives, formerly independent peasants were transformed into wage-labourers, with no control over agricultural decision-making and subjected to a harsh and unrewarding cooperative work system in which the leadership and militia formed privileged elites. In the "integrated" settlements relations with local people whose land and resources had been taken, were often strained, also leading to large-scale desertions.

The Beles Valley resettlement scheme has brought resettlers from the highlands to a completely different location in the lowlands. It has disintegrated their previous socio-cultural way of life and disrupted their production systems, causing multiple stresses. It had countless adverse effects on the lives and livelihoods of the resettlers, demanding stressful adaptation to the new setting. The resettlers encountered painful difficulties in adapting to the new socio-cultural, economic and biophysical environment and the concomitant changes in climate, farming practices, and food habits.

Climatically, the Beles Valley is hot and less hospitable, making the highlanders' adaptation even more difficult. Disillusioned by their expectations, resettlers in the Beles Valley began life in an impotent and unhappy manner, aggravated by the ravages of malaria, tuberculosis and other epidemic diseases. Their first contacts with the new sites were full of insecurity and precariousness, such that they felt their new conditions were a distress-

---

[5] For further details of wider assessment on the impact of involuntary resettlement on resettlers, see Cernea (1985, 1991, 1993, 1994, 1996a, 1996b, 1996c, 2000); Cernea and Guggenheim (1993); Cernea and McDowell (2000); Chambers (1970); Colson (1964, 1971); De Wet (1988, 1993, 1996, 2000); Cook (1994); Downing (1996); Mathur (1990, 1995); McDowell (1996); Meliczek (2000); Scudder (1973, 1985, 1991, 1993, 1996a, 1996b, 1996c, 1997a. 1997b, 1999); and Scudder and Colson (1979, 1982).

ing, painful, and traumatic experience. The unfavourable climatic conditions in the lowlands resulted in excessive mortality due to health problems (malaria and other epidemic diseases) and malnutrition. This fact is vividly described by Sivini (1986:233) as:

For the fifteen-week period that goes from October 12, 1985 to January 25, 1986, the weekly data relative to the mortality in the conventional settlement of Pawe in Gojjam confirm the existence of a highly critical situation, which seems to be above all connected with the climatic conditions. In fact, the phenomenon, while keeping itself at high levels, decreases as we move away from the rainy season. The ratio between deaths and population (calculated on the basis of arrivals) projected on an annual basis furnishes a mortality rate of 33.2 per cent for the first four weeks of the period in question, 21.4 per cent for the following seven weeks and 13.7 per cent for the last four weeks. A weighted annual mortality rate that assumes the first value as indicative of the rainy season (July-October), the second value indicative of the intermediate season (November and December, to which it actually refers) and the third, indicative of the better season (January-June), would be equal to 21.5 per cent.

Propaganda that described a glorified image of the new homes as if comforts were awaiting them deceived many of the resettlers. They repeatedly recalled their pre-resettlement living conditions in a positive light. Drought affected people of the north, and land-hungry people of the south-west abandoned their normal way of life and sought assistance in relief centres. The promises and guarantees provided by the government officials enabled them to decide on and join the scheme, removing the last doubts. These expectations raised during the recruitment stage were not fulfilled after arrival at the new sites, and created great disillusionment among the resettlers.

For instance, as I personally witnessed in June-July 1985, during the recruitment in the origins, resettlement was propagated by the local authorities with a glorified image of awaiting comfort and abundant fertile land to the chronically land-hungry Kambaata and Hadiyya peasants. They were told that the land would be cultivated by tractors; that fully furnished iron-roofed modern houses were already built awaiting them; and that they would be given plenty of food, clothing and necessary implements. Deceived by the propaganda, many peasants joined the scheme, discarding their property accumulated over generations. The would-be resettlers sold their domestic animals, grain, household furniture, dwellings, garden plants, and other related valuables at very low prices. Being recruited for the program, many of them used up the last of their money while waiting in the temporary shelters for transportation. Immediately after their departure for the promised land, their plots were redistributed to those newly married and others who suffer from serious land shortages.

However, the promises of the great expectations turned out to be totally untrue in the new locations. The initial contacts with the new sites were characterised by insecurity and precariousness. Life became hard in the new setting[6]. Following the instructions of the cadres, the resettlers had to build new houses because the ones built by the university students and staff during the campaign were crumbling. Hence, as stated above, they underwent a distressing, painful and traumatic experience, which brought about the breaking down of long established social structures, dismantling of production systems, and destruction of traditional coping mechanisms. Based on their on-site assessment in the Beles Valley in May-June 1986, Dieci and Roscio (1992:117) describe the general conditions as: "In the first half of 1986 the over-riding concern in the Beles area was the weakened state of the resettled populations due to the extreme hardship they suffered during resettlement and difficulties they encountered in adapting to the new environment, which was obviously greatest during the initial period of residence."

The resettlement scheme has increased state control over the resettlers, with government, party, and executing agencies taking control of their lives and socio-economic resources. At all levels, they were heavily guarded to prevent escape. Initially, religious holidays could not be freely observed due to the collective agricultural work. Free travel was absolutely impossible and it was strictly forbidden to travel out of the area. As I had personally witnessed in 1988, village-to-village travel was possible only through pass letters obtained from the village authorities. Agricultural collectivisation was imposed upon the resettlers and their labour time was strictly controlled according to the points system devised for producers' co-operative. Private trade was restricted. Individual initiatives were constrained. The overall administration of each resettlement village was put under a tight and paternalistic control of a village political cadre. Therefore, the Beles Valley resettlement scheme has involved "notable human costs higher than those caused by famine, in spite of large investments to rapidly install the infrastructures" (Sivini 1986:235).

---

[6] Although all resettlers felt similar horrifying experience at the initial phase in the new sites, it should also be noted that their attitudes substantially differed based on the reasons for resettlement such as voluntary, coercive, or those based on promises and incentives.

At the initial stages of the scheme, local social institutions that bind the multiple webs of community relationships along several lines were disintegrated in the new context. The resettlers were alienated from family and community control, and their social, political, and religious leaders were impotent to prevent the social disintegration and disruption of their livelihood affecting every one of them. The role of respected elders and religious leaders as facilitators of the whole process of marriage was disrupted. Initially, the roles of priests', *qaadi*'s, and other ritual leaders' spiritual duties were disrupted. The deep-rooted and long-established ritual process before, during and after the burial of the dead for the salvation of the soul was interrupted. The spiritual festive associations like *mahber* and *senbete* of the Orthodox Church followers were curtailed. The crucial roles of elders in the overall village community lives and livelihoods were absent. The administration of the village was left only in the hands of formally elected Peasant Association (PA) Committee members charged with the executive and judicial tasks of administering the new village.

The resettlers originated from culturally, linguistically, and climatically diverse areas of the country and resulted in interactions of different cultures of various ethnic groups previously isolated from each other. In the resettling process, in some of the villages resettlers belonging to the same ethnic groups are located together, whereas in others, resettlers belonging to different ethnic backgrounds are resettled together. As earlier described, resettlers from the north-central parts of the country were intensive cultivators of cereal crops with their main staple food being *injera*. The resettlers from the south-western part of the country were mainly *enset* (*Ensete ventricosum*) and tuber crops cultivators with an additional specialisation in income-generating activities, with their main staple food being *qotcho*.

Land in the resettlers previous locations, though small in size, was "privately" owned and the household was the main unit of production and consumption. Animal husbandry was practised. In the home areas, resettlers mostly belonged to one lineage, clan and ethnic groups living in neighbouring dispersed villages and hamlets. Village communities in the original areas have got long established social institutions, which have been underestimated and disintegrated in the resettlement context. Resettlement planning, explain Agneta et al.[7] (1993:275), "underestimated such key issues as the

---

[7] The five authors (Francesca Agneta, Stefano Berterame, Mariarita Caprici, Loredana Magni, and Massimo Tommasoli) who jointly contributed the chapter (in a volume edited by Michael M. Cernea and Scott E. Guggenheim) were expatriate employees of an Italian NGO called CISP, working at the initial phase of the project. After my employment in the NGO in June 1988 as a 'Research Assistant', I worked closely with Stefano Berterame and Loredana Magni, in data

role of the household economy as well as the potential of kinship relationships, of neighbour networks and of the common ethnic origin in order to sustain the resettlers' initiative." These institutional arrangements included important institutions such as *iddir* (both the legal framework and insurance of the local village community), which is intricately involved in the overall livelihood management of the community, as already pointed out. Moreover, people in the home areas were known under their respective parish, mosque, clan, or village groups. The kinship ties in the home areas were very strong and interwoven through the ancestral lineages. Above all, the community members in the previous home areas were coherently intimate with a sense of belonging and spiritual ties through a common origin which many resettlers referred to it as "a root area where one's umbilical cord is buried."

In contrast, the resettlement villages have people of diverse ethnic and religious backgrounds. The villages in the resettlement area are located in one place where groups of residential houses are laid in a grid pattern with only a 0.1 hectare homestead plot for each household (the only farm area managed by the farm household). In no case did an entire village community come from the same village and belonging to the same kin group members in the home areas. Institutions that bind the community's web of relationships along several lines in the origins such as neighbourhood, kinship, religious beliefs, work groups, land exchange, bond-friendship, fictive- and god-parenthood, and several other related were disintegrated and impoverished in the new context mainly at the initial stage (cf. chapter 9).

At the initial phase, resettlers did not have proper community village institutions and lack both religious and secular mutual associations. Free observations of religious holidays were constrained due to the difficulties they were encountering. The multi-purpose, long established kinship ties were altered in the new location, and there existed no kinship-based leadership. Both festive and reciprocal social organisations of production, which are key in the household and village economy of smallholder cultivation in the former home areas were disintegrated. Local community money-pooling mutual groups on rotating basis known as *iqqub* (in *Amharic*) were completely absent. The complex web of social networks, which bound the intricately interwoven intra- and inter-household and group relationships of the communities, no longer functioned. In other words, in the early days of resettle-

collection and analysis on diverse socio-economic and cultural aspects of resettlers from the entire resettlement villages as well as market trading and interaction data from weekly markets inside the resettlement area (e.g. L4, L7, L14 and R49) and those neighbouring the scheme area (e.g., Chagni, Gilgel Beles, Mandura, and Mambuk). For further details of the market exchange study, see Berterame and Magni (1988).

ment, the various communities' close bonds and webs of relationships along several local institutional arrangements were lost and their livelihood impoverished in the new setting.

Resettlement has affected the very family set-up of couples. On the one hand, either one of the partners abandoned her or his spouse right at the initial stage of choosing for resettlement, mainly influenced by either joining the scheme or remaining with consanguinal kin (mostly true for women due to the viri-local marriage). On the other hand, after tasting the bitter experience in the resettlement area at the early stage, again many resettlers with few or no children abandoned their partners partly for similar reasons. Resettlers got married without the usual proper ceremonies, due to the difficulties they were encountering. Thus, resettlement brought about the break-up of families, and those marriages which were established during the height of the problem were rather loose and resulted in abandonment and easy separation of partners. In particular, many of the abandoned or separated women have had difficulties in finding new partners in the resettlement site. There are more widows than widowers. Based on my personal observation, a woman's chance of re-marriage after having many children or late in life was very low in the area. In the case of divorce, men had higher chance of re-marriage than women had. In this aspect, resettlement has worsened the situation of women more than men.

The Beles Valley has only one harvest season a year. The rainfall in the new area is abundant and heavy, with frequent thunder, hailstorms and wind. On the other hand, the heat of the dry season is also very strong, with the resulting common wild bush fire that frequently destroys field crops. Such fires are unknown in the highlands. The highland crops and cropping season have been changed, and resettlers began adjusting to lowland farming systems. The hot environment in the lowlands had tremendous adverse effects on the adaptive adjustments of highland peasants.

In line with the change of the type of crops produced in the new context, the food habits of the resettlers were also changed. For the resettlers of south-west Ethiopia, whose main staple foods were *enset* and tubers, foods prepared exclusively out of lowland cereal crops are relatively new. They were not at all able to practice their intricate web of livelihoods based on *enset* culture in the new location because the climate of the new location is not conducive for growing *enset*. As a result, all *enset*-related rituals in their daily life are left only as memories, creating nostalgia and spiritual ties with the homelands. On the other hand, the northern Ethiopian resettlers have also re-adjusted themselves to the food prepared from crops they are newly introduced to in the lowlands. Both the southern and northern resettlers are equally critical of feeding maize porridge to their wives during maternity as opposed to the barley porridge in the origins of the northern peasants and *bu'illa* porridge (a Kambaata word for the best part of *enset* foods) of southern peasants. According to the respective resettlers, both *bu'illa* and barley have high nutritional and cultural values.

More than anything else, resettlement brought resettlers into direct contact with new communities. Resettlers were amazed by their first contact with the indigenous Gumuz in the new location. The autochthonous Gumuz used to lead a quite different socio-economic and cultural way of life as opposed to the one practised in the areas of the highland resettlers. They are also different in their darker pigmentation. Coupled with the difference in the socio-economic way of life as well as the marginalisation and expropriation of resources that belonged by tradition to the autochthonous Gumuz, there occurred fierce ethnic conflicts that caused loss of lives on both sides (cf. chapter 11). This is the bitterest experience for both the hosts and resettlers brought about by the inadequately planned resettlement scheme in contrast to their previous better secure way of life.

Many resettlers were forced to evacuate the Beles Valley because of the difficulties of adaptation to the inhospitable environment, new dietary habits imposed by the scheme, suffering caused by the prevalent diseases (malaria, tuberculosis, and asthma), lack of incentives to undertake agricultural activities, and nostalgia for homeland to reunite with separated families and relatives. As earlier described, the size of the resettled population dropped from 82,106 in 1987 and 1988 to 26,660 in 1993 and 1994 (cf. chapter 6, table 11).

After the 1991 political changes in Ethiopia, which brought about the downfall of the *Derg* regime and the formation of a new coalition Government of the EPRDF, part of the resettlers that remained in the scheme in the Beles Valley moved and reshuffled within the different villages inside the area. In addition, new populations searching for opportunities immigrated down the valley. Despite all the adversities, a substantial number of resettlers remained in the Beles Valley resettlement scheme area. The resettlers who remained in the area by then could be characterised as falling into three categories – those who have no alternative place of settlement either in their area of origin or elsewhere in the country, those who were incapacitated or weak, and those who had still seen opportunities in the resettlement areas and believed there was a livelihood to be made.

167

Impact on the Host Community: Displacement and Marginalisation of the Autochthonous Gumuz

Except for serious criticisms in rhetoric about the adverse effects of resettlement upon the livelihoods of the host populations in resettlement sites, it has had little consideration in practice. Salem-Murdock (1993:307) explains that "there has been little consideration of the effects of such forced movements on host communities. This general reluctance to investigate further into the welfare of host populations parallels the usual treatment of gender and social soundness analysis in project documents: mandated in policy and ignored in practice." He stresses a generally observed tendency of showing reluctance to investigate further into the welfare of the host communities, which are severely affected by the serious adverse effects of resettlement schemes at relocation sites.

Similarly, in the operations of the resettlement schemes, the host communities have been neglected in the relocation sites in Ethiopia in general and that of the Beles Valley in Metekel in particular. For instance, Kloos and Aynalem (1988:162) noted the impacts of state-sponsored emergency resettlement on the host communities of the receiving peripheral lowland areas (especially on those practising livelihood strategies different from that of the highlanders due to the unique ecological contexts) as: "In the haste in which the resettlement program was carried out, the indigenous shifting cultivation/hunting/gathering population was not considered in the development process, with the result that their resource base is being destroyed." Considering the impact of resettlement on the host autochthonous peoples at the relocation sites in the country's western peripheries, A. Pankhurst (1997:555) noted the following.

> For the local inhabitants the resettlement, which was imposed upon them without consultation, consent or compensation, dispossessed them of resources, forced changes in their settlement and livelihood patterns and threatened the environment upon which they depend. Particularly in the lowlands, the settlements have resulted in a further marginalisation of the local people who resorted to traditional strategies of avoidance in the face of state impositions. Relations with the settlers were primarily mediated by the exchanges in the markets, which were also the loci of conflicts. Despite minor benefits in terms of services, schools, clinics and roads, and the development of trade and small towns, the influx of settlers, the appropriation of land and other resources and the encroachment of the market economy has had negative economic effects on the subsistence economy and potentially disastrous long-term effects on the ecology.

The Gumuz in Metekel suffered a loss of resources, space and autonomy, without having had any say in the matter. The resettlement operation has taken away their traditional resources. As a result, they were pushed and retreated further into the remaining forest abandoning their former settlement, cultivation and fallow fields, and burial and ritual sites. The scheme alienated the Gumuz from their livelihood resources such as land, forest, and water. The appropriation of land by the scheme has denied them access to forest and other resources traditionally accessible to them. The scheme further increased population densities competing for natural resources (cf. chapter 5 "State-Sponsored Resettlement of the 1980s").

In the process of the resettlement exercise, all government and aid organisations involved in the program were preferentially treating the resettlers, marginalising the Gumuz. The scheme has disregarded the Gumuz and no single effort was made to incorporate them. They were neglected in the provision of all sorts of support extended to resettlers. Rather, armed soldiers and local Militia recruited from the resettlers guarded the resettlement area against local incursions on the scheme.

Following the resettlement program, the influx of immigrants coming to the area looking for opportunities has grown. This has increased the pressure on their land resources. The increased livestock of resettlers and later immigrants browsing inside the forests compacts the soils (making it difficult for shifting cultivation using simple traditional hand tools) and destroys the edible bamboo sprouts that serve as an important source of food for the autochthonous Gumuz

Critically aware of the negative consequences of the resettlement scheme upon their livelihood, the Gumuz showed hostile attitudes towards the resettlers. The hostilities between the two groups developed not only because the former lost part of their resources, but also because they have remained marginalised from the support extended to the resettlers. Additionally, the socio-economic and cultural differences between the two categories of people have also posed a potential threat to the conflicts. This could be either due to lack of clear understanding of each other's traditions and ways of lives, or completely uncompromising disregard and contempt to the "other's" way of life (reported usually true to the attitudes of the resettlers towards Gumuz).

Meanwhile, as a coping reaction towards the consequences of the wide range of encroachments, the Gumuz are showing changes in their livelihood strategies especially in the emerging renting land institutional arrangements of fallow fields with the plow cultivators (cf. chapter 12, section 12.4).

7.2 Environmental Impact

The Resettlement Scheme

Scudder (1999:360), in his 1999 Malinowiski Award Lecture, explains the serious adverse effects of resettlement on the environment based on his long-term socio-anthropological research on the Kariba resettlement scheme in Zambezi Valley as follows:

> My own research highlights the speed with which development-induced resettlement can cause environmental degradation when population densities exceed the carrying capacity of the land under existing systems of land and water use. In the Lusitu area of the middle Zambezi Valley, I estimate that the carrying capacity of the land was exceeded by at least a factor of three when 6,000 Gwembe Tonga were moved there in the late 1950s in connection with the construction of the Kariba Dam. Today, what was formerly a well-vegetated savannah woodland looks like a degraded Sahelian habitat on the edge of the Sahara. Occurring within a single generation, this transformation was the worst-case of environmental degradation [...].

Similar to the facts presented in Scudder's argument, the increased population density both by the resettlers and the influx of immigrants has dramatically increased pressure on the natural resource base in the Beles Valley resettlement scheme area. In addition to the increasing competition for natural resources, the different rivalling farming system of the highland resettlers (plow cultivation) against that of the autochthonous Gumuz (integral shifting cultivation), aggravated the damaging environmental consequences. Large areas of forests have been indiscriminately cleared, accelerating soil erosion, extinguishing the flora and fauna and creating an imbalance on the ecosystem of the area, which was originally covered with a dense forest of bamboo and other tree species.

However, the forest cover has been continuously cleared since the commencement of the resettlement scheme in 1985 up to the present for farmlands, village settlements, construction, fuel wood, charcoal production and other infrastructural construction. As a result, the forest cover has been swiftly diminishing and access to forest resources has become very scarce in many cases. At the moment, due to the pressure of increasing number and category of inhabitants both in the villages and the emerging small towns as well as construction activities taking place by private, government and non-government organisations, the demand for wood, bamboo, and thatching grass has dramatically increased in the area. Thus, as intermittently pointed out in this study, the ceaseless encroachment in general and the resettlement scheme of the 1980s in particular had been destroying the forests of the area.

The Immigrant Farmers

The adverse effects of the influx of immigrants on the natural environment and the livelihood of the local people are immense. As earlier stated, the number of the highland immigrant farmers moved into the resettlement area as of February-March 2001 is estimated to be 6,858 (cf. chapter 6 "Different Categories of Population", table 12). The land tenure status of these immigrant farmers has not yet been secured with official recognition by the local *woreda* administration. Ideally, it is the resettlers who are considered to be the legitimate owners of the land resources of the resettlement scheme area. The total number of former resettler population, as of February-March, 2001 is estimated to be 30,513 (cf. chapter 6, table 12). Compared with the resettlers, the capacity of the immigrant farmers is very strong since they moved to the valley "voluntarily" together with their livestock including traction animals. This enabled them to clear large plots of forestlands in the peripheries of the main plots of the resettlers, adding pressure on the forest resources of the area.

Additionally, the tenure insecurity of the immigrant farmers has acted as a serious cause of forest destruction, forcing them to focus more on short-term yield increase than preserving the resources for long-term use. As a result, they are accused of peeling off the barks of big mother trees in their field and drying and destroying them for expansion of farming fields. They are accused of the drying of these trees more than other farmers because of the temporary nature of their land holdings. The main explanation of the farmers about their action of peeling bark and drying indigenous mother trees is just to prevent the yield reduction of their crops under the shade of the trees. This act of indiscriminate destruction of the indigenous natural forest is causing grave consequences on the natural environment and the livelihood of the people.

The Tana-Beles Project

A year after the commencement of the Beles Valley emergency resettlement, on the 29th of March 1986, the Italian Government-funded project known as the "Tana-Beles Project" officially began its work. The basic objective of the Italian assistance was to develop a self-sustained economy for the region aimed at, in addition to emergency aid, economic self-sufficiency and self-management (Salini costruttori 1989:8f.). The first part of the project activities included: Supply of personal items to the resettlers; implementation and development of rain-fed agriculture and introduction of irrigated agriculture; and construction and expansion of the infrastructure (e.g., water supply, roads, health facilities, airport, radio communication, project centre, pipe-factory, agro-industrial factories, a big garage, warehouses, mechanised irrigation complexes, office and residential complexes, and two dams on the main and little Beles Rivers).

Except for its later serious drawbacks on the sustainability of its top-down and high-tech interventions, initially the operation of the project has greatly improved the emergency conditions of the resettlement area. Since the project was developed in the *Derg* regime's development policy framework, it had emphasised agricultural collectivisation. Additionally, the project was criticised for its high-tech centralised approach and severely constraining those small more adaptive and innovative small-scale initiatives of the household economy. Hence, critically commenting on these shortcomings of the project, Agneta et al. (1993:275) noted the following.

> The Beles project focused mainly on the infrastructural development of the area where people had already been moved, rather than proposing a range of solutions to basic problems such as the self-sustainability of the households, the diversification of the farming systems, the integration of the resettlement area into a regional economy, and the negotiation of conflicts deriving from host-settler disputes over land use and over the share of benefits resulting from the project.

Resettlers in the Beles Valley were assigned to work in the agricultural scheme that was collectively organised on a co-operative basis where their products were stored in the village warehouses and then distributed according to a point system classifying their labour efforts. The entire agricultural work was operated by the project, which carried out a mechanised tillage of around 23,000 hectares (Salini Costruttori 1989:14). The project enabled the different resettlement villages to have access to facilities that are not available in most Ethiopian rural villages. These facilities include an all-weather gravelled-road network of around 300 kilometres length which made all villages accessible; a pipeline of drinking water supplied from reservoirs; warehouses of 10,000 *quintals* capacity in each village; grain-mills and generators for mills; a modern regional hospital at the centre of the area and clinics in all villages; a malaria eradication centre; new corrugated sheet roofed housing; and primary schools. The project has managed to implement its multiple planned schemes including the road networks, agro-industrial processing facilities, pipe factory, health facilities, water supplies, the two dams, cleared fields, project management offices, residential quarters, project logistical base, and several related schemes.

The project's operational approach was based on highly centralised top-down decision making with massive interventions, having fundamental implications of artificial, rapid, and imposed socio-economic change relying on a strategy of collective production.[8]

The project's highly mechanised technology and capital-intensive co-operative agricultural development approach was not appropriate to the attainment of sustainability for the resettlers. Its operations encountered serious shortcomings after the 1991 political change. As stated above, several of its implemented schemes have collapsed after the change of the government and were not sustainable. Considering the environmental aspect alone, the project has indiscriminately cleared forest from both black waterlogged and red soil areas without proper land use planning. Those black soils used for rice production through mechanised tillage were left abandoned without forest cover after the collapse of the project. As a result, the large expanses of cleared, but abandoned black soil fields are exposed to soil erosion, causing serious implications on the microenvironment.

---

[8] A detailed account of the Italian aid funds granted to the "Tana Beles Project", according to Agneta et al. (1993:276f.), is described as follows: "For the Beles scheme, an initial grant of about 270 billion Italian lire was earmarked by the FAI (Italian Aid Fund), a special body set up by the Ministry of Foreign Affairs between 1985 and 1987 for emergency operations in Third World countries. As of July 1989, the funds already allocated and those meanwhile committed reached a total of over 406 billion lire, that is, about US$290 million. This figure includes: money spent by the main project (implemented by an Italian contractor, a principal consultant, and a monitoring structure surveillance); food aid; drugs supply; and NGO programs.

It is difficult to estimate the real per capita costs of resettlement in the Beles Valley. Even setting aside the costs covered by the Ethiopian government before the Italian project began and considering only the sum committed on the Italians, we obtain the remarkable figure of US$3,625 per capita so far allocated since the start of Italian aid in 1986. Because such an impressive amount of foreign financing went into the Beles Project, it is atypical of resettlement schemes in Ethiopia and conditions of life in the area should therefore be well above the average. That conditions remain so stark despite the enormous expenditure remains the most powerful argument for improving the understanding of how resettlement works."

On the other hand, the pre-1983 per capita cost of resettlement schemes in Ethiopia, according to Clay and Holcomb (1986, cited in Agneta et al 1993:276), is estimated at "1,400 Ethiopian *birr* (about US$676) for clothing, food, housing, and household material." Moreover, in the "Ethiopian Highland Reclamation Study", Samuels (1985, cited in Agneta et al. 1993:276) "puts the average cost of resettlement at 2,338 Ethiopian *birr* per capita (US$1,129) in Special Settlement Schemes and at 802 Ethiopian *birr* per capita (US$387) in Low Cost Settlement Scheme." (At the time of the estimate, the exchange rate of US$1=2.07 Ethiopian *birr*. However, now the exchange rate of US$1 for instance as of March 1, 2002 is 8.5611 Ethiopian *birr* based on a daily inter-bank foreign exchange market deals.)

The other two major implemented schemes of the project with serious environmental consequences were the two dams built on the main Beles River (meant for motor-pump irrigation) and little Beles River (major tributary to the main Beles and meant for potable water distribution in the entire scheme area).

The dam built on the main Beles River by the project was meant for irrigation. However, it is hard to believe that the intended objective of the dam was to irrigate fields up the slopes by pumping its waters using motor-pumps. It is easier simply to imagine how feasible would be the productivity and sustainability of the scheme in terms of cost-benefit analysis. The adverse effect of this dam is visible on the biotic resources mostly at the upper course of the river, which was flooded by the reservoir causing serious micro-environmental consequences.

The other dam built for the purpose of supplying potable water to the entire resettlement villages, is the one constructed on the Gilgel Beles River. The construction of the dam and its accompanying 180 km water pump installation scheme was one of the major components of the Tana-Beles project operations in the area. Of course, during the fresh period of project life, the intended objective of this component of the project functioned, and the villages managed to have access to potable waters from the installations.

However, the whole reservoir now has been totally filled with silt on top of which grasses and vegetation have fully grown. It was reported that draining the silt is impossible. Since the reservoir is completely full with silt, the river is flowing along a course created in the silt with no water reservoir. As a result, the potable water services to the villages are adversely affected and villagers are fetching water from rivers and streams.

The activities of the project attracted a considerable influx of people looking for opportunities. Private business activities have also brought to the area a certain distribution of cash that provided resettlers an increased purchasing power. The influx of the people for opportunities together with the complex establishments of the project facilitated the emergence of small towns, which at the beginning used to act as periodic rural market exchange centres and project management sites. On the other, as stated earlier, the influx of the immigrants added pressure on the resources of the area. Specially, the forest has been cleared for expanding farm plots, village settlements, infrastructure facilities, construction, fuel wood, charcoal production and other multiple needs aggravating the environmental consequences.

Chapter 8. Socio-Cultural Rearticulation and Livelihood Adaption

8.1 Socio-Cultural Rearticulation and Livelihood Reconstruction

After the initial phase of emergency and transition, resettlers in the Beles Valley who did not either succumb to illness or move away began adapting themselves to the new context. Entrepreneurial activities such as trade and market exchange were found to be one of the best and significant adaptive strategies. Considering the experiences of resettlers in the Beles Valley, Berterame and Magni (1988:271) noted: "The resettled groups after a first period of emergency and a lack of social and cultural references, reorganised themselves and developed a more or less adaptive behaviour towards the new context. The role of trade and markets in such a situation is central to satisfy the basic needs of the settler households."

Though markets signal economic activity in the new context, they were highly controlled by the authorities, being considered as distracting occasions which affect campaign co-operative work in the field. However, despite the repeated effort of the authorities to curtail them, markets emerged and displayed significant economic dynamism. Another important adaptive strategy pursued by the resettlers was working in handicraft activities of diverse types. Agneta et al. (1993:275) pointed out activities such as managing backyard plots[9], market exchange, and handicraft to be among the main adaptive strategies undertaken by the resettlers because the main field production was organised collectively under the system of producers' co-operatives.

As earlier noted, except for its later serious drawbacks on the sustainability, initially the operation Tana-Beles project greatly improved the emergency conditions of the resettlement area. However, the project's excessive handout approach created a dependency mentality and undermined resettlers' own efforts to achieve self-reliance. Despite the problems, the activities of the Tana-Beles Project attracted a considerable influx of people looking for opportunities and employment. Associated private business activities also brought to the area an injection of cash and investment leading to in-

---

[9] Based on my extended personal observation, the backyard plots (0.1 hectare) was the only field area under the full management of the households. Resettlers' farming experiences in the origins were reflected in the management of these backyard plots. For instance, the backyard management of south-western resettlers (Kambaata-Hadiyya-Wolaita) were mostly oriented towards cultivating maize, tubers (sweet potato, taro, and yam) and tobacco, part of which is meant for market exchange. Whereas, the backyard management of north-central resettlers (Amhara, Tigraway, Agaw, Oromo) were mostly devoted to maize cultivation meant for home consumption.

175

creased purchasing power. Through the influx of the people for opportunities and business activities together with the complex establishments of the project, small towns emerged as exchange centres at different locations in the area.

In the resettlement scheme, only those activities considered by the planners as marginal were left to the resettler households. In the absence of sectional support and encouragement, resettlers showed initiative and independence through the management of activities with conscious evaluations of the benefits of supplementary income. Despite the local authorities' efforts to hamper them, periodic markets developed to trade home gardening products, handicraft products, grain, livestock, spices and clothing. Resettlers opted for alternative adaptive strategies because the economy of ration was not sufficient to guarantee their survival. Their engagement in exchange, trading and similar socio-economic activities strengthened their social networks within the resettlement villages and neighbouring areas. So, resettlers proved to be innovative and dynamic in their adaptive strategies[10].

Rebuilding a social identity was one of the strongest needs felt in the new context (cf. chapter 10). Religious beliefs of the different ethnic groups began to be re-established. Ethnic identity was found to be important, and attempts were made to maintain it in the resettlement villages. Marriage was strengthened, particularly among resettlers who belonged to the same ethnic background. Through the marriage ties of the sons and daughters, affinal kin groups began being established between the families of the spouses. The different ethnic groups had shown integrative relations. However, the relations between the indigenous Gumuz and resettlers remained mostly in conflict (cf. chapter 11).

Marriage ceremonies, which in the early years of resettlement were conducted without the correct rituals and other associate practices, now take the form expected with respected elders and religious leaders once again playing the significant role in facilitating the process of marriage. The role of elders has regained importance in other aspects of village life. For example, elders in the respective communities now have a role in settling disputes arising between households, within households and at the village level. Increasingly, they advise, guide, and punish defaulters according to custom and take responsibility for teaching the importance of culturally accepted values

---

[10] For further details on the dynamic and innovative adaptive strategies of resettlers in the Beles Valley, see also Agneta et al. (1993), Berterame and Magni (1988), Dieci and Viezzoli (1992), Agdaw and Wolde-Selassie (1992), Dieci and Wolde-Selassie (1992),Betru and Wolde-Selassie (1995), and Wolde-Selassie (1997a, 1998, 2000a).

and norms. Elders encourage and motivate self-support among resettlers, they visit the weak and disabled, console the family of the deceased and perform other vital social services.

Associations based around the Orthodox, Protestant, Catholic churches, and Moslem mosques in the sites have emerged to extend support to their weaker members and in many cases have become the main source of livelihood. Hand-in-hand with the re-establishment of the different churches, the church leadership, comprised mostly of the elderly, has also re-emerged. They strongly preach to be faithful to one's own religion and observe the proper performances of followers respecting the percept of the religions. They perform the daily prayers of their religion for the salvation of the souls of the dead. Moreover, they have a key role in consoling bereaved families through their frequent prayers and visits. More than anything else, the very re-emergence of the belief systems has created a bright optimistic hope among the resettler communities and is contributing their adaptation.

Iddir, which was totally absent at the time of the resettlers' arrival, managed to be revitalised with the household as the basic unit for a membership. The present *iddir* of the villages are all across ethnic and religious boundaries based on the composition of the respective village inhabitants. Apart from the well-established *iddir* for burial and mourning, there are now *iddir* for oxen (a kind of insuring mechanism), and for transporting the sick to the hospital (the stretcher society). The different *iddir* are administered by an elected wise and respected *dagna* (chief), and those who fail to make contributions to the funds are punished severely (cf. chapter 9 for more detailed discussion).

Resettlers also managed to re-establish *mahber* and *senbete*, mutual religious festive associations mainly among the followers of the Orthodox Church. The *mahber* members meet once in a month in each other's houses, rotating in the name of a selected saint and enjoy food and drinks at the same time as performing prayers for their spiritual gratification. The *senbete* members meet every two weeks, rotating among members, holding feasts in the compound of the village church together with those disabled and weak members that come in search of food. At the same time, priests perform prayers. Both the *mahber* and *senbete* are formed across ethnic boundaries, and mutual support is extended to members as demanded both on good and bad occasions.

With the re-establishment of smallholder household production systems, resettlers' social organisation of production has also re-emerged. The social organisation of production among resettlers in the Beles Valley is centred around various work groups. These include *dabo* (festive labour), *wonfel* (reciprocal labour), *amicha* (affinal kin based festive labour), *balnjeera* (intimate friendship based festive labour which also known as *elfinna-qaso* among the south-western resettlers), *waari/maarfeja/toori* (supportive labour for the weak at the early hours in the morning before resettler-farmers go to their daily tasks), and *limmaano* (full-time supportive labour mostly for the disabled needy). These community level self-supportive organisations have re-emerged and further strengthened mainly based on the re-establishment of the smallholder cultivation managed by the households (cf. chapter 9).

In the present Beles Valley situation, resettlers have established complex social relations[11] both within the resettlement area as well as with the neighbouring population through marriage, religion, work groups, land exchange, bond-friendship, fictive parenthood, god-parenthood as well as on the basis of the individual's entrepreneurial ability in interacting with others. Individuals within the networks of relations exchange a great deal through their interaction. For instance, oxenless resettlers get support of oxen through their relations, and those without cash can gain access to loans. Based on established relations, some of the village resettler traders mobilise village-level grain purchase for merchants and earn commissions. In the field of agricultural activities, resettlers who have established better networks of social relations are capable of mobilising an enormous amount of festive labour, which makes a significant contribution to the success of livelihood strategies. Thus, the re-emergence of household economy coupled with the individual initiatives, innovation, and industriousness act as key elements in the resettlers' adaptation, re-vitalisation, and reconstruction of livelihoods even in the absence of properly established sectoral support. As resettlers adjust their social arrangements and their productive activities, there is witnessed a strengthening of socio-cultural rearticulation. This social rearticulation propelled economic recovery and livelihood reconstruction at large. A detailed account of the multiple social institutions and their vital role in securing livelihood in the new context is discussed thoroughly in the next chapter.

---

[11] Such vital complex networks of relations, according to Downing (1996), are the underlying social fabric and life-support mechanisms that were dismantled initially in the relocation process of resettlement (cf. chapter 2).

8.2 Modes of Livelihood in the New Context

Means of Livelihood[12]

After arriving in the Beles Valley since 1985 and having experienced around a decade of stagnation or even decline, resettler farmers are now showing remarkable flexibility and imagination, making the best of their access to and control over key resources such as land, livestock, labour, and cash income. In the present Beles Valley context, resettlers' livelihoods are based on both agricultural production as well as non-agricultural income-generating activities. The dominant agricultural activity is crop production together with substantial livestock raising, and crop-livestock integration. In addition, considerable horticulture and apiculture is practised, and many resettlers undertake on-farm and off-farm income-generating activities in order to diversify households' income sources.

Crop Production
Crop production is the main means of livelihood of resettler farmers, all of whom are plow cultivators. The major crops they produce include sorghum, finger millet, maize, sesame, ground-nuts, rice, chickpea, niger-seed, tobacco, and hot-pepper. In addition, they grow other crops on a lesser scale, such as cowpea, haricot beans, tobacco, cotton, sweet potato, taro, and cumin. The resettlers' seasonal cropping and labour calendar of activities are described in table 19.

Even though the magnitude differs on the basis of different ethno-cultural background, all women actively participate at all levels of field crop production activities. However, in the absence of their husbands, women heads of households shoulder a heavy responsibility of managing the household alone. Lack of male family labour, in the absence of adult sons, is the basic constraint that forces them to give out land on the basis of either sharecropping or rental arrangements.

---

[12] As already pointed out (cf. chapter 2 "Sustainable Rural Livelihoods"), a livelihood is defined as comprising the capabilities (what people can do or be with their entitlements), assets (including both material and social resources) and activities required for a means of living (Carswell 1997, Scoones 1998). Ellis (1998:4) elaborates a livelihood to be more than just income and explains as: 'A livelihood encompasses income, both cash and in kind, as well as the social institutions (kin, family, compound, village and so on); gender relations: and property rights required to support and to sustain a given standard of living'. A livelihood is considered to be sustainable if it can cope with, and recover from, stresses and shocks, maintain or enhance its capabilities and assets both now and in the future without undermining the natural resource base (Carswell 1997, Scoones 1998, Hussein and Nelson 1998).

Table 19: Seasonal Cropping and Labour Calendar of Activities

Months of the Year	Crop Production Activities
Megabit (March)	• Very late threshing; • Field clearing (cutting, up-rooting and burning bush from the field plot); • Preparing farm tools for plowing (plow, yoke, and others related); • Training young oxen; • Cutting roof-thatching grass; • Constructing or repairing residential houses and fencing; • Very early plowing; and • Manual hoeing/digging of plots by oxen-less farmers.
Miazia (April)	• Preparing backyard plot for planting; • Field plowing continues for various crops; and • Sowing sorghum, red finger millet, and maize after the middle of the month.
Ginbot (May)	• Sowing sorghum, red finger millet and maize; • Plowing for other crops; and • Planting groundnuts.
Sene (June)	• Peak planting/sowing month; • Plowing continues for other crops; • Sowing sesame, rice, black finger millet, groundnuts, cotton, hot-pepper and cow-pea; and • Early weeding of backyard plantations, sorghum and maize begins.
Hamle (July)	• Weeding of sorghum and maize continues; and weeding finger millet, sesame, ground-nuts, hot- pepper begins; and • Sowing black-finger millet, sesame, groundnuts, cotton, and hot-pepper is completed and weeding of the early sown same crops begins.
Nehase (August)	• Late sowing of sesame and hot-pepper is completed by the first week of the month; • Peak weeding of various crops demanding the highest field labour of the season; and • Sowing niger-seed.
Meskerem (September)	• Weeding activity continues; • Early sowing of chick pea; • Late sowing of niger-seed; and • Protecting crops against wild animals.

Tikimt **(October)**	<ul><li>Complete weeding except the final weeding (*Geraafo* (Amh.)) for sorghum;</li><li>Sowing chick pea;</li><li>Protecting crops against wild animals; and</li><li>Harvesting for maize, sesame, groundnuts, cowpea, haricot beans, and finger millet.</li></ul>
Hidar **(November)**	<ul><li>Main harvesting time for rice, groundnuts, finger millet, and early maturing sorghum;</li><li>Cutting hay for livestock;</li><li>Early threshing for sesame, ground-nuts, and related others; and</li><li>Early harvesting of sorghum.</li></ul>
Tahsas **(December)**	<ul><li>Peak harvesting, transporting, and piling season for sorghum, finger millet, and related others severely threatened by emerging bush fire outbreak;</li><li>Most busiest month of the crop season due to the fire outbreak and needs highest labour next to weeding; and</li><li>Early and medium threshing month.</li></ul>
Tir **(January)**	<ul><li>Peak threshing, transporting and storage month mainly for sorghum and finger millet;</li><li>Constructing granary and storage containers of various sizes; and</li><li>Early manual hoeing/digging of backyard plot by oxen-less farmers.</li></ul>
Yekatit **(February)**	<ul><li>Late threshing of finger millet and sorghum;</li><li>Main manual digging/hoeing of plots by oxen-less farmers;</li><li>Preparing different farm tools for the next season;</li><li>Early field plot clearing;</li><li>Training young oxen;</li><li>Constructing or repairing residence and fencing; and</li><li>Relative breath-taking period with weddings and several feasts.</li></ul>

Obviously, the livelihood of the resettler farmers depends upon the crops they produce meant both for consumption and exchange. Since they cannot grow everything needed for their life, they exchange part of their produce. They sell from their crops, buying other necessities. The basic items they buy include spices and legumes for sauce, clothing, medicines for humans and livestock. The income from the crops is also used to pay land-tax. Farmers also use the income to cover several costs of weddings, *iddir*, *mahber*, and other important social events. Moreover, they save from the income generated from crops mostly to buy livestock – the most important asset in their context. Among the livestock, oxen are the basic assets and key resources of the farming households. For farmers, traction oxen mean more income, which in turn leads the households towards further improvement in their social and economic status. The marketing of crops has a key role in the farmers' livelihood. In the area, farmers grow both food and cash crops. The main food crops are sorghum, finger millet, maize, and rice, whereas cash crops produced mainly for exchange include sesame, groundnuts, and niger-seed.

Animal Husbandry
Livestock raising is an important component means of the resettlers' livelihood. Most resettlers re-started life from scratch in the new context, because they have been moved and relocated mostly bare-handed. Their very existence was based on their monthly rations. In addition, the resettlement program itself was ideally viewed as a kind of leveller with a motto of collective agriculture. Except for the section of those resettlers from Gojjam who moved to the area with their livestock, many resettlers owned no livestock at the beginning. However, as the resettlers spent more time in the new context, they began re-introducing livestock, first, with smaller animals such as chicken and then, goats. Slowly they began owning livestock despite the severe threat of *trypanosomiasis*. The ownership of livestock, basically oxen, showed a tremendous increase with the increasing demand for draught animals with the re-introduction of smallholder farming as a result of the collapse of collectivisation. The concentration of livestock ownership has also varied with the increasing differentiation in the crop production and sources of income by the households due to the reintroduction of systems of individual ownership of farms by the households.

The draught animals (oxen) are one of the key resources of the farming households. Farmers also use cows for traction in the new context, at times pairing them with oxen. Moreover, some farmers were innovative enough to use donkeys for traction. They explained the multiple importance of donkeys as a) donkeys plow longer hours than oxen; b) donkeys are relatively more trypano-tolerant; c) they are cheaper and less risky; d) they do of course serve as pack animals; e) donkeys can be used for trading or can be rented to traders; and f) donkeys demand lesser care and fodder than oxen. However, it is difficult to plow with donkeys in the months of heavy rain when the fields are wet and muddy, in which the sharp and thin hooves of donkeys will be stuck in the muddy fields (in contrast to the broader and split hooves of oxen that resist muddy fields). According to resettler informants in the research sites, the immigrant farmers from Birr-Sheleqo in western Gojjam have introduced traction with donkeys to the area.

Resettler farmers who raise livestock depend mostly on the sale of, first smaller animals such as goats, sheep, and chicken; and then, cattle as the need for the income becomes higher. They opt for the sale of livestock mainly either due to lack of surplus crop produce or due to lower crop prices, which cannot generate the necessary income needed. But, they can also sell livestock for several other purposes. In addition, households owning quite a substantial amount of livestock (mostly resettlers from Gojjam) generate income from the sale of milk products, mainly butter.

On the other hand, apiculture is practised and used as an alternative source of income for those bee-keeping households as a sideline activity. The area is traditionally known for its honey and bee-resources. Many resettlers undertake bee-keeping as a supplementary activity to support and diversify the household income, apart from consumption. They use traditional bamboo-woven round hollow beehives for bee-keeping. In order to attract bees, they first hang the hives on the branches of big trees mostly inside a forest along the banks of rivers. Once the bees enter into the hives, farmers bring them home. At home, they arrange a place behind the residential house either constructing a high wooden platform and shelter or simply hanging the hives on the veranda. However, farmers complained about the very nature and behaviour of the bees of the area and called them *shifta* (bandits). This is because many of the bees are liable to go away when the honey is extracted. So they stressed that it is difficult to depend on apiculture as a reliable resource. On the other hand, it is also easy to get the bees since they readily enter the hives when they are hung on trees. The bee-keeping farmers complained about the bee-keeping because these bees are wild and not familiar with human harvesting of the honey. According to these farmers, the bees are more familiar with living and making honey in the caves of stones along rivers and in the hollow parts of big trees where the honey produced is not harvested away like those domesticated in the bee-hives. Since these places are less accessible, the bees can safely stay without people taking their honey.

Entrepreneurship
By entrepreneurship is meant those micro-business activities performed by the members of the households either to diversify the income of the household or for mere survival. The local markets in the resettlement area are nodal points where the resettlers and the town dwellers, the highlanders and lowlanders, and resettlers and neighbouring inhabitants meet, interact and exchange products. In addition, these markets serve as meeting places for the resettler population with different ethno-cultural backgrounds from the different villages within the resettlement area for conducting both marketing and non-marketing activities. These market-places are places where multiple

183

micro-business activities take place. Out of the many entrepreneurial activities undertaken, the main ones include grain trade, livestock trade, and several other petty trading activities.

Those pulse crops such as field pea, feba-beans, vetch (*guaya* in Amharic), and lentils as well as cereals such as barley, wheat, and *teff*, which do not grow in the resettlement site, are brought to the area by grain traders from the neighbouring highland areas. Many resettler family members are engaged in this activity. Some of these traders perform a two-way task taking out cheaper grain from the resettlement area and bringing in the expensive grain to the area in exchange based on demand. Many better-off farmers in villages buy and gather grains from the village farmers and channel it to the big traders, earning commissions and thereby profiting from their service.

Trading cattle and goats is performed mostly by rich farmers, who are capable of running the enterprise as a means of income diversification. However, some medium but active farmers make arrangements with similar traders of the neighbouring areas and run the business jointly. Here, even those poor members engaged in the accompanying of the livestock can also get a share after the sale of the animals. Many of the inhabitants in R8 and R9 benefit from their linkages with those goat traders of Gondar coming through Jawe – an area that borders theirs. At times, they buy it from the traders themselves at a cheaper price and sell it back at a higher price, making substantial profit.

Women trade malt and flour. In order to sell malt, they first buy the grain, process it, and after a couple of days they produce malt by transforming its value and sell back, making a substantial profit. Moreover, they buy grain (cereals), take it to the grain mill, get it milled and then sell the flour, generating a modest income. On the other hand, men buy livestock (cattle, sheep and goats) butcher them in the open market or in a shop and sell the meat, making profit out of it. Distilling local spirit (*araqe*) and brewing *borde* and *tella* (main local beers prepared from sorghum, finger millet and maize in that context) are main income-generating sources for women on market days. Such an activity is done mostly in the dry months after completing harvest. The dry season is a time when grain is abundant. It is also a period of relative rest-taking and "leisure" after the heavy field labour and is full of local feasts. It is also a time when the purchasing power of customers is higher. Women are also engaged in the selling of the spirits which they bring from relatively cheaper neighbouring areas. However, women of the families following either Protestant Christianity or Muslims are neither engaged in brewing and distilling local alcoholic drinks nor in the sale for generating income.

As the smaller towns in the area grew in size, many poor farmers and their families began selling fuel wood to the dwellers. Farmers skilled in charcoal production are making attractive income mostly selling it to the town dwellers. Basically most farmers of food-deficit households depend highly on the sale of charcoal and fuel wood to the small town centres as a component source of their livelihood. A grass variety grown in some of the villages located in waterlogged areas is useful for making hand-woven grass-cords used for construction of local residential houses. Weaving the grass-cords and building the houses are performed in the dry months of the year after completing field harvests. As a result, farmers mostly from villages in those waterlogged areas are engaged in the production of grass-cords using the grass variety collected from the nearby fields and bush, and sell them mainly in the local market centres generating substantial amount of income.

Almost all inhabitants of the area (including both the town dwellers and residents in the villages) use dry grass to cover the roofs of their residential houses. Moreover, the same grass is also used to cover the roofs of the different offices in the area. Since the area is very hot, houses covered with grass are cooler and preferred for residences and offices. So, the roofs of those houses or offices covered with corrugated iron sheet metal are converted, their roofs being thatched with the grass layer upon the iron to make them cooler, friendly and hospitable. As a result, the demand for the dry roof-thatching grass is very high. However, the proper type of such grass is mostly in abundance in those heavy black soil villages and scarce in red-soil villages. In addition, the early dry months are the best time for cutting such grass. Otherwise, the prevalent forest/bush fire can easily destroy it. Therefore, in addition to home use, many farmers harvest this grass during the early dry months and store it in their compound.

The dense forest once covering the whole area of the present resettlement villages has been continuously cleared over the last fifteen years for farmland, villages, fuel wood, residential construction and other infrastructure buildings. As a result, the forest has been swiftly diminished and its easy access has also become difficult except for some of those bordering villages. At the moment, due to the increasing number and category of the inhabitants of both the villages and towns as well as construction activities taking place by private, government, and non-government organisations, the demand for wood and bamboo has increased dramatically in the area. Due to this fact, in addition to the home use, many farmers in the villages collect bamboo and construction wood from far-away forests and store them in their compounds. Then, by selling the bamboo and wood, they generate substantial income.

Many resettler families are engaged in undertaking diverse petty-trading activities to augment their household income. Among others, the main petty entrepreneurial activities include trading spices, vegetables and fruits, honey, butter, coffee, tobacco, and sundry items. Trading products like onion, garlic, and potato are mainly brought from the highland areas such as Chagni by truck-owners mostly by wholesalers. Then, local resettler traders buy from them and re-trade in the open local markets as well as in the villages. Many of the traded vegetables and fruits are the produce of the resettlers in their irrigated plots. Crops like wheat, barley, feba-beans, field-pea, vetch, and *teff* are mostly brought by the traders from the highland areas of Gojjam and Gondar. Coffee comes from outside the area mainly from Chagni market. Honey is partly the product of the resettlers but also comes from all the bordering areas of Metekel and Gondar. Sundry items are brought to the area through an extended network of traders starting from Addis Ababa. Tobacco leaves are mainly the produce of the resettlers. Ginger is also produced and sold by the Gumuz. Members of the resettler households trade these and other items in the local open markets of the area.

Income generated from seasonal casual or daily labour in the fields of better farmers in the peak seasons of weeding and harvesting is the basic source of livelihood for the poor but able farmers. Almost all healthy poor farmers and their family members of working age engage in daily labour activities in order to generate income and cope with the food shortage of the households.

Daily wage employment in the fields of better farmers is an important emerging source of income for many low-income food-deficit families. Job-seeking farmers of both sexes of working age come out early in the morning to a roadside usually with their hand tools (mainly at peak weeding and harvesting seasons) and await the employers who will pick them on the basis of prior working experience and physical strength. In the selection, women are preferred for weeding finger millet, rice and sesame; whereas, men are highly preferred for weeding sorghum and harvesting all crops. The ones who have not been selected by the employers will disperse after a while. Sometimes the same farmer who has rented out his land will be hired as a daily labourer in his own rented-out field. Some households send only part of the household labour to generate income while others are performing in the family plot. The daily employment opportunities are open in the fields of better farmers, immigrant farmers, town dwellers, Tana-Beles Project and investors. Daily employment, mostly by low-income food-deficit households, is found to be the best alternative income-generating source.

Agricultural Production Strategies[13]

In agricultural production, resettlers apply diverse but at the same time integrated production strategies, including cultivation of plots by their own draught animals, manual digging and hoeing, exchange of oxen and labour, exchange of oxen for cash and grain, exchange of land and oxen, exchange of grain and labour, exchange of labour for labour, sharecropping land, renting land, obtaining oxen through social networks, use of household labour, festive and reciprocal labour mobilisation, hiring farmer(s) for a cropping season, and hiring labour in peak seasons. While some of these practices would have been followed in the areas of origin, what we are seeing in the Beles Valley are combinations of strategies which formerly were not considered.

Cultivation of Plots with Their Own Draught Animals

Farmers who own oxen, a key resource used for farm traction, use them on the basis of several arrangements. For instance, those farmers who own an ox for two pair them with others belonging to farmers of the same category or with those who individually own an ox and use them turn by turn. The pairing arrangement is more or less the same for those who own an ox for two and those who own an ox individually. However, those who own a pair of oxen and above do not necessarily look for pairing. Even in cases where farmers own three oxen, mostly they plow with a pair allowing one of the oxen to rest, and rotating the animals. But, in some cases, the third ox will be paired with another ox owned by other farmer(s). Farmers who manage to own an ox are the ones who are capable of at least producing enough food for the households in normal circumstances. On the other hand, farmers with a pair of oxen or more are mostly surplus producers. Thus, the ownership of oxen allows the households to cultivate their plots on time and efficiently, contributing towards their increased productivity.

---

[13] Anthropological research on agricultural production strategies of the smallholder farming households, Barlett (1980a) explains, will enable one to see closely the diversity within the farming families as well as their social and natural decision-making environment (which are affected by the resources available to the households) in its holistic complexity. For more details see Barlett (1980a, 1980b).

Manual Digging and Hoeing

Oxen-less healthy and strong farmers manually hoe their backyard plot as well as part of their field main plot by using simple hand-tools. Since manual digging demands much labour, they usually apply reciprocal labour called *wonfel* usually within the same category of farmers. In order to expose the hoed field to the sun, the manual digging begins early in the months of late January and February. Due to lack of oxen, they cannot properly plow. They sow crops in the second manual cultivation as the early rains come. Farmers in this category are mostly poor and complained about their suffering from hardship. As a result, many have become easy victims of prevalent diseases such as malaria and tuberculosis. The remaining part of their plot is cultivated on the basis of either sharecropping-out or renting-out land arrangements. In a few cases they can also get oxen through personal relations and manage to cultivate it. The manually cultivated plot is not large enough, and the households usually face food shortages unless supported by other coping mechanisms.

Exchange of Oxen and Labour

Due to the prevalence of *trypanosomiasis*, oxen in the Beles Valley are the most delicate as well as precious resources of those households that own them. Farmers take care when exchanging oxen for labour. In most cases, the oxen owner will not simply give out oxen in exchange for labour, but he will come together with the oxen either to plow or to closely supervise fair plowing. Oxen are not only exchanged for labour for plowing, but also for threshing. Oxen owners do not favour exchanging oxen for labour in which the animals will be used for the heavy threshing of finger millet. When oxen lack closer care, they are easily vulnerable to the attack of *trypanosomiasis*. Compared with the human labour, oxen's labour is very expensive. In order to get a pair of oxen's labour for one day, five days of human labour is demanded. A daily human labour cost is usually 4 to 6 *birr*; whereas, a daily minimum cost of a pair of oxen is not less than 20.00 *birr*. Unless forced by circumstances, oxen owners prefer to hire daily labourers in cash rather than exchange oxen for labour. The request for exchange of labour for oxen mainly comes from the oxen-less farmers.

Exchange of Oxen for Cash and Grain

Renting-out oxen for cash is the least prevalent practice among the farmers of the villages. Oxen owners, after completing their field activities or when extra oxen time is available, rent-out a pair of oxen for 20.00 *birr* in the village mainly to village government employees such as teachers and health workers who got land from farmers through different arrangements. If the village is near the towns, it is the town dwellers who usually rent-in oxen from farmers (at times a pair of oxen for a day is rented-out to a town dweller at an average of 50.00 *birr*). However, oxen rental arrangements of town dwellers are most frequently with immigrant farmers who own many oxen.

On the other hand, farmers rent-in oxen in exchange for grain that will be paid after harvest. Both oxen-less and oxen-owning farmers (who need additional oxen) practice the renting-in arrangement. Here, a farmer who rents-in an ox for a full agricultural season will usually pay six *quintals* (600 kg) of grain after harvest. The type of grain paid can be either the direct harvest using the ox or according to the agreement of the parties involved. According to my resettler informants in Pawe, principally oxen rental arrangements are made between the neighbouring Agaw (Gojjam) farmers and resettlers (the latter being the ones who rent-in oxen for grain).

Exchange of Land and Oxen
Oxen-owning farmers plow land of oxen-less but strong and healthy farmers. After plowing and sowing the field, all the remaining activities till threshing will be left to the land-owning farmers. The latter take full charge of repeated weeding, field crop protection against wild animals, harvesting and the like. The oxen-owners come only at the threshing stage. Finally, they share the produce on the basis of a 1:2 ratio – one-third for the oxen owner and two-thirds for the landowner who covered the highest field labour. The oxen-owner gets a share of the produce simply for his oxen's labour. Moreover, oxen-owners plow fields of landowners on the basis of sharing half of the land they cultivated for that particular year. After completing the field preparation and sowing, the two parties share the field equally and take charge of undertaking all the remaining field activities independently in the respective fields up to the final harvesting and threshing. Thus, oxen enable the owners to get a share of land. Meanwhile, lack of oxen force the landowners to share-out land for oxen.

Exchange of Grain and Labour
Oxen-owners, after sharecropping-in the land of physically weaker farmers, sometimes become unable to cover the necessary labour demanded to perform the field task. As a result, they will be forced to make arrangements with farmers who are capable of providing labour demanded at all levels of field cultivation after sowing. In such a case, the first arrangement with the landowners is usually to share the produce on the basis of a 1:3 ratio (one-

fourth for the land-owner and three-fourths for the sharecropper) because weaker landowners are not capable of providing the labour demanded. Then, the oxen-owners re-share from their share on the basis of a 1:2 ratio (one-third for oxen-owner and two-thirds for the labour provider). For instance, if the produce from such plots is twenty *quintals*, the share among the partners is five *quintals* for landowner, five quintals for the oxen-owner, and the remaining ten quintals for the labourer. Here, the labourer gets half of the produce from the plot because he does not own the plot. Had he owned the land, his share would have been even more.

In addition, in the busy peak-harvesting season intensified by the frequent threat of bush-fire outbreak, the labour demand in many of the fields is very high. In this busiest period, every household is busy harvesting, so mobilising labour is usually difficult. Due to the high demand, there can also be a shortage of daily labourers. As a result, those farmers who cultivated many fields, but who are not capable of harvesting on time, give out the fields to other farmers who can manage to harvest, pile, and thresh (together with the owner) the crop on time. The labour providing farmers' share the produce on a 1:3 basis (one-fourth for the labourers and three-fourths to the owner).

Exchange of Labour for Labour
This form of exchange concerns human labour, which is mainly practised by women heads of households who need male labour in exchange. In the area, some of the field activities such as plowing, part of harvesting, piling, and threshing demand strong male labour. In order to get male labour in exchange for those activities, women perform activities such as field levelling, weeding, and transporting harvest in the fields of male farmers. Moreover, even male farmers who need special skills of neighbouring farmers provide their labour in undertaking one activity and in exchange get the skilled labour. For instance, in order to get the service of a farmer skilled in roof thatching, the former may provide labour support in other activities of the latter.

Tenancy Arrangement
Sharecropping of land is a very common arrangement. In this form of arrangement, weaker as well as most oxen-less poor farmers share-crop-out land for oxen-owners. The amount of share of the produce varies according to the labour contributed throughout the field activities. The parties also share the other inputs accordingly. The higher share of inputs and especially labour at all levels of field activities entitles a higher share of produce. If all

the production costs are fully covered by the sharecropper, the most common form of sharing the product of a fertile plot is on the basis of 1:3 (one-fourth for the land-owner and three-fourths for the inputs provider). Based on the agreement of the parties as well as the location and fertility condition of the plots, the ratio of sharing the produce can vary. Landowners prefer to sharecrop-out land to those farmers considered hardworking. Those who sharecrop-in are mostly the better farmers of the village owning oxen. Immigrant farmers who are not entitled land right but live in villages are also major sharecroppers.

In addition to sharecropping, renting land is frequently practised in the area. The rental arrangement is both in cash and in kind, the latter dominating. In the cash rental arrangement, the average cost of a 0.75-hectare plot of land is 150.00 *birr* for one cropping season and paid immediately based on interviews with Pawe informants as well as personal observation. Those households who rent-out land mostly do it as a last resort when faced with difficulties and, at times, to use the money for petty-trading activities. Those who rent-in land are better-off farmers of the village and town dwellers in the nearby towns. On the other hand, renting-out land for grain is quite common; and a 0.75-hectare plot of land on the average is rented-out for three to three-and-half *quintals* of finger millet or sorghum for one cropping season to be paid after harvest. Both parties appreciate this form of arrangement. The landowner considers it a risk-free arrangement with no worry about crop failure. The other party also considers it a free arrangement so flexible for making decisions to grow whatever the household needs. In addition to the weak and poor farmers, some of those who specialise in different activities also opt for renting-out land in kind. For instance, it was observed that a rich wood-worker whose wife is a potter rented-out land for three-and-half *quintals* of finger-millet in order to allot enough time for his craft activities, which got a better return.

Access to Oxen Through Social Relations
Using established social relations with the farmers of the village as well as with those in the neighbouring areas, some farmers managed to obtain oxen free of charge to cultivate their field plots. The oxen-owning farmers are also socially obliged to provide the necessary support in case requested by members of the village. Farming households with affinal and consanguinal relations with oxen-owners get oxen support accordingly. Farmers who have managed to establish strong links with the neighbouring Agaw (Gojjam) farmers obtain oxen for plowing their plot. In addition, resettlers who have closer relations with the immigrant farmers get oxen support upon request.

However, oxen obtained through social relations are mostly used to cultivate only one's own plot and are rarely used to cultivate sharecropped-in or rented-in plots.

Household Labour

Labour is one of the key resources of the farming households. Those households that have grown-up children's labour are better off than those without enough field labour. Both male and female labour is equally important in the field agricultural production activities. Those better off households, which have enough labour within the family do not have to apply labour-mobilising mechanisms as much. They rather rely mostly on the household labour, saving the extra expenditures spent on the organisation of labour mobilising feasts. On the other hand, average and poor households with adequate household labour employ part of that labour in daily labour or other income-generating activities to augment the household's production.

When family labour is considered in terms of the household development cycle, infant children up to the age of five stay under the household's closer care. Male children serve as shepherds, fetch firewood, go to school, and support the field activities of their fathers. Whereas female children serve in cleaning the house and fetching water, go to school and support the activities of their mothers. The adult males perform duties of plowing, cultivating, weeding, harvesting, threshing, etc. On the other hand, adult women undertake all tedious household chores. During the peak agricultural activities, all grown-up members of the household participate in the field activities. Old men and women play elderly roles and undertake lighter duties of the respective sexes and guide the young using their accumulated experience. In the late old age, they become powerless and need attendance by the closer family members. However, as personally observed in the fieldwork, in the absence of closer relatives who will take care of them, they become weak and helpless dependants due to the disintegration and weakened state of many of the traditional social institutions.

Labour Mobilisation

During demanding seasons of peak labour, farmers of all categories apply different labour-mobilising mechanisms such as festive, reciprocal, and generous support. The festive labour is mostly organised by the well-to-do farmers, who are capable of spending resources (mainly grain) for the organisation of feast to mobilise *dabo* or *jigi* labour. Other farmers voluntarily pool labour and undertake activities jointly, rotating in the fields of members known as *wonfel* or *qanja*. Furthermore, the village farmers provide free labour to support the weaker members or those members who temporarily encountered difficulties usually at the early hours before going to their respective field activities known as *waari* or *maarfeja*. The local names of the institutions stated above are all in Amharic (cf. chapter 9 "Work Group").

Hiring Farmers for a Cropping Season

Better-off farmers who continuously demand additional labour hire a full-time farmer(s) for a full cropping season. Most of the farmers hired in this manner come from the neighbouring areas of Gojjam and Gondar. The employers give the hired farmers food and full accommodation. The term of hiring farmers is both in cash and in kind (the latter being dominant). In the few cases of cash-hiring, farmers hired for a cropping season are usually paid 500.00 *birr* on the average in addition to food and accommodation. However, the predominant form of hiring arrangement is for a share of one-fourth of the produce from all crops exclusively cultivated by the hired farmer using the oxen of the owner. The hired farmer, under a close monitoring of the owner, undertakes the farm activities throughout the cropping season in the field he is assigned and gets the agreed share of the produce at the end of the cropping season.

Usually the hiring period ranges from the beginning of February to the end of January. Even though it is not a frequent practice, women can also have the opportunity to be hired in the same way. However, hired women cannot perform those farm activities that demand exclusive male labour. In the Beles Valley context, the heaviest field activity is repeated weeding, for which women are highly preferred for their weeding meticulously, particularly finger millet and sesame. The main form of hiring a woman is for a share of one-fifth of the produce of her labour at the end of the cropping season. Mostly these women are the ones who come to the villages as dependants of the relatives already residing there. According to village farmers, while hiring women, having a blood relation with either of the spouses is preferred to avoid suspicion that might arise from wives since they stay longer in the field together with the husbands.

Hiring Labour in Peak Seasons

Hiring labour on a daily basis is the most predominant practice of rich farmers during peak seasons. The practice is welcome by both parties. The better farmers get easy access to the labour they demand simply by picking from the roadside. The available labour allows them to complete their field task on time and efficiently. The daily labourers are mostly hired for 4.00 *birr* a day paid immediately at the end of the day. They are also given the daily meal in the field. The poor households use daily labour as part of the main source of their livelihood. As a result, early in the morning, the job seekers with their hand tools (usually sickles) come to the roadside in the centre of the village and stay there until picked by the employers. As personally observed in the field, on the crossroad juncture of three villages (L9, L23, and L45), labourers of working age of both sexes gathered on the roadside waiting for daily employers. Since it was a time when the schools were closed, some of the job seekers were students who will use the income to support the costs of their school expenses. Some are young girls, who explained that they use the income to buy local jewellery and clothing. Many who have given-out their plots either on sharecropping or renting-out arrangements, are there to use the income for purchasing food for their households since it is a food-deficit period. Some of the labourers were there to augment the household income, leaving behind part of their household members to work in their own household plot. Part of these labourers had completed weeding their plots and were using their time to generate additional income. Most of the job seekers were from the food-deficit households. Apart from the better-off village farmers, town dwellers and the Tana-Beles Project were also hiring those job seekers.

Synthesis of Agricultural Production Strategies

The diverse agricultural production strategies applied by the resettlers are inter-related in various situations[14]. Those resettlers who manage to own a key resource like oxen have a better opportunity to cultivate more plots of land. They exchange oxen for land mainly in a form of sharecropping and/or land rental arrangements. Oxen are also exchanged for labour for the oxenless members both for plowing and threshing. Having cultivated large plots of land, richer resettlers, in the absence of enough household labour, are forced to draw labour through labour mobilising mechanisms (festive labour), hiring farmer(s) for a full cropping season, and/or hiring wage labourers only during the peak seasons. In contrast, average farmers mostly rely on their household's own labour. During peak seasons, they usually pool reciprocal labour among farmers of the same type. Many of the average farmers

---

[14] Here, the idea of "situational logic" noted by Prattis (1987:19) that considers "man as strategiser" reflects certain light on the dynamic synthesis of the diverse agricultural production strategies. Situational strategies of individuals (in this case significantly applicable to the smallholder resettler farming households), Prattis argues that, enable them to hold a location within any given socio-cultural structure influence their decision-making in a number of alternative ways based on their access to and control over resources (in this case such as land, labour, cash, draught animals and social capital). For more details see also Prattis (1973).

own a single ox or jointly own one ox, and use it pairing with that of others to cultivate their field plots on a rotating basis. They also pool their oxen in the same way for threshing.

On the other hand, oxen-less farmers mostly give out field plots for oxen-owners on the basis of sharecropping and land rental arrangements. The ratio of sharing the produce in the sharecropping arrangement is dependent upon the share of the production cost by the parties. If the parties share equal production costs, they share the product equally. Otherwise, the one that contributed higher production cost will take a higher share of the product. Land rental arrangement is practised both for cash and in-kind for grains. In the in-kind rental arrangement, the cultivator will give the agreed amount of grain after harvest. Poor farmers are forced to rent-out land mainly for lack of key resources like oxen and/or field labour. Having disposed-off their land on sharecropping or rental arrangements, many of the able-bodied re-settlers usually engage in daily wage labour during the peak seasons. However, some of the oxen-less resettlers get oxen through their individual social networks of relations that enable them to cultivate the whole or part of their plots. Moreover, some of the strong ones manually dig and hoe part of their plots, usually pooling reciprocal labour pooled from within similar house-hold types. Moreover, oxen-less farmers who have managed to cultivate their plots through several mechanisms exchange their labour for oxen to be used in threshing. Sometimes, women in the absence of male labour exchange their labour mostly in the weeding for male labour for harvesting and threshing. Therefore, the diverse agricultural production strategies applied by the differentiated resettler households are interrelated with each other in several contexts.

Livelihood Strategies[15] and Socio-Economic Differentiation
Although the state-sponsored resettlement of the 1980s ideally tried to act as an "equaliser" and "leveller" at the initial phase of its operation providing equal ration, homestead plots, housing, clothing, farm hand-tools, free social

---

[15] As earlier discussed (cf. chapter 2 "Sustainable Rural Livelihoods"), Scoones (1998:9) explains three broad clusters of rural livelihood strategies as agricultural intensification/extensification, livelihood diversification, and migration which are often heavily reliant on livelihood resources, which include natural, economic/financial, human, social and other capital. Scoones (1998:9) further notes, rural livelihood strategies to cover a broad range of options open to rural people to pursue: livelihood either from agriculture through the processes of intensification or extensifica-tion; or diversify to a range of off-farm income earning activities; or move away and seek a liveli-hood, either temporarily or permanently, elsewhere; or more commonly, pursue a combination of the strategies together or in sequence.

services, etc. together with the communal form of production system, in practice, the reality was otherwise. The fact of diversity in the very dynamics of the resettlers' lives and livelihoods in the new setting contradicts with the very idea of imposed levelling. This idea runs counter to the heterogeneity of backgrounds and positions prevalent among the resettlers that joined the program. Right from the very beginning, resettlers differed on the basis of ethno-cultural backgrounds, occupational skills, individual behaviour, physical strength, food habits, religious beliefs, literacy background, contextual wealth, access to opportunities (employment), and assignment of positions in the local leadership. In the present Beles Valley context, resettlers showed a widening socio-economic differentiation. [16]

During the fieldwork period, it was observed that resettler farmers have increasingly differed in the ownership of basic resources such as land, livestock, labour, and cash income. Based on extended interviews with resettler informants and my personal observation, they are classified and differentiated into five broad household categories according to local community standards and include:

- Very rich (high surplus),
- Rich (moderate surplus),
- Medium (self sufficient),
- Poor (food deficit), and
- Poorest (weak and dependent).

The boundaries of the household typologies are not at all fixed. Rather there exists a continuous flux of ascending and descending in the rankings.

The successful livelihood strategies that act as the basis for the resettlers' livelihood adaptation[17] and eventual socio-economic differentiation include

---

[16] Explaining somewhat similar socio-economic differentiation and heterogeneity of smallholder farming households, (Ellis 1988:6f.) noted the following: "Peasants are not a uniform, homogeneous, set of farm families all with the same status and prospects within their communities. On the contrary, peasant societies are always and everywhere typified [...] by internal differentiation along many lines. The word 'differentiation' here signifies that differences of social status, like many other aspects of peasants, are not static, timeless feature. Social structure changes over time according to the nature of forces acting on peasant society and to the adaptation of individual families to those forces." For more details see also Ellis (1998).

[17] As earlier described (cf. chapter 2"Sustainable Rural Livelihoods"), Scoones (1998:6) explains livelihood adaptation as "the ability of a livelihood to be able to cope with and recover from stresses and shocks" in which those who are unable to cope are inevitably vulnerable and unlikely to achieve sustainable livelihoods. Livelihood adaptation can be either positive, if it is by choice, reversible, and increases security; or negative, if of necessity, irreversible, and fails to contribute

smallholder farming household tailored production practices, agricultural intensification, household income diversification, recreated and adapted networks of social relations, remittances, economising, risk aversion, and innovation. However, it remains the case that women-headed households are more vulnerable than other types of households. This is in part due to the lack of labour and social support within the household, and also an inability to call on social networks beyond the household. In the absence of their husbands, women shoulder the responsibility for managing the households alone and are obliged to enter into tenancy arrangements through either sharecropping-out or renting-out their land.

Smallholder Farming Household Tailored Production Practices

The collapse of communal cultivation and the re-establishment of an individual production system through land privatisation after the end of the *Derg* government has widened the resettlers' socio-economic differentiation. The land privatisation has widened the difference between the rich and poor. It has brought to the fore inequality between the weak and the strong. The very perception of the weak and strong differed on the issue of the change of government and land tenure. The weak are in favour of the communal cultivation time of the former government. They feel highly nostalgic about the communal period when they were entitled to their ration and were secure. However, now they feel highly resentful, disappointed, and hopelessly sunk in misery. Nostalgic for the past, they said: *Albaash aguraashachin hedoal!* (Amh.), which literally means "our feeder and clothier has gone!" or "our patron has gone!" To the contrary, the perception of the better-off farmers is against the collective agriculture and favoured the individual production system managed by families that liberated them to enjoy the results of their labour. This individually managed household production system is considered as one of the basic factors that brought increased socio-economic differentiation of resettlers.

In the current Beles Valley context, resettlers differ in their access to and control over key resources such as land, labour, oxen, and cash income. Almost all resettlers have equal access to the 0.1 hectare backyard and 0.75 hectare main plots. However, some of them who by chance had lands of marginal quality have abandoned them. In those villages where there is a potential for more cultivable land, capable farmers have prepared additional

---

reducing vulnerability (Davies and Hossain 1997:5). Livelihood adaptation, according to Davies and Hossain (1997:5), is also defined as "the dynamic process of constant changes to livelihoods which either enhance existing security and wealth or try to reduce vulnerability and poverty."

plots by clearing forest and bush. Farmers in the better category generate income from both on-farm and off-farm activities, whereas farmers in the poor category are highly constrained, eking out a meagre existence applying diverse coping mechanisms. Moreover, farmers differ in their ownership of household assets.

Agricultural Intensification and Household Income Diversification[18]

As earlier discussed, agriculture is the main livelihood of farming households and grow both cash and food crops, raise livestock, and produce apiculture and horticulture. Most of the better farmers are intensive agriculturists, performing enhanced and strengthened farming of diverse production. The production of such farmers is so abundant that they use it both for consumption and generation of on-farm income that will be used for further improvement of their livelihood.

In the Beles Valley area, there exists substantial potential for generating income from diverse sources. Farmers produce cash crops such as sesame, groundnuts, and niger-seed exclusively for sale. They also produce food crops both for home consumption and sale. They keep bees and also grow some horticulture products. They raise livestock for traction, manure, consumption, income and status. Moreover, except those families in the weak and disabled category, many of the farmers in the other differentiated types are engaged in entrepreneurial activities. The five markets of the resettlement area as well as the neighbouring markets of Mambuk, Deq, Gilgel-Beles, Mandura, Chagni, and Kuyissa are the main markets where entrepreneurial activities take place. These are contact places of the population of resettlement and neighbouring areas with heterogeneous and multiple economic, social and cultural backgrounds. Some farmers perform entrepreneurship even inside their own villages. The entrepreneurial items are multiple and transacted among the population of diverse background. In addition,

---

[18] Based on the *Embu* peasants in Kenya, Haugerud (1984:26) identified somewhat similar findings and notes that diversification out of agriculture to be the major source of dynamism in the rural economy acting as a cause and consequences of socio-economic differentiation of smallholder farming households. Haugerud explains that cash earned from off-farm income generating activities helps poor households (with inadequate resources) to meet minimum consumption needs; to medium households, it supplements the farm income by providing crucial additional income; and for a few wealthy households, it is an important link to extra-local markets and institutions that permit entry into the sphere of accumulation through land purchases and/or acquisition of commercial loans. This clearly shows household income diversification to be the main differentiating factor of the rural economy. Coupled with household income diversification, access to key resources such as land, labour and cash that in turn are also determined by the social and political ties contribute towards socio-economic differentiation.

198

the seasonal and daily employment opportunities in the area are sources of substantial income. In addition, farmers pursue different handicraft activities as sideline occupations that enable the household to generate income. For the poor, income-generating is a means of eking out mere survival. However, for the better-off, diversifying income is a means of further improvement.

Physical Strength and Domestic Dynamics
Households with healthy, strong and working-age members make use of the labour in the agricultural production as well as for generating income, contributing for further betterment of the farming family. In contrast, households with many weak dependants and children below a working age are highly constrained and become quite vulnerable to easy impoverishment. Farmers commented on such dependants as: *Lasira yaalderrese, lamabil yaalaanese*; (Amh.) which literally means "one who is not of a working age, but capable of consuming food." Apart from undertaking the usual home chores, women (including young girls of working age) intensively participate at all levels of field agricultural production activities. In most cases, women are more active in undertaking diverse petty trading activities especially in the poor and medium households. They are also the ones who are mostly engaged in the transporting and selling of charcoal and fuel wood in the towns. The males do the chopping and are engaged in the preparation of charcoal. Based on observation and discussions with different groups of informants, women have an enhanced contribution to the well-being of the households through their multiple roles in the productive, reproductive and community activities. Moreover, men and women of old age undertake light jobs and elderly tasks, at the same time guiding the young with their accumulated experience. Close family members attend, those elderly of late old age. However, the ones without closer attendants are weak and destitute, becoming dependent upon the charity of the village communities.

Types of Soils and Location of Farmland
The soils of Beles Valley are broadly categorised as red and black. The drained light black soils are highly liked by the farmers for the possibility of double harvest, the second harvest being chickpea. However, the heavy waterlogged land is very difficult to cultivate by the present technology of the farmers. So, farmers whose field plots are located in the waterlogged soil have abandoned them and are left without field plots in most cases. On the other hand, the red soil is highly preferred by farmers because of its easy cultivation as well as the possibility of producing major cash and food crops.

However, the fertility level of red soil varies from one location to the other even within the village. Some plots are highly infested by striga weed; and some others are located in the peripheries highly prone to destruction by wild animals. Thus, farming households are differentiated on the basis of ownership of fertile, infertile, and waterlogged soils as well as differing locations of the field plots.

Networks of Social Relations
Resettlers have established close relations with others within the resettlement area as well as with the neighbouring population through marriage, religion, work groups, land exchange, bond-friendships, fictive parenthood, god-parenthood as well as on the basis of the individual's entrepreneurial ability in interacting with others. Individuals with networks of relations exchange lots of things through their interaction. For instance, oxen-less farmers get use of oxen through their relations. Those who look for a grain or cash loan at times of difficulty get easy access through their relations. Some traders at times leave livestock with friends among the farmers. These farmers take the animals on instalment and pay for them after selling, making a profit. Farmers who also have better relations with others can mobilise enormous festive labour.

Earlier Resource Position and Remittances
Although many of the farmers who joined the resettlement as a last resort were barehanded and began life from scratch, others had substantial resources according to my informants in Pawe. For instance, resettlers from Gojjam moved to the valley with their livestock. Some resettlers from South Shewa managed to have money from the sale of their assets at home. Even a few of the resettlers from famine stricken areas had some amount of money from sale of relief rations (grain and clothing). Once they arrived at the resettlement sites, members of resettlers who were selected for various leadership positions in the villages and those who had close relations both with them and the village cadres have benefited from the village relief resources. Initially, the cadres favoured those closer to them in assigning light jobs and providing better rations. Later when the Tana-Beles Project began its operation, the village elected officials favoured those closer to them, enabling seasonal employment in the project and at the same time getting equal ration without actually working in the fields. Behind such action, some of the elected officials were alleged of sharing from the income in the form of a bribe. In all respects, the elected officials were the most privileged category of resettlers throughout the communal cultivation period. Many of the re-

strictions applied to others, including freedom of movement from-and-to the area of origin, were not applicable to them. However, with the current possibility of free movement after the change of the government in 1991, many resettlers managed to meet relatives in the original area and collected remittances. These means enabled resettlers to buy important key assets like oxen or smaller livestock. The importance of remittances is mostly higher at the initial stage after the re-establishment of smallholder cultivation. On the other hand, a few other resettlers who had left behind in the original area part of their assets with their relatives, later sold them, returned to the valley, and bought basic assets like oxen.

Ethno-Cultural Background[19]
As earlier described, the ethnic backgrounds of resettlers in the valley are diverse. These resettlers differed in the push and pull factors that made them join the resettlement program. The northern resettlers from Wollo, Tigray, and North Shoa were pushed by the devastating famine. But, resettlers from South Shoa and Gojjam were pushed mainly by shortage of cultivable land. Many of the resettlers were also deceived and pulled by the extremely idealised propaganda image of the selected sites as being furnished with all facilities necessary for livelihoods. Upon arrival, all were disillusioned and became destitute as stated earlier. The resettlers from Southern Shoa mainly have a background of *enset* culture and tuber crops. Resettlers from all other areas have a highland crop production background. So, the different backgrounds have an influence upon the adaptive re-adjustments of resettlers in a new context (cf. chapter 7 "Impact on the Resettlers: Socio-Cultural Disintegration and Livelihood Impoverishment"). Resettlers also differed in their religious backgrounds, having different self-help mechanisms (cf. chapter 9 "Religious Belief").

Savings and Economising
Some resettler households managed to save gradually even from their ration throughout the early phase of resettlement. At one stage, they bought chickens, and then goats. Step by step, through goats, they passed to an ox for two, and then to oxen, and finally to other many more livestock, gradually achieving the present rich and very rich levels. On the other hand, there are some who are weak in economising even today and remained poor as a result. Those weak people in economising are accused of their 'extravagant' expenditure on food, alcoholic drinks, smoking, and unplanned movements

---

[19] See also Agneta et al. (1993)

of back-and-forth to origins. Resettlers at all levels strongly stressed economising as a basis for improvement. Therefore, step-by-step savings and economising of scarce resources to alternative ends are considered as key basis for the socio-economic differentiation of farming households.

Risk Aversion and Innovation
Farmers cultivate diverse crops in their fields. In their cultivation, prime attention is given to food crops basically meant for home consumption in order to avoid the risk of purchasing food crops from the market. Cash crops are mainly cultivated on plots remaining food crops. In order to avoid the risk of death of their oxen by the prevalent *trypanosomiasis,* some farmers sell their oxen immediately at the end the season's cultivation and buy at the beginning of the next season.

Moreover, better farmers take the risk to introduce new crops to the villages. For instance, based on my personal observation, one very rich resettler farmer in L29 took the risk of introducing new large-scale sesame cultivation to his village. Out of this he managed to generate a substantial amount of money at the end of the harvest, contributing much to his further advancement.

Farmers are also innovative enough in the identification of plowing with donkeys, which are less prone to attack by *trypanosomiasis* in comparison to oxen and provide multiple services to the households. As earlier stated, based on observation and discussion with the innovative farmer who introduced farming with donkeys to the village, donkeys are found to be highly practical and less risky in the fact that they are cheaper than oxen, plow longer hours than oxen, can be rented out to traders or used for trading by the owner, and serve the households as pack animals. Therefore, both risk taking and risk aversion in different contexts as well as innovation are among the important factors of the socio-economic differentiation of resettlers' households.

Synthesis of Strategies for Socio-Economic Differentiation
Almost all the factors discussed above that contributed to the increasing social differentiation of the resettler households in the new context are inextricably interrelated in many aspects. Obviously, many of the resettlers began life from scratch in the relocation site. However, some of them differed in their earlier resource positions. For instance, according to informants, many of the resettlers who joined the program due to land shortage were not barehanded like those pushed by famine. Resettlers pushed by famine and land shortage also differ in their physical strength as well. Based on information obtained from informants, there existed differences in the

mation obtained from informants, there existed differences in the resource position even among resettlers pushed by famine. Some of them sold rations (food and clothing) and a few collaborated in mini-tasks in the temporary shelters while preparing for the move, getting better provisions. Apart from this, some of the resettlers from Gojjam joined the scheme moving their livestock resources. So, resettlers differed in their earlier resource positions right from their arrival at the new location. Even though life was painful and traumatic during the initial phase of transition, resettlers showed increasing differentiation as they went through adaptive re-adjustments.

Access to opportunities in the different positions of the village leadership has created advantage for a few in comparison to all other resettlers. Based on the intimate or informal relations to the village authorities, some resettlers got causal employment opportunities in the different rehabilitation programs of the area, at the same time getting equal rations. In order to extend their employment duration, some of them used to share their income with the village authorities in the form of bribes as noted earlier. Many resettlers were innovative enough and engaged in activities such as entrepreneurship, home gardening, and handicrafts that were considered to be marginal by the planners of the collective field agriculture.

Here, the contribution of ethno-cultural backgrounds is worth mentioning. Due to the land shortage in the homelands, resettlers of Kambaata and Hadiyya were used to undertaking diverse sideline income-generating activities in order to augment the meagre farm produce. Using this background, many of them engaged in entrepreneurial activities while making adaptive re-adjustments.

On the other hand, some resettlers mostly from the north, cultivated small plots at the far peripheries of the main fields as well as along the rivers and streams working in the late evenings after the daily field communal labour thus generating substantial produce. Additionally, some resettlers regularly made savings from their rations through reduced consumption and began buying smaller livestock as a result. Individual resettlers who were good in establishing networks of relations within their own groups or with the community neighbouring them also showed a difference in their adaptive re-adjustments. These and other related factors contributed a great deal towards the initial remarkable increase in the differences among the resettlers in their economic considerations.

However, a tremendous leap in the increased differentiation of resettlers began with the collapse of collectivisation and the re-establishment of smallholder cultivation after the 1991 political change in the country. The land privatisation and smallholder household tailored production systems played a crucial role in the increased dynamics of socio-economic differentiation. Almost all resettlers obtained equal access to land. However, they differed in the type of soil and location of the field plots. Some resettlers acquired more fertile fields near the village, while others got less fertile and/or waterlogged heavy black soil plots. Some got plots at the peripheries very far from the village, which demanded longer walking hours and also being exposed to attacks by wild animals. Even though each resettler got an equal amount of land, they differed in their access to other key resources like oxen, labour, and cash income. As a result, those resettlers who got better access to key assets have better control over resources.

Due to lack of oxen and field labour, many resettlers give-out land to oxen-owners. Even those who have household labour but lack oxen are often forced to exchange land on sharecropping arrangements. Those individual resettlers who are entrepreneurial in their social networks of relationships with the resettler and neighbouring population are able to obtain and generate resources that contribute to their difference. Furthermore, oxen-owning resettlers are the ones that undertake intensive agricultural production. At the same time, they have easy access to mobilise or hire the labour demanded for their field agricultural production as well as clearing larger field plots in the peripheries (mostly making use of the oxenless but physically strong and healthy resettlers in the villages). Thus, through the cultivation of larger plots, they produce abundant yield and generate substantial on-farm income that undoubtedly enables them to show further improvement. Those who undertake both on- and off-farm income-diversification activities integral with intensive cultivation are the ones who are making a wider socio-economic difference within the resettler farmers. They are highly innovative and skilled in entrepreneurial performance and social networks of relationships. They are also both risk-taking and risk-averse. Thus, the diverse basic strategies for the socio-economic differentiation of resettler farmers are interrelated with several aspects of life in a new context.

Chapter 9. Role of Local Institutions in the Pursuit of Livelihood Adaption

As discussed earlier, the resettlement scheme has dismantled the entire complex web of local institutions[20] and the very social fabric of the resettlers, detaching them from social bonds in the face of the relocation process[21]. This disintegration had increased the uncertainties and desperation of the resettlers. However, as the resettlers went through adaptive readjustments, they began re-instituting local institutions, which in turn played vital roles in the process of their livelihood adaptation in the new setting. Through the rearticulation of local institutions, the uncertainties in the daily lives of resettlers were reduced and stable livelihood reconstruction strategies were attained.

The early disarticulation and the later rearticulation of local institutions enabled the often-invisible complex web of institutional arrangements and their multiple roles to be visible to outsiders as well. Meaningful re-instituting processes of institutions were properly realised with the collapse of collectivisation and reestablishment of smallholder production systems. Resettler households embedded in these local institutional frameworks channel access to different livelihood resources, which are essential for their livelihood strategies. The livelihood strategies are in turn linked to the multiple institutional settings upon which the households are embedded. These

---

[20] Institutions, North (1991:97) explains, are a humanly devised set of rules or constraints that structure social, economic and political interactions that determine both what people are prohibited from doing, and under what conditions people are permitted to undertake certain activities. North (1990:3f.) also notes that institutions have been devised by societies throughout history in order to guide human interaction, to create order, to reduce uncertainty, and to provide structure to everyday life as a framework within which human interaction takes place (cf. chapter 2 "Local Social Institutions").

[21] Involuntary resettlement, Downing (1996:34) explains, disintegrates the underlying social fabric, dismantles vital social networks and weakens life-support mechanisms of the resettlers by debilitating their authority systems and capacity to self-manage and cope with uncertainty. In the words of Downing, those involuntarily relocated "people may physically persist but the community that was is no more." Additionally, describing similar empirical accounts based on his Kariba studies, Scudder notes: "At Kariba women bemoaned the fact that they would have to leave the gardens, and especially the garden shelters, that had passed through the female line over generations. Shrine custodians feared that sickness would follow them if they left the area with which their ancestors' authority was associated. Adults did not wish to leave the graves of their ancestors and complained that they were being thrown away by government into an unfamiliar and hostile hinterland far from their beloved Zambezi river." (cf. chapter 2 "Review of Definitions and Concepts").

livelihood strategies enable the households to establish differing degrees of food security, social security, and the entire livelihood security at large.

In the process, resettlers managed to re-establish complex institutional networks first within their village and then at different levels including the entire resettlement area as well as the neighbouring host communities. The re-instituting process was practised through neighbourhood, kinship and marriage, religious belief, work groups, sharecropping, bond-friendship, and other related networks of relationships. In the present Beles Valley context, the five broadly differentiated household types such as very rich, rich, medium, poor, and poorest/weak practice diverse livelihood strategies based on multiple local institutional arrangements. The following description and analysis reveals the role of local social institutions in the pursuit of resettlers' livelihood adaptation and interactions. Their local institutions and livelihood strategies are interrelated. In the process of the pursuit of resettlers' livelihood security, the vital roles of local institutions are manifested in mediating and channelling access to livelihood resources, providing strong social security or safety nets, and facilitating local self-governance. However, in spite of all the enormous potentials, some critiques of local institutions need to be recognised in certain contexts.

9.1 Types of Local Social Institutions[22]

Those rural local institutions of the relocated peasants discussed include those complex webs of institutions based on neighbourhood, marriage and kinship, religious beliefs, production work groups, sharecropping, and bond-friendships. It is difficult to categorise local institutions into typologies in a strict sense due to complex interrelations among them. The following typologies are simple groupings of local institutions in order to facilitate the thematic discussions of this report.

Neighbourhood

The neighbourhood institutions include the most important *iddir, elders' council* and *iqqub*. In the present context, communities have instituted two new neighbourhood institutions known as *yelimaat qan* "development day" and *yetsidaat qan* "sanitation day". The operation of these two is closely coordinated together with the community and the formal peasant association (PA) committee members.

---

[22] All italicised terms representing the different local institutions in this chapter are stated in Amharic unless otherwise indicated in other local languages.

(*A*) *Iddir/Qire/Seera*[23]*:* It is the most predominant mutual self-help institution of the communities in the villages. Initially, at the time of their arrival, resettlers did not have a proper *iddir*. As they went through adapting to the new context, they managed to re-establish it. After the political change in 1991 and the collapse of collective cultivation alongside with the re-establishment of smallholder household production system, community institutions began strengthening with proper strong *iddir* being formed and beginning to function in diverse contexts. These *iddir* include the predominant *yeafer iddir* (for burial and mourning), *yekebt iddir* (for oxen and cows), *yeqaareza iddir* (for transporting the sick), *yebeetsira iddir* (for house construction) and *yezemed iddir* (among relatives) and *balinjeera iddir* (among close friends). The household (headed either by male or female) is a basic unit for membership in an *iddir*. The *iddir* of the villages are instituted across ethnic and religious boundaries based on the composition of village inhabitants.

Yeafer iddir is a mutual community institution meant to organise a burial of a dead member and assist the bereaved family. It is administered by an *iddir-dagna*. When death occurs in a member's family, it will be announced. Until the corpse is buried, all members will be engaged in performing diverse duties related to the burial. According to my Pawe informants, these shared tasks undertaken include announcing the death to those close to the deceased in the neighbouring areas, collecting a contribution of cash and in-kind from members (usually 2-3 kilos of food grain and 50 cents to one *birr*), digging the grave, burying the corpse, constructing shade for mourners, chopping fuel wood, attending guests, roasting or boiling grain, preparing coffee, etc. Members participate in the mourning and consoling the bereaved family for several days. Moreover, members voluntarily extend support to the deceased family in the field during peak agricultural season if the death has jeopardised the field activities of the family.

Those members of the village community who own traction oxen and milking cows have established *yekebt iddir* to cooperage with and mutually support each other during the death of their livestock as an insurance mechanism. When a member's ox or cow dies, usually an estimated 75% (400-600 *birr* for an ox and 300-500 *birr* for a cow) of the actual price of the animal will be paid, mostly after harvest. In case of the death of oxen, there

---

[23] *Iddir and qire* are equivalent and widely used variant terms in Amharic. *Seera* is the equivalent term for *iddir* in Kambaata and Hadiyya languages. It is the legal framework and insurance of the local village community. For more details, see (Dejene 1993, Pankhurst and Endrias 1958, Singer 1980).

207

exists an option according to the owner's preference. Usually, twelve oxen days' labour service will be extended in the field plowing if the owner who lost an ox prefers a payment in kind.

Most of the communities live in villages very far away from a hospital. In this less hospitable area for highland resettlers, cases of sickness are quite frequent. As a result, the villagers established *yeqaareza iddir* (stretcher *iddir*) for transporting sick family members. In some cases, this is a sub-section of the main *yeafer iddir*.

Due to a problem with termites, residential houses of villagers cannot last very long. So, villagers are forced to build their residences quite frequently. As a result, they established *yebeetsira iddir* for supporting each other in house building. In order to build a house, all members will bring wood for the wall and bamboo for the roofing. Then, they complete building both the wall and the roof, pooling their labour. The owner performs those remaining tasks such as cutting the grass, thatching the roof, and related finishing activities.

Yezemed and *baalinjeera iddir* is a special form of village *iddir* established among those closely related members of the community on selective terms based on kinship (mostly affine) and intimate friends and provides multiple services to its members. It is established either separately among relatives or friends alone or jointly. For instance, the case presented below explains the functions of a joint one because of the demands of the new context where intimate links on the basis of the two institutions are emerging and in a process of strengthening. Thus, a case of such *iddir* explained by its members is stated as follows:

A Case of Yezemedina Balinjeera Iddir in Village L9

Initially, we were only four when the *iddir* was first established two years ago. We needed this institution in addition to the main *yeafer iddir* due to our closer relations, which demanded extra self-help among us. First each one of us contributed five kilos of grain and stored it. Then, it was sold and we began collecting contributions in cash. Today, the number of members composed of close friends, affined and blood relatives has increased to forty. Our present sum of money has reached two thousand *birr*. When death occurs, we pay from the sum but we replace it immediately by collecting extra contributions of one *birr* and one kilo of grain each. Our monthly contribution of one *birr* each is regularly collected to raise the sum of the money. The money has increased fast together with its important credit service for members. A member can take credit against the money at a ten percent interest rate per year basis and can run different forms of income-generating activities. The interest rate is twelve

times cheaper than the local usurers who demand usually a ten percent interest rate per month. Additionally, sick members are entitled to interest-free credit. However, this credit service is limited only to the members.
Source: Resettler informants in village L9 (August-September 1999)

In all the different *iddir*, members mutually support their weaker members like the sick, elderly, orphan, and the disabled in activities such as cultivation of their backyards as well as construction of their residential houses.

(B) Elders' Council: The role of the *elders' council* regained importance in all aspects of the village community life. Based on the customary traditions of the community, elders settle conflicts arising at intra-household, inter-household, village and above village levels; advise and punish defaulters according to custom; teach and stress the importance of culturally accepted values and norms; encourage and motivate self-support and self-esteem by showing consideration for those weaker members; advocate sharing and co-operation; visit the sick and disabled; console the deceased family; facilitate marriage and inheritance cases; and play several other related important roles among the village community.

(C) Iqqub[24]: It is a voluntary money-pooling institution rotating the sum among the members either weekly, bi-weekly or monthly. Based on observation and discussions with community members, *iqqub* is practised much less than *iddir*. According to village informants, it is practised among a few young traders mostly during the dry season when off-farm income-generating activities are common. Since pooling money is one of its prime functions, *iqqub* demands strong mutual trust among its members. In the Beles Valley context where resettlers with diverse backgrounds are residing together, developing the required strong mutual trust for re-instituting *iqqub* seemed to have needed more time. Apart from the stated factor of background diversity, members of the community have also tried to explain part of the reason for the delay to be the prevalence of diseases (mostly malaria and tuberculosis) and the less hospitable nature of the lowland climate in the Beles Valley. Due to the reported health hazards, community members seem to rationalise the risk of engaging in pooling money in a rotating *iqqub*. However, more detailed factors for the less frequent practice of *iqqub* need further investigation.

---

[24] For more details, see Dejene (1993)

(*D*) *Village Development and Sanitation Days* (*yelimaatinna yeteena qan*): Local institutions facilitate and mediate the achievement of collective goals of the community. The innovative local institutions that have communal goals for the entire village community are best represented through village development and sanitation days. These are occasions in which the village inhabitants voluntarily perform diverse tasks of collective importance to the community. These activities include cleaning the village by draining waters so as to control mosquitoes; cleaning springs and fencing the surroundings; engaging in common weeding of the dangerous weed striga (*Striga spp;* locally known as *aqenchira* or *qittign* (Amh.)) at its immature stage from the field plots of villagers; constructing soil conservation bunds in areas susceptible to erosion; construct fences around the village clinic and school; constructing the residential houses of teachers, health workers and development agents including fencing the compounds; cleaning, repairing and constructing fences and work in the compounds of churches and mosques; extending generous support to the sick, disabled, and weak members of the community by constructing their residences and cultivating at their backyards; and so on.

The views and perceptions of the villagers towards the importance of the tasks on these occasions are very positive, and the participation of the community is voluntary and very high as a result of its practical common benefit to all the members. It is primarily a self-governed voluntary institution where the activities are performed by empowering the community. The elders, religious leaders, peasant association leaders, and all community members are fully involved at all levels. It is a special form of community-based institution with a strong base on community values, ethics, norms, conventions, and rules for their own collective goals.

Religious Belief
The different religious denominations of the resettlers have re-emerged, the dominant religions of the area being Orthodox Christianity, Islam, Protestantism, and Catholicism. Hand-in-hand with the re-establishment of the different religions, their leaders, mostly older people, have also regained importance. Their role and influence has become much stronger in putting pressure on their respective faith followers. They strongly preach to be faithful to one's own religion and observe the proper performance of the daily routine prayers of their religion. They perform prayers for the salvation of the souls of the dead. Moreover, they have a key role in soothing, cooling and consoling the grief of the bereaved families through their frequent

prayers and visits. More than anything else, the very re-emergence of the belief systems has created a very bright optimistic hope and gratification among the resettler communities, contributing a lot to the stable adaptation.

As part of the spiritual gratification, followers of the respective religions extend support to their weaker members, which in many cases is considered to be their main livelihood sources. The very preaching of each denomination motivates and encourages its followers to show affection, consideration, and sympathy to the needy. The Orthodox Church followers feed the poor through *senbete* feast consumed in the compounds of the churches.

The Muslims contribute *Zakat*[25] (locally called *zeka*, and is ideally an alms contribution of one-tenth of one's wealth) for supporting their weaker members. The Protestant and Catholic church followers fixed a date (usually Wednesdays) locally known as *yetesfa sira qan* (hope work day) in which they extend voluntary support to the weaker members and perform several activities including plowing and cultivation at their backyards, construct and repair their residences and compounds. The religious leaders mostly perform multiple spiritual and secular village day-to-day tasks forming part of the village elders.

Particularly among the followers of the Orthodox religion, *mahber* and *senbete* social institutions are widely practised. *Mahber* is formed by a group of selected members in the name of a selected saint. It is an association where the members organise a large feast every month on a rotation basis. Apart from enjoying its recreational nature of feasting and celebrating, members also support each other in several aspects of their daily lives. They support a member and his family during hardship and high labour demand during peak field activities as demanded. Moreover, *senbete* is organised by a group of the followers of the same religion where one or two members

---

[25] *Zakat*, according to the *Shorter Encyclopaedia of Islam*, is "the alms-tax, one of the principal obligations of Islam" prescribed for Muslims to pay "on the following kinds of property: 1. crops of the field, which are planted for food; 2. among fruits [...]; 3. camels, cattle, sheep and goats [...]; 4. gold and silver; 5. merchandise. On the first and second class the *zakat* is to be paid at once at the harvest, on the last three after one year's uninterrupted possession; a condition for liability to *zakat* is the possession of a certain minimum (*nisab*). On the first and second class the *zakat* is 10% [...]. There are complicated rules for the third category, which [...] take into consideration not only the number but also the kind of animals; the *nisab* is 5 camels; or 20 cattle, or 40 sheep or goats; the animals are only liable to *zakat* if they have grazed freely during the whole year and not been used for any work. The *zakat* on the fourth and fifth category is $2^1/_2$%; the *nisab* for precious metals is calculated according to the weight and amounts [...]; the value of merchandise must be estimated at the end of the year in gold or silver; in this case also there is liability to *zakat* only if the precious metal or merchandise has been kept for a full year unused 'as treasure' " (Gibb and Kramers 1961:654f.).

prepare food (*daabbo*) and drink (*tella*) every two weeks or once a month on a rotating basis. The food and drink is brought to the compound of a church, and members feast after the proper prayer together with the weak members who come looking for food or even reside there. Moreover, there exist important religious affiliation institution such as god-parenthood (*kristinna abbaat*). Through these institutional arrangements, multiple reciprocal supports are exchanged based on the resulting intimate interactions.

Kinship and Marriage
In the context of resettlement villages, peasants who do not belong to the same consanguinal kinship unit or even belong to different ethnic groups are living together. However, a few groups with a substantial number of members related by patrilineal kinship have come to the area and live either in the same or different villages. These kin members have stronger and closer ties and communicate with each other during important occasions. They managed to re-establish kinship ties, although not in the same magnitude as before relocating. On the other hand, since the resettlers' arrival at the new location, affinal kinship has been progressively emerging among different families through the marriages of their children. Marriages, which were at first practised without the usual proper ceremonies at the earlier stages, have almost fully regained "traditional" performances, and the whole process has begun to be organised and attended ceremonially according to the resettlers' respective socio-cultural backgrounds.

Among others, *amicha* (literally "affinal kinship") has become an important institution for labour mobilisation between the families of father-in-laws and son-in-laws. It has a very high image and value for the status of both parties. After informing the son-in-law of his need for the labour support, the father-in-law prepares an abundant feast including food, drinks, and animals to be slaughtered. Cognisant of this fact, the son-in-law mobilises the support of all his close members. Then, he comes with his group to the field of his father-in-law and courageously tries to complete the work to the full satisfaction of his affine. On the other hand, the son-in-law and his group will be carefully attended and fed to the best by the father-in-law's family. Usually, the feast continues over-night and the father-in-law prices for the worthiness of his son-in-law with gifts of various sorts, which strengthens the household of the new couple. This institutional arrangement is usually practised among relatively better-off households predominantly among those resettlers from north-central parts of the country (mainly Amhara). Moreover, kinship is one of the basic traditional institutions where families closely support their fellow members on multiple occasions.

Work Group

As already pointed out earlier, the major mutual community labour mobilising local institutions in the area include *dabo/jigi, wonfel/qaanja, amicha, baalinjeera* (also named *elfinna-qaso* in Kambaata and Hadiyya languages among the south-western resettlers), *waari/maarfeja/toori,* and *limmaano. Dabo/jigi* is a festive labour activity mostly organised by better-off farmers capable of offering a feast to mobilise labour. *Wonfel/qaanja* is a reciprocal labour pooled mostly by average farmers to perform tasks jointly on a rotating basis. *Amicha* (affinal kinship) can also refer to a work group of respective relatives. *Baalinjeera* (*elfinna-qaso*) is an intimate friendship-based festive labour activity and is similar to *amicha. Waari/maarfeja* is free labour support to the weaker members or to those who temporarily have encountered difficulties and usually is performed at early hours before going to the respective fields. *Limmaano* is full-time free labour support extended to the sick, disabled, and weak members of the community. These community level self-support institutions of resettlers have re-emerged and been strengthened mainly based on the re-establishment of the smallholder cultivation managed by the households, demanding mutual support.

Bond-Friendship[26]

The village community members have established institutional networks of relationships with others within the neighbourhood or beyond through intimate friendship on the basis of individual entrepreneurial ability in interacting with others. Individuals with networks of relations exchange a lot through their interaction. For instance, oxenless farmers get to use oxen. Those in need of cash and grain loan get easy access through their relations. Farmers faithful to each other based on their friendship take livestock from traders on instalment and pay after selling, making a substantial profit. As already pointed out, farmers who have better relations with others can mobilise enormous festive labour participants. Thus, mutual bond-friendship (*wodaajinet*) is one of the important institutions that can channel a member's access to multiple livelihood resources.

Tenancy Arrangements

The two predominant tenancy arrangement institutions are sharecropping and renting land locally known as *mareet maagaazaat*. These arrangements are means in which the main plots of weaker and oxen-less poor farmers are

---

[26] It is a widespread phenomenon in Ethiopia. For instance, for detailed description of the practice among the Gurage, see Shack (1963).

cultivated for mutual benefit of both parties (cf. chapter 8 "Tenancy Arrangement"). Through these arrangements members of the community practice complex forms of exchange systems such as oxen and labour, oxen and cash/grain, land and oxen, grain and labour, and labour and labour (cf. Chapter 8 "Agricultural Production Strategies" for further details).

9.2 The Role of Local Institutions in Securing Livelihood

Resettled farmers within the aforementioned institutional arrangements exchange indispensable resources through their interactions. The central role of the local institutions is manifested in mediating and channelling access to livelihood resources, providing strong social security or safety nets, and facilitating local self-governance.

Mediate and Channel Access to Livelihood Resources[27]

Local institutions mediate and channel the resettler households' access to a wide range of livelihood processes and serve as gateways to livelihood security. They are held together in social capital upon which people draw in the pursuit of livelihoods. The socio-economically differentiated resettler households have varying access to different livelihood resources based in part on the prevailing local institutional arrangements. These households are embedded in several institutional settings and operate in multiple institutions that fulfil different functions in different contexts.

Resettler households' access to key livelihood resources were enhanced through the re-establishment of institutional networks of relationships[28]. The different resettler household categories practice differing livelihood adaptation and coping strategies regulated by the institutional settings. For instance, the livelihood strategies of the very rich households mostly have favourable local institutional opportunities for further improvements. Their livelihood strategies are based on institutional arrangements such as sharecropping-in and renting-in land; mobilising large festive labour (*dabo*,

---

[27] As already pointed out in figure three (see chapter 2), Scoones (1998:4) explains that in a given context the ability to perform the multiple rural livelihood strategies (based on the combination of livelihood resources so as to achieve an outcome of livelihood adaptation) is mediated by institutional processes. His analytical framework of sustainable rural livelihoods emphasises the fundamental importance of local institutional and organisational contexts as central in influencing sustainable livelihood outcomes.

[28] This empirical account, based on the experiences of resettlers observed in the field, holds true and strengthens the consideration of local institutions as the social cement of human interaction as well as their vital role in enabling access to livelihood resources (Davies and Hossain 1997:24 cited in Scoones 1998:12; cf. chapter 2 "Local Social Institutions").

amicha, and *baalinjeera*); hiring-in farmers for a cropping season and daily labour during peak seasons; generating income from diverse sources (cash and food crops, livestock and its products, interest from cash and grain loans, trading grain and livestock, etc.); exchanging oxen for labour; exchanging oxen for cash and grain; exchanging oxen for land; and exchanging grain for labour. In their social rankings, they are very respected and extend generous welfare support to the weak members of the village through several local institutional arrangements. They organise large feasts on annual holidays. In the case of Orthodox Christians, they organise large feasts on those occasions such as *mahber, senbete,* and *kristinna* (feast organised on the occasion of the baptism of babies) where the weak members visit for feasting.

Meanwhile, the rich households have moderate institutional opportunities for further improvement. Their livelihood strategies are based on arrangements such as sharecropping-in land; renting-in land; hiring-in a farmer for a cropping season; occasionally hiring daily labour at peak seasons; mobilising festive labour (*dabo, amicha,* and *baalinjeera*); generating moderate income from diverse sources; exchanging oxen for labour; and exchanging oxen for land. They also provide generous support to the weak members through several local institutional settings and do organise moderate feasts on important occasions in which the weak visit and feast.

Less extensive, the production strategies of medium households depend on institutional arrangements such as pooling reciprocal labour through *wonfel* or *qaanja.* These households generate average income from diverse sources to augment the field produce and organise feasts only on major occasions. However, they seldom mobilise festive labour. They do not demand welfare support of others and can only occasionally extend moderately generous support to the weak members of their neighbourhood.

On the other hand, the main coping strategies of poor households are based on institutional arrangements such as exchange of land for oxen; exchange of labour for grain; exchange of labour for oxen; taking grain and cash loan; getting access to inputs and oxen through social networks; and collecting support from friends and neighbours. In addition, the poor households get access to oxen and/or credit (cash/grain loan) through local institutions such as bond-friendship, fictive/foster-parenthood, god-parenthood, affinal kinship, and *yezemedinna balinjeera iddir.* However, the survival strategies of the weak and dependent households are based on institutional arrangements of basically the generous handouts of the village community as well as visiting places of feasts for mere existence. Thus, the poorest families mainly survive on generous welfare support of the better households.

Provide Strong Social Security and Safety Nets

Local institutional arrangements provide strong social security and safety nets for the community. *Iddir* is the most important exemplary institution. Through *yeafer iddir*, funeral processes are facilitated and closely attended, financial expenses are covered, and multiple forms of solidarity and support are offered to the mourning family. As earlier explained, those cattle-owning members mutually support each other through *yekebt iddir*. *Yebeetsira iddir* enables community members to construct residences with fewer burdens. *Yeqaareza iddir* allows transporting their sick members and helps in saving lives. Members of *yezemedina baalinjeera iddir* use their institutional resources for fulfilling several goals of self-help in their daily lives in addition to extending extra mutual support during funeral and mourning. Membership in the basic neighbourhood *iddir* is equally open to all village community members without any status differentiation.

The religious belief institutions are basically meant for the spiritual gratification and social security of the community. Members of *mahber* and *senbete* have secure social cohesion and extend mutual support within each. Through the religious institutions, followers extend several welfare supports to their weaker members. Specially, the poorest and weak are socially secure through their institutional affiliations in the respective religions. The priests and *qaadi* play key roles in creating and maintaining cohesive relationships in the community. In their spiritual role, they have a strong capacity for applying pressure in conflict resolution. They also play an important role of maintaining stability within the community through their prayers, believed to mediate the worldly and heavenly. Through their prayer for the salvation of the souls of the dead, they soothe and console bereaved families.

The role of elders in the lives of the village community is indispensable. The conflict resolution capacity of elders is vital in creating stability and security inside the entire village community. Lasting conflict resolution without the direct and active role of elders is unimaginable. Elders are the prime facilitators in the process of extending welfare support to the weak members of the community through their traditionally most valued blessings. They advocate important values of mutual trust, Cupertino, and sharing – and this provides security for the village community in general and the weaker members in particular. Using their traditional wisdom, elders care for the safety and security of all the community members.

Facilitate Local Self-Governance

Local institutions, in the course of their existence, have a well-established and traditionally proven role of facilitating forums for democratic local self-governance through popular participation and community empowerment. Local institutions are freely initiated by the community without any external pressure and serve as forums for discussions of common concern. They facilitate a free, safe, and enabling environment, serving as vehicles of community participation. They enhance the freedom of community members as masters of their own affairs. Local institutions' relative independence from the state bureaucracy provides the community a certain freedom and liberty in their action. Membership in local institutions is entirely free from state interference. Since the loyalty and accountability of local institutions are to their community, they boost the trust, motivation, and self-esteem of the community. Thus, local institutions reveal the local community's proven capacity to organise and manage its own affairs.

Local institutions open up greater opportunities of participation at the local level of decision making especially for those marginal groups of the community such as the poor, women, and other marginalised minority groups such as artisans. The participation of the poor and other marginal groups facilitates better empowerment and representation for community level decision-making processes that would produce benefits, which lead to the alleviation of poverty and to enhanced livelihood security.

The different types of local institutions have an indispensable significance in the processes of local-level community self-governance. For instance, the council of elders customarily discusses issues of community concern in public, taking into consideration the freely expressed views of their community. Their conflict-resolving mechanism is considered to be fair and binding with careful compromise and tolerance, preventing either litigant from being a total looser or a complete winner. The other equally important role of the council of elders is observed in the management of common resources such as grazing areas, village forests, front yards, footpaths, and similar commonly owned properties, though their customary role seemed to have been neglected in some cases by the peasant association leaders. However, in most of the villages, the peasant association administrators cannot make a final decision with respect to defaulters before the traditional elders exhaust their methods through the appropriate local institutions.

In all the study villages, the formal peasants' association administrators confirmed the fact that without the elders' councils, their formal role would have been insignificant. The most frequently cited case in the Beles Valley context was the comparison of self-governance between the time of "political cadre administration" at the initial stage of resettlement and the present situation. During the cadre administration, almost all the local institutions were dismantled together with the population relocation. So, directly after relocation, the cadres, whose rule was that of malevolent absolute dictators, were the only authorities in village affairs. A case of the brutal forms of punishments committed by the cadres against the innocent resettlers is stated below:

A Case of Local Cadre Administration in L22 Village

At the early stages of the resettlement process in the Beles Valley, movements of resettlers outside the village without pass letters from village authorities were absolutely impossible and cause severe punishments by the cadres if identified. In 1977 E.C. (1985/86), a few months immediately after arrival, resettlers from the village who went to buy spices from the nearby Worke market became victims of cadre punishments. They were publicly brutally beaten and arrested in the village prison. Then, part of them were made to dig deep wells of their length; others were ordered to bring chopped 40 loads of fuel wood for cadres; some others were also ordered to bring 60 pieces of forked polls from the forest. Then, they were left completely naked pitilessly in the heavily burning sun of a lowland climate. Some are lifted to the top of a tukul and pushed to fall by rolling down; others were forced to carry 50 kg of ration to Pawe militia training centre about 40 km away from the village.

In 1978 E.C. (1986/87) w/ro Gormishe Medile, who was found by the cadre mourning for her husband who died by accident falling from a tree, was unsympathetically punished. She was ordered by the cadre to perform intensive labour work of collecting gravelled stones from the Beles river and paved a safe dry passage in front of the houses of cadres for three days.

In 1980 E.C. (1987/88) seven settlers who participated in the unloading of grain from Relief and Rehabilitation Commission (RRC) truck were accused of theft only for distributing scattered leftover grain seeds on the loading surface of the truck were publicly beaten and left bleeding in the burning sun. Six of them died few weeks later and only one was surviving at the time of interview.

Source: Resettler informants in village L22 (July-August 1995)

In the views of the resettlers, local self-governance has an important meaning based on the background of the horrible experiences they went through. Under the new formal local cadre administration, the communities had no freedom to make decisions whatsoever by themselves. Their complex indigenous institutions of social interactions were disarticulated increasing their stresses.

The community has strong hatred to those days. This situation has somehow changed with the political change and then the beginning of an improved rearticulation of local institutions. For instance, *iddir* creates a best forum for discussing issues of common good. Members, while attending a mourning family, discuss and settle matters concerning the entire community or its members. Since *iddir* is equally open to all types of households, everyone has a better chance of participating publicly in one way or another. It is one of the main occasions where many issues of community concern are discussed. The whole process of electing leaders, voting, running meetings, keeping discipline, and managing the entire discussion procedures reveals the fact of proven local community potential in governing the affairs of the entire community.

Therefore, the more the community is empowered at a local level, the better will be their self-governance and popular participation, which is a fertile ground for livelihood adaptation. The above case material shows that local institutions facilitate the functioning of local self-governance, which in turn channels access to productive resources in the process of securing livelihoods. However, the local communities in the study setting still demand further more enabling environment for popular participation and empowerment on their own affairs. An excessive top-down interference of the state in the local community affairs is a severe disabling factor and a major bottleneck for community participation. Thus, creating an enabling environment for local institutional arrangements through practical empowerment of the local community is very important for enhancing their livelihood security.

9.3 A Critique of Local Institutions

In spite of the infinite potential functions in multiple settings as explained in the foregoing part, local institutions do have limitations in certain contexts that need recognition. North (1990) states that institutions structure incentives or disincentives in human interaction by defining and limiting the set of choices of individuals. So, in the dynamics of institutional *inclusion* and *exclusion*, local institutions could suppress opportunities for some members of the community (for example, the poor, women, and other marginal groups) while enhancing those of other members through channelling differential access to livelihood resources.

Institutional arrangements are key elements in determining distinct liveli-hood strategies pursued by poor households compared to rich households. Similarly, social proscription creates differences in the livelihood options available for marginal groups. Participation in different local institutions usually assumes some sort of ascribed or achieved preconditions such as residence in village community, wealth, gender, religion, kinship, ethnicity, and crafts. Whether individuals meet these conditions determines their ac-cess to the resources these institutions govern. In the case of Beles Valley, although membership is open to all members, most *iddir* require residence in the given village. Festive *mahber* is formed among better-off households. *Amicha* is restricted to affines. *Senbete, zeka* and *yetesfa sira qan* (hope work day) are restricted to followers of respective religious denominations.

A strong sense of belonging along ethnic lines is noticed implicitly or ex-plicitly in several institutional settings. Certain implicit segregation and elements of exclusion from some institutions is noticed on marginal groups like the potters. Except those who are heads of households, women generally have relatively less institutional access to livelihood resources. Usually, women form those limited gender-specific institutions such as *wonfel*. Cus-tomarily, women are rarely noticed as members of *elders' council* in the village.

Moreover, the role of local institutions should not be over-exaggerated beyond their capacity in the local context. The multiple significance of local social institutions does not mean that they are holistic enough in all contexts *per se*. Some of the local institutions have proven ability in specific func-tions. The boundaries created through the inclusion and exclusion of mem-bership in the institutions should be noted where institutional arrangements circumstantially either restrict or broaden access to ranges of livelihood re-sources.

The argument is that local institutions should be strengthened by integrat-ing them with appropriate new ideas as preconditions in interventions that would enhance community livelihood security. Moreover, local institutions that have proven successful at propelling the pursuit of resettlers' economic recovery and livelihood adaptation in the Beles Valley resettlement scheme even in the absence of proper sectoral support should be consciously consid-ered and revitalised both by researchers and planners instead of importing ideas and schemes that are completely alien to local conditions.

PART FOUR: GUMUZ AND RESETTLERS – ETHNIC IDENTITY, CONFLICT, AND COEXISTENCE

Chapter 10. Ethnic Identification of the Gumuz and Highland Resettlers

This chapter tries to present the ethnic identification dimensions of the Gumuz and highland resettlers. In the local identity politics of "inclusion versus exclusion" or "we/us" and "they/them," the identification process of *"who against whom and why?" [...] "who belongs to whom and why?"* (using the expressions of Schlee 2000:89, emphasis added) questions are attempted to be examined in the study context.

10. 1 Profile of Multi-Ethnic Composition

The profile of multi-ethnic composition in Metekel is diverse and complex. Before the arrival of the state-sponsored resettlers of the 1980s, Metekel was inhabited by several ethnic groups with their own distinct languages, socio-economic formations, and cultures, which include the Gumuz, Shinasha, Agaw, Oromo, Amhara (Gojjam, Gondar, and Wollo, including early immigrants since the 1950s), and Kumfel (*Qollegna* Agaw). Of these ethnic groups, the Gumuz are a relatively numerous but politically less powerful autochthonous group as already discussed in part two.

Table 20*: Major Ethnic, Language, and Religious Groups Inhabiting Metekel Other than the State-Sponsored Resettlers of the 1980s

No.	Major Ethnic Groups	Population	Language Family	Dominant Religious Background*
1	Gumuz	66,965	Nilo-Saharan	Traditional belief system
2	Shinasha	32,038	Omotic	Orthodox
3	Oromo	27,050	Cushitic	Orthodox, Protestant
4	Amhara	21,900	Semitic	Orthodox, Islam
5	Agaw	17,155	Cushitic	Orthodox, Islam

Source: CSA, 1996 (Based on the 1994 Population and Housing Census of Ethiopia)
* Researcher's personal observation and impression

Table 21: Ethnic Background of Population Inhabiting the Beles Valley Resettlement Area

Ethnic Background	State-Sponsored Resettlers of the 1980s			Immigrant Farmers of the 1990s			Small Town Dwellers			Total Population		
	No.	%	%	No.	%	%	No.	%	%	No.	%	%
Amhara W.	10682	51.0	-	577	8.7	-	1033	13.2	9.4	12292	34.7	25.4
Amhara Sh.	5564	26.6	-	-	-	-	477	6.1	4.3	6041	17.1	12.5
Gojj.	4469	21.4	-	5712	86.3	-	4711	60.2	42.9	14892	42.1	30.8
Gon	210	1.0	-	331	5.0	-	1605	20.5	14.6	2146	6.1	4.4
Total	*20925*	100	*68.6*	*6620*	100	*96.5*	*7826*	100	*71.2*	*35371*	100	*73.1*
Kambaata	3661	12.0		58	0.8		615	5.6		4334	9.0	
Hadiyya	3410	11.2		60	0.9		538	4.9		4008	8.3	
Oromo*	1399	4.6		48	0.7		110	1.0		1557	3.2	
Wolaita	443	1.4		-	-		-	-		443	1.0	
Tigraway	313	1.0		12	0.2		219	2.0		544	1.1	
Agaw (Seqota)	362	1.2		-	-		-	-		362	0.7	
Agaw (Gojj.)	-	-		60	0.9		1549	14.1		1609	3.3	
Others	-	-		-	-		134	1.2		134	0.3	
Total	**30513**	**100**		**6858**	**100**		**10991**	**100**		**48362**	**100**	

Source: Wolde-Selassie Abbute survey (February – March 2001)
*Mainly from North Shoa and some from Wollo
W. = Wollo
Sh. = Shoa
Gojj. = Gojjam
Gon. = Gondar

As earlier pointed out in the introductory chapter, the ethnic profile in Mete-kel can be broadly grouped into four sub-categories and include (1) the autochthonous Gumuz; (2) the long-standing highland neighbours such as Shinasha, Amhara (Gojjam/Gondar), Agaw (Gojjam), and Oromo; (3) early immigrants from Wollo since the 1950s who are predominantly Amhara; and (4) the state-sponsored resettlers of the 1980s that include Amhara (Wollo, Gojjam, Gondar, and North Shoa), Kambaata, Hadiyya, Agaw (Wollo-Tigray/Seqota) and Tigraway. Apart from the stated four, those residents in the small towns of the area, in particular the Beles Valley are accordingly considered as an important additional sub-category.

The profile of these major ethnic, religious, and language composition of populations inhabiting Metekel is described in tables 20, 21, and 22. Some of the contents of these tables have already been pointed out in the previous parts of this study (cf. chapters 1 and 6).

More specifically, the state-sponsored resettlers of the 1980s indicated in the table 21 can be categorised into the three major language families. Those in the Semitic language family include Amhara and Tigraway; in the Cushitic include Kambaata, Hadiyya, Oromo, and Agaw; and the Omotic include Wolaita.

Table 22: Religious Background of the Population Inhabiting the Beles Valley Resettlement Area

R. B.	State-Sponsored Resettlers of the 1980s			Voluntary/ Displaced Immigrants of the 1990s			Small Town Dwellers			Total Population		
	No.	%	%	No.	%	%	No.	%	%	No.	%	%
C. P. T.	1648	7.3	5.4	-	-	-	594	7.0	5.4	2242	6.3	4.6
	4793	21.2	15.7	148	3.3	2.1	506	6.0	4.6	5447	15.3	11.3
	22613	*100*	*74.1*	*4501*	*100*	*65.6*	*8496*	*100*	*77.3*	*35610*	*100*	*73.6*
M.	7900	25.9		2357	34.4		2495	22.7		12752	26.4	
T.	30513	100		6858	100		10991	100		48362	100	

Source: Wolde-Selassie Abbute survey (February – March 2001)
R. B. = Religious Background; O. = Orthodox; C. = Christian; P. = Protestant; M. = Muslim;
T = Total

It is against such a contextual multi-ethnic and religious background that the discussion in this part of the study attempts to examine the ethnic identification of Gumuz and highland resettlers.

10.2 The Gumuz: Ethnic Identity

The *Bega*[1] and the *Shuwa*[2] Identity
The Gumuz make strong boundary dichotomization between *we* and *they*. They refer to their group members as *Bega* (our people) and all other highland neighbouring members as *Shuwa* (others). The latter include Amhara,

---

[1] *Bega* is an *emic* designation used by the Gumuz, referring to their group members. The two ethnic terms *Bega* and Gumuz are used interchangeably throughout the study.

[2] *Shuwa* is an *etic* categorical designation used by the Gumuz, referring to the members of their highland neighbours. The terms *Shuwa* and highlanders or 'highland resettlers' are used interchangeably throughout the study.

Shinasha, Agaw, Oromo, and all other highland resettlers in Metekel usually without differentiation. The other local equivalent term for *Shuwa* is *qay*[3]. In this study, the terms *Bega* and *Shuwa* are used interchangeably used while designating the respective groups.

In the process of ethnic identification, several features were articulated to mark the socio-cultural distinction of the Gumuz (*Bega*) identity against the highland neighbours (*Shuwa*). Some of these identity markers articulated include the popular genealogical myth of common origin and historical experiences; occupation of divergent ecological niches as lowlanders versus highlanders and the differing modes of livelihood; differing belief systems, marriage systems, and patterns of authority; overt physical features such as pigmentation and bodily scarification; and other identification symbols such as language, costume and folklore. Additionally, various features of ethnic stereotyping are used to label identifications.

Origin Myth and Historical Experiences
Genealogical metaphor of common origin and historical experiences are perceived by the Gumuz as key factors expressed in the process of shaping the *Bega* identity as distinct from *Shuwa*. According to the popular origin myth, once upon a time, twin sons were born from a mother. One of the sons was black and the other was fair. As they grew up, they competed for power in the presence of a local assembly. First, they were given a mule for racing. The *Shuwa* galloped well but the *Bega* fell from his mule. Then, they were offered to choose from bow and arrow, and spear and shield. The *Shuwa* chose the spear and shield, while the *Bega* took the bow and arrow. Later, they were made to choose between porridge and *injera* as their staple food. The *Bega* took porridge while the *Shuwa* took *injera*. Then, they were asked to settle either in the central highlands or towards the lowlands and the periphery. The *Shuwa* selected to settle in the highlands, to the right, and the *Bega* selected the lowlands, to the left. Thus, the Gumuz claim genealogically to have originated from a common ancestor with their *Shuwa* neighbours, but they differed in their choices from the very beginning.

The historical aspects such as the ceaseless external encroachment, ruthless subjugation, and enslavement of the Gumuz by the central highlanders are strongly emphasised in the process of shaping and maintaining the *Bega* identity. Such experiences are a shared element of the Gumuz and a crite-

---

[3] The term *qay* ("red") is used as a literally translated local Amharic equivalent for the Gumuz term *Shuwa* to refer collectively to those "fair-pigmented" highlanders in comparison to the "darker pigmented" Gumuz.

rion, which strictly excludes their *Shuwa* neighbours. A long-time exposure of the Gumuz to slave raiding by the highlanders combined with their increased pressure on the land resources forced them to escape and retreat farther to the inaccessible lowlands. Several Abyssinian kings conducted devastating and destructive campaigns to subjugate and enslave the Gumuz. The Gumuz were frequently raided for their young men and women. According to the oral accounts of the Mandura and Dangur Gumuz informants, the shocking experiences of the slave raids by highlanders witnessed during the early years of some of the living informants was the cutting of one of the enslaved's strong leg tendons, preventing escape. These horrible experiences of enslavement have a strong influence in the consciousness of inclusion and ethnic boundary maintenance process of *Bega* identification against the extreme exclusion of *Shuwa,* polarising them based on deep-rooted suspicion and mistrust. (cf. chapter 3, section 3.1 for detailed description Gumuz ethno-history).

Features of Ethnic Stereotyping

Various ethnic stereotyping features are used to label the *Bega* identity against *Shuwa*. The *Shuwa* dichotomise, thus polarising their identity by referring to the Gumuz with a derogatory generic term, *Shanqilla*[4], signalling stigma and implying contemptuous inferior status. The Gumuz also in turn refer to the *Shuwa* with the generic hatred term *Mittiha*[5]. The highly polarised dichotomization in the *Bega* identification is strongly based on the exclusion of the *Shuwa,* deeply reflected in the stated references of ethnic stereotyping. Equally interesting ethnic stereotypes used to mark the boundaries between the *Bega* and *Shuwa* are expressed in behavioural labels. The *Bega* characterise the behaviour of the *Shuwa* as brutal, greedy and insatiable and as people who used to attack, intrude and plunder their property. They consider the *Shuwa* as cruel, heartless and inhuman people who used to brutally raid and enslave them. *Bega* developed a deep-rooted hatred and are usually suspicious of the *Shuwa*, whom they consider as treacherous, unreliable, and double-crossing people who viciously hurt them. For *Bega*, the *Shuwa* are greedy intruders who ceaselessly encroach on their resources, infringing their rights. Behavioural practices such as telling lies and stealing were said to be totally unknown among the *Bega* before the intrusion of the

---

[4] Derogatory generic term ascribed by highlanders to designate the Gumuz for their darker pigmentation.
[5] Critical generic term ascribed by the Gumuz to the neighbouring highlanders and connotes their cruelty and brutality.

Shuwa and even today in those areas least encroached by the latter, the granaries of the former are left in the field away from the village, proving the absence of theft. The *Bega* consider the *Shuwa* as untrustworthy and insatiably exploitative where the boundary rift between the two seems to remain very wide. Such a mistrust and wide boundary rift is noticeable in multiple contexts. For instance, according to the interpretation of my Gumuz research assistant, Wubalta Enno, during the fieldwork some Gumuz members in Mandura were sceptical of the effectiveness of the 1999 and 2000 polio vaccinations offered free of charge. Their suspicion, in their perception, was of the unusual behaviour of the *Shuwa* to offer something of real value free of charge. So, some were sceptical of getting their children vaccinated, considering that 'had the medicine really had the stated preventive value, the *Shuwa* would not have given it free of charge.'

Identity Markers[6]

Those several presumed identity markers articulated to express socio-cultural distinction of the *Bega* against the *Shuwa* are reflected in the occupation of divergent ecological niches as lowlanders versus highlanders; differing modes of livelihood; egalitarian versus hierarchical patterns of authority systems.

The different ecological niches used by the *Bega* and the *Shuwa* are often cited as one of the main attributes of their difference. Since the Gumuz inhabit the lowlands, their entire way of life is manifested in their adaptation to the hot-humid-tropical climate in the lowland ecological niche with topography of undulating gentle slopes, plains, and valley bottoms. Shifting cultivation and the gathering of wild forest foods, hunting, fishing, and honey collection, form the main sources of subsistence to the Gumuz (cf. chapter 3.4; chapter 4 "Shifting Cultivation and Multi-Niche Management Strategy" and "'Fire' as Resource Management Strategy"; and chapter 5 "Impact on the Livelihood, Resource Management and the Environment"). The *Shuwa* predominantly inhabit the mid- and high altitude areas and their mode of subsistence is based on mixed farming of plow cultivation and animal husbandry (cf. chapter 8 "Means of Livelihood"). Patterns of authority among the Gumuz are ideally egalitarian (cf. chapter 3 "Elders and Patterns of Authority"), whereas patterns of authority among their *Shuwa* neighbours, are considered to be hierarchical, based on either achieved or ascribed status.

---

[6] For more detailed discussions on the distinctions of ethnic identity markers such as symbols, emblems and features based on East African examples, see Schlee (1994:129-133).

Identity Symbols

In addition to the identity markers stated above, those socio-cultural attributes articulated to mark the *Bega* identity expressed through symbolic implications include sister-exchange marriage; traditional belief systems; and language, costume, and folklore.

Sister-exchange[7] is the most elaborate form of marriage among the Gumuz (cf. chapter 3 "Marriage and Kinship System"), which is different from the type of marriage practised by their *Shuwa* neighbours (mostly arranged through bride-price and exchange of various forms of marriage gifts). Sister exchange marriage is a very elaborate age-old arrangement practised among the clans with an ideology of "fair balance" with a symbolic implications of durable bonding between clans exchanging women as well as those lending and borrowing girls for marriage within the clan[8]. The sister-exchange in the marriage and kinship systems of the Gumuz is considered as a symbol of their persistent identity. It is a means of their survival strategy used for preserving their identity from the penetration of the more powerful neighbouring highlanders through their goods and cash systems (James 1975:94).

The Gumuz are followers of a *traditional belief system* (cf. chapter 3 "Traditional Belief Systems and Spirit Mediums"), whereas their *Shuwa* neighbours are predominantly followers of Orthodox (monophysite) Christianity together with a significant number of followers of Islam. The *Bega*

---

[7] For more detailed description and discussion of sister-exchange marriage among the Gumuz to the south of *Abbay* River, see James (1975, 1986).

[8] James (1975:86) explains that the Gumuz have "the most elaborate and internally coherent system of sister-exchange marriage. The exchanges take place between patrilineal clans, and they are normally arranged by clan elders, who have considerable authority over the younger men and women. If a marriage takes the form of an elopement and there is no subsequent exchange, it is described as 'stealing' and could provoke violent retaliation. The matter may be put right a few years later when an exchange girl is found, or even in the next generation, when a daughter may be used in an exchange, as her mother should have been.

Elaborate arrangements may be made for borrowing and lending girls for exchange within the clan or between closely linked clans. When you borrow a girl from a clansman to exchange for a wife, you should eventually give your own daughter (whose birth is made possible by the exchange) back to your clansman or his son as a replacement; your daughter can then herself be exchanged. There are sets of debts linking people over the generations, both between clans and within clans. Once an exchange-marriage link is made it is fairly durable in itself; if one wife dies, a replacement may be found (and even a second replacement if the first replacement dies) [...]. It is common for a widow to be inherited by one of her husband's brothers. Fathers exercise a fairly strict control over the marriage of their daughters, allocating them to one or another son or nephew, or even exchanging them for a second wife for themselves.

Everyone among the Gumuz is caught up in this network of exchanges; there is no alternative mode of marriage contract [...]. As can be imagined, marriage arrangements among the Gumuz are major political matters, linked both with feuds between clans and with peace-making."

consider their traditional belief system as one of the distinguishing features of socio-cultural differences. The ideologies of their lives and livelihood are symbolically marked in their traditional belief systems and worldview reflecting the attributes of complex nature-culture interconnections.

Equally important overt cultural attributes, among others, considered by the *Bega* as identity markers with symbolic labels are *language, costume, and folklore*. Cultural attributes such as language, dress, and ritual procedure are considered as merely symbolic labels denoting the different sectors of a single extensive structural system (Leach (1954:17, cited in Schlee 1994:132). As stated earlier, linguistically, the Gumuz belong to the Koman group of the Central-Sudanic branch in the Nilo-Saharan language family (cf. chapter 3, section 3.1), whereas their *Shuwa* neighbours belonging to Semitic (Amhara), Cushitic (Oromo and Agaw), and Omotic (Shinasha) language families.

In their custom of costume, Gumuz women wear a cotton skirt wrapped around their waist extending down to their knees and most of the time, leaving the upper part of the body nude. Interviews with Gumuz in Mandura provide evidence that wearing full dress of the neighbouring *Shuwa* women and the shallow over-wear shawl (*natala*) is perceived by the Gumuz women as crazy and deviant behaviour and as showing disrespect to their traditional way of life. Gumuz women wear strings tightly tied around their arms on two places below the shoulder and above the elbow. On special occasions women make leather strings cut from fresh skins of goats ritually slaughtered to celebrate ceremonial events and tightly tie them around their legs. An example of such a ritually celebrated occasion is an event to mark a bride's virginity in which the groom offers a goat to the singing, dancing, and chanting womenfolk of his and the girl's natal village. Women also wear ornaments such as strings of coloured beads around their necks, iron rings on their fingers, large earrings, suspended and fixed iron ornaments on their nose, and bracelets both on their arms and legs. Girls at their puberty wear over their skirts thin strings of leather tassels wrapped around their waists and suspended on their buttocks at the back as a decoration and provide an attractive rhythm on the occasions of traditional dances and chants. They also smear ochre mixed with castor bean on their hair. The women carry goods balanced on a stick over their shoulders, in suspended nets tied on both ends into which large gourds, baskets and bags containing the load are fit. In contrast, the *Shuwa* women differ in their costume and carry loads on their backs.

On the other hand, the style of clothing worn by Gumuz men is not easy to describe because of the influence of a combination of autochthonous,

European, highland Ethiopian, and the Sudan sources. However, adolescent youth wear local daggers inserted into a dagger-sheath tightly tied together with packed strings of leather tassels suspended on either side of their waist. The dagger is used both for defence and cutting meat, whereas the dagger together with the suspended strings of leather tassels is used like a rattle to provide the rhythm singing and dancing.

Unlike most of their Orthodox Christian *Shuwa* neighbours, whose priests are relatively familiar with written literature, the Gumuz are primarily non-literate people, who fully depend on orally transmitted traditions and are rich in folklore such as poetry and prose narratives. Their folklore has been woven from the substances of their experiences and portrays their struggles with the mysteries of existence as well as their explanation about the unknown in order to create order and reason. Apart from its extensive artistic value, the folklore expresses their struggle for their rights, wars and conflicts they have had with their neighbouring ethnic groups, their resistance struggle in defending and safeguarding their human and land resources, and their perceptions and explanations of the secrets of nature, life, and death. Thus, while articulating the *Bega* ethnic identity against that of their *Shuwa* neighbours, the Gumuz refer to their language, costume, folklore and related overt cultural features as marks that distinctly dichotomise them from their neighbours in the identification and boundary maintenance of their ethnic identity.

Identity Emblems
Bodily scarifications are considered as evident symbolic identity markers – emblems. Removing the two central lower incisors by the Rendille of Kenya, Schlee (1994:132) explains, marks a highly visible identity emblem of the group. Additionally, removing all the four lower incisors among the Anywaa (both sexes) and six deep cuts on the faces of Nuer men (known as *gar* in the Nuer language) denote clearly observable identity symbols and emblems of the respective groups[9].

Similarly, among the Gumuz, bodily scarifications mark clearly visible identity symbols and emblems of their ethnic group members. Apart from designating as identification symbols, the overt physical scars serve as a mark of beautification especially in the case of women. Men mostly have scars on both the left and right sides of the upper cheeks, whereas women

---

[9] Personal communication with Dereje Feyissa who is conducting his research on Anuak and Nuer in Gambella. He observed a declining trend in the practices by both ethnic groups especially in areas proximate to Gambella town.

mostly have decorative scars on their backs, cheeks, stomach, and upper arms. The bodily scarification is performed on boys and girls at puberty. These bodily scars are referred to locally as *moqqota*. The traditional practitioner of *moqqota* is known as an *ittemoqqota*. The different bodily scars have different shapes and are referred to by different names. Bodily scars on cheeks are called *moqqotlissa*; scars on the back of women are called *moqqotbongua*; scars on the abdomen of women are called *moqqotaiila*; scars on the upper arm are called *moqqotqo'ea*; and scars on the lower arm are called *moqqota'ea*. According to informants, a Gumuz, especially without a proper facial scar, is not considered a *Bega*. Either he is not a *Bega* or is someone who was born outside their area from parents taken as slaves. These different bodily scars are considered overt identification marks while articulating the *Bega* identity over against that of the *Shuwa*.

10.3 Identity Dimensions among the Highland Resettlers

Apart from the broad autochthonous Gumuz (Bega) versus highland resettlers (Shuwa) identification dichotomy in the Beles Valley and its environs, the latter are in turn differentiated into various levels and layers of identity dimensions. These include early immigrants of the 1950s versus state-sponsored resettlers of the 1980s and later immigrants of the 1990s; state-sponsored resettlers versus later immigrants; north-central versus south-western resettlers; the Amhara, Oromo; Tigraway, an Agaw (Seqota) within the north-central resettlers; the Kambaata, Haddiya and Wolaita within the south-western resettlers; and further differentiation along kinship and geographical space in the home and resettlement areas.

Highlander Resettlers (*Qay*) versus Gumuz (*Tiqur*)

The broader categorical identification boundary is dichotomised as *qay* (fair pigmented highlanders) and *tiqur* (dark pigmented Gumuz) mainly according to the highlanders' designation. This general level of identification considers all highland resettler plow cultivators in one inclusive category while excluding the autochthonous Gumuz on the basis of an overt physical feature, namely pigmentation. In other words, the dichotomy seems to be divided as "outsiders/immigrants" versus "autochthonous."

However, it has to be noted that the Shinasha are considered as the second "autochthonous" ethnic group of Metekel in the ethnic politics of the present state. Nevertheless, in the perception of the Gumuz, the Shinasha are categorically identified more as part of the *Shuwa*. Although the two groups have lived neighbouring each other for a long time, the Gumuz do not seem comfortable with their alliances with the Shinasha because the latter belongs fully to *Shuwa* in many of the basic features delineated to the category. Among many distinguishing features, the Shinasha are mostly strong adherents of Orthodox Christianity. For instance, no case of inter-marriage is reported at all by members of the two ethnic groups. The Shinasha mainly inhabit the mid-altitudinal ecological niche, while the Gumuz inhabit mostly the lowland ecological niche. The two also differ in their farming systems since the Shinasha are mainly plow cultivators, which was said to be of a later introduction. The Shinasha are considered as strictly endogamous within their ethnic group members but exogamous in marrying women from outside one's own clan. Meanwhile, the highland resettlers perceive the Shinasha with suspicion for their ambiguous position of political alliance with the Gumuz, viewed as a strategy devised to exclude all the other highlanders from competing for economic, social, and political resources and gains in the area.

Immigrants of 1950s versus Resettlers of 1980s and Immigrants of 1990s

The next level of categorical identification focuses on the case observed in the Beles Valley and its environs within the highland resettlers. The groups in this category can be differentiated into three sub-categories. The first group includes those early immigrant farmers of the 1950s from Wollo, Gojjam, and Gondar who settled along the environs of the present Beles Valley resettlement scheme area. Of these early immigrant farmers, those from Wollo are Muslim while those from Gojjam and Gondar are Orthodox Christians. Moreover, those early Wollo immigrants originally trekked together with their fellow members, most of whom had settled in areas around Dibati. The second group includes those state-sponsored resettlers of the 1980s, who form the majority of the present Beles Valley inhabitants with diverse ethnic backgrounds, including Amhara (Wollo, Gojjam, Shoa and Gondar), Kambaata, Hadiyya, Wolaita, Oromo, Tigraway and Agaw (Seqota). Finally, the third group includes those displaced immigrant farmers of early spontaneous immigrant settlers of Wollo around Dibati in the 1950s (displaced as a consequence of ethnic conflict with Gumuz in their earlier settlement areas) as well as those voluntary immigrant farmers from Gojjam and Gondar who are locally known as *zellan* (which literally means 'nomads' for their large livestock husbandry). The immigrant farmers in the latter category came to the Beles Valley in the 1990s following the 1991 political change in the country as already described earlier in part three.

The early immigrants of Wollo, Gojjam, and Gondar since the 1950s identify themselves as broader inclusive group under the common ethnic label of Amhara. They ideally kept to the minimum their differences of origin from different geographical locations as well as their differences in belief systems in Islam and Orthodox Christianity. In this context, their Amhara ethnic identification is mobilised and instrumentalised specially to defend and protect their group members by excluding the autochthonous Gumuz, with whom ethnic conflicts were quite common. However, under the broader Amhara collective identification, each immigrant group segmented along respective sub-group collectivities in which, among other things, intermarriage across groups was less common. In other words, their strongly mobilised collective identification seems to be based on contextual needs of the circumstances. In such a situation, when the state had brought around eighty thousand resettlers to the area in the 1980s, the early immigrants were initially delighted, considering themselves new-comers as categorically in the same broad collective identity against the autochthonous Gumuz. The early immigrants considered the new-comers as an asset that would strengthen their number and capacity, increasing their security from feared attacks by the Gumuz.

Under the broad *qay* (non-Gumuz) collective identity, further layers and levels of differentiation began emerging in the relations between the early immigrants and new resettlers. Referring to the same original area as a background, the early Wollo immigrants showed preferential identification with the new resettlers from Wollo. On the other hand, those early Gojjam immigrants showed the same attitude to new resettlers from Gojjam as those from Gondar. Mostly, manipulating these social networks along common original geographical locations, the immigrants contributed multiple social, psychological, and economic resources through customary institutional arrangements in the process of the latter's adaptation in the new setting.

However, as the resettlers went through early adaptive readjustments and began showing economic recovery, elements of implicit envy began emerging among the early immigrants against the resettlers as tough competitors both in their production and exchange interests. The excessive support extended to the resettlers by both the state and aid organisations (neglecting all others in the neighbourhood) has also created implicit and explicit resentment and noticeable distance. Moreover, the state-sponsored resettlers also suffered significant discrimination and stigma referred to by the very local term *safaari*/resettler), signalling the negative contemptuous meaning of weak and helpless newcomers who are not self-reliant but existing under the "baby-care" of the state and aid organisations' generosity and handouts.

Hence, the resettlers later developed strong resentment and hatred to the very term *safaari* and rather preferred very much to be called *gabare* (farmer).

Once the later displaced and voluntary immigrant farmers of the 1990s immigrated into the area, the early immigrants showed an increased tendency to preferentially identify with them rather than with the state-sponsored resettlers. In the case of early Wollo immigrants, increased preferential identification with those displaced immigrants from around Dibati was based on not only tracing the same spatial origin but also temporally significant, referring to their former common trekking together in the 1950s in search of cultivable land, leaving behind their home areas. On the other hand, those early immigrants from Gojjam and Gondar have also showed increased preferential identification with the later voluntary immigrants from the respective areas. Most of these immigrants came on their own without special care of the state and settled mainly along the peripheral villages abandoned by the resettlers and in areas proximate to the early immigrants. Moreover, the later immigrants are identified as closer to the early immigrants because of their stronger social and economic set-up than the state-sponsored resettlers. Intermarriage was reported between the later immigrants from Wollo settled in village R104 with those early immigrants residing around Mambuk. Both are strong adherents of Islam.

Resettlers of 1980s versus Immigrants of 1990s

Despite their sub-differentiation along the causes of their immigration (displaced or voluntary) to the area, the immigrants of the 1990s are collectively identified belonging to the same broad category. Among others, the factors that influence their categorical identification include both temporal and spatial issues. The temporal aspect is reflected in their arrival at around the same time, whereas the spatial aspect designates their settlements being mostly located at the peripheries of the resettlers' villages and cultivation fields. Moreover, their land tenure insecurity issue played a strong role in the inclusion within the same category where ideally the true owners of land resources in the area are said to be those state-sponsored resettlers. One exception is those displaced immigrants in village R104 who settled in a village totally abandoned by resettlers with the approval of the then provisional committee.

As intermittently discussed throughout the study, following the 1991 political change in the country, bloody ethnic conflict with Gumuz emerged both around Dibati with early immigrants from Wollo and inside Beles Valley with resettlers reaching its climax in 1994. On the one hand, many of the

233

early immigrants settled around Dibati were displaced and moved to a temporary shelter at Chagni. On the other hand, many of the resettlers in the Beles Valley abandoned their villages, abruptly returning to their original areas. Most of those who remained in the area were reintegrated into the existing villages located either in the centre or those in relatively safer locations within the area.

Due to the dramatic consequences of the ethnic conflict, a provisional committee chaired by a person named *Molla Lakew* administered the area. During this period, those displaced from Dibati were informed about vacant villages through their fellow early immigrants around Mambuk. Then, a group of elders led by the late *Sheh Yisa Yesuf* visited the area and contacted the chairman of the committee. Together with the chairman, the elders visited the vacant village at R104 and got the approval of the chair to move into the village. The elders went back to their people and returned together with their fellow members and settled in the village with full recognition of the authorities. As they immigrated into village R104, part of the former resettlers' villages of R105 and R103 were also given to them. Those who joined them within the first two years were accommodated with a share of land.

Today, their *kebele* forms one of the formal local administrative units of the district. Interestingly enough, their kebele is divided into ten smaller village hamlets known as *Berber, Yekuas, Berejet, Dawunt, Wadila, Masera, Shimel Mender, Zigih, Dawur* and *105*. The ten names represent part of their identification marks brought with them and maintained in their culture and history of migration beginning from Wollo, then to around to Chagni and Dibati, and finally to their present location in the Beles Valley. Of the stated ten, the first six names, *Yekuas, Berejet, Dawunt, Wadila* and *Masera,* are names maintained from their original areas from Wollo when they left the area in 1950s. These six names were maintained from the origins as village names in their last settlement areas around Dibati as well. The next three names, *Shimel Mender, Zigih* and *Dawur* are maintained from their last settlement areas around Dibati (the first two names) and Chagini (the third name). Finally the last name, *105* shows a new name incorporated from their recent settlement in the present location inside the Beles Valley.

Initially, the resettlers welcomed the immigration of the later immigrant farmers because they brought livestock with them. The immigrants' cattle provided hope to the mostly weakened resettlers by allowing them to envisage possibilities of human and livestock adaptation in this malaria and *trypanosomiasis* infested area. Since resettlers had lost contacts with cattle in the new setting, they were excited to observe cattle browsing in the area and even just by being able to see and smell the dung itself. They welcomed the immigrants with livestock both as traction animals as well as producers of milk and milk products. However, as the new immigrants with their better resource position and physical strength began showing rapid wealth accumulation, the resettlers started being resentful and "envious." Their resentment of the newcomers' competition for resources was reflected in the resettlers' call for the local authorities to remove immigrants. The resettlers claim to be the true owners of the resources because they were the ones who created the conditions for human habitation of the area.

In their relations with the resettlers, a preferential identification was practised between immigrants and resettlers from Wollo, Gojjam, and Gondar respectively. Immigrants from Gojjam and Gondar are mostly adherents of Orthodox Christianity, while those from the Dibati area (formerly from Wollo) are adherents of Islam. However, when it comes to sharing the land resources, resistance was observed on the part of the resettlers. At times, fierce conflicts occurred between immigrants and resettlers originating from the same area. For instance, a serious conflict broke out over land claims in the abandoned village of R102 between displaced immigrants settled in village R104 and resettlers in villages R101 and R127 – even though both are from Wollo, and differed only in the time of their relocation. The conflict was resolved through the intervention of local authorities. R102 was allocated to resettlers of R101 and R127, while the immigrants in R104 were allocated additional areas of parts of R103 and R105 although part of the latter two was claimed back by the autochthonous Gumuz. No intermarriage case was reported between the immigrants and resettlers from Wollo, most of whom are followers of Islam.

Despite the conflicts due to resource competition and absence of intermarriage, there is still strong preference for those who are from the same original areas. Referring to the deep-rooted linkages to the early and later immigrants as well as resettlers of the same origin, my resettler informant from Wollo residing in RUS51 resettlement village used a popular folk saying as: *Yesaw ager saw kammiyagorsegn, yeagere/yewonze saw yinkesegn!* which literally means "instead of a hand-feeding by an outsider, I would prefer a bite by my own fellow countryman." In this particular situational context, my informant wanted to extend a message of in-group inclusiveness and sense of close belonging of all those from Wollo at the exclusion of all others.

Identity Dimensions among the Resettlers of 1980s

North-Central versus South-Western Resettlers
The state-sponsored resettlers are broadly dichotomised into two identification categories of north-central and south-western groups. Apart from the broader common geographical locations of their original territories, the socio-cultural differences of the two groups are articulated through several local stereotypes. The two identifications are locally labelled as Amhara versus Kambaata. The first label is based on the numerical dominance of the Amharic speakers, whereas the latter label is based on the first part of the former provincial name Kambaata and Hadiyya, the original area of south-western resettlers.

The dichotomization of the two groups is expressed significantly on the basis of their differing backgrounds as those with cereal crop production versus those with *enset* and root crops production. It was noted that south-western resettlers are considered as better in home garden management, while those from the north-central are better in field crops cultivation. This characterisation holds plausible justification. In the origins of the south-western resettlers, the backyards are intensively cultivated and managed with perennial plantations of *enset*, fruit plants, and other root crops like cassava and taro, whereas the same is not true in the origins of north-central resettlers. The north-central resettlers perceive the others rather contemptuously for the latter's excessive engagement in sideline income-generating activities, allegedly showing weakness and lack of proper attention in the main field crop cultivation. On the other hand, those from the south-west consider the others as rigid intensive field crop cultivators due to their alleged lack of awareness of lucrative sideline exchange and subsidiary income-generating activities.

No significant inter-marriage is observed between the two groups, the reasons for which being explained in the local stereotypes. The south-western resettlers do not want to give their women to others because the latter's men are considered as unsympathetic to women because they make them to work longer hours in the field. They also do not want to marry women from others because the latter's women are not effective entrepreneurs. However, the north-central resettlers' version of the local stereotype is different. They do not want to marry the women from south-western resettlers because these women are weak in the field activities, which is very important in the farming family. Moreover, the two groups vary in religious denominations.

236

The north-central resettlers are mostly followers of either Orthodox Christianity or Islam, whereas those from the south-west are primarily followers of Protestantism and Catholicism. In the present context, the followers and priests of Orthodox Christianity noticeably stigmatise both Protestants and Catholics. Their resentment is based on the consideration of the former as followers of alien religions (locally termed as *matte* (Amh.)), posing a threat to Orthodox Christianity.

Ethnic Identification among the North-Central Resettlers

The north-central resettlers are further differentiated, identified, and dichotomised into different ethnic groups within the collective identification category. The different ethnic groups identified in the category include Amhara, Oromo, Tigraway and Agaw (from Seqota). Among other things, they are differentiated along respective languages. One step further, the Amhara are in turn differentiated and identified as territorial groups from Wollo, Gojjam, North Shoa, and Gondar. Again, the level of differentiation and identification goes further on specific localities within the same larger territorial group. For instance, those who come from Wollo identify themselves as Borana, Raya, Ambasell, Bati, etc[10]. The level of identification goes on provincial, district, local parish or village, hamlets and down to individuals. According to one of my resettler informants from Wollo, they prefer to select marriage partners from within those resettlers who had come from common or neighbouring villages. If that is not possible, the search will continue with those from the same district; if not, they will continue searching with those from the same province. Finally, if the search within the previous levels is not possible, then a search from the same regional background is considered, though it seems not quite common. If one fails to find a suitable partner along the stated lines, he will visit the home area.

On the other hand, there exist several crosscutting identifications from which selections are made depending on the situational contexts. For instance, those who follow the same religion such as Islam or Orthodox Christianity identify themselves with the followers of the respective religion through inclusion in diverse local religious institutions. Moreover, those who come from neighbouring original areas have preferential inclusion. For example, the Amhara, who came from Raya in north Wollo identify more inclusively with the Tigraway of Raya than the Amhara who came from

---

[10] The stated identification names in the home areas, according to Braukämper (1980, ch. 3 "Seasonal Calendar of Livelihood Activities"), are mostly names of Oromo ancestors, which reveal a probable shift from Oromo to Amhara ethnic consciousness.

south Wollo, depicting the importance of spatial dimensions in identification process. Similarly, resettlers coming from southern Wollo closely identify with those coming from neighbouring North Shoa than those from north Wollo. Closer identification also exists between resettlers from west Wollo and east Gojjam, who are divided only by the Abbay River. In their new context, resettlers are observed preferentially identifying themselves circumstantially more with their neighbours residing in the same resettlement village under various institutional arrangements (such as membership in a local *iddir*, religious associations, etc.) than with those who have come from the same original area but settled in a different village. The complex networks of local institutional arrangements of the community act as an important factor of situational identification.

The languages of Agaw resettlers from Seqota (Wollo-Tigray) and the Agaw of Gojjam residing along the environs of the resettlement area are not mutually intelligible. These two groups are considered to have the same historical origins. They ended up occupying different territorial areas due to historical circumstances. However, there is no significant and noticeable preferential identification of the two groups now residing closer to each other (the one inside the resettlement village and the other right next to it in the environs). No case of inter-marriage was reported. Rather, the Agaw of Seqota identify very closely with those Tigraway and Amhara resettlers of Raya who have come from the neighbouring original areas. Similarly, the Tigraway from Raya have closer ties with those Agaw and Amhara resettlers coming from neighbouring original areas. The Agaw of Seqota and Tigraway ethnic groups are numerically not many and cannot form their own villages. Hence, they are incorporated into villages together with the Amhara from the same neighbouring home area in north Wollo.

The Oromo resettlers from south Wollo and north Shoa are mainly resettled in a single resettlement village L23. They are all followers of Islam and form a relatively intact group maintaining many of their cultural features of their home areas including language, religion, costume, and related customary institutional arrangements. Similarly, members of the Oromo ethnic group show preferential close ties with those neighbouring Amhara resettlers of south Wollo and north Shoa.

Ethnic Identification among the South-Western Resettlers
The south-western resettlers are in turn further differentiated and identified into the different ethnic groups of Kambaata, Hadiyya, and Wolaita within the larger collective identification category. Both Kambaata and Hadiyya form the majority of the south-western resettlers, whereas the Wolaita are

less in number. They share villages mostly with the Hadiyya because they came together with the Hadiyya mostly from Sike district, which is predominantly inhabited by Hadiyya and bordering the Wolaita in the areas of origin. Despite their respective socio-cultural differences articulated in terms of language, culture, history, folklore and other contextual circumstances, these three groups have a strong coherence among themselves especially in the new setting due to their origin from the same geographical location. They are predominantly followers of either the Protestant or Catholic religion. However, there are some among them who are followers of either Islam or Orthodox Christianity. There is widespread inter-marriage between the Kambaata and Hadiyya ethnic groups in both the areas of origin and in the resettlement area.

In the case of all three ethnic groups, kinship and identification in clan membership has strong significance. For instance, among many crosscutting identifications between Kambaata and Hadiyya, clan membership is the most important[11]. Even in the new context where the resettlers' social structure is not as intact in terms of clans and kinship as in the place of origin, there exists a strong need to form closer inclusive identification based on these grounds. Those resettlers belonging to the same clan consider themselves as close kin and visit each other wherever they live in the entire resettlement area. The clan membership is stressed to be a far more important factor of close identification than membership in an ethnic group. Clan members are called for their company during all important family events such as birth, circumcision, marriage and death. For instance, when death occurs in one of the clan member's family, other clan members were informed first through messengers selected from the local *iddir*. The burial will be performed after the arrival of clan members. They accompany the deceased's family usually for one week, sharing the grief to the family. Members of the neighbourhood *iddir* usually attend for three days. Those members of the same ethnic group, visiting the family only in normal relations mostly return immediately.

In the context of clan member identification a family with many clan members considers themselves more secure than those with fewer or no clan members, the latter being rather desperate. Interestingly, many of the clans are spread across the ethnic boundaries of both the Kambaata and Hadiyya. Depending on the circumstances, there exist preferential identification with a clan member in another ethnic group than with someone simply a common member of the same ethnic group. Many of the resettlers resentfully stressed

---

[11] Braukämper has recorded some of the clan names of Hadiyya and Kambaata (1983).

lack of strong clan memberships and attachments in the resettlement setting, making them mostly nostalgic for their home areas.

On the other hand, those stigmatised occupational handicraftsmen in these ethnic groups, locally called *Fuga,* perceived their situation in the new context rather differently. The women are potters, while the men are mostly woodworkers. In the home areas, they perform economically and ritually important functions (through handicrafts production and ritual services during important life events) but are socially segregated and despised groups from the rest of the society, restricted to endogamous marriage (Braukämper 1983, chapter 3 "Seasonal Calendar of Livelihood Activities"; Wolde-Selassie 2001b). In the new setting, except their fellow country folk, the others do not discriminate and despise them. They are treated as equals like any of their neighbours, getting all the benefits extended to resettlers. Through their additional handicrafts skills, they became even wealthier than in their former position in the home areas. This resulted in some of their fellow country-folk being jealous and envious well as being contemptuous of the potters' unusual improvement of the quality of life and wealth accumulation. As a result, the handicraftsmen developed a strong resentment to one's own fellow country-folk, who discriminate against them, and usually prefer to establish ties with others who do not discriminate but honour them for their skills and services. I personally observed that one *Fuga* craftsman has married an Agaw woman from areas neighbouring the resettlement area. She was observed, making pottery products by learning the skill from the traditional potters. The other *Fuga* women appreciated her efforts and improving skill in pottery production. These *Fuga* families have unanimously stressed the fact that their economic situation and social status has improved in the new setting, which is attributed to lack of discrimination by others.

Chapter 11. Ethnic Conflicts and the *Mangina* Institution

11.1 Intra-Ethnic Relations

Intra-Ethnic Integration
This importance of membership in a clan is repeatedly observed and noted during the fieldwork in multiple intra-Gumuz relations and interactions in their daily lives such death and mourning (a male visiting clan member has to fire a bullet twice or more based on his lineage closeness), defending and avenging attacks on other clan members as well as in all important life events such as birth, circumcision (men), marriage and other related ritual

events. For instance, my Gumuz assistant Wubalta Enno is almost always asked about his clan background by most of our Gumuz informants, particularly in the first introductions. In other words, a Gumuz person without a clan membership does not exist. As earlier described, a number of clans form larger territorial groups such as the Gumuz of Mandura, Dangur, Gublak, Guba, Dibati, and Wombera as well as even much broader territorial categories of the Gumuz of Metekel, Kamashi, Metemma, and the entire Gumuz ethnic group as a whole (cf. chapter 3 "Family, Neighbourhood/Commune and Clan").

Intra-ethnic clan interactions are crucial for the very survival and coexistence of the different groups as a community, and relations are held with mutual recognition according to their tradition. Violation of such recognition results in severe inter-clan feuds. Normally, the neighbouring clans in their respective territories[12] co-exist peacefully with a respectful recognition of each other in their interactions with individual members as well as among groups. At a lesser scale, intra-clan lineage relations are also handled with care and recognition. In their fairly egalitarian system, any Gumuz member is considered as fully equal to any other fellow member or neighbour.

Intra-Ethnic Conflicts
The potential causes of severe cyclical intra-ethnic conflict include: adultery, belief in evil eye, and insults of an individual or a group, abducting girls, and claims for a return or replacement for exchanged sisters in marriage. Aysheshim (1987:32) notes similar observations of adultery, rape, incest, insults, and refusal of debt payments serving as serious causes of homicide among the Gumuz. My interviews with Mandura and Dangur Gumuz informants confirm that adultery is dealt with by punishments including the death penalty. When an individual belonging to another clan commits adultery, the chance of easily resolving the emerging conflict will be very remote. Showing overt contempt for or insulting an individual or a group has grave repercussions of resorting to serious conflict that may accordingly

---

[12] Ideally, all clans are reported to occupy localised respective territories. However, in reality the neatly localised clan territoriality seems difficult, and there are cases where members of same clans are observed in different territorial units. According to Gumuz informants, clan members residing outside clan territories are those who joined other clans on the full consent of the latter accepting the former to share their territories only in peaceful way. Even in such a case, the status of those who joined from outside is subordinate to the clan members who claim to be the true owners. Hence, every Gumuz prefers to stay together inside his clan territory, among other things, for security and honour unless otherwise forced to leave by circumstances such as intra-clan and inter-clan retaliatory feuds.

cause a number of casualties. Abducting girls has a serious risk of causing bloody hostility because getting a wife is possible only in exchange for a sister. Girls' virginity is highly valued in the exchange marriage, and lack of it acts as a cause of severe conflict. Moreover, a claim for a return of an exchanged sister or replacement in case of divorce or early death of either of the sisters before bearing children causes inter-clan tension.

As already pointed out, belief in evil-eye is the most serious source of tension (cf. chapter 3 "Belief Systems"). Once the intra-ethnic clan conflicts emerge and begin claiming lives, the chance of easy resolution remains difficult due to resorting to cyclical and endless revengeful actions by the members of the feuding clans. In the case of a death where the cause is believed to be due to an evil-eye, serious inter-clan conflict will emerge that results in bloodshed unless intervened immediately by wise elders from neutral clans.

Incest is one of the severest causes of bitter intra-clan lineage conflicts. During my recent fieldwork period (October 2000 to April 2001), I was informed by one of my informants in the Metekel Zone of a case of a group of Gumuz from Bulen *Woreda* being arrested for their alleged action of burying alive one of their male fellow members. The victim had allegedly and incestuously deflowered a young girl of his lineage. According to the explanation of my informant, the furious kinsmen dug a hole in the ground and buried him alive instead of wasting a bullet shooting him.

The same informant explained about a serious conflict emerged between clan members that exchanged young wives on an occasion of a mourning ceremony. Of two exchanged wives, one is married to an old man, while the other is married to a young person. The one married to an old man in the exchange system was said to have shown contempt to her old husband and returned to her natal village. Her return to the natal village caused a claim to return the wife given in her exchange or a replacement. However, her husband had considered her contemptuous abandonment as humiliation and disgraceful shame to him and his clan group. The angry husband avenged himself by firing at his wife's brother that received a wife in exchange for her, and killed him on the mourning ceremony. The killer was then shot and killed on the spot by close clan member of the dead. The situation deteriorated further into fighting between clan groups and is said to have resulted in four deaths and more people wounded. The practice of retaliation feuds that target any male member of each other's groups creates complex tensions that involve any male member of the conflicting clans. This makes the conflicts more protracted.

A documented case of inter-clan conflict that occurred between two Gumuz clans, part of which has been personally observed and documented throughout my extended fieldwork stay in the area is described as follows. *Maataaba* and *Dimtsatse* clans used to live near to each other. Previously, they had good relations and exchanged women in marriage. The source of their relatively extended cyclical conflict emerged before five years. A young woman of *Dimtsatse* clan married in exchange to a *Maataaba* clan was shot dead by her senior co-wife's son while preparing food for the family. The son killed this younger wife of his father in order to avenge him for insulting his mother as lazy. The *Dimtsatse* clan members, angered by the death of their innocent clan member, went to *Maataaba* village and killed one male member in revenge. Then, neutral clan elders intervened and attempted to resolve the conflict by getting the clans to refrain from actions that would cause further tension.

However, sometime after a year, *Maataaba* and *Dimtsatse* clan members exchanged insults in a Pawe village L4 marketplace, the source cause of which was said to be the earlier conflict. As a result, later the same day, the *Maataaba* clan members killed a *Dimtsatse* clan member. Immediately, a few hours after the action, *Dimtsatse* clan members followed and killed one male *Maataaba* clan member in revenge. Then, the tension increased because of the refusal of *Maataaba* clan to resolve the matter by immediate mediation. This is because *Maataaba* considered themselves to be the looser because two of their clan members were killed and a woman of their clan who was exchanged for the deceased young woman now lives with *Dimtsatse* clan. Again after a while one evening in 1996, *Maataaba* clan members attacked *Dimtsatse* clan at Manjeeri village and killed one and wounded another member. However, out of the attackers two were killed on the spot and one was wounded in a retaliation attack by the *Dimtsatse* clan members. Again, the attack caused another loss for the *Maataaba* clan and they refused to settle the matter through mediation until they could balance their losses. Since then, their hostilities and tensions increased, pushing both groups to take maximum care and vigilance against each other. Group members will not cross each other's territory. Nor will group members travel in a direction which is near to the other. However, in between, the *Dimtsatse* clan showed its willingness to resolve the matter through peaceful mediation, which was repeatedly rejected by *Maataaba,* which claimed to have sustained losses. A personally observed detailed account of part of the conflict resolving processes of the same case is presented in chapter 11 subsection "Intra-Ethnic Conflict Resolution".

11.2 Inter-Ethnic Relations

Uneasy Coexistence between the Gumuz and Resettlers

The intensity of both conflicting and integrative relations between the Gumuz and their highland resettler neighbours are mainly determined both by the long-standing and present interactions of the two categorical groups in different contexts. In order to facilitate a closer understanding of the dynamics of inter-ethnic relations in the area, an attempt is made to approach the inter-ethnic relations from a broad dichotomy of the Gumuz on the one hand and their highland resettler neighbours on the other hand. The basis for the dichotomy of the two categories has been explained in the preceding part.

The inter-ethnic relations between the Gumuz and the highland resettler neighbours are mainly polarised with differing magnitudes of ethnic tensions and hostilities. The ethnic polarisation and the resultant boundary rift between the two collectivities has remained very wide especially based on the long-standing political power relationships that placed the Gumuz at an inferior, stigmatised and marginal position. Hence, the Gumuz are discriminated and ascribed a lower status by their *Shuwa* neighbours and, as stated earlier, referred to by an externally defined pejorative and derogatory categorical and generic term *Shanqilla*. Today, for Gumuz, a reference by the term *Shanqilla* is an intolerable insult that acts as one of the main causes of bloody ethnic conflicts in the area. Thus, the expression of the Gumuz ethnic identity and the resultant prevalent conflicting relations with their highland neighbours has been shaped in such highly polarised and stratified circumstances based on historical, economic, political and cultural factors used to designate contextual differences that dichotomise boundaries between the *Bega* and the *Shuwa*.

Inter-Ethnic Conflicts

Causes of Inter-Ethnic Conflicts
The most frequently mentioned serious causes of inter-ethnic conflicts between the *Bega* and *Shuwa* are the experiences of slave raids in the past and the resultant implicit and explicit prejudice and mistrust at present; contempt and stigmatisation expressed in the categorical reference of the Gumuz with a derogative term *Shanqilla*, as repeatedly stated earlier; exploitative relationships in the past and a prevalent unequal exchange at present; and the ceaseless encroachment on the land resources. The slave raiding that victimised the Gumuz has imprinted in their minds a deep-rooted enmity toward their neighbouring highlanders (Aysheshim 1987:61). Additionally, as noted

earlier, competition over natural resources since the conquest of the area by the central state is considered as the most serious cause of conflict between the Gumuz and their neighbours including the state-sponsored resettlers. Whenever Gumuz explain their predominantly conflicting ethnic relations and uneasy coexistence with their *Shuwa* neighbours, they always show elements of deep-rooted suspicion and mistrust towards the latter.

As earlier described, the Gumuz are critically aware of the consequences of both slow and rapid encroachments upon their land resources continuously pushing them further to the inaccessible peripheries throughout the different past regimes up to the present day. In spite of their being pushed as "defenceless" victims in the struggle throughout the past regimes, they used to take frequent defensive and revenge attacks upon the expanding enemies and then retreat further down into the inaccessible lowlands in fear of more organised raiding and plunder from the highland expansionists. During the *Derg* regime, among other things, the Gumuz faced the bitterest experiences of the adverse effects of the massive state-sponsored resettlement scheme.

According to the perceptions of the Gumuz, the state-sponsored resettlement is considered as parts of the already ongoing encroachment process, only at its highest scale and occurring rapidly. The Gumuz do not make any distinction among long-time highland neighbours, early immigrants, state-sponsored resettlers, and later immigrants – categorically labelling all as *Shuwa* with similar attributes. Due to its severe adverse consequences on their life and livelihoods, the Gumuz showed hostile attitudes towards the resettlement scheme by disapproving of it. They began expressing their grievances[13] by attacking resettlers located in those villages bordering them. Similar conflict and hatred continued slowly throughout the period up to the fall of *Derg* regime. Low-scale frequent causalities have been occurring since the resettlers' first arrival. However, the already volatile relations between the Gumuz and resettlers burst out into an open ethnic conflict that resulted in bloodshed claiming considerable human lives on both sides immediately after the 1991 political change in the country. The detailed account is described in chapter 11 sub-section "Conflicts between the Gumuz and the Resettlers of the 1980s".

---

[13] Gebre (1995:23) notes the causes of the grievances and complaints of the Gumuz as: "(1) settlers came there without their knowledge and permission, (2) they have been pushed into the bush from their established residence and farmland in favour of settlers, (3) the recurring clashes with the settlers resulted in a great loss of human life and property, (4) settlers destroyed their forests and wildlife causing ecological destruction, and (5) following the settlement program, people from the highland began to come in great numbers and settle on their land as a matter of right."

Conflicts between the Gumuz and Highland Neighbours

Those relatively long-standing highland neighbours of Gumuz include Amhara, Agaw, Shinasha, and Oromo. Almost all the ethnic groups rarely seem to be truly sympathetic with Gumuz in their relations. Rather, their basic interest lies in the exploitation the latter's resources. Below, an attempt is made to delineate briefly the profile of the uneasy coexistence of Gumuz with each one of them.

(*A*) *Gumuz and Amhara:* The relation of Gumuz and Amhara is characterised by hostility and seems to be more polarised than that with all other groups. My Gumuz informants in Mandura and Dangur emphasised their historical experience of slavery and the repeated invasion and plunder by the Amhara armies under different regional monarchs, and the central state during the imperial regime. After the 16th century, the centre of state was in Gondar, and the Gumuz of Metekel were very close to its influence. In order to bring the land, its resources and the people under control, states Taddese Tamrat (1988:12-14) that the kings such as Sarsa-Dengel (1563-97), Susenyos (1607-32), Fasiledes (1632-67), Yohanes (1667-83), and Iyasu the Great (1683-1706) successively conducted devastating and destructive campaigns on the Gumuz, achieving a final breakthrough and incorporating into the ancient system of indirect rule by appointing neighbouring Agaw chiefs (under patron-client relationship) over them. This lasted up to the overthrow of the imperial regime by the *Derg* in 1974. Wendy James (1986) considers the documentary accounts of early scholars such as James Bruce, Henry Salt, and Charles T. Beke who have witnessed the fact that the Gumuz lived in the highlands of the present central and southern parts of Gojjam in the eighteenth and early nineteenth centuries (cf. chapter 3, section 3.1). These accounts try to point out that, in the process of the exploitative expansion of the highland Amhara, the Gumuz were forced to move gradually down to the lowlands in the far western periphery of the country in search of greater safety. As earlier stated, the prevalence of prejudice with explicit and implicit categorical ascription of inferior and marginal status to the Gumuz by the Amhara further nurtured the creation and maintenance of deep-rooted hatred and mistrust.

(*B*) *Gumuz and Agaw:* The relation between the Gumuz and Agaw is likewise characterised by conflicts. The Gumuz were indirectly ruled under the Agaw chiefs, appointed by the Amhara. According to the Gumuz informants, the Agaw raided them for slaves, pushed them away to the peripheries and exploited them and plundered their property (in the name of land tax) directly encroaching upon their land. In the nineteenth century, Charles

Beke recorded an Agaw tradition that asserts the Gumuz to be the previous occupiers of Agaumidir, but had been displaced by the Agaw (Beke 1945 quoted in Pankhurst 1997:91). The Gumuz that I spoke to said that as close neighbours, the Agaw have been able to approach the Gumuz cleverly: they have learnt to speak the Gumuz language, and to maximise their material gains from the relationships subtly. The Gumuz perceive the Agaw as deceivers. They are aware of exploitative relationships and lack full trust, viewing the Agaw with suspicion.

On the other hand, there exists a group neighbouring the Gumuz locally known as Kumfel[14] (a term considered to signal contempt and stigma in their own account). The variant reference name preferred in the *emic* perception of the group is *Qollegna* Agaw as noted earlier. They are locally well known for their traditional honey production. Their honey production culture has been rooted in the long tradition where trees with numerous local beehives are known under family names and inherited by descendants in the lineage through generations. Since they are engaged in honey production, part of their livelihood is dependent on the forest resources. Hence, the impact of their honey production on the forest resources is not harmful. The relations of Gumuz with Kumfel need further investigation. No case of any severe conflicting relations between the two groups was noted. It seems that they are labelled as a minority group being ascribed a lower status by Amhara and other highlanders although not as discriminatory as *Shanqilla*.

(*C*) *Gumuz and Shinasha:* Although it is perceived with a lower tone and scale, the relations of Gumuz with the Shinasha is also said to be troubled with tensions of conflict and uncomfortable co-existence. Both the Shinasha

---

[14] Kumfel, Simoons (1960:43) notes, are "a small Christian Agow-speaking group, occupy few villages at elevations from 3,000 to 6,000 feet in the dry forest country along the valley of the Dinder River at the southern edge of Begemider and Semyen (later Gondar). According to their traditions, the Kumfel came from the Atchifer and Kumbil (the derivation of the word Kumfel?) districts of Godjam Province a century ago at the invitation of King Theodore. Amhara of the highland of K'wara nearby claim, on the other hand, that the Kumfel are descended from slaves set free by Theodore and allowed to settle along the Dinder. Because they believe the Kumfel to have been slaves, the Amhara are very contemptuous of them and regard them as only a little more acceptable than the Wayt'o fishermen of Lake T'ana. The physical appearance of the Kumfel casts little light on the problem of their origin, for some of them are quite Negroid and others indistinguishable from the peoples of the highland [...].
The Kumfel country contains an abundance of wild and semi-domesticated bees, and the traveler knows when he is approaching a Kumfel village by the presence of cylindrical beehives tied high in the branches of trees, some as far away as five or six miles from the village. Honey is an important trade item for the Kumfel today, and when they first settled in the Dinder valley they even paid their taxes in honey."

247

and the Gumuz informants agree that they had severe conflicts in the past that had driven the Gumuz from their earlier locations now inhabited by the Shinasha. The Gumuz attribute the relatively lower scale and frequency of hostilities with the Shinasha to the latter's mainly hoe-cultivation system, which has lesser adverse effects on the forest resources. However, the Gumuz still consider the Shinasha with suspicion, pointing out the latter's similarity and strong association with the *Shuwa* categorical identification (e.g., fully followers of Orthodox Christianity, fair pigmentation, costume, and other associated elements of socio-economic and cultural resemblance). The Gumuz perceive Shinasha's present alliance in the local politics as a strategic instrumental inclusion to compete for the Gumuz resources by excluding all the others in the *Shuwa* category.

(D) Gumuz and Oromo: The relation between the Gumuz and Oromo (inhabiting three of the seven *woreda* in Metekel Zone such as Dibati, Bulen, and Wombera) is almost similar to that of Shinasha, but with reportedly lesser tension and hostility than with the Agaw and Shinasha. Although the Gumuz do not attribute equally brutal treatment to the Oromo (like that of Amhara and Agaw), they are again sceptical in their relations with them as well. The basic factor of their uneasy co-existence is again encroachment on the land resources and other exploitative relationships based on the prevalent power politics of the dominant and the subjugated, the latter of which is predominantly true of the autochthonous Gumuz.

Conflicts between the Gumuz and Immigrants of the 1950s
The relations between the Gumuz and spontaneous settlers have been one of the most hostile, resulting in frequent bloody conflicts after the latter's immigration[15] from Wollo to the area since the 1950s. The ceaseless immigration of the Wollo peasants (especially in areas inside Mandura, Dibati, and Bulen *Woreda* of Metekel) pushed the Gumuz away from their land resources. In addition, the different farming system of Wollo peasants coupled with the local stereotypes associated with their habitual and indiscriminate cutting of tree resources contributed to their worsening relations. Since the Wollo peasants usually feel insecure because of their numerical minority, they regularly pull more immigrant countrymen both for security and economic survival, which in turn exerted more pressure on the land resources of the Gumuz. In such inimical relationships, the two sides pursue retaliatory

---

[15] For more details on the history and reasons of immigration of Wollo peasants to Metekel in the mid-nineteen twenties, see Berihun (1996).

248

inter-ethnic avenging feuds that evoke an atmosphere of tensions that polarise the rift between the two groups. Regular ethnic conflicts have been quite common between the two since the Wollo settlers' early immigration days. However, the worst of all conflicts is the one that occurred in the years from 1992 to 1994 following the political change of the country in 1991. This ethnic conflict claimed numerous lives from both sides and destroyed enormous property, displacing many of the Wollo peasants from the conflict zone.

The main cause of the conflict was attributed to vindictive measures taken by the Gumuz for all the past losses and grievances influenced by the new state policy on ethnicity, which structured administrative boundaries along ethnic lines. As a result, the bloody ethnic conflict ran for two successive years and worsened the plight of the immigrant population, displacing around 10,490 Wollo spontaneous immigrant settlers (Wolde-Selassie 1996b:11). This severe conflict sparked in January 1992 by an alleged attack of Gumuz on Wollo immigrants, continued up to 1994. Its adverse impact on human lives and property is described below based on the accounts of the immigrants[16] as:

> According to the estimation of some of my Wollo informants, about 329 persons were killed and elders, children, and disabled persons were burnt alive with their houses. A total of 6833 rural houses, 185 mosques that are made of grass roofs, one church, five elementary schools and a service cooperative shop were burned during the conflict. About 1792 cattle and too many sheep and goats were looted. In addition, the harvest both stored at home and at the field were destroyed (Berihun 1996:119).

As pointed out earlier, many of these farmers displaced due to the ethnic conflict immigrated to the Beles Valley, seeking for better security near the Metekel Zonal Administration centre and looking for adequate farm land and pasture for their livestock (cf. chapter 6 "Different Categories of Population" and chapter 7 "The Immigrant Farmers"). A detailed account on how this conflict was resolved is described in chapter 11 sub-section 11 "Conflict Resolution between the Gumuz and Immigrants of 1950s".

---

[16] It should be noted that the casualty and property damage figures described show only those reported accounts from the immigrants on their side. However, similar accounts estimating the effects of the same conflict on the part of Gumuz are not available.

Conflicts between the Gumuz and the Resettlers of the 1980s

The relations between the Gumuz and state-sponsored resettlers are characterised by worse hostilities, causing bloody conflicts that have claimed lives on both sides. The ethnic conflict, mistrust, and hatred continued slowly throughout the period up to the fall of the *Derg*. The already volatile relations between the two groups then burst out into an open ethnic conflict[17] that resulted in bloodshed claiming considerable human lives on both sides immediately after the 1991 political change in the country. Some of the major inter-ethnic conflict accounts that occurred between the two groups are described below using materials from my informants in Pawe.

The cases are based on both primary accounts of those who personally witnessed one or several of the incidents as well as on secondary accounts. My informants include the Gumuz, the resettlers, informal accounts of officials in Pawe Special *Woreda* and Metekel Zone, staff and employees of government and non-government organisations, and residents of small towns in the area. Except for those estimates that seem almost plausible, it is very difficult to consider the casualty figures as accurate. Due to the extreme sensitivity of the ethnic conflicts that happened, almost all informants provided their accounts as confidential and none of them wanted to be identified

---

[17] A summarised account of this severe ethnic conflict, according to Gebre (1995:24), is given as: "In December 1991, the Gumz invaded resettled villages and killed 58 Kembata and Hadia settlers. Informants stated that on September 18, 1993, Gumz gun-men killed some 20 settlers in a market place, in village 4. This happened because, according to Gumz informants, few days earlier a wife of Gumz local leader and another young boy were brutally killed by settlers. On 21 September 1993, settlers organised themselves and started arresting important Gumz and Shinasha officials at Zonal level. Some officials escaped the arrest by taking refuge with the Gumz armed force camping next to the administration building. The next day, EPRDF/government army requested the Gumz force to surrender, while the settlers were taking measures (including death penalty) against the imprisoned officials. When the Gumz militia refused to surrender, the government army is said to have resorted to force to settle the problem. Some 20 Gumz militia men are said to have escaped death of the estimated total 70. On the same day, settlers advanced to the nearby Gumz communities and destroyed villages, appropriated property, and pushed the Gumz further to the bush. During the three days clash over 50 Gumz, few government soldiers, and few settlers are said to have died.

The local government officials have been asked for confirmation of the above incidents. Although they agree definitely to the report that clashes broke out, they claim to have no concrete evidence regarding the type and nature of casualties."

(cf. The description of my own findings so far about the same severe conflict as presented in the main text as *cases one, two and three* based on the accounts of several informants composed of different resident categories in the area. I have attempted to substantiate the highly sensitive information on this ethnic conflict since its emergence up to March 2001 as part of my extended investigation in the area both as a practitioner and researcher since June 1988 up to the present. Yet, my description of this ethnic conflict should not be considered as complete and final at all.)

openly. Many have carefully reminded me, indirectly signalling a warning of its sensitivity, stating: "These are serious issues one should not openly tell an outsider without strict precaution. However, since I/we have known you for a long time and consider that you may not use it for any hidden goals that might backfire and cause serious setbacks, I/we share the information just for your knowledge." Many of the interviews on the issue were conducted privately. I was unable to find any official reports on the cases of the conflicts. Thus, it should be noted that these not yet openly unfolded cases of ethnic conflicts remained still extremely sensitive, many people considering the very topic as a sort of fearsome taboo, which should not be violated lightly.

(A) Case One
The bloodiest conflict caused by a sudden attack of the Gumuz on December 27, 1991 (*Tahsas* 18, 1984 E.C) in L4 village claimed the lives of an estimated 54 Hadiyya and Kambaata resettlers, who were buried in a mass grave. The cause for the action was explained as just intending to expel the resettlers from the lands the Gumuz had lost. However, the Gumuz informants explained the cause of this bloodshed as not deliberate. According to their account, the incident was based on a spontaneous and emotional action taken in retaliation to the death of one of their members killed by a bullet fired by a resettler during a *tazkar* ceremony commemorating the death of an old Gumuz man. This resettler was said to have joined them from L4 Kambaata and Hadiyya resettlers' village. His gunshot was not a deliberately targeted action to kill the Gumuz but it happened by mistake. The gunshot was simply intended to show respect to the occasion according to the Gumuz tradition. It is explained that the angered Gumuz gathered from the area to attend the ceremony killed that resettler on the spot and turned their indiscriminate attack on the nearby resettlers causing the above stated casualties.
Additionally, the next day on December 28, 1991 (*Tahsas* 19, 1984 E.C.), the Gumuz again attacked Kambaata and Hadiyya resettlers in village L3 at night while they were in a prayer program of a Protestant church. This attack caused an estimated nine deaths and left many wounded.

(B) Case Two

The other heavy ethnic conflict occurred on September 11, 1993 (*Meskerem* 1, 1986 E.C) in which Gumuz gunmen attacked the L4 village market causing an estimated eight dead and twenty-six wounded. Some informants estimated the casualty around twenty dead and nineteen wounded. The alleged cause of the attack, according to the resettlers, was attributed to the incitement of the local administrators appointed from the Gumuz and Shinasha ethnic groups in order to remove the resettlers from the area.

(C) Case Three

On the pretext of response to the above two cases, the resettlers organised themselves and began taking retaliatory actions on September 22, 1993 (*Meskeram* 12, 1986 E.C.) that continued for a number of days, resulting in a loss of many lives from the Gumuz and some from Shinasha. Some resettlers who were alleged to have been supporting or spying for the latter were reportedly shot to death. The retaliatory action of the resettlers first targeted the Gumuz and Shinasha officials appointed at the local administration where three of them accused of inciting the violence were reported to have been shot dead. Following that, fighting broke out inside the Pawe administration centre (at Almu) between the Gumuz militia who refused to surrender and the EPRDF fighters, claiming lives on both parts. Then, an indiscriminate pursuit and plunder of the Gumuz living in the estimated eight peasant associations neighbouring the resettlement scheme area continued for a number of days, causing casualties on both sides but with more destruction of property and lives among the Gumuz. On the other hand, some of the Gumuz fighters who escaped from Pawe took as hostages non-Gumuz living in Gublak, who were reported later to have been executed. However, the horrifying situation has somehow been put some how under control with strong involvement of the forces of the central state. As a result, the regional state capital was transferred from Pawe to Assosa. The conflict area has begun to be administered by a provisional committee of the residents in the entire area. People from both groups suspected of inciting and causing the conflict were arrested at Chagni. Then the state authorities recruited members from all ethnic groups for cadre training, in the meantime facilitating the efforts of a multi-ethnic elders groups which were attempting to settle the conflict. Since then, no major conflict has occurred up to the present. As a consequence, the resettlers evacuated massively the area and returned to their places of origin.

(D) Case Four
There were lower-scale conflicts in different parts of the resettlement area particularly bordering the Gumuz both before and after the above major conflict. In 1993, one Saturday morning, a resettler was said to have been killed by a Gumuz near Abbat Beles village while collecting his harvest in the field. It was a market day at Abbat Beles. As a result of the killings, the angry resettlers avenged by suddenly attacking those Gumuz in the market where an estimated six were killed. After two months, in order to avenge their losses, the Gumuz attacked a village market at R49 on Saturday where it is reported that one resettler was killed and three wounded. What makes these conflicts worse is the nature of avenging. Either party generally avenges any male members of the other group (mostly innocent ones) simply within the *qay* versus *tiqur* (*Shanqilla*) category.

(E) Case Five
In May 1995, resettlers from villages R49 and RUS51, who went to the nearby forest to collect construction wood were attacked by Gumuz, two being reported to have been killed and one wounded. The wounded one managed to reach the village and informed people there about the incident. The angry resettlers brought the dead back to their village. In such a situation, the furious resettlers observed Gumuz men on a truck coming from Mambuk and driving along the main Chagni to Guba highway that connects their villages. They immediately stopped the truck, brought the Gumuz down and attacked them severely, reportedly killing two on the spot and seriously wounding two others. Of the wounded, one was reported dead later in Pawe hospital.

(F) Case Six
In November 1992, there occurred conflict between Gumuz of Aypapa village and the resettlers of R101 and R127 villages. An ox owned by a resettler had damaged crops in the Gumuz field. While searching for the ox, one of the owner's neighbours came in contact with the Gumuz whose crops had been damaged. Then, the two were said to have exchanged insults. Upon returning to the village with the ox, the neighbour reported to the owner how he managed to escape from a fu-

rious Gumuz who allegedly wanted to attack him. The angry owner took up his gun, blew his trumpet, calling on the villagers to follow him because he is going to attack. In the conflict, he killed the Gumuz but at the same time, other Gumuz immediately killed him on the spot. His neighbour was wounded. Later, the EPRDF forces intervened and the conflict was stopped.

(G) Case Seven
Intermittent low-level conflicts have been quite common between the Gumuz of *Maataaba* and the resettlers of village L134. As part of many earlier cases, recently around the end of 1999, there occurred a conflict that claimed one resettler dead and two others wounded. This time, through the pressure of the local authorities, those Gumuz alleged to have committed the casualties were said to have been handed over to the authorities by the Gumuz village community.

11.3 The *Mangima*: Traditional Institution of Conflict Resolution

Mangima is the most important traditional institution for resolving inter-ethnic as well as intra-ethnic clan and lineage level conflicts. A lower scale *mangima* for resolving intra-clan lineage level conflicts is in many cases easily managed by the clan's elders. However, a much more complex higher scale *mangima* is convened to resolve serious intra-ethnic conflicts between or among rival feuding clans as well as to resolve inter-ethnic conflicts that emerge between the Gumuz and their non-Gumuz neighbours.

Intra-Ethnic Conflict Resolution
In order to resolve the aforementioned severe intra-ethnic clan conflict between *Maataaba* and *Dimtsatse* clans in Mandura *Woreda* (explained in chapter 11 sub-section "Intra-Ethnic Conflicts"), a *mangima* peace-making ritual was convened, the case of which is presented here. As pointed out earlier, two of my specific field research sites are located within these two feuding clans, and I had the opportunity to observe personally the ritual performances of resolving the conflict through the *mangima* institution in December 2000.

After relentless mediation efforts of clan elders recruited from neutral clans that have no any earlier unresolved conflicts with either of the two feuding clans, the parties agreed to resolve peacefully. Here, it should be emphasised that particularly close male relatives (mostly brothers) of the deceased from the loser clan need to agree with their clan elders before the whole clan group accepts the mediation offer. As a result of the agreement of the brothers of the deceased from the *Maataaba*, the first stage *mangima* was convened in 1998 (for the series of inter-clan conflicts that occurred in 1996 and before as stated in chapter 11 sub-section "Intra-Ethnic Conflicts"). This stage is basically meant to get the parties to refrain from taking any action that will cause further hostilities.

Cessation of Hostilities Stage
On the occasion of the first phase *mangima,* which was meant for cessation of hostilities, those who committed the killings on both sides were not present personally, in order to avoid emergence of unexpected and spontaneous violence. Only those close relatives, especially brothers of both the victims and killers, who are key members of the peace-making process, appeared on the occasion together with adult male clan members. As part of the *mangima* process, a ritual was performed at a neutral middle location outside the villages of the two clans. Since *Dimtsatse* had killed more members from *Maataaba*, the *mangima* elders from third party clans have charged the former to provide two oxen and a goat for performing the ritual.

At this cessation of hostility stage, the *mangima* ritual process focused specially on swearing by both parties to refrain from taking any actions that could provoke and inflame further hostilities. As they began performing the ritual, first the goat was slaughtered with the blessings of elders symbolically meant to appease the spirits of the area for the success of the *mangima* process. Then, the two oxen were slaughtered. Before consuming the meat, the swearing (*gicheha* (Gum.)) ritual was performed using the following six different items. These swearing items were *soil from a termite hill, a bullet, a thorn, woven palm, a leaf of a gourd plant, and a front leg bone (radius) of the goat.* The core members of the swearing process were close patrilineal relatives of both the deceased and killers from the two sides stated above. *First,* the two parties touched the soil brought from termite hill and swore, saying: "If we violate this cessation of hostility agreement, let us die and be buried." *Second,* the two parties stepped on the bullet put on the ground and swore saying: "If we violate this cessation of hostility agreement, let it be that our bullets will not shoot their targets, rather we be targeted by the others." *Third,* the two parties held the thorn and swore saying: "If we violate this cessation of hostility agreement, let thorns pierce our feet, cause swelling on our bodies and kill us." *Fourth,* the two parties held the woven palm fronds and swore saying: "If we violate this cessation of hostilities agreement, let we die and our corpses be wrapped in woven palm and buried." *Fifth,* the two parties held the leaf of a gourd plant and swore saying: "If we violate this cessation of hostility agreement, let our bellies swell like a gourd and die." Finally, *sixth*, the two parties held the front leg bone of the slaughtered goat and broke it together in the meantime swearing: "If we violate this cessation of hostility agreement, let us be killed, our bones being broken in the same way." Once the swearing process was completed, the elders added further blessings of good wishes for its success. Then, all participants consumed the meat on the spot in public. At the end, the first stage *mangima* was completed with further blessings from the elders.

Main Peace-Making Stage
The two feuding clans refrained from taking any action that violates their agreements a result of the first stage *mangima*. After a closer assessment of the positive progress for two years following the cessation of hostilities agreement, the mediating elders brought the parties into re-establishing normal peaceful relationships by organising the main and next stage *mangima* in December 2000.

The second and main stage *mangima* is meant for full reconciliation and creating peaceful co-existence between the two clans. In contrast to the early stage *mangima* that is performed in a neutral location away from the villages of the two clans, the main stage *mangima* ritual is performed in both villages of the feuding clans in turn, on two different occasions. This main stage *mangima* is performed through extended rituals of bringing the warring parties to enter each other's houses. The process includes exchanging friendly kissing and consuming feasts prepared for the occasion by the families of the brothers (or close male relatives) of those brothers either have killed or were killed during the conflict period.

In this main stage *mangima*, the leading invitation offer should come first from the clan that caused more casualty or lost fewer members. Hence, the *Dimtsatse* clan took the lead of inviting the *Maataaba* clan adult male members. Before this occasion, the peace-making elders completed the mediation process by convincing the *Dimtsatse* clan to offer a girl without claiming one in exchange to compensate and balance the losses of the *Maataaba* clan.

On the occasion, the *Dimtsatse* clan organised big feast in the houses of the brothers of those who had committed the killings. Once again, those who caused the causalities will remain hidden to avoid an unexpected disturbance of the peace process. The *mangima* ritual performance began early in the morning after the *Maataaba* clan members arrived at *Dimtsatse* clan village for the first time since the first conflict emerged in 1996. As part of commencing the occasion, they first visited all families of the *Dimtsatse* clan who had lost their family members since 1996 one by one, expressing proper mourning ritual by firing bullets and performing all the necessary formalities. The deceased's' families on their part showed all the formalities as for a fresh mourning occasion.

After the visit to the deceased families had been completed, then the two parties facilitated by elders, went to the nearby Pawe River. Before crossing the river, elders took a pinch of pounded bark of a ritual tree mixed with sorghum flour and touched every one of the two clans members by dipping it in the river water. Only those who were touched crossed the river, exchanging friendly kisses while doing so. This ritual at the river symbolises that all those evil spirits which had caused the conflict between the two clans must go away with the river water to an unknown destination. In other words, it is cleaning away polluting spirits. After crossing the river and reaching the immediate front-yard of the warring parties, the process of touching necks was repeated, and the men exchanged friendly kisses once again before entering into the house. Once they entered, a goat was offered by one of the brothers, which was immediately slaughtered. As coffee was roasted and boiled, the *keya* (local brew) specially prepared for the occasion was served. Two litres of local distilled alcoholic (*araqe*) drink was also offered. Finally, the roasted goat meat was consumed. Throughout the whole process, elders were blessing intermittently. The same process was repeated in all brothers' families of those who took the action turn by turn in the village. Completing the process through cordial treatment, the *Maataaba* clan members returned to their village.

The *mangima* will be completed after the *Maataaba* clan members invite the *Dimtsatse* in a similar way on a convenient date facilitated by the elders. A date was not fixed immediately. However, my *Maataaba* informants told me that they will inform the *Dimtsatse* of the date through the mediating elders after the necessary preparations are completed in the future. It seems to take a number of months or even a few years before they will organise the return invitation, because until end of March 2001 the *Dimtsatse* had not yet been invited. Hence, due to the resolution of the intra-ethnic clan conflict between the *Maataaba* and *Dimtsatse* clans thoroughly through the traditional *mangima* institution, they have somehow begun rearticulating their normal interactions.

Inter-Ethnic Conflict Resolution

Conflict Resolution between the Gumuz and Resettlers of 1980s
Through the application of the traditional peace-making *mangima* institution, the inter-ethnic conflict between the Gumuz and resettlers was to some

257

extent managed to be resolved, partially facilitated by the EPRDF cadres. The resettlers called the peace-making process *shimgilinna*. However, I maintained the native term *mangima,* because the ritual performance was conducted applying the traditional practices of the Gumuz. According to my resettler informants in Pawe, who were part of the peace-making process, the traditional practices of the Gumuz were adopted in order to communicate better with, considering that "the autochthonous know best" and since they will fully abide by the outcomes. Resettlers stressed the *mangima* institution of the Gumuz as the most binding, learning from the experiences of those long-standing neighbours and earlier immigrants. Two cases of *mangima* peace-making practices (one of high scale to settle major conflict and the other of low scale for settling relatively small scale conflict) are presented below.

(*A*) *A Higher Scale Mangima:* The bloody inter-ethnic conflict noted above between the Gumuz and resettlers was resolved, at least for the moment, through high level, complex and extended peace-making process – especially by the relentless efforts of selected elders from both parties under the title "reconciliation of Gumuz and Amhara." The ethnic variant name Amhara was used in the title to refer to the resettlers since most of them are from the Amhara ethnic group. The peace-making elders were composed of fifteen from Gumuz, fifteen from Amhara, and three from Agaw. The Agaw elders acted as neutral facilitators and middlemen in the peacemaking. The consultation processes of the elders' peace-making efforts were monitored by the local state authorities as well as members of the defence forces who were assigned to follow its results closely because of the sensitivity of the whole volatile situation.

Once the elders reached agreement to resolve the differences between the two groups, a ritual for cessation of hostilities was performed near the main bridge over the Beles River. For the peace-making ritual performance, the Gumuz offered two goats and the Amhara offered an ox. Of the two goats, one was slaughtered near the main Beles River meant to appease the spirits of the area and believed to bring a lasting peace. The second goat was slaughtered for consumption by the Muslim participants at the end of the ritual. The ox was slaughtered for all non-Muslim participants. While the meat was roasted, a swearing ritual was performed through the facilitation of elders. Right from the very beginning up to the end, elders were intermittently giving blessings, wishing lasting peace between the warring parties.

Five objects were brought for symbolic significance of the performing of swearing ritual process. These are a bullet (*tiyyit*), a thorny plant known as *qontir* in Amharic (*Capparis tomentosa Lam.*), a piece of stone (*dingay*), dry donkey-dung (*faandiya*), and a front leg bone (radius) of a goat. As the ritual performance proceeded, *first* the two parties stepped on the bullet and swore saying: "If we violate this cessation of hostility agreement, let it be that our bullets will not shoot their targets but the others' will target us." Then, they exchanged their bullets one from each group as a mark of resuming friendliness. In other words, the bullet symbolises death for the violating party. *Second*, the two parties touched the *qontir* plant and swore: "If we violate this cessation of hostility agreement, let us die by being pierced and halted by the *qontir* and fall under the target of the others." *Third*, the two parties held a piece of stone and swore: "If we violate this cessation of hostility agreement, let we loose all our senses as humans and become mute like stones." *Fourth*, the two parties held dry donkey-dung and swore: "If we violate this cessation of hostilities agreement, let we become as light as the pieces of dry donkey-dung and disappear with the winds." Finally, *fifth*, the two parties held the radius and broke it, swearing: "If we violate this cessation of hostility agreement, let us be killed, our bones being broken in the same way." Usually, a peace-making and reconciliation ritual performed by breaking bones is believed to the most binding and lasts longest. Thus, once the swearing process was over, the elders added further blessings and the meat was consumed on the spot by all participants. Since then, no major conflict has occurred

This high scale ethnic conflict coupled with the special situation of the resettler population in the new contextual setting enabled the granting of the Beles Valley resettlement scheme area a special autonomous status under the name Pawe Special *Woreda*. As a result, the Pawe district, which was previously fully administered under the Metekel zone, was empowered with more autonomy and delegated direct access to the regional state council (crossing the zonal ladder). Since then, the resettlers have been represented by four elected representatives of their own members (three from north-central resettlers and one from south-western resettlers) in the regional state's council as part of the special autonomy.

(*B*) *A Lower Scale Mangima:* In order to resolve a conflict between the Gumuz of Aypapa near Mambuk and resettlers of villages R101 and R127 noted above as case six in the previous section, comparatively lower scale *mangima* was conducted. Since both sides sustained equal casualties of one death each, they agreed to settle the conflict according to traditional mediation. Elders were selected from the two groups. Members of the EPRDF fighters and cadres were also reported to have facilitated the immediate mediation efforts of the elders. This conflict was attempted to be handled with care lest it otherwise ignite further cyclical vindictive conflicts on a broader scale.

For the performance of the *mangima* ritual, each side contributed one goat. Both went to the nearby river. Of the two key persons of the peace-making process, one was represented by the brother of the dead from the Gumuz side. On the other side, since the dead resettler had no brother, a close friend from the deceased's original area (north Wollo) represented from the resettlers' side. After the blessing and good wishes of the mediating elders, the first goat was sacrificed as part of the belief meant to appease the spirits of the area for provision of amicability between the groups. Then, the second goat was slaughtered. The representatives of the parties were made to touch the blood with their hands and swear: "If we fail to abide by this settlement, let us suffer casualties and die, our blood flowing in the same way." Again, the two representatives stepped on the blood bare-footed and swore, repeating the same. Once more, they stepped over the blood and then back and swore, repeating the same. Afterwards, two Kalashnikov guns were laid on the ground and the two stepped over them and back and swore: "If we fail to abide by the settlement, let our guns not shoot at their targets, rather others will target us." Finally, the goat's radius was held together and broken, at the same time the men swearing: "If we fail to abide by this set-tlement, let us be killed, our bones being broken in the same way." At every interval, the peace-making process was intermittently endorsed with the blessings of elders and approval of the participants. Finally, the meat was roasted and consumed by all participants. Since then, no casualty has oc-curred between the two groups.

Conflict Resolution between the Gumuz and Immigrants of 1950s
According to informants especially in Dibati *Woreda* (some of whom were part of the peace making process), this ethnic conflict was mediated and resolved by the involvement of a selected multi-ethnic council of elders fa-cilitated and monitored by the EPRDF cadres. Two groups of elders were formed for resolving this equally large-scale ethnic conflict. The first group of elders, composed of three Shinasha, three Agaw, two Gumuz, and one Amhara elders, was assigned to handle the case in the areas around Mandura *Woreda* from Metekel and bordering Guangua *Woreda* (Chagni) of Agauawi zone in the Amhara region. The second major group of elders, composed of five Shinasha, ten Agaw, four Oromo, seven Amhara, and seven Gumuz elders, was assigned to handle the severe large-scale ethnic conflict cases around Menta-Wuha, Dibati, and Zigam located mostly in Dibati *Woreda*.

Under this broader elder's council, a supportive sub-committee of elders was established in the respective peasant associations of the entire ethnic conflict area.

The consultation processes and progress of the elders' peace-making efforts were regularly reported to the local state authorities, who were assigned to follow closely the results due to the extremely sensitive situation. Once the elders managed to reach agreement from all parties to resolve the conflict peacefully, they first attempted to restore the return of looted property from both parts and people were reportedly disarmed, removing guns considered "illegal" in co-ordination with the local authorities. Then, a high level peace-making ceremonial ritual was organised at Chagni town. The swearing of the conflicting groups for cessation from actions that ignite further interethnic conflict was performed at the peace-making ritual. The whole detailed process of peace-making ritual performed to resolve the conflict between the Gumuz and Wollo spontaneous settler farmers was reported to be quite similar to the *mangima* procedure described about the peace-making process between resettlers and Gumuz in the Beles Valley as described above. As part of the ceremonial ritual, five oxen were slaughtered with the blessings of elders at Chagni town and consumed by the attending parties from the conflicting ethnic groups. The five oxen were reportedly provided by the local authorities as part of the facilitation efforts. It was meant to handle the delicate problem exerting maximum care because the situation had already begun getting out of control, claiming many lives and destroying huge amounts of property. Since then, no major conflict of the scale has been reported. As a consequence, there was further restructuring of the boundaries between the Metekel and Agauawi Zones of the two federal states by incorporating most of the peasant associations inhabited by the Wollo immigrants of the 1950s into the Amhara National Regional State, which were previously under the Benishangul-Gumuz National Regional State.

11.4 Ethnic Relations and the Role of the State

Although dealing deeply with the role of the state in the complex issues of inter-ethnic relations is beyond the scope of this study, some points with direct relevance to the subject in the context under discussion are attempted to be presented. The present government seems to have instrumentalised ethnicity in the country in general and in Metekel in particular. Metekel, as explained above, is a context of complex ethnic relations. However, the state's very ethnicity policy does not seem to have a clear knowledge of the

261

extent of its complexity both at conceptual and practical levels. In such a multi-ethnic complex context, local physical administrative boundaries are demarcated along ethnic lines without serious consideration of the fluidity of ethnicity in the practical grounds. Hence, the state ethnicity policy itself, which lacks conceptual and practical clarity, can be considered to be equally accountable for igniting these bloody inter-ethnic conflicts of higher scale with widespread hostilities.

However, after suffering its worst effects, the same state authorities attempted to play significant roles by trying hard to handle these sensitive and delicate ethnic conflicts that emerged getting out of easy control. The role of the state authorities was reportedly stressed in their relentless facilitation and manipulation exerted to the local respected elders' efforts of peace making through their traditional institutions. Thus, as a result of the tireless efforts of traditional elders, the bloody ethnic conflicts have been somewhat resolved – at least temporarily. Mainly, it is after this important landmark role of elders in ethnic conflict resolution that the state authorities seem to have realised the power of a local solution to such sensitive ethnic problems. Nevertheless, the efforts of the state authorities role of facilitation especially through provision of logistics (such as transportation for selected elders engaged in the mediation and arranging consultation venues) and follow-ups should not be of course underestimated. In certain cases, my Dibati informants (who were some of the peace-making elders) reported that the local political authorities have provided ritual performance animals. For instance, the oxen slaughtered at the Chagni peace-making ritual (to resolve the conflict between the Gumuz and Wollo immigrants) were reported as being provided by the local branch of the ruling EPRDF party. Moreover, the whole conflict-mediation process was also reported as being closely monitored both by the local political cadres and representatives from the defence forces stationed in the area. After the situation had somewhat cooled down, the state authorities began working hard training a number of cadres in several rounds, recruiting men from different ethnic groups in an attempt to contain the ethnic conflict problem as well as part of the state's ethnicity politics with its larger objectives and goals.

The major political alliance in Metekel is formed between Gumuz and Shinasha, considered as the two local 'native' major ethnic groups; though there still exists complex politics in it. Primarily the two ethnic groups share major local administrative positions. This has created implicit and explicit resentment by all other resident groups of the area. There is a deep-rooted wider rift between those who are considered as the original inhabitants of the area and those considered as newcomers from outside (*matte*). To a limited extent, it is only the Pawe Special *Woreda* that seems to enjoy a relative autonomy as a consequence of the terrible ethnic conflict stated above. The *woreda* has direct access to the region crossing the zonal chain and has elected representatives in the Regional State Council. As already pointed out, in the Regional Council, those ethnic groups entitled to hold seats through their elected representatives are: Gumuz (33 seats), Berta (24 seats), Shinasha (6 seats), Mao and Komo (4 seats), and Pawe state-sponsored re-settlers (4 seats – 3 representing Amhara resettlers and 1 representing Kambaata and Hadiyya).

However, in such an ethnically complex setting, the role of the formal state institutions on the issues of ethnicity and ethnic relations is by far out-weighed by the role of the traditional informal institutions, as pointed out in the preceding part. In matters pertaining to ethnic relations, the local authori-ties in all my study *woreda* informally confirmed the fact that, had it not been for the relentless efforts of community elders through informal institu-tional arrangements in differing settings, they would not have managed to handle issues related to such a complex and fluid subject of ethnicity at all. In other words, they implied that the role of the state in ethnic relations without the primary role of traditional institutional arrangements is futile.

The approval by my informants from the local authorities noted above was witnessed by a number of the ongoing practices and facts on the actual contexts of the area. For instance, following the reconciliation experiences of those large-scale inter-ethnic conflicts through the traditional *mangima* institution, several low and medium scale peace-making committees com-posed of local elders were formulated to settle inter-ethnic disputes facili-tated by and integrated with the local authorities.

A case example for such a committee entitled to find local compromising solutions for inter-ethnic conflicts is the one formed in inter-ethnic conflict-prone locations between the three resettler villages of *R104*, *R101* and *R127* in Pawe Special *Woreda* on the one hand and the Gumuz of Aypapa village in Dangur *Woreda* on the other. This rather permanent conflict-monitoring as well as conflict-resolving committee has ten members composed of two elders from Aypapa Gumuz, two elders from later immigrants' village of *R104*, two elders from resettlers' villages of *R101* and *R127* (one from each), two representatives from Pawe Special *Woreda* (which include the *woreda* police commander and the security sector chief), and two representatives from Dangur *Woreda* (which include the *woreda* police commander and the security sector chief). There are also other similar committees formed between the Mandura *Woreda* (in Metekel Zone of the Benishangul-Gumuz National Regional State) on the one hand and the Guangua and Dangila *Woreda* (in Agauawi Zone of the Amhara National

Dangila *Woreda* (in Agauawi Zone of the Amhara National Regional State) on the other. In such an ethnically complex plural context, these joint committees were reported to have contributed a lot to the stability and peace making process in such an area where peaceful co-existence between the Gumuz and their neighbours has been troubled and perturbed by prevalent tensions and hostilities.

Chapter 12. Inter-Ethnic Integration and Coexistence

Despite the prevalent conflicting inter-ethnic relations and uneasy co-existence, there is also some existing and emerging ethnic integration across ethnic boundaries in different contexts with differing magnitudes. These contexts of ethnic interactions and mutual relations include local market exchanges, bond-friendships, sharecropping arrangements, religious conversions, neighbourhood, and similar other local informal institutional arrangements.

12.1 Local Market Exchange

Exchange of products in the local markets is an important component of the Gumuz means of livelihood. Most of the Gumuz are first order producer-sellers who bring to local markets their own produce and sell them to direct consumers or traders, who in turn take the goods out of the area into second order or extended networks of sellers. Except exchanging for basic subsistence, no trading for accumulation has been observed among the Gumuz. They sell several items in such local markets as Chagni, Mandura, Gublak, Mambuk, L4 resettlement village, L7 resettlement village, Kuyyisa, and Gilgel Beles inside the main study area. In these markets, I observed them selling such crops as finger millet, sorghum, cotton, ginger, nigerseed, hot pepper, pumpkin, maize, yam, *oppa*, *endaha* , *kakima* (edible wild leaves), *kuya* (wild fruit), and several others; such domestic animals as goats, sheep and chicken; different handicraft products; and *keya*. The local market exchange places are existing, emerging, and expanding centres of mutual inter-ethnic interactional contexts between the Gumuz and their neighbours.

The Gumuz informants in Mandura and Dangur *Woreda* stressed the expansion of local market[18] exchanges as a positive element of encroachment.

---

[18] Similar observation on the importance of the market place in creating closer relations was noted between the Gumuz and the Wollo immigrant peasants of the 1950s settled around Menta-Wuha area, formerly parts of the Dibati *Woreda* (Berihun 1996:98). Nevertheless, in some of the market places, the Gumuz were usually observed trading at a relatively "distanced" locations on

They approved the increased and improved local market exchange that brought about noticeable change upon their livelihoods as the most important positive effect. Although most of the services are not primarily targeted to their benefit, the Gumuz also noted considerable improvements in infrastructure and services such as transportation, potable water, education, health services, and grain mills. Despite the conflicts which emerged as a consequence, these changes have equally served as contexts of integration and mutual interaction directly or indirectly. However, these limited positive effects cannot at all be compared with the enormous adverse effects of encroachment.

12.2 Mutual Bond Friendships

Mutual bond friendship[19] (*wodaajinet*) between the Gumuz and their neighbours is also an important existing and emerging form of mutual interaction across ethnic boundaries. It had already existed in the past and is also dynamically bonding mostly at a micro-level individuals belonging to either of the groups. These individually established acquaintances have been further extended in a network of friend-of-friends relationships between neighbouring ethnic groups on the differing circumstantial contexts of individual entrepreneurial ability in interacting with others. Individuals with networks of relations mutually exchange a lot through their interaction across ethnic boundaries. For instance, *Bega* and *Shuwa* friends intentionally visit each other. They enjoy each other's company during important life events such as happy and sad occasions like festivities and mourning. Those in need of loans of cash and grain get easy access through their friendship relations. Through friendship, the *Shuwa* get access to sharecropping arrangements with the Gumuz. Bonded friends act as nodal figures in channelling information and resolving misunderstanding and conflicts. Mutual bond-friendship is one of the important institutions between the Gumuz and *Shuwa* that can channel the bonded friends' access to multiple livelihood

---

the peripheries of the markets, whereas the non-Gumuz were observed mainly trading in the centres.

[19] Despite the predominantly conflicting inter-ethnic relations, Berihun (1996:100) has also noted somewhat similar cases of existing individual friendly relations between the Gumuz and the Wollo immigrant peasants around Menta-Wuha area (formerly parts of the Dibati *Woreda*). These individual friends across ethnic groups show mutual concern for one another (including their families) such as invitations on important social occasions. However, even in such contexts, the Wollo immigrant settlers have been reported taking economic advantage of their Gumuz friends, especially in obtaining land either free of charge or with minimum payments typically indicative of the prevalent unequal exchange between them.

resources. However, the Gumuz seem to be sceptical of the trustworthiness of their friendships with their neighbouring *Shuwa*. They seem to lack full trust on the friendship with *Shuwa* neighbours due to the latter's deception of their friends with unequal exchange mostly aimed at unsympathetic intentions of over-exploiting the Gumuz.

12.3 Traditional *Michu* Institution

The traditional *michu* institution, considered to have come to Metekel with the Oromo from south of Abbay River, is the most intimately binding friendship institution ritually established between members belonging to the same or different ethnic groups. In other words, it is both an inter-ethnic and intra-ethnic clan intimacy institution. Mostly, *michu* is established between members with no close blood relations. The deeper meaning of binding friendship with *michu* connotes a formation of relations with an extra lasting intimacy and belongingness between the *michu* friends and families. The *michu* established between individuals has an extended importance of closely binding the respective group members of the two individuals. *Michu* is most commonly practised in Dibati, Bulen and Wombera *Woreda*, which are inhabited by the Oromo ethnic group members interspersed with other ethnic groups.

There are three forms of *michu*. The first is a *michu* friendship established between the opposite sexes of youth with an equivalent meaning of *kenfer-wodaj* ("boyfriend/girlfriend"). The second form of *michu* is one established between already closer friends just to add emphasis and to hide secrets from others. This form of *michu* is said to be established even between consanguines. Here, a person who committed acts of crime goes to his friend, confesses his secrets and requests a *michu* to seal the secret. In the absence of anyone else, the two first each prick the tip of one of their little fingers and let the blood pour out and swear, saying: "If any of us leak or disclose this secret to the public, let the blood of the one who does it pour out and causing him to die." Then, they will keep the secret hidden throughout their life. The third and the publicly established *michu* institution is the one that is ritually established between non-consanguines at intra-ethnic or inter-ethnic levels.

The third and main form of *michu* is a key case in point here and depicts features of mutual intra-ethnic and inter-ethnic interactions across boundaries. Members who want to establish *michu* will first assess each other's qualities very well and agree to do so. Then they organise a feast and inform others of their wish to respected elders to process the ritual, calling the company of their other close members. On a fixed date, the right hand index fingers of the two friends will be pricked. Then the two hold tightly at each other's fingers so that the blood of the one will enter into the other. After this *michu* ritual is performed, the two friends are considered to have the same blood and remain extra-intimate as equal to and at times even more closely related as blood relatives. This *michu* is reported to have been established between members of the Gumuz, Shinasha, Oromo, Agaw, and Amhara especially in Dibati, Bulen and Wombera *Woreda* as stated above. Once *michu* is established, the two families are considered close relatives and cannot intermarry. They share close relations between each other, one seeking the company of the other during most life events. Above all, both families bonded together through the *michu* play key roles in resolving conflicts and mediating any form of misunderstandings and conflicts that might emerge at different intra-ethnic and inter-ethnic levels.

12.4 Tenancy Arrangements (Renting Land)

Tenancy arrangements, mainly renting Land[20] between the Gumuz and their neighbours in general, and highland migrant resettlers in particular, is a practice that has existed as mutual inter-ethnic relations with differing magnitude in the past, and in recent years its scale is even highly increasing. However, in those areas away from encroachment pressure, land renting arrangements are least practised or even not known at all.

The practice is widespread however in those Gumuz areas under the pressure of high external encroachment. Here, it is to be recalled that the encroachment pressure has brought about a short fallow period due to limitations in land resources. This in turn has introduced among the shifting cultivators a claim of ownership to an earlier cleared field left fallow. Therefore, mostly it is this fallow field which is rented-out out by the Gumuz claimant to highland immigrant oxen-plough cultivators. The usual terms of renting land arrangement are an exchange for grain where an estimated one-hectare of farm land is rented out in exchange for an average 300-500 kg of grain (mainly finger-millet or sorghum) depending on the fertility of the land.

---

[20] Similar practices of renting land arrangements are also observed and reported between the Gumuz and Wollo immigrant settlers around Dibati, especially in areas bordering the villages of the two ethnic groups (Berihun 1996:106; he uses the term sharecropping instead). Nevertheless, he notes, such relations that seem advantageous in times of peaceful coexistence between the residents of the two ethnic groups along the proximate villages, are also at the same time areas of severe disadvantages during times of inter-ethnic conflicts, exposing them to be easy victimisation.

Specifically, in the process of a renting land arrangement, the Gumuz and the immigrant plough cultivator agree first on the details of the terms of exchange. Then, the final approval and decision are made in the presence of Gumuz elders. After harvest, the tenancy arrangement partners share the products on the basis of the terms fixed in their earlier agreement. However, there exists a predominant mistrust on the part of the Gumuz, who condemn the immigrant highlanders as unfaithful and deceivers. They complain about the immigrants' frequent failure and deceptive character in fulfilling their agreement that mostly ignite conflicts, which in many cases are resolved through the intervention of elders. The attitudes of those Gumuz members who practice renting-out land seem positive towards the arrangement.

An interesting case in point concerns the experiences of the tenancy arrangement occurring between the Gumuz of Wondbil village in Mandura *Woreda* and their state-sponsored resettler neighbours of L134 village in Pawe Special *Woreda*. Over the last four years, there has been an enormous increase in land renting arrangements.

My resettler informants in village L134 confirmed the fact that the Gumuz farming system is ecologically friendly. Getting access to the Gumuz land in tenancy arrangement means accessing what to them is a "virgin" land with a potential of higher yield. For instance, one resettler farmer of the village compared the fertility of the farm fields owned by a Gumuz and a resettler, stating: "Instead of farming five hectares of our poor lands, it is much better to farm a single hectare of rented-in land from the Gumuz." Since the farmlands of the resettlers were cleared by bulldozers and used for a relatively long period without rest, they are less fertile. According to the views of resettlers, had it not been for the tenancy arrangements with the Gumuz, they would not have even managed to feed their families. So, through several local institutional arrangements, many of the village plow-cultivating farmers have rented-in fallow lands of the neighbouring Gumuz.

As a result, the search for tenancy arrangements between the Wondbil village Gumuz and the L134 village resettlers has enormously increased. Competition has emerged within the resettlers to rent-in land from the Gumuz. As a consequence of the competition, quarrelling and conflicts began among the resettlers. For instance, in the 1999-2000 cropping season, one resettler farmer made a tenancy arrangement with a Gumuz. Another resettler went to the same Gumuz and requested the same land. However, the Gumuz refused the latter's bribes and told him that he cannot change his decision. The latter resettler farmer returned to the village and quarrelled with the first farmer. The village elders faced problem trying to solve the conflict between the two resettler farming families. So, they consulted the elders of the Wondbil Gumuz, requesting their support.

The Wondbil village Gumuz elders came to the resettlers' village in order to help resolve the conflict between the farmers. They managed to resolve the differences between the two farmers, applying and performing a lower scale ritual of their traditional *mangima* conflict resolving institution. In order to ease the situation and create amicable relations, they gave other land in tenancy arrangement to the second resettler farmer.

Another case personally observed in the same resettler village L134 was a large meeting of the whole village community *iddir* members. The issue under discussion was concerning grazing land. This grazing land where the resettlers' cattle used to graze belongs to the neighbouring Wondbil village Gumuz. However, one resettler member of the village obtained this land from the Gumuz in a tenancy arrangement. As a result, the village cattle lost their grazing area. The village resettlers requested the person who rented-in the grazing land to quit his arrangement with the Gumuz. Nevertheless, he reacted by not withdrawing his arrangement, justifying his position by explaining that unless the Gumuz provide this land willingly to the village inhabitants, they can rent-it-out to any other person from another village even if he quits the arrangement as requested. Of course, the resettlers were well aware of the fact that the Gumuz will not compromise on this land issue and considered consulting them a futile attempt. So, they put more pressure on their fellow resettler to withdraw his arrangement so that they can use the land for grazing just by understanding. The resettler found it difficult and refused to withdraw the arrangement. Then, the resettlers resorted to imposing the customary institutional sanction of excluding him from the village *iddir*. In other words, if they imposed the traditional sanction, the resettler's family will be banned from getting all the amenities in case anything bad (death, sickness, destruction of property by fire or thunder, etc.) happens to his family. He reacted by pleading that the attempted proposal of the severe *iddir* sanction was unfair for the wrong he had not committed. His plea was of course supported by some of the fellow villagers. Even some of the villagers indicated the effort as a sabotage incited by some villagers who themselves failed to get this land in a tenancy arrangement from the Gumuz. This was reflected in the very difference of opinion among the villagers themselves. The meeting personally observed to discuss the case was so intense, at times even going beyond the context aimed at the state's lack of proper land-use policy in the area, which had originally caused their suffering from shortage of grazing land. Each side attempted to justify the matter but failed to reach a persuasive conclusion to sanction and exclude the resettler out of the community *iddir*.

12.5 Religious Conversion and Inter-Marriage

The Gumuz have been influenced in differing degrees by the religions of their neighbours. For instance, those Gumuz neighbouring the dominantly Orthodox Christian highlanders have been appreciably influenced by the religion. Islam influences the Gumuz near the Sudan border. On the other hand, the Gumuz of Metekel bordering the present Kamashi Zone of the previous Wollega region along the Abbay River are said to have been relatively influenced by elements of Protestant (evangelical) Christianity from the south. Those Gumuz converts to Orthodox Christianity seem to oscillate between the practices of their traditional belief system and Christianity, and are not considered as strong adherents to it. Usually, the *Shuwa* neighbours establish local religious institutional relations in a form of god-parenthood and as members of religious associations such as *mahber* and *senbete*. In most cases, through such institutional arrangements, the *Shuwa* neighbours get easy access to the land resources of the Gumuz, who still suspect the true nature of their relations since they mostly result in unequal exchanges. So, even in such contexts, the Gumuz do not feel to have been considered as equals.

Inter-marriage between the Gumuz and *Shuwa* neighbours is not yet prevalent. The only noticeable inter-ethnic marriages observed are between the Gumuz men (usually elite townsmen) and Agaw women. However, the Gumuz women are rarely observed and reported inter-marrying with their neighbouring *Shuwa* men. Those "elite" Gumuz who have married Agaw women gave as one of the reasons for not marrying a Gumuz women the following argument – their in-laws would not allow them to take their wives (i.e., the elites' wives) out of their (again, the elites') villages for any purpose, lest they no longer be available for return in case the brother-in-laws' wives (the elites' sisters) are found wanting. This is because of the traditions associated with the exchange marriage, which demands maintaining the two exchanged wives in the respective clans. In other words, maintaining the two within the clan villages that exchanged wives proves securing a demand for a return of exchanged women to their natal village or replacements by clansmen in case of death, divorce, or lack of fertility. In certain cases, such demands are reported to extend into the fertility rate of the two exchanged women. In such an extreme case, it is reported that a group that got few children from exchanged women demands additional women for balancing the fertility. Hence, exchanged women should remain within their virilocal villages based on the traditional demands of one's natal clans.

However, the Gumuz women's explanation of the aforementioned "el- ites'" marriage preference with the non-Gumuz women is different from that of the men's version stated above. Gumuz women reportedly alleged such practices of their men as contemptuous, referring to the latter's bias attrib- uted to one's fellow women in the villages to be less fit as partners in the towns and cities. Nevertheless, the inter-marriage with Agaw women signals positive interactions between the two groups who have lived for a longer period neighbouring each other.

12.6 Networks of Relationship

As pointed out earlier, in areas of frequent contacts, both *Bega* and *Shuwa* have established several local institutional networks of relationships whereby important experiences were shared and exchanged. Apart from those contexts stated above, the Gumuz and non-Gumuz interact in multiple contexts that include wedding and mourning "festive" occasions, field la- bour mobilisation, employment and work settings, schools, and similar oth- ers. In their daily interactions, both have exchanged important experiences with each other. For instance, the Gumuz gained experience from the non- Gumuz in practices such as oxen-plowing, timber production, milking cows, brewing local beer (*tella*), preparation of *injera* and *wot*, cultivating vegeta- bles in the home gardens, and several related practices. On the other hand, the non-Gumuz gained some experience from the Gumuz in shifting cultiva- tion production practices and food habits such as gathering forest foods like *endaha, kimaa, kakima*, and *echa* for sauce preparation; planting *oppa* and pumpkin; consumption of bamboo sprouts; field cultivation using simple digging hand tools (e.g., *teba*) to maintain soil fertility; using red finger- millet seed variety; and brewing *keya*.

Moreover, many Gumuz children have been observed attending Gumuz as well as non-Gumuz village elementary schools. At times, these Gumuz children who attend non-Gumuz village schools were noticed playing impor- tant roles of bridging the two communities. For instance, Gumuz pupils coming from *Mataabaa* Gumuz village and learning at the L29 resettler village elementary school have played an important mediation role in set- tling a conflict that emerged between the two communities as a result of Gumuz field crop destruction by resettlers' cattle. The pupils managed to bring together their Gumuz and non-Gumuz parents with the facilitation of their teachers.

Members of Gumuz who are employees of the zonal and *woreda* offices also act as nodal contacts between their village communities and the outsiders. The Gumuz are mainly employed as guards and messengers in the different offices due to lack of educational background demanded for professional positions as stated earlier. These lower level employees mostly commute between their villages and the small towns where they work, enhancing their nodal roles. They also have better access to information in their respective offices. For instance, at times those plough cultivators who want to sharecrop land from Gumuz approach these employees for information. Hence, they serve as important nodal points in the interaction networks of the two communities.

Therefore, there are many areas of existing and emerging networks and contexts of inter-ethnic interaction and mutual coexistence between the *Bega* and *Shuwa* in the entire Metekel in general and the Beles Valley in particular. However, these existing and emerging inter-ethnic integration between the *Bega* and *Shuwa* are quite overwhelmed by the prevalent inter-ethnic conflicts and uneasy coexistence.

PART FIVE: ANALYSIS, SYNTHESIS AND CONCLUSION

Chapter 13. Analysis and Synthesis of Findings and Theoretical Considerations

13.1 Analysis and Synthesis of Findings

The Autochthonous Gumuz

The autochthonous Gumuz, whose livelihood is based on shifting cultivation combined with gathering, hunting, fishing, and honey collection, have an accumulated traditional ecological knowledge and natural resource management systems. They have holistic relationships with their natural environment and view it endowed with sacred meanings. The ethnographic evidence complements what Seeland (1997:103) conceptualises indigenous peoples' ecological knowledge as the "interconnections of nature and culture". The traditional ecological knowledge and natural resource management systems of Gumuz are reflections and abstractions of life-experiences drawn from the appropriation of nature to constitute their culture. The findings also validate the arguments of Appiah-Opoku and Mulamoottil (1997) that consider indigenous ecological knowledge as a body of intimate knowledge of the environment through living in close contact with nature.

The indigenous environmental thought, ecological knowledge, and resource management systems of the Gumuz can be best understood in close amalgamation with their traditional belief systems. In their worldview, the land resources are perceived as the ingenuous gift, blessing, and creation of *yamba* (the supreme deity), considering them to be the source of life and livelihood to the past, present and future generations. *Yamba* is believed to have provided them with the knowledge of proper use and management of natural resources as well as the responsibility of transferring them to the next generation. The diverse resources are also believed to have their respective *missa* (poly-spirits) that ensure safe and proper use and management of each resource where violations result in severe retribution from the respective *missa*. Additionally, the natural resources are considered as their ancestral heritage.

The composite mesh of ecological thought, knowledge, and belief systems of the Gumuz supports Berkes' (1999:13) conceptual consideration of traditional ecological knowledge and resource management systems as a

273

"knowledge-practice-belief complex." The ethnographic evidence revealed from the Gumuz experiences confirms the fundamental significance of traditional belief systems in the understanding of indigenous ecological knowledge and management systems. What is noted about their belief systems further complement the conceptual orientation stressed by Lovelace (1984:198) whereby cultural beliefs are considered as crucial aspects of human ecology often providing interpretations for survival relating human adaptations to their environment. Additionally, the experiences of Gumuz hold true to what Marshall (1994:138) considers indigenous ecological thought as "web of nature," identifying autochthonous peoples with their nature and its creatures where he notes the natural and cultural being harmoniously bonded. Based on the ethnographic evidence, the environmental thought, ethical values, and ecological knowledge of the autochthonous Gumuz are dynamically blended in their traditional belief systems and worldviews that serve as basis for their adaptive natural resource management system.

The diverse ranges of natural resources are managed skilfully, making use of natural processes so as to maintain the fragile agro-ecosystem. The traditional ecological knowledge is the foundation for shifting cultivation. Shifting cultivation is also found to be an important natural resource management strategy where the fields are shifted in order to use and conserve consciously the rich nutrients of the natural vegetation-soil complex. In the successive phases of shifting cultivation, the cropping field plot is considered as the first stage in the transition back to forest because it is skilfully managed to re-establish forest and vegetation. By maintaining the natural forest and vegetation ecosystem, the other equally important natural resource components such as soils, waters and wild animals are managed in a sustainable way.

The shifting cultivation practice of the Gumuz substantially validates the consideration of integral shifting cultivation as not only an agricultural system but also a most important natural resource management system (Warner 1991:9; Permpangsacharoen 1999:3). Their shifting cultivation system fully constitutes to "integral swiddener," one of the two types of shifting cultivation identified by Conklin (1957:2) because they practice a resource use and management system based on "traditional, year-round, community-wide, self-contained and ritually sanctioned way of life." In contrast to the integral swidden farming practices, which in this case is true of the Gumuz, the "pioneer swiddeners" include peasants practising partial swidden predominantly based on economic interests having strong socio-cultural ties outside the area, using the swidden to supplement the permanent field agriculture

(Conklin 1957:3). According to Warner (1991:10), the pioneer swiddeners belong mostly to the land-hungry immigrants who do not have enough knowledge of the forest ecosystem and use farming methods from their area of origin rather than those suited to the area of resettlement area. Since the two systems have different impacts on the natural environment, the distinction between the two forms of swidden farming is very important. In the realities of my research context, what Conklin termed as "integral" and "pioneer" have relevance because two differing and rivalling forms of farming systems – plow cultivation and shifting cultivation – have been identified causing totally different impact on the fragile agro-ecosystem.

The sedentary plow cultivation farming systems of the encroaching highland resettler farmers have been identified as causing adverse consequences on the natural environment. The plow cultivation demands clean fields clearing off trees, including removing the roots for smooth traction. As opposed to the plow cultivation, the shifting cultivation is integral to the forest ecosystem. Shifting cultivation maintains the re-vegetation potential of trees without removing and destroying the roots of those trees cut down. So, the integral shifting cultivation practised by the Gumuz is crucial to the environmental stability and better conserves the forest.

The indigenous institutions enshrined within their environmental thinking and knowledge systems ensure smooth management of natural resources in an environment friendly and ecologically stable manner. On the basis of their accumulated knowledge, respected Gumuz elders as well as those magico-religious persons like *gafia* are primarily responsible for enforcing clusters of institutional arrangements. As earlier discussed, the community elders, above all others, make the natural resource conservation, regulation, and allocation decisions according to tradition. In their natural resource tenure system, ownership of natural resources is vested upon the whole community where resources should only be used for the benefit of *both* the present and future generations. Since natural resources do not belong to only one generation, they cannot be privately possessed or controlled by any single members of the community – only the produce thereof. Ideally, the Gumuz do not view vital natural land resources as a commodity to be exchanged for profit making.

The challenges affecting the indigenous ecological knowledge of autochthonous peoples in the face of today's market economy, Berkes (1999:151f.) explains, is their noticeable engagement in activities differing in type and intensity from the indigenous patterns of resource use. Berkes notes that the overzealous attempt to portray all indigenous peoples as natural conservationists has been increasingly becoming unrealistic due to loss of control of resources, breakdown of land use and knowledge systems, population growth, commercialisation, and technological change. However, despite all these challenges faced, many autochthonous peoples do still maintain resource use and management practices that are sustainable, environmentally friendly and protective to the biodiversity.

Along a similar line of the above Berke's argument and conceptual orientation, the ethnographic evidence reveals significant ongoing and emerging changes that have noticeable effects on the indigenous natural resource management systems of Gumuz mainly all along the encroachment pressure areas. In those areas of excessive encroachment, the Gumuz, are facing severe stresses in trying to maintain their land resources and strategies of natural resource management based on their indigenous knowledge systems. The stresses are basically resulting from reductions in their traditional territories due to widespread encroachment pressure, constriction of their land resources by the state, political forces, technological changes, and to a certain extent internal growth of their own population. As a result, pressure and competition over their land resources has enormously increased, causing severe stresses on their indigenous ecological knowledge and resource management systems.

However, in those relatively inaccessible areas not seriously affected by encroachment pressure, the indigenous ecological knowledge and resource management systems of Gumuz are still intact. Meanwhile, they are also strong adherents of their traditional belief systems. Despite the pressures they have been facing, the evidence reveals the enormous significance of the indigenous ecological knowledge systems of Gumuz in their strategies of natural resource management.

As discussed earlier, the Gumuz are one of the minority ethnic groups totally marginalised from the centre and located at the periphery being vulnerable to encroachment on the land that belonged to them by tradition across regimes up to the present. Due to the ceaseless process of gradual and rapid encroachments, they have been facing pressures of deprivation from their land resources being pushed farther to the peripheries, where their basic source of life, livelihood, and culture are now threatened. As a result, their indigenous ecological knowledge and adaptive natural resource management system are under the stress of excessive encroachment and have been neglected by policy planners even today.

The various regimes of the central state were all reluctant to recognise their land resource rights by entitling them to special legal provisions to attain greater resource tenure security. Based on bias, misconception, and lack of proper understanding of the ways of life and livelihood of the autochthonous Gumuz, the development policy planners and state authorities at different levels were observed increasingly promoting permanent agriculture. In such a paternalistic top-down elitist approach, the latter are imposing pressure to eradicate the shifting cultivation and the multi-niche holistic livelihood strategies of the Gumuz substantially validating what Berkes (1999:176) termed 'positivist-reductionist-simplistic approach' which mistakenly considers "professionals know best", neglecting the traditional knowledge and practice. In order to realise the promotion of permanent agriculture through the introduction of oxen traction and extension services as well as provision of other social services, the regional state has planned a resettlement program meant to resettle the Gumuz in accessible areas. As detailed earlier, my Gumuz informants in Mandura and Dangur stressed lack of their genuine participation in the matter and listed the inevitable severe consequences of the envisaged schemes that would undoubtedly endanger their way of life and livelihood (cf. chapter 5 "State Policies and the Human and Natural Environment"). The basic premise for the envisaged plans of resettlement and conversion to ox-plow cultivation is the misconceived consideration of the traditional way of life and livelihood practices of the autochthonous Gumuz as insignificant, backward, and a hindrance to speedy development.

The Highland Resettlers

The broad category of highland resettlers includes differentiated population sub-categories of (*i*) long-standing highland neighbours of the Gumuz, (*ii*) early spontaneous immigrants of the 1950s mostly from Wollo, (*iii*) state-sponsored resettlers of the 1980s, (*iv*) voluntary and displaced immigrants of the 1990s, and (*v*) those immigrant residents in small towns. Although the complex and dynamic interplay of all the stated sub-categories are broadly assessed with differing intensity, the key emphasis of this study is on the state-sponsored resettlers of the 1980s.

The Beles Valley resettlement in Metekel is one of the biggest schemes that hosted highland resettlers as a consequence of both drought and famine in 1984 and 1985 (cf. chapter 6, section 6.1). Before the arrival of resettlers, an estimated 18,312 autochthonous Gumuz, who as a result of the resettlers' coming were displaced and pushed further to the peripheries dispossessed of their land resources, inhabited the scheme area. Subsequently, the resettlement scheme brought a total of 82,106 highland peasants at a peak of the operation to a completely different location in the lowlands of the Beles Valley (cf. chapter 5 "State Sponsored Resettlement of the 1980s"). Propaganda that described a glorified image of the new homes as if comforts were

277

awaiting them deceived most resettlers. Due to the various forms of coercion applied during recruitment, the traumatic experiences they encountered and the disillusionment due to the denial of expectations, the relocated peasants in the new location began life in an impotent and famished manner aggravated by the ravages of malaria, tuberculosis, and other epidemic diseases.

The resettlers' first contacts with the new sites were full of insecurity and precariousness, where they felt their new conditions were distressing, painful, and traumatic – substantially complementing the multifaceted physiological, psychological, and socio-cultural stresses considered by Scudder (1973:51). The resettlers encountered *physiological stress* through the increased morbidity and mortality rates aggravated by the ravages of epidemic diseases. They faced *psychological stress* due to trauma of family break-ups, grieving for lost family members as well as the home villages, which many of them considered as "a place where one's umbilical cord was buried" and anxiety about their uncertain future in a completely new setting. Moreover, they encountered *socio-cultural stress* associated with painful and distressing experiences of breaking-up of long established social structures, dismantling of production systems, and destruction of traditional coping strategies. Most essentially, these composite stresses very much complement what Colson and Scudder (1982:274f.) have considered a transition stage in their four-stage processual conceptual model of analysing resettlement as a sequence of stages. In responding to the multifaceted stresses, the resettlers attempted to cling to some familiar elements persisting from their origins through what Scudder (1973:53) has called "a process of cultural involution." Furthermore, the initial stressful relocation and transition stage experiences of the resettlers' holds true to Mathur's (1995:17) perception of resettlement as "an unmitigated disaster when viewed from the views of the resettlers," pointing out that "no trauma can be more painful for a family than to get uprooted from a place where it has lived for generations and to move to a place where it may be a total stranger."

Substantially validating the conceptual thoughts and the experiences pointed out by De Wet (1988:182), the natural and socio-cultural environments of the resettlers in the Beles Valley have been changed significantly due to the very long distance they underwent, moving from predominantly highland original areas to a completely lowland environment. This aggravated their stress. Hence, the physical and socio-cultural spatial changes that the resettlers underwent in the Beles Valley context strengthens De Wet's (1993:322) *spatial approach* demonstrating the resettlers' differing behavioural patterns and reactions to the stresses of long-distance relocation.

In the entire resettlement scheme area, the resettlers were heavily guarded at all levels to prevent them from escaping the increased state control imposed over them. Initially, religious holidays could not be freely observed due to the collective agricultural work. Free travel was absolutely impossible. The resettlers were strictly forbidden to leave the area. Even travel within the scheme area from one village to the other was possible only with pass letters obtained from the village authorities. They could not freely express themselves about their horrible misery and suffering in the new context. Their rights to freedom of speech were violated and denied, since access to communicate with them by any independent institutions was totally banned. Moreover, collectivisation was imposed upon them, and their labour time was strictly controlled according to the point system devised for producers' co-operatives. Individual household initiatives were constrained. The overall administration of each resettlement village was put under the tight and paternalistic control of a village political cadre.

Primarily, the resettlement scheme dismantled and disintegrated the resettlers' *traditional social institutions* and *organisations*, which serve as the very social fabric of the communities and mesh the web of their socio-cultural relationships. Already at the very beginning, the entire complex web of local institutions was disarticulated, and the relocated peasants were detached from their institutional heritage and left completely stripped of their social fabric in the face of the poorly-thought-out displacement and relocation process. These complex institutional linkages upon which the community's interactions are based were utterly neglected by the planners and implementers of the resettlement scheme. The uncertainties and desperation in the resettlers' daily lives had increased due to the disintegration of the infinite web of institutional settings upon which they were linked in manifold ways. The resettlers seriously felt the disarticulation of social institutions, resulting in their manifold stresses being severely aggravated. This evidence supports what in Cernea's (2000:30) terminology is called "social disarticulation" as one of the eight sub-processes in his "impoverishment risk and reconstruction model" of involuntary resettlement. In the process of relocation, the resettlers' previous social fabric is torn apart in the new context, dismantling their patterns of social organisation and disrupting their life-sustaining social networks significantly validating Cernea's conceptualisation explained above.

The dismantled social institutions and organisations of resettler peasant households are considered as the central concepts of Scoones' (1998:4) rural livelihood model, revealing as they do their multiple and crucial roles in mediating and channelling rural households' livelihood resources and livelihood strategies. The disintegration of these institutions and organisations of the people involuntarily relocated in the Beles Valley scheme validate both Scoones' and Cernea's conceptualisations of the indispensable roles of "social capital" where its loss compounds with the loss of natural, economic and human capital causing severe consequences in their lives and livelihoods.

Additionally, social disintegration through the weakening state of life-support mechanisms, debilitating capacity of self-management, and the collapsing social fabric of resettlers, according to Downing's (1996:34) argument, is expressed as: "The people may physically persist but the community that was is no more." The ethnographic evidence revealed from the field substantially complements what Downing conceptualised as a *social geometry model* considering the *social spatial-temporal* dimensions of resettlers undergoing forced resettlement. Compatible with his concepts, initially resettlers in the Beles Valley under the multiple stresses of the transition stage (cf. Scudder 1973) were traumatically bewildered and attempted helplessly to find an answer to basic questions such as "who are we?" and "where are we?" Similar to what Downing has noted, the socially defined "space, time and personages" of resettlers is changed significantly (especially at the initial stage) in the new social and physical context of the Beles Valley (as detailed in a number of chapters in the preceding parts of this study). In *spatial* terms, their settlement pattern has tremendously changed, including its associated social significance of space from the hamlets and villages in the home areas. In *temporal* terms, significant changes are observed among the youth, adults, and elders in their differing roles, authority systems and access to and control over the social and economic resources in relation with the new socio-economic systems in the new context. In the sequential intersections of time, space, and personage terms, many of the ritual activities used to mark important life events, such as birth, circumcision, marriage, and death have changed tremendously due to the social disintegration caused by the resettlement scheme. So, the findings revealed from the Beles Valley resettlers' experiences of the initial socio-cultural disarticulation holds true to Downing's (1996:48) *social geometry model* (cf. chapter 2 "Social Spatial-Temporal Approach/Social Geometry Model"). Validating and strengthening Downing's key conceptual questions of resettlers ("who are we?" and "where are we?"), the Beles Valley evidence revealed the fact that resettlers questioned similarly for identification due to the fundamental loss and disruption of the familiar in a completely new human and physical environments.

Nevertheless, as the resettlers went through adaptive readjustment, they began re-instituting local institutions, which in turn played central role in the process of their livelihood adaptation in the new setting. With the rearticulation of local institutions, the uncertainties in the daily lives of resettlers were reduced and stable livelihood reconstruction strategies were attained. The early disarticulation and the later rearticulation of local institutions enabled these often-invisible complex webs of institutional arrangements and the multiple roles to be vividly visible to outsiders as well. The meaningful re-instituting process of local institutions was properly realised with the collapse of collectivisation and reestablishment of the smallholder production system managed by the households. In the process, resettlers managed to re-establish complex institutional networks first within their villages and then at different levels including the entire resettlement area as well as in the areas of the neighbouring host communities. The livelihood adaptation process was practised through re-establishing institutional arrangements such as neighbourhood, marriage and kinship, religious beliefs, work groups, tenancy arrangements, bond-friendship, and related other complex social networks of relationships.

The ethnographic evidence revealed concerning the initial disintegration and the re-establishment of resettlers' social institutions and organisations substantially supports Cernea's (2000:40-42) views of community reconstruction and social rearticulation. After the initial phase of emergency and transition for around a decade, resettlers in the Beles Valley who did not either succumb to illness or move away began adapting themselves to the new context and showed profound positive effects of reconstructing local social institutions and organisations (cf. chapter 9). Resettler households embedded in these local institutional frameworks channelled access to different livelihood resources, which are essential for their livelihood strategies. These livelihood strategies are in turn linked to the multiple institutional settings upon which the households are embedded. The livelihood strategies enable the households to establish differing degrees of food security, social security, and the entire livelihood security at large. Thus, in the process of the pursuit of livelihood adaptation by the relocated peasant households in the new context, the central roles of *local institutions* are manifested in mediating/channelling access to livelihood resources, providing strong social security or safety nets, and facilitating local self-governance.

The excessive encroachment that occurred during a number of political regimes, and in particular the massive state-sponsored resettlement scheme of the 1980s is primarily responsible for the environmental degradation in the study area. The pressure on the natural resources by several interest groups caused adverse effects on the ecology of the area. The evidence from the environmental impact of the Beles Valley scheme holds true to what Scudder (1999:360f.) noted about the environmental degradation caused by the resettlement in his seminal longitudinal study of Kariba scheme in the middle Zambezi Valley due to the extreme population pressure (both resettlers and immigrants) exceeding the carrying capacity of the land. Scudder compares the present environmental degradation situation of the scheme area, which came to be like a Sahelian habitat within a single generation, whereas it had formerly been a well-vegetated savannah woodland. If the present excessive pressure proceeds unabated, the same will be fully true of the Beles Valley. Similarly, the experiences of immigrants in the Beles Valley substantially supports what Scudder (1997:696) noted concerning the pressure from immigrants in resettlement schemes elsewhere. The indiscriminate destruction of the forest resources in the Beles Valley scheme area has been causing an imbalance of the stability in the entire agro-ecology and the natural environment through increased soil and water erosion, intensified heat and wind, decreased waters in rivers and streams, scarcity of wild animals and aquatic resources in the waters, scarcity of shade trees and windbreaks, and increased soil depletion.

However, despite its compatibility with Scudder's and Cernea's grand theories of involuntary resettlement in several aspects, the findings from the Beles Valley resettlement scheme differ with each of them to a substantial degree in certain aspects. Cernea's *impoverishment risks and reconstruction model* identifies eight sub-processes of impoverishment as key variables of resettlement: *landlessness, joblessness, homelessness, marginalisation, increased morbidity and mortality, food insecurity, loss of access to common property and services, and social disarticulation.* Nevertheless, this important list of sub-processes fall short of incorporating explicitly the environmental consequences of resettlement although his model's key argument is livelihood reconstruction, which should undoubtedly depend on the ecological contexts of the relocation settings. On the other hand, Colson and Scudder's *processual analysis of resettlement as a sequence of stages* formulates four successive stages of the relocation process, namely *the recruitment stage (stage one), the transition stage (stage two), the stage of potential development (stage three) and the handing over or incorporation stage (stage four).*

In his later work Scudder (1993:130-135) divides the previous first stage into two (a first stage precedes the awareness of the local people of their impeding removal; and a second stage involves site preparation when the

282

local people begin to realise their potential removal) and identifies five stages. Since there is no major difference between the two divisions, the four-stage division is considered in the analysis of data in this study. The Beles Valley findings are fully compatible with the first two of the four stages. However, the findings tend to challenge some elements of the later stages as not compatible with the Beles Valley case. The key argument lies in the model's conceptual consideration of the third stage being a level that can only be reached and sustained by the next generation. Although the environmental sustainability remains valid, reaching the third stage predominantly by the second generation does not hold true to the actual experiences in the Beles Valley. In the latter's case, already first generation resettlers even in the absence of proper sectoral support mechanisms underwent the stated initial multiple stresses, but showed ingenuity, innovation and entrepreneurial adaptive abilities. They did this to such an extent that they developed significant socio-economic differentiation within an average of only *one* decade. So, the ethnographic evidence from the Beles Valley showed substantial difference with respect to the third and fourth stage arguments, which are assumed to be reached only by the second generation (who have grown up in the new relocation area). To a considerable extent, resettlers in the Beles Valley relatively managed to achieve their socio-economic recovery fairly well as well as community formation and self-management in much less than a generation (whose relocation commenced within the duration from 1985 to 1988), challenging significantly the applicability of Scudder and Colson's seemingly highly generalised third and fourth stage arguments.

The Gumuz and Resettlers: Identity and Ethnic Relations

The inter-ethnic relations in the study area are quite complex, predominantly characterised by features of ethnic stratification and polarisation (cf. chapter 10, section 10.1). The ethnic identification processes of the autochthonous Gumuz and highland resettlers described and discussed consider a complementary combination of both moderate *primordialist* and *constructivist* conceptual approaches to ethnicity and ethnic relations. In the local complex dynamic identity politics of defining peoplehood considering the principles of "belongingness versus difference/distinction" or "inclusion versus exclusion" in the research context, both approaches hold important plausible arguments that are reflected in the discussion and analysis of the ethnographic accounts of the study groups.

In the ethnic identification process of dichotomization and maintenance of boundary between *we/us* and *they/them*, the Gumuz identify their group members as *Bega* (our people) and categorically refer all other neighbouring non-Gumuz ethnic groups' members as *Shuwa* (others), usually without differentiating them. The expression of Gumuz ethnic identity is mainly shaped and articulated in an ethnically polarised and stratified context based on historical, economic, political and cultural factors used to signal contextual differences that dichotomise the boundaries between the *Bega* (*we/us*) and their neighbouring *Shuwa* (*they/them*). These defining features of "inclusion versus exclusion" or "in-group versus out-group" membership of *we/us* and *they/them,* in the collective identification processes of *"who is against whom and why?"* [...] *"who belongs to whom and why?"* (using once again the expressions of Schlee 2000:89, emphasis added) are explained and described in the accounts of the following main factors. These factors articulated in the interactional contexts, which allowed the Gumuz to label and draw the socio-cultural distinction of the *Bega* identity over the *Shuwa* include the historical and genealogical metaphor of common origin and life experiences; occupation of divergent ecological niches as lowlanders versus highlanders and the differing modes of livelihood; differing belief systems, marriage systems, and patterns of authority; overt physical features such as "skin pigmentation" and bodily scarification; and other obvious cultural features such as language, costume, and folklore.

These socio-cultural features articulated to distinguish the *Bega* identity against that of their neighbouring *Shuwa,* substantially fits in with what Geertz (1996:40-45) termed "primordial ties" of ethnicity. Geertz enumerates the defining elements of his "primordial ties" concept to include assumed blood ties, race, language, religion, region and custom. The ethnographic evidence on the *Bega* identification significantly validate Geertz's *primordial* concepts in their reference to the common apical ancestor described in an origin myth from twin brothers and the associated power contest ritual that deeply widened the rift between them and their neighbouring *Shuwa*. An equally important factor is the categorical reference to the *Bega* by the contemptuous, stigmatising and derogative term *Shanqilla* for their darker "skin pigmentation" ascribed by the *Shuwa* neighbours in the *ethnic stereotyping,* signalling inferior status with elements of "racial" discrimination based on physical features. On the other hand, the *Bega* in turn refer to the *Shuwa* with an externally defined categorical ascription of a "hatred" generic term *Mittiha,* connoting hatred due to the alleged cruelty and brutality of all "fair skin pigmented" non-Gumuz neighbours (*qay*). Additionally, the *Bega* refer to their language and traditional belief systems as identification markers, which differ very much from the languages spoken and the religions followed by the *Shuwa*. As to the ecological niche inhabited, the *Bega* identify themselves with the lowland eco-system associated with its distinct livelihood system as opposed to that of *Shuwa's* inhabitation primarily of mid-and highland eco-systems associated with different livelihood system. The *Bega* also refer to their traditional customs (such as ritual practices during all important life events like birth, marriage, and death), folklore (such as circular dance and body movements below the waist), and bodily scarification as identification markers against the *Shuwa,* whose customs and traditions are considered to be completely different. As noted above, the findings from the *Bega* and *Shuwa* data substantially validate the significance of some elements of the moderate *primordialist approaches* to ethnicity implying the essential essence of the above articulated attributes in the group members' cognition of emotional bonds and affective ties. Hence, the persistent maintenance of the *Bega* ethnic identity against the excessive external pressure and subjugation further strengthens the above arguments.

In certain cases, extending this *primordialist* argument to the extreme, some informants from the two groups expressed the rarely existing practice of inter-marriage between them in the local stereotype, questioning as: "Could a sheep and a goat copulate? How could a sheep and a goat crossfertilise?" This reply from the *Bega* and *Shuwa* informants in Pawe, Mandura and Dangur *Woreda* questioned back my inquisitive question concerning the rare practice of inter-marriage between the members of the two groups, showing the extreme sentiment as if the two groups are "biologically differing species." However, this argument of expressing their difference as "biologically differing species" seems to a large extent a socio-cultural construction of difference in order to exclude members of either of the group to the extreme as a result of suspicion and contempt prevailing based on age-old repressive relationships. Running counter to this "biological" argument are the occasional cases where the Gumuz "elite" members marrying women from the *Shuwa* (specially Agaw women). However, cases of Gumuz women marrying *Shuwa* men are rarely noted.

Elements of moderate primordial ties are noted among several ethnic group members. One interesting case of such a tie noted in the field is about a Shinasha man who heads one of the departments in the Metekel Zone. He was born and brought up in an area of Metekel where an Oromo language (*Oromigna* in Amharic or *Oromiffa/Afaan Oromoo* in Oromo) is spoken. He speaks *Oromigna* as a mother tongue and does not speak the Shinasha language at all. Except for his upbringing in a spatially and socially different Oromo speaking context, he fully identifies with Shinasha ethnic group members, and hence is entitled to share the political power representing the Shinasha. Though this case could also be considered as instrumentalised ethnicity, it undoubtedly validates the lingering implicit and explicit primordial ties beneath his current identity.

Although the primordial sentiments of ethnicity either thinly linger or strongly persist in the cognition, perception and emotion of the members of ethnic groups, ethnic identification is equally articulated depending on the circumstances. The persistence of primordial elements and the socio-cultural construction of ethnicity depending on situations are admitted by the most influential constructivist Barth (1969:29) in his equivocal statement referring to the problem of variation about the simultaneous characteristics of ethnic labels. He states: "Particularly where people change their identity. this creates ambiguity since ethnic membership is at once a question of source of origin as well as of current identity." As noted earlier, the central tenets of Barth's constructionist approach to ethnicity and ethnic groups focus on "the ethnic boundary that defines the group, not the cultural stuff that it encloses," which is accredited as an "intellectually liberating paradigm shift" (Cohen 1994:59). The dichotomization and maintenance of boundary between the *Bega* and *Shuwa* revealed in this study complements Barth's seminal concept of ethnic boundaries.

In accordance with Barth's boundary concept, for instance, the highland resettlers' category is further differentiated at various levels based on circumstantial identifications and alliances. The different sub-categories of the highland plow cultivators (that include those who have neighboured the Gumuz for a long time, the early immigrants of the 1950s, the resettlers of the 1980s, the later immigrant of the 1990s, and the immigrant small-town residents specially since the 1980s) identify together and form a strong alliance against the Gumuz – especially in situations of ethnic conflicts of "autochthonous" versus "outsiders."

However, as ethnographically detailed in chapter ten, each of the stated sub-categories maintains its boundary depending on the circumstances and intended objectives and goals of the respective group members. Here, both the spatial and temporal factors of the circumstances need to be stressed due to their roles of articulating and maintaining the boundaries of each sub-group. Those long-standing neighbours emphasise their earliest occupation of the spaces neighbouring the autochthonous Gumuz in the inclusion process of setting a boundary by excluding others. In addition, their faith in the Orthodox Christianity acted as a strongly strengthening factor. The early immigrant resettler farmers refer temporally to their arrival since the 1950s and spatially from the same original areas and settling in the present destination areas. The later immigrants have similar spatial and temporal feelings to those of the early immigrants. However, the state-sponsored resettlers feel that only they went through the hurdles of the adverse effects of resettlement in addition to their time of arrival together and settlement in the present space strengthening their sub-categorical boundary. Again, one step down, the resettlers are further differentiated first along their original regional locations as north-central versus south-western; and then further to specific ethnic, clan, lineage and small territorial units. At every level, those assumed, existing, and/or emerging features are articulated that account for the group members' *inclusion* versus *exclusion*, dichotomization, and boundary maintenance of *we/us* versus *they/them* as well as changing alliances and identifications depending on the circumstances. These multiple-level circumstantial identifications considerably support what Salamone and Swanson's (1979:169f.) noted as: "very small differences will be magnified by a group wishing to remain unique from another group while major differences will be ignored by that same group should it wish to emphasise its solidarity with another group."

Yet, there are several crosscutting ties of identification and alliance of the different groups in the interactional and transactional contexts witnessing Barth's consideration of the fluidity of the boundary concept. For instance, crossing the most polarised dichotomization of *Bega* and *Shuwa* boundary, the Shinasha (one of the long-standing neighbours of Gumuz that belong to the *Shuwa* category) formed alliances with the Gumuz in the inter-ethnic conflict that emerged in the area following the 1991 political change. The obvious reason of this alliance is reported as based on competition for resources (economic, political, and social), aimed at excluding all other *Shuwa* members. The Shinasha showed alliance with the Gumuz because they were also entitled a status of "autochthonous" to the area in the instrumentalised present ethnic politics of the state. However, the Gumuz seemed rather suspicious and sceptical of this alliance and many considered it as instrumental with intended goals in resource competition rather than truly affectionate identification. Several cases of crosscutting relations are also noted along lines of belief in same religion and same or proxy original areas as well as settlement in the same village or neighbourhood as pointed out in the ethnographic text in part four.

The *Bega* versus *Shuwa* categorical dichotomization holds true to the concepts that Jenkins (1994:200f.) termed as "groups and categories" in which he considers the concept of "groups" rooted in internal definition, while the concept of "categories" as externally defined. He states that "[... S]ocial groups define themselves, their name(s), their nature(s) and their boundary(s), social categories are identified, defined and delineated by others [... S]ocial identity is the outcome of the conjugation process of internal *and* external definition." Considering Jenkins' concepts, *Bega* could be taken as an internal definition because it is the name given by the Gumuz to their fellow members. On the other hand, *Shuwa* could be considered as a categorical non-contemptuous term externally defined and ascribed by the Gumuz to all non-Gumuz highland neighbours. In the meantime, the pejorative term *Shanqilla* could be considered as a categorical term externally defined and ascribed to the Gumuz as well as other Nilotic group members signalling strong stigma and inferior status. The contemptuous equivalent term ascribed by the Gumuz to the *Shuwa* is *Mittiha,* signalling mistrust for the latter's alleged cruelty and inhumane plunder and depicts the power relations between the two broad groups. The use of these value-laden terms further supports Jenkin's concepts termed as "categorisation and power."

The encroachment and the resultant competition over resources has always increased enmity, hence serving as one of the major root causes for inter-ethnic tension and uneasy coexistence between the *Bega* and the *Shuwa,* as intermittently discussed throughout the study. The ethnographic evidence substantially support and validate Barth's concept of the linkage of ethnicity to the concept of niche and resource competition, emphasising divergent adaptations. As pointed out in this study, the *Bega* inhabit mostly the lowland ecological niche based on different strategies of livelihood, articulating different socio-cultural features that forms the basis of their ethnic identity against their neighbouring *Shuwa*. On the other hand, the *Shuwa* mostly inhabit the mid- and highland ecological niche using different strategies of livelihood.

Apart from encroachment on the land resources, the other frequently stressed causes of inter-ethnic conflicts between the *Bega* and *Shuwa* include the preoccupation of the former with past slavery experiences associated with the contemptuous reference by the derogative term *Shanqilla*. The Gumuz view and perceive that their interaction with the *Shuwa* is mostly one of being exploited, with unequal exchange relationships. Hence, they usually signal an element of innately deep-rooted mistrust while explaining the prevalent conflicting ethnic relations and uneasy coexistence with their *Shuwa* neighbours. As a component part of the process of encroachment on the land resources of the Gumuz in Metekel, the state-sponsored massive emergency resettlement scheme of the 1980s in the Beles Valley has been acting as one of the major factor in the prevalent inter-ethnic conflicts between the Gumuz and resettlers. These widespread inter-ethnic conflicts are attempted to be resolved through the traditional conflict resolution institution known as *mangima* (Gum.). However, despite the predominant conflicting relations, there are also some existing and emerging integrative interactions across ethnic boundaries in different contexts.

The findings of this study, especially on the *Bega* identification and persistent maintenance of their ethnic group solidarity, substantially complements Spicer's (1971) concept of "persistent identity systems" that is also reconsidered by Scott (1990) as an "oppositional model of ethnic solidarity" or "explanatory model." The relentless persistence of the *Bega* ethnic identity marking a strongly intact group could be accounted for by their hardened identification going through stiff hurdles of exploitative historical experiences of "opposition" and subjugation, which has been stigmatising, marginalising, and enslaving them. This persistence of distinctive *Bega* identity maintenance against the *Shuwa* significantly validates to a large extent Spicer's and Scott's conceptual considerations revealing the facts about their "high degree of ethnic solidarity" and the associated "high primordial sentiments" based on the "high level of opposition" they suffered under the repression of their *Shuwa* neighbours. Hence, the distinctive *Bega* ethnic identity has been maintained intact, surviving all the inhumane plunder and domination of the expansionist conquerors.

Therefore, the *Bega* versus *Shuwa* ethnic identification and relations revealed in this study substantially complement the arguments of Spicer and Scott that consider primordial ties to circumstances in an attempt to resynthesise *primordial* and *circumstantial* approaches to ethnicity. Thus, the findings based on the ethnographic accounts so far attempted to verify ethnicity to be both *primordial* and *circumstantial,* providing indicative direction for formulating further research questions that would advance our conceptual understanding through future cross-cultural research.

13.2 Centrality of Local Institutions in the Adaptations and Interactions of Hosts and Resettlers

The ethnographic details described and discussed in this study, among many other things, attempt to reveal the key role of local social institutional dynamics and processes in the livelihood adaptations and interactions of the autochthonous and resettler populations in the research setting. The attributes of the institutionally embedded adaptations and interactions of the two main study categories of peoples are detailed in a number of chapters throughout the entire study. Based on the findings, a synthesised account of my arguments expressed in an attempt to contribute towards strengthening the existing conceptual approaches as well as offering new insights into the centrality of local institutions[1] in the livelihood adaptations and interactions of host populations and resettlers are discussed in the following sub-sections.

Livelihood Maintenance and Adaptation of the Autochthonous Gumuz
As earlier discussed and described (cf. part two), the incessant encroachment across different political regimes had been adversely affecting the human and natural resources of the autochthonous Gumuz. In the past, the slave raiding by the highlanders severely affected the human resources of the Gumuz. Their livelihood system has been affected due to the age-old encroachment pressure of the highlanders that has been persistently pushing them to the peripheries up to the present, stripping of their traditional land resources. The Gumuz have been facing and reacting to these challenges through their local institutional mechanisms. Under their strong institutional arrangement mainly facilitated by elders and spirit mediums, the Gumuz are organised intact where the customary norms oblige members (especially men) to take defensive and revengeful actions against outsiders, protecting their members from attacks. It is usually after a heavy revengeful attack against the encroachers (usually in the night), that they retreat farther into the inaccessible forests in fear of more organised and better equipped plunder of raiding from the highlanders.

The sister-exchange marriage institution of Gumuz facilitated the persistent maintenance of their identity, preserving their institutional embeddedness in such kinship and marriage relations, constraining the socio-economic and cultural penetration of the highlanders. The institutional embeddedness in the sister exchange marriage system strengthens James' (1975:94) consideration of the same institution as the deep-rooted and symbolically significant survival strategy of the Gumuz against the penetration of the goods and cash systems of the more powerful neighbouring highlanders.

Despite the adverse effects of the pressures from the encroaching plow cultivators, the Gumuz persistently maintained their system of integral shifting cultivation, which is central to their indigenous natural resource management system. In doing so, they have also maintained significantly the associated institutions used for regulating natural resource use and management as well as their modes of livelihood irrespective of the emergent

---

[1] Institutions consist of cognitive, normative, and regulative structures that shape social behaviour and provide meaning to it (Scott 1995:33, cited in Nuijten 1999:3). For more detailed account on the review of the conceptual considerations on local institutions, see chapter 2 "Local Social Institutions".

changes in certain aspects. The multiple local institutions (social, economic, cultural, political, religious) provide meaning in social life and articulate the attributes that mark the Gumuz identity. Such central significance of local social institutions in the life, livelihood and identity of the Gumuz strongly strengthens Appendini, Nuijten and Rawal (1999:11) arguments, considering the roles of local social institutions as "providing inputs for productive activities, providing forms of social security, providing elements which are central to people's identity and meaning in life."

Resettlers' Livelihood Adaptation
In the dislocation and relocation process of resettlement, the social fabric and life-sustaining mechanisms of the resettlers were disintegrated. At the initial stages of the resettlement scheme, local social institutions that bind the multiple webs of community relationships along several lines were dismantled, detaching the resettlers from their complex web of institutional arrangements. This disruption had increased the uncertainties and desperation of resettlers, making highly visible the central place of local institutions in their entire lives and livelihood. This seriously felt visibility of the often invisible local institutions, dismantled through the involuntary relocation, could be compared with an American saying, "you don't know what you've got till it is gone, gone[2]." In the extreme case, the same could also be compared with a situation where a peaceful life is disrupted at a time of warfare.

The ethnographic evidence detailed in a number of chapters in this study (cf. chapters 6, 7, 8 and 9) reveals the centrality of local institutions in resettlers' livelihood adaptation. The findings strengthen the significance of those conceptual approaches on the social impacts of resettlement. The disintegration of social institutions in the process of involuntary relocation is termed by different authors as "social disarticulation" (Cernea 1996, 2000); "physiological, psychological and socio-cultural stress" (Scudder and Colson 1982); disintegration of "spatial-temporal" determinants of resettlers – socially constructed spaces, times and personages (Downing 1996); and disruption of "physical-spatial" settings of resettlers' behavioural patterns – changes in the socio-cultural, economic, political and demographic contexts (De Wet 1993)[3].

---

[2] Personal communication with Mr. Kim Dammers, my American friend and doctoral candidate in Ethnology.

[3] For more detailed description and discussion of each conceptual approach, see part one, chapter 2.

After going through the initial severe troubles of adaptive readjustments, the resettlers began re-instituting local institutions, which in turn played vital roles in the process of their livelihood adaptation in the new setting. The reestablishment of these local institutional arrangements facilitated and mutually strengthened a complex web of social relationships within the resettlers as well as with those neighbouring populations of the resettlement scheme area, and considerably complements the theoretical perspective of *social networks* (cf. chapter 2 "Local Social Institutions"). Through the rearticulation of local institutions, the uncertainties in the daily lives of resettlers were reduced and stable livelihood reconstruction strategies were attained. Additionally, the central roles of these social institutions are manifested in mediating and channelling access to livelihood resources, providing strong social security or safety nets, and facilitating local self-governance (cf. chapter 9). *Hence, the livelihood recovery and adaptation of resettlers have been propelled with the rearticulation of local social institutions. This key finding of the study offers new insights into the centrality of local institutional dynamics and processes in an involuntary resettlement context as well as puts forward a crucial conceptual contribution concerning the vital role of local institutions in resettlers' livelihood adaptations. Based on the ethnographic evidence of this study, I strongly argue* for *the central significance of local institutions in the resettlers' lives and livelihood adaptation* against *their sheer neglect by resettlement planners and implementers.*

Hosts' and Resettlers' Interactions

The intra- and inter-ethnic relations within and across the two categories of peoples are mediated and networked through complex web of local social institutions (cf. chapters 10, 11 and 12). On the one hand, the intra-ethnic identifications as well as interactions within the autochthonous Gumuz are embedded in their local institutions (e.g. institutional arrangements such as kinship and marriage, belief systems, elders and spirit mediums, and neighbourhood commune). For instance, the clan is one of the most important kinship-based institution that serves as an intra-ethnic identity marker of the Gumuz. In addition, inter-clan interactions are crucial for the very survival and coexistence of the different Gumuz clans where their relationships are held with mutual recognition. Violation of such mutual recognition according to their traditional patterns results in severe inter-clan feuds, which in turn is managed by a key traditional conflict resolution institution known as *mangima* (cf. chapter 11).

On the other hand, the identifications as well as interactions within the resettlers are also embedded in and mediated through their local institutions.

As already described and explained, the highland resettelers' category is further differentiated into a number of sub-categories, who in turn are again divided into different ethnic, territorial, and kinship groups. Meanwhile, the interactions within the highland resettlers are embedded in their local social institutions such as neighbourhood, religious, friendship, and work groups, crossing the ethnic divide (cf. chapter 9).

Despite the predominance of conflicts, the interactions between the autochthonous Gumuz and the state-sponsored resettlers are networked through local institutions (cf. chapter 12). The prevalent conflicts between the two groups are mediated through the traditional *mangima* institution (cf. chapter 11). In areas of frequent contacts, the two groups have established several local social institutional arrangements. One of the most important local institutional arrangement of mutual interaction that has been binding the Gumuz and resettlers is the tenancy arrangement where the former rent-out land to the latter based on existing and emerging networks of relations (cf. chapter 12.4). Therefore, the ethnographic evidence from this study demonstrates the centrality of local institutional dynamics and processes in the interactions of the autochthonous Gumuz and highland resettlers.

Chapter 14. Conclusion

This study examines the impact of the encroachment of highland plow culti-vators that occurred on the land resources of the autochthonous Gumuz in Metekel during a number of political regimes, mainly focusing on the par-ticular case of the massive state-sponsored resettlement scheme of the 1980s in the Beles Valley. It tries to reveal the complex socio-cultural, economic and environmental changes brought about by the scheme in the area. By principally focusing on the impact of the resettlement scheme, the study presents the differing strategies of livelihood and adaptive resource man-agement; the local knowledge; the traditional ecological knowledge and worldviews; the human and environmental impacts of resettlement; the cen-trality of local institutions in the process of adaptations and interactions; and the ethnicity, ethnic conflict, and coexistence of the two categories of popu-lations. The *autochthonous Gumuz* (host population), the *resettlers* (relo-cated peasantry from the highlands), and the *ecology* are all affected by the resettlement scheme.

The resettlement program affected the autochthonous Gumuz. The scheme displaced an estimated 18,000 of them to the peripheries from around 250,000 hectares of their traditional land. The scheme has also af-fected the resettlers and around 80,000 of them were brought to the Beles

Valley from north-central and south-western parts of the country. The inter-actions of the two groups of populations are equally affected by the scheme in which their relations are predominantly characterised by mistrust and hostilities.

In the aftermath of the 1991 political change in Ethiopia, the living con-ditions in the area have been reshaped in large degree by severe ethnic con-flicts that emerged between the Gumuz and resettlers, causing on the one hand spontaneous evacuation of a number of the state-sponsored resettlers, while on the other it increased in-flow of immigrants from the neighbouring areas. This change has further aggravated the ecological conditions in the area both by the increased number of immigrants and by other interest groups linked to the new rain-fed agricultural "investment" schemes. The Gumuz view the scheme as part of the age-old encroachment process – only organised at a higher scale and speed. Meanwhile, they have traditional secular and religious institutions that have enabled them to persist, maintain-ing their identity in the face of the heavy external pressure.

The Gumuz have special holistic relationships with their natural envi-ronment, endowing it with sacred meanings. Their traditional ecological knowledge and natural resource management systems are blended with the traditional belief systems. The indigenous institutions enshrined within their environmental ethic and knowledge systems ensure smooth management of natural resources in an environmentally friendly and ecologically stable manner. In their tenure system, ownership of natural resources is vested upon the whole community, and land resources are used and managed to the benefit of the present *and* future generations.

The Gumuz have been most vulnerable to a continuous encroachment on their land resources that belonged to them by tradition from time immemo-rial. They are one of the minority ethnic groups marginalised from the centre and located at the periphery. Due to the persistent process of gradual and rapid encroachments across regimes (imperial expansion, continuous push of highland plow cultivators, state farm, resettlement, and now "investment"), they have been facing pressures of deprivation from their land resources, now threatening their basic source of life, livelihood, and culture. The vari-ous regimes of the central state were all reluctant to recognise their land resource rights by entitling them to special legal provisions to attain greater resource tenure security. State policies and planners have neglected their indigenous ecological knowledge and natural resource management systems even today.

As a result of the combined impacts of state policies of various regimes, encroachment pressure over the natural resources in Metekel from several interest groups has drastically increased, severely affecting the natural environment as well as the Gumuz lifestyle. The pressure and destruction of forest resources in the area have been causing various environmental consequences by creating instability in the entire agro-ecology. The loss of forest upsets the livelihood of the autochthonous inhabitants by disrupting their natural resource management systems.

This study attempts to point out that during *the imperial regimes prior to 1974*, the Gumuz had been facing ruthless encroachment pressures from the highland Ethiopian expansionists, who pushed them further down to the peripheries in the lowlands of Metekel. The encroachments of neighbouring highlanders and spontaneous settlers continued throughout the *Derg* regime *(1974-1991)*. Moreover, two forms of rapid encroachment were undertaken during the *Derg* regime. These are the "Beles State Farm" and the "1980s massive government sponsored emergency resettlement program" that destroyed a great amount of the natural resources in the area. Under the present post-1991 regime, still a considerable amount of land resources are being leased to private investors without thorough topographic, soil, vegetation type, and other socio-economic investigation, thus causing adverse consequences on the autochthonous population and the environment.

The influx of encroaching resettlers and immigrants bringing completely different farming systems from the highlands has been causing much more damage to the natural resources of the fragile lowland agro-ecosystem than the ecologically friendly integral livelihood and management practices of the Gumuz ever have. The ethnographic evidence reveals the potential of indigenous environmental thought and knowledge of the Gumuz in their sustainable natural resource management systems.

The relocated resettlers are severely affected by the resettlement program as well. The scheme dismantled their customary local institutions that serve as the very social fabric of the communities. The ethnographic evidence of the study tries to offer insights into the central role of *social institutions* and *organisations* in the pursuit of the resettlers' livelihood adaptation. Initially, the complex web of local institutions was disarticulated, and the relocated peasants were detached from their institutional heritage in the face of the displacement and relocation process. The complex institutional linkages through which the people's interactions are bound were utterly neglected by the planners and implementers of the scheme. This uncertainties and desperation in the resettlers' daily lives had increased due to the disintegration of the infinite web of institutional settings by which they were tied in manifold ways. The disarticulation of local institutions was seriously felt by the resettlers – but remained invisible to and neglected by the outside local resettlement authorities. As a result, the many stresses of the resettlers were severely aggravated in the new context. However, as the resettlers went through adaptive readjustment, they began reinstituting local institutions, which in turn played multiple key roles in the process of their livelihood adaptation in the new setting. Therefore, with the rearticulation of institutions, the uncertainties in the daily lives of the resettlers were reduced, and stable livelihood reconstruction strategies were attained.

The early disarticulation and the later rearticulation of institutions enabled the often-invisible complex web of local institutional arrangements and the multiple roles to become visible to outsiders as well. A meaningful re-instituting process of institutions was properly realised with the collapse of collectivisation and the re-establishment of a smallholder production system managed by the households. In the process, resettlers managed to re-establish complex institutional networks first within their village and then at different levels including the entire resettlement area as well as the neighbouring host communities. The reinstituting process was practised through neighbourhood, kinship and marriage, religious belief, work groups, share-cropping, bond-friendship, and other related complex networks of local institutional relationships.

Households embedded within these local institutional frameworks are channelled access to different livelihood resources essential for their livelihood strategies. The livelihood strategies are in turn linked to the multiple institutional settings in which the households are embedded. The livelihood strategies enable the households to establish differing degrees of food security, social security, and the entire livelihood security at large. In the present institutional context of the Beles Valley, the broadly differentiated five smallholder farming household types that include very rich (high surplus), rich (moderate surplus), medium (self-sufficient), poor (food-deficit), and poorest (weak/dependent) practice diverse livelihood strategies.

Local institutions and livelihood strategies of rural households are dynamically interrelated. In the process of the pursuit of relocated peasant households' livelihood security, the key roles of local institutions are manifested in mediating/channelling access to livelihood resources, providing strong social security or safety nets, and facilitating local self-governance. Thus, this study tries to reveal the role of local social institutions in the pursuit of relocated peasant households' livelihood adaptations. In spite of all the enormous potentials, some limitations of local institutions should also be recognised in certain circumstances.

The inter-ethnic relations between the autochthonous Gumuz (*Bega*) and highland resettlers (*Shuwa*) in the multi-ethnic setting of Metekel are quite

296

complex, depicting features of ethnic differentiation and polarisation. The inter-ethnic relation between the *Bega* and the *Shuwa* is mainly characterised by polarised interactions at various levels of ethnic tensions. Apart from the encroachment on the land resources, the other frequently stressed causes of inter-ethnic conflicts between the *Bega* and *Shuwa* include the un-erased memory of past slavery experiences associated with the contemptuous reference by the derogative term *Shanqilla*. The *Bega* perceive that their interactions with the *Shuwa* are rather exploitive through unequal exchange relationships. They show deep-rooted mistrust while explaining the prevalent conflicting relations and uneasy coexistence with their *Shuwa* neighbours. The expression of *Bega* identity is mainly shaped in such an ethnically polarised context used to signal both essential and circumstantial differences in order to maintain the boundaries between them and their neighbouring *Shuwa*.

Despite the predominantly conflicting relations, there are also significant existing and emerging mutual interrelations across ethnic boundaries in different contexts and with differing magnitudes. The interactions between the two categories of populations are mediated through local institutions. The contexts of mutual relations include local market exchanges, bond-friendships, tenancy arrangements, religious conversions, neighbourhood, and other related networks of relations.

The present government's ethnicity policy itself appears to be equally accountable for re-igniting the severe inter-ethnic conflicts and widespread tensions in the study area. After suffering its initial severe consequences, the state authorities tried hard to manage the ethnic conflicts by manipulating and facilitating the efforts of traditional institutions. It is through the relentless attempts of traditional elders (with facilitations of local authorities) that those severe ethnic conflicts have been contained (at least for the moment). Nevertheless, a deeper understanding of the ethnicity situation as well as of thoroughly detailed causes and consequences of ethnic conflicts and their management in the complex multi-ethnic context of Metekel demands further deeper cross-cultural research.

The ethnographic details described and discussed throughout this study attempt to reveal the socio-cultural, economic, and ecological changes brought about by the encroachment of highland resettlers in Metekel. In particular, the massive state-sponsored of resettlement of the 1980 has a severe impact on the autochthonous Gumuz, highland resettlers, and the ecology in the Beles Valley and its environs. The study tries to offer new insights into the centrality of local institutional dynamics and processes in the adaptations and interactions of autochthonous populations and immigrant settlers. It presents conceptually significant arguments manifested from a local institutional perspective for studying the impacts of resettlement on hosts and resettlers. It shows the centrality of these institutional arrangements in planning and implementing resettlement schemes. Meanwhile, it also attempts to contribute to the existing literature gap on the host population in studies of resettlement in which to date such studies have no more than mentioned the host population because all major resettlement concepts and practices have narrowly focused mainly on resettlers. At length, the study tries to depict the peculiar features of the politically mandated mass relocation of the 1980s in Ethiopia in comparison to mainly development-induced resettlement schemes and presents important ethnographic evidence, which on the one hand strengthens several aspects of existing concepts and equally challenges them on a number of grounds, offering new insights on the other hand. It also tries to contribute to the anthropological literature on resettlement in general as well as to the ethnographic studies of western Ethiopia (Metekel) and the Ethio-Sudan borderland areas. Finally, these findings could also be used for formulating possible further future research questions for the advancement of anthropological approaches to resettlement.

Bibliography

Acronyms and Abbreviations in the Bibliography

AAU	Addis Ababa University
ARTF	Agricultural Research Task Force
BGNRS	Benishangul-Gumuz National Regional State
CISP	Comitato Internazionale per lo Sviluppo dei Popoli (International Committee for the Development of Peoples)
CPAR	Canadian Physicians for Aid and Relief
CSA	Central Statistical Authority
DFID	Department for International Development
EMA	Ethiopian Mapping Authority
EPA	Environmental Protection Authority
FDRE	Federal Democratic Republic of Ethiopia
FAO	Food and Agricultural Organisation
IDR	Institute of Development Research
IDS	Institute of Development Studies
IES	Institute of Ethiopian Studies
LUPT	Land Use Planning Team
MoA	Ministry of Agriculture
MPO	Metekel Planning Office
MZAD	Metekel Zonal Agricultural Department
MZCA	Metekel Zonal Council Archive
n.d.	No Date
NSCRP	National Study Committee of Receiving Provinces
PHCC	Population and Housing Census Commission
ONCCP	Office of the National Committee for Central Planning
PDPU	Population and Development Planning Unit
PHCE	Population and Housing Census of Ethiopia
RRC	Relief and Rehabilitation Commission
SAERP	Sustainable Agriculture and Environmental Rehabilitation Program
ECA	Economic Commission for Africa
WARDIS	*Woreda* Agriculture and Rural Development Integrated Services
NWZADO	North-Western Zonal Agricultural Development Office

299

Unpublished Sources

Aysheshim Medfu

1987   "Crime and Custom: With Specific Reference to Shanqilla National-
ity." B.A. Senior Essay in Law. Addis Ababa: AAU.

Berihun Mebrate

1996   "Spontaneous Settlements and Inter-Ethnic Relations in Metekel,
Northwestern Ethiopia." M.A. Thesis in Social Anthropology. Addis
Ababa: AAU.

Berterame, Stefano and Loredana Magni

1988   "Local Markets and Exchanges in the Beles Valley Resettlement
Area." In: *Proceedings of the Workshop on Famine Experiences and
Resettlement in Ethiopia. Dec. 29-30, 1988.* Addis Ababa:
AAU/IDR.

Betru Haile and Wolde-Selassie Abbute

1995   "Diagnostic Study on Household Food Security in the Beles Valley."
Addis Ababa: CISP.

BGNRS

1996b   "Basic Data of Development Sectors." Assosa: BGNRS. Mimeo
(Text in Amharic).

Birner, Regina

1997   "Decision-Making in Agricultural Production: Limitations of the
Formal Models, Intra-Household Decision-Making, Commercial and
Co-operative Decision-Making." Göttingen: Institute of Rural De-
velopment, University of Göttingen.

Blench, Roger

2000   "Nilo-Saharan Language Listing: Circulated for Comment." Cambridge.

Davies, Susanna

1997   "Livelihood Adaptation." Paper for Workshop on *Making Livelihoods Work – Women, Men and Children in Rajasthan.* Brighton:
IDS.

Dessalegn Rahmato

1989   "Rural Resettlement in Post-Revolutionary Ethiopia: Problems and
Prospects" In: ONCCP. *Conference on Population Issues in Ethio-
pia's National Development: Report of Conference Proceedings.*
Vol., II. Addis Ababa: PDPU/ONCCP. Mimeo.

De Wet, Chris
1996   "Reconstructing Resettlement: Some Research Suggestions for Developing and Combining Scudder's and Cernea's Approaches to Resettlement." A Paper Presented at the *International Conference on Reconstructing Livelihoods: Towards New Approaches to Resettlement*, September 1996. Oxford: Refugee Studies Programme, University of Oxford.

2000   "Can Everybody Win? Economic Development and Population Displacement." A Paper Prepared for '*Workshop on Involuntary Resettlement: Risks, Reconstruction and Development.*' *Rio de Janeiro July 30 – August 5, 2000. Symposium I and Workshop 18, 10th World Congress of Rural Sociology*. Rio de Janeiro: Brazil.

Elias Negassa
1992   "The Ill-Conceived Settlement Program and Its Consequences." A Paper Presented at the *Ethiopian Rehabilitation Campaign Donor's Conference. May 25-26, 1992*. Addis Ababa: RRC.

Gebre Yntiso
1995   "Survival Strategies and Difficulties: The Case of Gumz Communities in Beles Valley." Addis Ababa: CISP.

Haugerud, A.
1984   "Household Dynamics and Rural Political Economy among the Embu Farmers in the Kenya Highlands." PhD Dissertation. Evanston: Northwestern University.

James, Wendy
1976   "Notes on the Gumuz (Shangalla) of the Blue Nile Valley." A Type-Written Manuscript in the Author's Possession.

n.d.   "From Aboriginal to Frontier Society in Western Ethiopia." In D.L. Donham and Wendy James (eds.) *Working Papers on Society and History in Imperial Ethiopia: The Southern Periphery from the 1880s to 1974*. Cambridge: African Studies Centre.

Jemal Mohamed
1996   "The Resettlement Programme in Ethiopia with Particular Emphasis on Asosa Project 1979-1994." B.A. Senior Essay in History. Addis Ababa: AAU.

Lupt-Nwazado-Moa
1987   "Socio-Economic Evaluation of the Current Land Use in the Middle Beles Valley." Unpubl. ms.

301

Kaufman, Stuart J.
2000   "Peace-Building and Conflict Resolution." A Paper Prepared for Conference on *Living Together After Ethnic Killing: Debating the Kaufmann Hypothesis. NJ, 14 October 2000'*. New Brunswick: Rutgers University.

Kidane Mariam Demellew
1987   "The Shanqilla of Metekel: Some Tentative Notes." B.A. Senior Essay in History. Addis Ababa: AAU.

MPO
1993   "A General Natural Resources Survey of Metekel Administrative Region (Part I and II)." Chagni: MPO.

Mulugeta Gebre Hiwot
1996   "A Study of Agricultural Land Use in Kebele L3 of Pawe Resettlement Center." B.A. Senior Essay in Geography. Addis Ababa: AAU.

MZAD
1999   "Study on Basic Agricultural Data in Metekel Zone." Pawe: MZAD. (Text in Amharic).

MZCA
1992   "Metekel." Chagni. (Text in Amharic; No Archival Document Number).

NSCRP
1988   "Report of the National Study Committee of Receiving Provinces." Addis Ababa: NSCRP, Council of Ministers. (Text in Amharic).

Pankhurst, Richard
1976   "The History of Bareya, Shanqilla and Other Ethiopian Slaves from t he Borderlands of the Sudan." Paper Submitted to the *Conference of Ethiopian Feudalism*. Addis Ababa: Institute of Ethiopian Studies, AAU.

Scudder, Thayer
1996a   "Advancing Theoretical Perspectives on Resettlement." A Paper Presented at the *International Conference on 'Reconstructing Livelihoods: Towards New Approaches to Resettlement, September 1996*. Oxford: Refugee Studies Programme, University of Oxford.

Sisay Muhe
1988   "The Reaction of Gumuz Towards Resettlement Programme: With Particular Reference to Matama Gumuz Settlement." B.A. Senior Essay in Sociology. Addis Ababa: Addis Ababa University.

Studio Pietrangeli
1988   "Tana Beles Project – Master Plan no. 2B." Rome.

302

Taddese Berisso
1995   "Agricultural and Rural Development Policies in Ethiopia: A Case Study of Villagization Policy among the Guji-Oromo of Jam Jam Awraja." Ph.D. Dissertation. East Lansing: Michigan State University.

Taddesse Tamrat
1988   "Nilo-Sahara Interactions with Neighbouring Highlanders: The Case of the Gumuz of Gojjam and Wollega." In: *Proceedings of the Workshop on Famine Experience and Resettlement in Ethiopia. December 29 – 30, 1988*. Addis Ababa: Institute of Development Research, AAU.

Wallmark, Patrik
1976a   "The Basic Occupations of the Say: A Nilotic Tribe in Northern Wollega, Ethiopia." Nakamte.
1976b   *"The Religion and Popular Belief among the Say in Northern Wollega, Ethiopia."* Addis Ababa.

Wolde-Selassie Abbute
1991   "The Consequences of Resettlement: The Case of Southwestern Shoa Resettlers in the Metekel Resettlement Scheme." Addis Ababa. (Text in Amharic).
1996a   "Report on a Mission to Identify Facts about Rural Community Water Supply in Region Six (Assosa)." Addis Ababa: CISP.
1996b   "Assessment of Socio-economic Context and Rural Community Water Supply in the Metekel Zone." Addis Ababa: CISP.
1997a   "The Dynamics of Socioeconomic Differentiation and Change in the Beles Valley Resettlement Area, Northwestern Ethiopia." M.A. Thesis in Social Anthropology. Addis Ababa: AAU.
1997b   "Land Rights and the Minorities: The Case of the *Gumz* in *Metekel*, Northwestern Ethiopia." In: *Papers of the Workshop on 'Access to Land and Resource Management in Ethiopia'. Nov., 28-29, 1997*. Addis Ababa: IDR, AAU.
2001a   "Identity, Encroachment and Ethnic Relations: The Gumuz and Their Neighbours in Metekel, Northwestern Ethiopia." A Paper Presented at a Conference on *Changing Identifications and Alliances in North-Eastern Africa* Halle/Saale, 5-9 June, 2001. Halle/Saale: Max Planck Institute for Social Anthropology.

Yimer Yesuf
1996   "A History of Qeto Resettlement Area (1985-1995)." B.A. Senior Essay in History. Addis Ababa: AAU.

Published Sources

Abdussamad H. Ahmad

1988   "Hunting in Gojjam: The Case of Metekel 1901-1932." In: *Proceedings of the Eighth International Conference of Ethiopian Studies.* Vol. I, pp. 237-44. Addis Ababa: Institute of Ethiopian Studies.

1995   "The Gumuz of the Lowlands of Western Gojjam: The Frontier in History 1900-1935." In: *Africa.* Anno L, 1:53-67.

Agdaw Asfaw and Wolde-Selassie Abbute

1992   "Utilization of Horticultural Products in the Beles Valley Resettlement Villages." In: Paolo Dieci and Claudo Viezzoli (eds.) *Resettlement and Rural Development in Ethiopia: Social and Economic Research, Training and Technical Assistance in the Beles Valley.* Milano: Franco Angeli.

Agneta, Francesca, Stefano Berterame, Mariarita Capirci,
Loredana Magni and Massimo Tommasoli

1993   "The Dynamics of Social and Economic Adaptation During Resettlement: The Case of Beles Valley in Ethiopia." In Michael M. Cernea and Scott E. Guggenheim (eds.) *Anthropological Approaches to Resettlement: Policy, Practice, and Theory.* Boulder: Westview Press.

Agneta, Francesca and Massimo Tomassoli

1992   "Pre-School Education and Priests' Schools in Pawe Resettlement Area." In: Paolo Dieci and Claudo Viezzoli (eds.) *Resettlement and Rural Development in Ethiopia: Social and Economic Research, Training and Technical Assistance in the Beles Valley.* Milano: Franco Angeli.

Alfredsson, G.

1993   "Minority Rights and a New World Order." In: D. Gomien (ed.), *Broadening the Frontiers of Human Rights.* Oslo: Scandinavian Press.

Appiah-Opoku, Seth and George Mulamoottil

1997   "Indigenous Institutions and Environmental Assessment: The Case of Ghana." In: *Environmental Management.* 21, (2): 159-171.

Appendini, Kirsten, Monique Nuijten and Vikas Rawal

1999   *Rural Household Income Strategies and Interactions with the Local Institutional Environment: A Methodological Framework.* Rome: FAO (Internet: http://www.fao.org/sd/Roan0021.htm).

Banks, Marcus
1996 *Ethnicity: Anthropological Constructions*. London: Routledge.
Banuri, T. and F. Apffel Marglin (eds.)
1993 *Who will Save the Forests?* London: Zed Books.
Barlett, P. F.
1980a "Adaptive Strategies in Peasant Agricultural Production." In: *Annual Review of Anthropology*. 9: 545-573.
Barlett, P.F. (ed.)
1980b *Agricultural Decision Making: Anthropological Contributions to Rural Development*. San Diego: Academic Press, Inc.
Barth, Fredrik
1969 "Introduction." In: Fredrik Barth (ed.). *Ethnic Groups and Boundaries: The Social Organization of Culture Difference*, pp. 9-38. Boston: Little, Brown and Company.
1994 "Enduring and Emerging Issues in the Analysis of Ethnicity." In: Hans Vermeulen and Cora Govers (eds.) *The Anthropology of Ethnicity: Beyond 'Ethnic Groups and Boundaries.'* Amsterdam: Het Spinhuis.
1998 "Preface to 1998." In: Fredrik Barth (ed.), *Ethnic Groups and Boundaries: The Social Organization of Culture Difference*, pp. 5-7. Reissued 1998. Illinois: Waveland Press.
Beauclerk, John et al.
1988 *Indigenous Peoples: A Field Guide for Development*. Oxford: Oxfam.
Beke, Charles T.
1844 "Abyssinia – Being a Continuation of Routes in That Country." In: *Journal of the Royal Geographical Society*. XIV: 1-76.
1845 "On the Languages and Dialects of Abyssinia and the Countries to the South." *Proceedings of the Philological Society*. II: 89-107.
Bender, M. Lionel.
1975 *The Ethiopian Nilo-Saharans*. Addis Ababa: Artistic Printers.
1983 "Introduction." In: M. Lionel Bender (ed.), *Nilo-Saharan Language Studies*. East Lansing: African Studies Center, Michigan State University.
Berdichewsky, Bernardo (ed.)
1979 *Anthropology and Social Change in Rural Areas*. The Hague: Mouton Publishers.

Berkes, Fikret
1988   "Environmental Philosophy of the Chisasibi Cree People of James Bay." In: M. R. Freeman and Ludwig N. Carbyn (eds.), *Traditional Knowledge and Renewable Resource Management in Northern Regions*. Alberta: Boreal Institute for Northern Studies.
1993   "Traditional Ecological Knowledge in Perspective." In: Julian T. Inglis (ed.), *Traditional Ecological Knowledge: Concepts and Cases*. Ontario: Canadian Museum of Nature.
1999   *Sacred Ecology: Traditional Ecological Knowledge and Resource Management*. Philadelphia: Taylor and Francis.
2001   "Religious Traditions and Biodiversity." *Encyclopedia Biodiversity*. 5: 109-120.
Berkes, Fikret and Carl Folke
1997   "Linking Social and Ecological Systems for Resilience and Sustainability." In: Fikret Berkes and Carl Folke, *Linking Social and Ecological Systems: Management Practices and Social Mechanisms for Building Resilience*. Cambridge: Cambridge University Press.
Berkes, Fikret, Nina Kislalioglu, Carl Folke and Madhav Gadgil
1998   "Exploring the Basic Ecological Unit: Ecosystem-like Concepts in Traditional Societies." In: *Ecosystems*. 1: 409-415.
BGNRS
1996a   *Proclamation No.2/1996 - Formulation of Benishangul Gumuz National Regional State Constitution Proclamation. Lissane Hig Gazeta* 1st Year No.3. Assosa, 1st July. (Text in Amharic and English).
BGNRS
1999   *Investment in Benishangul-Gumuz*. Assosa: BGNRS. (Text in Amharic with English Summary).
Boissevain, J. and J. Clyde Mitchell (eds.)
1973   *Network Analysis: Studies in Human Interaction*. Mouton: Mouton and Company.
Brandon, K. and M. Wells
1992   *People and Parks: Linking Protected Area Management with Local Communities*. Washington, D.C.: The World Bank.
Braukämper, Ulrich
1980   *Geschichte der Hadiya Süd-Äthiopiens. Von den Anfängen bis zur Revolution 1974*. Studien zur Kulturkunde 50. Wiesbaden: Franz Steiner Verlag.
1983   *Die Kambata: Geschichte und Gesellschaft eines südäthiopischen Bauernvolkes*. Wiesbaden: Franz Steiner Verlag.

306

Bruce, James
1813 *Travels to Discover the Source of the Nile. Vol. IV.* 3rd ed. Corrected and Enlarged. London: Longman.
Brüne, Stefan and Volker Matthies (eds.)
1990 *Krisenregion Horn von Afrika.* Hamburg: Institut für Afrika-Kunde.
Brush, Stephen B.
1996 "Whose Knowledge, Whose Genes, and Whose Rights?" In: S. B. Brush and D. Stabinsky. (eds.), *Valuing Local Knowledge: Indigenous People and Intellectual Property Rights.* Washington D.C.: Island Press.
Budge, E. A. Wallis
1928 *A History of Ethiopia: Nubia and Abyssinia.* London: Methuen.
Carswell, G.
1997 *Agricultural Intensification and Rural Sustainable Livelihoods: A "Think Piece." IDS Working Paper. 64.* Brighton: IDS.
Cernea, Michael M.
1991a "Involuntary Resettlement: Social Research, Policy, and Planning." In: Michael M. Cernea (ed.), *Putting People First: Sociological Variables in Rural Development.* 2nd ed. Oxford: Oxford University Press.
1993 "Disaster Related Refugee Flows and Development Caused Population Displacement." In: Michael M. Cernea and Scott E. Guggenheim (eds.), *Anthropological Approaches to Resettlement: Policy, Practice, and Theory.* Boulder: Westview Press.
1994 "African Population Resettlement in Global Context." In: Cynthia C. Cook (ed.) *Involuntary Resettlement in Africa: Selected Papers from a Conference on Environment and Settlement Issues in Africa.* Washington: The World Bank.
1996a "Understanding and Preventing Impoverishment from Displacement: Reflections on the State of Knowledge." In: Christopher McDowell (ed.), *Understanding Impoverishment: The Consequences of Development-Induced Displacement.* Oxford: Berghahn Books.
1996b *Social Organization and Development Anthropology: The 1995 Malinowski Award Lecture.* Washington: The World Bank.
1996c "Bridging the Research Divide: Studying Refugees and Development Oustees." In: Tim Allen (ed.), *In Search of Cool Ground: War Flight and Homecoming in Northeast Africa*, pp. 293-317. London: James Currey.

307

2000   "Risks, Safeguards, and Reconstruction: A Model for Population Displacement and Resettlement." In: Michael M. Cernea and C. McDowell (eds.), *Risks and Reconstruction: Experiences of Resettlers and Refugees*. Washington D.C.: The World Bank.

Cernea, Michael M. (ed.)

1985   *Putting People First: Sociological Variables in Rural Development.* Oxford: Oxford University Press.

Cernea, Michael M. and Christopher McDowell (eds.)

2000   *Risks and Reconstruction: Experiences of Resettlers and Refugees.* Washington D.C.: The World Bank.

Cernea, Michael M., and Scott E. Guggenheim (eds.)

1993   *Anthropological Approaches to Resettlement: Policy, Practice, and Theory.* Boulder: Westview Press.

Cerulli, Ernesta

1956   *Peoples of Southwest Ethiopia and Its Borderland.* London: International African Institute.

Chambers, Robert (ed.)

1970   *The Volta Resettlement Experience.* New York: Praeger.

Cheesman, R. E.

1968   *Lake Tana and the Blue Nile: An Abyssinian Quest.* London: Frank Cass.

Clay, J.

1988   "Villagisation in Ethiopia." In: J. Clay et al. (eds.) *The Spoils of Famine: Ethiopian Famine Policy and Peasant Agriculture.* Cambridge: Cultural Survival.

Clay, Jason W. and Bonnie K. Holcomb

1986   *Politics and the Ethiopian Famine 1984-1985.* Cambridge: Cultural Survival.

Cohen, Anthony P.

1994   "Boundaries of Consciousness, Consciousness of Boundaries." In: Hans Vermeulen and Cora Govers (eds.) *The Anthropology of Ethnicity: Beyond 'Ethnic Groups and Boundaries'.* Amsterdam: Het Spinhuis.

Cohen, Ronald

1978   "Ethnicity: Problem and Focus in Anthropology." In: *Annual Review of Anthropology.* 7: 379-403.

Colson, Elizabeth

1958   *Marriage and the Family among the Plateau Tonga of Northern Rhodesia (Kariba Studies, Vol. I).* Manchester: Manchester University Press.

1960   *Social Organisation of the Gwembe Tonga*. Manchester: Manchester University Press.
1963   "Land Rights and Land Use among the Valley Tonga of the Rhodesian Federation: The Background to the Kariba Resettlement Programme." In: D. Biebuyck (ed.), *African Agrarian Systems*. Oxford: Oxford University Press.
1964   "Social Change and the Gwembe Tonga." In: *The Rhodes-Livingstone Journal*. 35: 1-13.
1971   *The Social Consequences of Resettlement: The Impact of Kariba Resettlement Upon the Gwembe Tonga*. Manchester: Manchester University Press.

Conklin, H. C.
1957   *Hanunoo Agriculture: A Report on An Integral System of Shifting Cultivation in the Philippines*. Rome: FAO.
1961   "The Study of Shifting Cultivation." In: *Current Anthropology*. 2 (1): 27-61.

Cook, Cynthia C. (ed.)
1994   *Involuntary Resettlement in Africa: Selected Papers from a Conference on Environment and Settlement Issues in Africa*. Washington: The World Bank.

CSA
1996   *The 1994 Population and Housing Census of Ethiopia: Results for Benishangul-Gumuz Region. Volume I Statistical Report*. Addis Ababa: PHCC/CSA.

Davies, Susanna and Naomi Hossain
1997   *Livelihood Adaptation, Public Action and Civil Society: A Review of the Literature. IDS Working Paper 57*. Brighton: IDS.

Dejene Aredo
1993   *The Informal and Semi-Informal Financial Sectors in Ethiopia: A Study of the Iqqub, Iddir, and Savings and Credit Co-operatives*. Nairobi: African Economic Research Consortium.

Dessalegn Rahmato
1988   "Settlement and Resettlement in Metekel, Western Ethiopia." In: *Africa*. (Dell'Istituto Italo-Africano). XLIII: 211-242.

De Wet, Chris
1988   "Stress and Environmental Change in the Analysis of Community Relocation." In: *Human Organization*. 47 (2): 180-187.

309

1993   "A Spatial Analysis of Involuntary Community Relocation: A South African Case Study." In: Michael M. Cernea and Scott E. Guggenheim (eds.), *Anthropological Approaches to Resettlement: Policy, Practice, and Theory*. Boulder: Westview Press

Dieci, Paolo and Claudo Viezzoli (eds.)

1992   *Resettlement and Rural Development in Ethiopia: Social and Economic Research, Training and Technical Assistance in the Beles Valley*. Milano: Franco Angeli.

Dieci, Paolo and Vittorio Roscio

1992   "The Need for a Grass-Roots Approach: The CISP Development Project in the Beles Area." In: Paolo Dieci and Claudo Viezzoli (eds.), *Resettlement and Rural Development in Ethiopia: Social and Economic Research, Training and Technical Assistance in the Beles Valley*. Milano: Franco Angeli.

Dieci, Paolo and Wolde-Selassie Abbute

1992   "The Planning of Home Gardening Activities in the Beles Valley Resettlement Villages." In: Paolo Dieci and Claudo Viezzoli (eds.), *Resettlement and Rural Development in Ethiopia: Social and Economic Research, Training and Technical Assistance in the Beles Valley*. Milano: Franco Angeli.

Donham, Donald and Wendy James (eds.)

1986   *The Southern Marches of Imperial Ethiopia*. Cambridge: Cambridge University Press.

Dorst, Jean and Pierre Dandelot

1970   *A Field Guide to the Larger Mammals of Africa*. London: Collins.

Downing, Theodore D.

1996   "Mitigating Social Impoverishment When People are Involuntarily Displaced." In: Christopher McDowell (ed.), *Understanding Impoverishment: The Consequences of Development Induced Displacement*. Oxford: Berghahn Books.

Eller, Jack and Reed Coughlan

1996   "The Poverty of Primordialism." In: John Hutchinson and Anthony D. Smith (eds.), *Ethnicity*. Oxford: Oxford University Press.

Ellis, Frank

1988   *Peasant Economics: Farm Households and Agrarian Development*. Cambridge: Cambridge University Press.

1998   "Household Strategies and Rural Livelihood Diversification." In: *Journal of Development Studies*. 35 (1): 1-38.

EMA

1988   *National Atlas of Ethiopia*. Addis Ababa: EMA.

310

EPA
1997   *Environmental Policy*. Addis Ababa: Environmental Protection Authority, FDRE.

Evernden, N.
1993   *The Natural Alien: Humankind and Environment*. 2nd ed. Toronto: University of Toronto Press.

FAO
1978   "Shifting Cultivation." In: *Forest News for Asia and the Pacific*. 2 (2): 1-26.

Federal Nagarit Gazeta
1996   *Investment Incentives, Council of Ministers' Regulation No. 7/1996* (Second Year, No., 29, July 1996). Addis Ababa.

Fukui, Katsuyoshi and John Markakis (eds.)
1994   "Introduction." In: Katsuyoshi Fukui and John Markakis (eds.) *Ethnicity and Conflict in the Horn of Africa*, pp. 1-11. London: James Kurrey.

Garretson, P. Peter
1980   "*Manjil* Hamdan Abu Shok (1898-1938) and the Administration of Gubba." In: Tubiana, Joseph (ed.), *Modern Ethiopia: From the Accession of Menilek II to the Present. Proceedings of the Fifth International Conference of Ethiopian Studies. Nice / 19-22, December 1977*, pp. 197-210. Rotterdam: CNRS.

Geertz, Clifford
1973   *The Interpretation of Cultures*. New York: Basic Books.
1996   "Primordial Ties." In: John Hutchinson and Anthony D. Smith (eds.), *Ethnicity*. Oxford: Oxford University Press.

Gibb, H. A. R. and J. H. Kramers (eds.)
1961   *Shorter Encyclopaedia of Islam*. Leiden: E. J. Brill.

Giddens, A.
1979   *Central Problems in Social Theory: Action, Structure and Contradiction in Social Analysis*. London: McMillan.

Gil-White, Francisco
1999   "How Thick is Blood? The Plot Thickens...: If Ethnic Actors Are Primordialists, What Remains of the Circumstantialist/Primordialist Controversy?" In: *Ethnic and Racial Studies*. 22 (5): 789-820.

Gray, A.
1996   "Indigenous Resistance to Involuntary Relocation." In: Christopher McDowell (ed.), *Understanding Impoverishment: The Consequences of Development-Induced Displacement*. Oxford: Berghahn Books.

Greaves, T. C.
1996　"Indigenous People." In: D. Levinson and M. Ember (eds.), *Encyclopedia of Cultural Anthropology*, pp. 635-38. New York: Henry Holt and Company.

Grosby, Steven
1996　"The Inexpungeable Tie of Primordiality." In: John Hutchinson and Anthony D. Smith. (eds.), *Ethnicity*. Oxford: Oxford University Press.

Haberland, Eike and Helmut Straube
1979　"Nordost-Afrika." In: Hermann Baumann (ed.), *Die Völker Afrikas und Ihre Traditionallen Kulturen – Teil II: Ost-, West- und Nordafrika*, pp.69-156. Wiesbaden: Franz Steiner Verlag.

Habte Mariam Marcos
1975　"Amharic Summary." In: M. Lionel Bender. *The Ethiopian Nilo-Saharans*. Addis Ababa: Artistic Printers.

Hansen, Art and Anthony Oliver-Smith (eds.)
1982　*Involuntary Migration and Resettlement: The Problems and Responses of Dislocated People*. Boulder: Westview Press.

Hurni, Hans
1990　"Agrarentwicklung und Umweltprobleme in Äthiopien." In: Stefan Brüne and Volker Matthies (eds.), *Krisenregion Horn von Afrika*. Hamburg: Institut für Afrika-Kunde.

Hutchinson, John and Anthony D. Smith (eds.)
1996　*Ethnicity*. Oxford: Oxford University Press.

Hussein, K. and J. Nelson
1998　*Sustainable Livelihoods and Livelihood Diversification. IDS Working Paper 69*. Brighton: IDS.

Irwin, Lee
1968　"Some Notes on Saysay Culture." In: *Journal of Ethiopian Studies*. 4 (1): 131-139.

Isaacs, H.
1975　*The Idols of the Tribe*. New York: Harper.

James, Wendy
1975　"Sister Exchange Marriage." In: *Scientific American*. 233 (6): 84-94.
1986　"Lifelines: Exchange Marriage among the Gumuz." In: Donald Donham and Wendy James (eds.), *The Southern Marches of Imperial Ethiopia*. Cambridge: Cambridge University Press.

James, Wendy, Gerd Baumann and Douglas Johnson (eds.)
1996　*Juan Maria Schuver's Travels in North East Africa 1880-1883*. London: The Hakluyt Society.

Jenkins, Richard

1994 "Rethinking Ethnicity: Identity, Categorization and Power." In: *Ethnic and Racial Studies*. 17 (2): 197-223.

1996 "Ethnicity etcetera: Social Anthropological Points of View." In: *Ethnic and Racial Studies*. 19 (4): 807-822.

1997 *Rethinking Ethnicity: Arguments and Explorations*. London: Sage Publications.

Klausberger, Friedrich

1975 "Bashanga, das Strafrecht der Baga-Gumuz." In: *Ethnologische Zeitschrift Zürich*. 1: 109-126.

Kuls, Wolfgang

1962 "Land, Wirtschaft und Siedlung der Gumuz im Westen von Godjam (Äthiopien)." In: *Paideuma*. Band VIII, Heft I: 45-61.

Kunstadter, P.

1978 "Ethnic Group, Category and Identity: Karen in Northwestern Thailand." In: C. F. Keyes (ed.), *Ethnic Adaptation and Identity: The Karen on the Thai Frontier with Burma*. Philadelphia: ISHI.

Kurimoto, Eisei

1992 "Natives and Outsiders: The Historical Experience of the Anywaa of Western Ethiopia." In: *Journal of Asian and African Studies*. 43: 1-43.

1996 "People of the River: Subsistence Economy of the Anywaa (Anuak) of Western Ethiopia." In: Shun Sato and Eisei Kurimoto (eds.), *Essays in Northeast African Studies*. Osaka: National Museum of Ethnology.

Leach, Edmund

1954 *Political Systems of Highland Burma*. London: Athlone Press.

Llobera, Josep R.

1999 *Recent Theories of Nationalism*. Barcelona: Instituto de Ciencies Politiques i Sociale.

Lovelace, George, W.

1984 "Cultural Beliefs and the Management of Agroecosystems." In: A. Terry Rambo and Percy E. Sajise (eds.), *An Introduction to Human Ecology Research on Agricultural Systems in Southeast Asia*. Laguna: University of Philippines at Los Banos.

Marshall, Peter

1992 *Nature's Web: An Exploration of Ecological Thinking*. London: Simon and Schuster.

1994 *Nature's Web: Rethinking Our Place on Earth*. First U.S. Edition. New York: Pragon House.

313

Mathur, Hari M.
1995   *Development, Displacement and Resettlement: Focus on Asian Experiences*. New Delhi: Vikas Publishing House.
Mathur, Hari M. (ed.)
1990   *The Human Dimension of Development: Perspectives from Anthropology*. New Delhi: Concept Publishing Co.
McDowell, Christopher (ed.)
1996   *Understanding Impoverishment: The Consequences of Development-Induced Displacement*. Oxford: Berghahn Books.
Meheret Ayenew
1994   "The Ketto Resettlement: A Brief Comparative Survey of the Land Tenure System, 1985/86 and 1993." In: Dessalegn Rahmato (ed.) *Land Tenure and Land Policy after the Derg: Proceedings of the Second Workshop of the Land Tenure Project. No. 8*. Trondheim: Institute of Development Research/Addis Ababa University.
Meliczek, Hans
2000   *Land Settlement: Experiences and Perispectives*. Eschborn: GTZ.
Mengistu Woube
1995   "Southward-Northward Resettlement in Ethiopia." In: *Northeast African Studies*. 2 (1): 85-106.
Mitchell, J. Clyde
1973   "Networks, Norms and Institutions." In: J. Boissevain and J.C. Mitchell (eds.), *Network Analysis: Studies in Human Interaction*. Mouton: Mouton and Company.
1974   "Social Networks." In: *Annual Review of Anthropology*. 3: 279-299.
Moran, Emilio F.
1987   "Socioeconomic Considerations in Acid Tropical Soils Research." In: Management of Acid Tropical Soils for Sustainable Agriculture: Proc. No.2. IBSRAM. Bangkok, Thailand, pp. 227-244.
North, Douglass C.
1990   *Institutions, Institutional Change and Economic Performance*. Cambridge: Cambridge University Press.
1991   "Institutions." In: *Journal of Economic Perspectives*. 5 (1): 97-112.
Nuijten, Monique
1999   *Institutions and Organising Practices: Conceptual Discussion*. Rome:FAO.(Internet: http://www.fao.org/sd/rodirect/roan0020.htm).

Pankhurst, Alula
1989   "The Administration of Resettlement in Ethiopia since the Revolution." In: Abebe Zegeye and S. Ishemo (eds.) *Forced Labour and Migration: Patterns of Movement within Africa.* London: Hans Zell Publishers.
1990   "Resettlement: Policy and Practice." In: Siegfried Pausewang et al. (eds.) *Ethiopia: Options for Rural Development.* London: Zed Books.
1992   *Resettlement and Famine in Ethiopia: The Villagers' Experience.* Manchester: Manchester University Press.
1997   "When the Centre Relocates the Periphery: Resettlement During the Derg." In: Katsuyoshi Fukui et al. (eds.), *Ethiopia in Broader Perspective: Papers of the 13th International Conference of Ethiopian Studies, 12-17 December, 1997.* Vol., II, pp. 540-58. Kyoto: Kyoto University.
Pankhurst, Richard
1997   *The Ethiopian Borderlands: Essays in Regional History from Ancient Times to the End of the 18th Century.* Lawrenceville: The Red Sea Press.
Pankhurst, Richard and Endrias Eshete
1958   "Self-Help in Ethiopia." In: *Ethiopia Observer.* 2 (2): 354-364.
Permpongsacharoen, Witoon (ed.)
1999   "In Defence of Swidden." In: *Watershed* 5 (1): 2-3.
Plant, R.
1994   *Land Rights and Minorities.* London: Minority Rights Group International.
Prattis, J. I.
1973   "Strategising Man." In: *Man.* 8: 46-58.
1987   "Alternative Views of Economy in Economic Anthropology." In: J. I. Prattis (ed.), *Beyond the New Economic Anthropology.* London: The McMillan Press.
Rehm, Sigmund and Gustav Espig
1991   *The Cultivated Plants of the Tropics and Subtropics: Cultivation, Economic Value, Utilization.* Weikersheim: Verlag Josef Margraf.
Salamone, Frank A. and Charles H. Swanson
1979   "Identity and Ethnicity: Ethnic Groups and Interactions in a Multi-Ethnic Society." In: *Ethnic Groups.* 2: 167-183.

315

Salem-Murdock, Muneera
1993   "Involuntary Resettlement: A Plea for the Host Population." In: Michael M. Cernea and Scott E. Guggenheim (eds.), *Anthropological Approaches to Resettlement: Policy, Practice, and Theory.* Boulder: Westview.

Salini Costruttori
1989   *Tana-Beles Project Ethiopia,* 1989. Salini Costruttori.

Salt, Henry
1814   *A Voyage to Abyssinia and Travels into the Interior of that Country, Excuted under the Orders of the British Government in the Years 1809-1810.* London: Frank Cass.

Samuels, J. C.
1985   *Resettlement Strategy Proposal, Ethiopian Highlands Reclamation Study, Working Paper No. 28.* Addis Ababa: Ministry of Agriculture, FAO.

Schlee, Günther
1994   „Ethnicity Emblems, Diacritical Features, Identity Markers: Some East African Examples." In: David Brokensha (ed.), *A River of Blessings: Essays in Honor of Paul Baxter.* Syracuse: Syracuse University.
2000   "Identitätskonstruktionen und Parteinahme: Überlegungen zur Konflikttheorie." In: *Sociologus.* Heft 1:64-89.

Schweizer, Thomas
1997   "Embeddedness of Ethnographic Cases: A Social Networks Perspective." In: *Current Anthropology.* 38 (5): 739-760.

Scoones, Ian
1998   *Sustainable Rural Livelihoods: A Framework for Analysis.* IDS Working Paper 72. Brighton: IDS.

Scott, George M.
1990   "A Resynthesis of the Primordial and Circumstantial Approaches to Ethnic Group Solidarity: Towards an Explanatory Model." In: *Ethnic and Racial Studies.* 13 (2): 147-171.

Scott, W.
1995   *Institutions and Organizations.* Thousand Oaks, CA: Sage.

Scudder, Thayer
1962   *The Ecology of the Gwembe Tonga.* Manchester: Manchester University Press.
1968   "Social Anthropology, Man-Made Lakes and Population Relocation in Africa." In: *Anthropological Quarterly.* 41 (3): 169-176.

1973 "The Human Ecology of Big Projects: River Basin Development and Resettlement." In: *Annual Review of Anthropology*. 2: 45-61.

1985 "A Sociological Framework for the Analysis of New Land Settlements." In: Michael M. Cernea (ed.), *Putting People First: Sociological Variables in Rural Development*. Oxford: Oxford University Press.

1991 "A Sociological Framework for the Analysis of New Land Settlements." In: Michael M. Cernea (ed.), *Putting People First: Sociological Variables in Rural Development*. 2nd ed. Revised and Expanded. Oxford: Oxford University Press.

1993 "Development-Induced Relocation and Refugee Studies: 37 Years of Change and Continuity among Zambia's Gwembe Tonga." In: *Journal of Refugee Studies*. 6 (2): 123-152.

1996b "Resettlement." In: D. Levinson and M. Ember (eds.), *Encyclopedia of Cultural Anthropology*, pp. 1111-1115. New York: Henry Holt and Company.

1996c "Development-Induced Impoverishment, Resistance and River-Basin Development" In: Christopher McDowell (ed.), *Understanding Impoverishment: The Consequences of Development-Induced Displacement*. Oxford: Berghahn Books.

1997a "Social Impacts." In: Asit K. Biswas (ed.), *Water Resources: Environmental Planning, Management and Development*. New York: McGraw Hill.

1997b "Resettlement." In: Asit K. Biswas (ed.), *Water Resources: Environmental Planning, Management and Development*. New York: McGraw Hill.

1999 "1999 Malinowski Award Lecture - The Emerging Global Crisis and Development Anthropology: Can We Have an Impact?" In: *Human Organization*. 58 (4): 351-364.

Scudder, Thayer and Elizabeth Colson
1979 "Long-Term Research in Gwembe Valley, Zambia." In G. M. Foster et al. (eds.), *Long-Term Field Research in Social Anthropology*. New York: Academic Press.

1982 "From Welfare to Development: A Conceptual Framework for the Analysis of Dislocated People." In: Art Hansen and Anthony Oliver-Smith (eds.), *Involuntary Migration and Resettlement: The Problems and Responses of Dislocated People*. Boulder: Westview Press.

Seeland, Klaus (ed.)

1997   *Nature is Culture: Indigenous Knowledge and Socio-Cultural Aspects of Trees and Forests in Non-European Cultures.* London: Intermediate Technology Publications.

Shack, William A.

1963   "Religious Ideas and Social Action in Gurage Bond-Friendship." In:
Africa. 33,3:198-208.

Shils, Edward

1957   "Primordial, Personal, Sacred and Civil Ties." In: *British Journal of
Sociology.* 7: 113-45.

Sillitoe, Paul

1998a   "What, Know Natives? Local Knowledge in Development." In: *Social Anthropology.* 6 (2): 203-220.

1998b   "The Development of Indigenous Knowledge: A New Applied Anthropology." In: *Current Anthropology.* 39 (2): 223-252.

Simoons, Frederick J.

1960   *Northwest Ethiopia: Peoples and Economy.* Madison: The University of Wisconsin Press.

Singer, N. J.

1980   "The Relevance of Traditional Legal Systems to Modernization and
Reform: A Consideration of Cambata Legal Structure." In: J. Tubia-
na (ed.), *Modern Ethiopia. From the Accession of Menilek II to the
Present. Proceedings of the Fifth International Conference of Ethio-
pian Studies. Nice 19-22, December 1977,* pp. 537-55. Rotterdam:
CNRS.

Sivini, Giordano

1986   "Famine and Resettlement Program in Ethiopia." In: *Africa.*
(Dell'Istituto Italo-Africano). XLI: 211-242.

Skolimowiski, H.

1981   *Eco-Philisophy.* London: Boyars.

        Sokolovskii, Sergey and Valery Tishkov

1996.   "Ethnicity." In: Allan Bernard and Jonathan Spencer (eds.), *Encyclopedia of Social and Cultural Anthropology,* pp. 190-93. London:
Routledge.

Spicer, Edward H.

1971   "Persistent Cultural Systems: A Comparative Study of Identity Systems That Can Adapt to Contrasting Environments." In: *Science.*
174: 795-800.

Stauder, Jack
1971   *The Majangir: Ecology and Society of a Southwest Ethiopian People*. Cambridge: Cambridge University Press.
Steingraber, S.
1988   "Integrated Settlement in Gambella: Armed Uprisings and Government Reprisals." In: J. Clay, et al. (eds.), *The Spoils of Famine: Ethiopian Famine Policy and Peasant Agriculture*. Cambridge: Cultural Survival.
Tadros, Helmi R.
1979   "The Human Aspects of Rural Resettlement Schemes in Egypt." In: Bernardo Berdichewsky (ed.), *Anthropology and Social Change in Rural Areas*. The Hague: Mouton Publishers.
Thompson, Richard H.
1989   *Theories of Ethnicity: A Critical Appraisal*. New York: Greenwood Press.
Tirfe Mammo
1999   *The Paradox of Africa's Poverty: The Role of Indigenous Knowledge, Traditional Practices and Local Institutions – the Case of Ethiopia*. Lawrenceville: The Red Sea Press.
Unseth, Peter
1985   "Gumuz: A Dialect Survey Report." In: *Journal of Ethiopian Studies*. 18: 91-114.
1989   "Selected Aspects of Gumuz Phonology." In: Taddese Beyene (ed.), *Proceedings of the Eighth International Conference of Ethiopian Studies. Vol. II*. Addis Ababa: Institute of Ethiopian Studies.
Uphoff, N.
1986   *Local Institutional Development: An Analytical Sourcebook with Cases*. West Hartford, Connecticut: Kumarian Press.
Van den Berghe, Pierre
1981   *The Ethnic Phenomenon*. New York: Elsevier.
1986   "Ethnicity and the Sociobiology Debate." In: John Rex (ed.), *Race and Ethnicity*. Milton Keynes: Open University Press.
1996   "Does Race Matter?" In: John Hutchinson and Anthony D. Smith (eds.), *Ethnicity*. Oxford: Oxford University Press.
Varma, S.C.
1985   *Human Resettlement in Lower Narmada Basin*. Bhopal: Narmada Valley Development Authority, Government of Madhya Pradesh.

Verdery, Katherine
1994 "Ethnicity, Nationalism, and State-making – Ethnic Groups and Boundaries: Past and Future." In: Hans Vermeulen and Cora Govers (eds.), *The Anthropology of Ethnicity: Beyond 'Ethnic Groups and Boundaries.'* Amsterdam: Het Spinhuis.

Vermeulen, Hans and Cora Govers (eds.)
1994 *The Anthropology of Ethnicity: Beyond 'Ethnic Groups and Boundaries'.* Amsterdam: Het Spinhuis.

Wallmark, Patrik
1981 "The Bega (Gumuz) of Wollega: Agriculture and Subsistence." In: M. Lionel Bender (ed.), *Peoples and Cultures of the Ethio-Sudan Borderlands*, pp. 79-116. East Lansing: Michigan State University.

Warner, Katherine
1991 *Shifting Cultivators: Local Technical Knowledge and Natural Resource Management in Humid Tropics.* Rome: FAO.

Warren, D. Michael, L. Jan Slikkerveer and David Brokensha (eds.)
1995 *The Cultural Dimension of Development: Indigenous Knowledge Systems.* London: Intermediate Technology Publications.

West, P. and S. Brechin (eds.)
1991 *Resident Peoples and National Parks.* Tucson: University of Arisona Press.

Westphal, E.
1975 *Agricultural Systems in Ethiopia.* Wageningen: Centre for Agricultural Publication and Documentation.

Williams, J. G. and N. Arlott
1980 A Guide to the Birds of East Africa. London: Williams Collins.

Wolde-Selassie Abbute
1998 The Dynamics of Socio-Economic Differentiation and Livelihood Strategies: The Case of Relocated Peasants in the Beles Valley, North-Western Ethiopia. *Discussion papers No. 26. Goettingen: Institute of Rural Development, University of Goettingen.*

2000a "Social Re-Articulation after Resettlement: Observing the Beles Valley Scheme in Ethiopia." In: Michael M. Cernea and Christopher McDowell (eds.), *Risks and Reconstruction: Experiences of Resettlers and Refugeess*, pp. 412-30. Washington D.C.: The World Bank.

2001b "Socio-Economic Role and Status of Handicraftsmen among the Kambaata of Southern Ethiopia." In: *Aethiopica.* 4: 96-120.

Appendices

Appendix 1. Detailed Statistical Data on the Population Background in the Beles Valley Resettlement Scheme Area (Pawe Special *Woreda*)

Table 1: Local Administrative Sub-Centres, *Kebeles* and Villages of the Pawe Special *Woreda**

Local Administrative Sub-Centres, *Kebele* and Villages of the Pawe Special *Woreda*			
Four Adminis-trative Sub-Centres	**Present Twenty *Kebele* Admini-stration (Post 1991)**		**Former Villages/Towns under Resettlement Administration (Pre-1991)**
1		1	*Almu* Town	*Almu* Town
	Almu	2	Abbat Beles	Abbat Beles, L1, L2, RDS51
		3	L3	L3, L4
		4	*Felege Selam* Town	*Felege Selam* Town (L4)
		5	L28	L28, **L29***
		6	L134	L131, L132, **L134***
2	Addis Alem	7	*Addis Alem* Town	*Addis Alem* Town (L7)
		8	L30	L5, L6, L7, L30
		9	L17	L17, **R8*, R9***
		10	**L23****	**L9**, L10**, L23**, L45****
		11	R7	R6, R7
3	L14 (*Addis Zemen*)	12	L12 (*Debre Work*)	L11, L12, L13
		13	L14 (*Addis Zemen*)	L14, L15, L16, L130
		14	L21 (*Addis Beles*)	L20, L21, L22
		15	L24	L24
		16	L26	L26
4	LUS51 (*Mekane Selam*)	17	R4	R2, R3, R4, R5
		18	RUS51 (*Mekane Selam*)	R46, **R49*,** RUS50, RUS51
		19	R101	R101, R127, R102
		20	R104@	R104@, R103@, R105@

Source: Pawe Special Woreda Administration (February - March 2001)
**The researcher's main study sites
*The researcher's study sub-sites
@Village abandoned by state-sponsored resettlers and occupied by later immigrant farmers
L - Villages on the left side of Beles River; R – Villages on the right side of Beles River
RUS – Right upside villages; RDS - Right downside villages

---

* This same table is also used in the main text (table 10). Its placement here is intended to show the structure of the local administration units so that the reader can easily understand the details of the next tables listed as part of the appendix.

Table 2a: The 1980s State-Sponsored Resettler Population

No.	Present Kebele Admini-stration	Former Re-settle-ment Villages	Heads of Households			Family Members			Total
			Male	Fem.	Total	Male	Fem.	Total	
1	Abbat Beles	Abbat Beles	48	45	93	44	34	78	171
		L1	128	47	175	199	217	416	591
		L2	151	48	199	234	279	513	712
		RDS51	62	18	80	60	70	130	210
		Total	389	158	547	537	600	1137	1684
2	L3	L3	119	20	139	503	531	1034	1173
		L4	85	6	91	300	375	675	766
		Total	204	26	230	803	906	1709	1939
3	L30	L5	166	24	190	277	354	631	821
		L6	103	20	123	217	183	400	523
		L7	138	17	155	216	336	552	707
		L30	316	98	414	688	960	1648	2062
		Total	723	159	882	1398	1833	3231	4113
4	L23**	L9**	160	40	200	214	216	430	630
		L10**	167	49	216	154	259	413	629
		L23**	236	58	294	352	507	859	1153
		L45**	151	62	213	262	355	617	830
		Total	714	209	923	982	1337	2319	3242
5	L12 (Debre Work)	L11	194	18	212	420	466	886	1098
		L12	242	29	271	471	497	968	1239
		L13	87	24	111	156	195	351	462
		Total	523	71	594	1047	1158	2205	2799
6	L14 (Addis Zemen)	L14	100	20	120	65	95	160	280
		L15	59	15	74	62	101	163	237
		L16	103	12	115	300	390	690	805
		L130	23	16	39	52	71	123	162
		Total	285	63	348	479	657	1136	1484
7	L21 (Addis Beles)	L20	70	17	87	75	86	161	248
		L21	71	13	84	96	136	232	316
		L22	52	8	60	80	99	179	239
		Total	193	38	231	251	321	572	803
8	L24	L24	385	125	510	943	1112	2055	2565
9	L26	L26	160	36	196	337	397	734	930
10	L28	L28	120	41	161	200	231	431	592
		L29*	218	76	294	152	321	473	767
		Total	338	117	455	352	552	904	1359
11	L134	L131	90	20	110	340	310	650	760

No.	Present Kebele Administration	Former Re-settlement Villages	Heads of Households			Family Members			Total
			Male	*Fem.*	*Total*	*Male*	*Fem.*	*Total*	
11	L134	L132	47	3	50	120	130	250	300
		L134*	**147**	**40**	**187**	**200**	**213**	**413**	**600**
		Total	*284*	*63*	*347*	*660*	*653*	*1313*	*1660*
12	L17	L17	86	21	107	121	154	275	382
		R8*	**42**	**3**	**45**	**100**	**125**	**225**	**270**
		R9*	**56**	**4**	**60**	**120**	**180**	**300**	**360**
		Total	*184*	*28*	*212*	*341*	*459*	*800*	*1012*
13	R4	R2	32	12	44	70	72	142	186
		R3	131	33	164	250	349	599	763
		R4	63	12	75	89	111	200	275
		R5	67	30	97	54	100	154	251
		Total	*293*	*87*	*380*	*463*	*632*	*1095*	*1475*
14	R7	R6	109	13	122	99	151	250	372
		R7	150	47	197	228	318	546	743
		Total	*259*	*60*	*319*	*327*	*469*	*796*	*1115*
15	RUS51	R46	100	40	140	215	200	415	555
		R49*	**129**	**74**	**203**	**400**	**462**	**862**	**1065**
		RUS50	200	75	275	225	350	575	850
		RUS51	154	34	188	381	444	825	1013
		Total	*583*	*223*	*806*	*1221*	*1456*	*2677*	*3483*
16	R101	R101	120	20	140	206	254	460	600
		R127	40	15	55	90	105	195	250
		Total	*160*	*35*	*195*	*296*	*359*	*655*	*850*
17	R104	R104@	-	-	-	-	-	-	-
Total			*5677*	*1498*	*7175*	*10437*	*12901*	*23338*	*30513*

Source: Wolde-Selassie Abbute survey /February – March 2001/
**The researcher's main study sites
*The researcher's study sub-sites
@Village abandoned by the state-sponsored resettlers and occupied by later migrant farmers

Table 2b: Voluntary/Displaced Immigrant Population

			Voluntary/Displaced Immigrant Population						
No	Present Kebele Ad-minis-tration	Former Re-settle-ment Villages	Heads of Households			Family Members			Total
			Male	*Fem.*	*Total*	*Male*	*Fem.*	*Total*	
1	Abbat Beles	**Abbat Beles**	10	6	16	10	12	22	38
		L1	10	-	10	19	26	45	55
		L2	59	20	79	100	114	214	293
		RDS51	1	-	1	2	2	4	5
		Total	*80*	*26*	*106*	*131*	*154*	*285*	*391*
2	L3	L3	5	-	5	6	9	15	20
		L4	9	2	11	45	10	55	66
		Total	*14*	*2*	*16*	*51*	*19*	*70*	*86*
3	L30	L5	37	8	45	119	107	226	271
		L6	11	-	11	37	32	69	80
		L7	21	7	28	42	40	82	110
		L30	6	2	8	12	20	32	40
		Total	*75*	*17*	*92*	*210*	*199*	*409*	*501*
4	**L23****	**L9****	4	3	7	15	18	33	40
		L10**	24	3	27	22	18	40	67
		L23**	12	-	12	18	21	39	51
		L45**	5	2	7	12	14	26	33
		Total	*45*	*8*	*53*	*67*	*71*	*138*	*191*
5	L12 (*Debre Work*)	L11	-	-	-	-	-	-	-
		L12	-	-	-	-	-	-	-
		L13	-	-	-	-	-	-	-
		Total	*-*	*-*	*-*	*-*	*-*	*-*	*-*
6	L14 (*Addis Zemen*)	L14	74	6	80	167	234	401	481
		L15	7	-	7	10	18	28	35
		L16	39	1	40	110	130	240	280
		L130	25	2	27	81	92	173	200
		Total	*145*	*9*	*154*	*368*	*474*	*842*	*996*
7	L21 (*Addis Beles*)	L20	21	-	21	47	70	117	138
		L21	28	-	28	56	73	129	157
		L22	26	-	26	56	57	113	139
		Total	*75*	*-*	*75*	*159*	*200*	*359*	*434*
8	L24	L24	*4*	*-*	*4*	*6*	*7*	*13*	*17*
9	L26	L26	*1*	*-*	*1*	*-*	*1*	*1*	*2*
10	L28	L28	17	11	28	13	13	26	54
		L29*	**60**	**19**	**79**	**22**	**24**	**46**	**125**
		Total	*77*	*30*	*107*	*35*	*37*	*72*	*179*
11	L134	L131	20	-	20	40	60	100	120

No	Present Kebele Administration	Former Re-settlement Villages	Heads of Households			Family Members			Total
			Male	*Fem.*	*Total*	*Male*	*Fem.*	*Total*	

Combined below:

No	Present Kebele Administration	Former Re-settlement Villages	Heads of Households — *Male*	Heads of Households — *Fem.*	Heads of Households — *Total*	Family Members — *Male*	Family Members — *Fem.*	Family Members — *Total*	Total
11	L134	L132	14	2	16	40	40	80	96
		L134*	40	15	55	6	4	10	65
		Total	*74*	*17*	*91*	*86*	*104*	*190*	*281*
12	L17	L17	48	5	53	84	127	211	264
		R8*	29	6	35	110	135	245	280
		R9*	39	4	43	144	128	272	315
		Total	*116*	*15*	*131*	*338*	*390*	*728*	*859*
13	R4	R2	-	-	-	-	-	-	-
		R3	8	-	8	10	16	26	34
		R4	41	3	44	121	144	265	309
		R5	49	4	53	81	118	199	252
		Total	*98*	*7*	*105*	*212*	*278*	*490*	*595*
14	R7	R6	14	1	15	26	36	62	77
		R7	36	4	40	98	88	186	226
		Total	*50*	*5*	*55*	*124*	*124*	*248*	*303*
15	RUS51	R46	6	2	8	-	-	-	8
		R49*	15	3	18	26	22	48	66
		RUS50	20	2	22	24	34	58	80
		RUS51	-	-	-	-	-	-	-
		Total	*41*	*7*	*48*	*50*	*56*	*106*	*154*
16	R101	R101	30	20	50	36	38	74	124
		R127	20	23	43	18	31	49	92
		Total	*50*	*43*	*93*	*54*	*69*	*123*	*216*
17	R104	R104@	*290*	*41*	*331*	*632*	*690*	*1322*	*1653*
Total			*1235*	*227*	*1462*	*2523*	*2873*	*5396*	*6858*

Title of table: **Voluntary/Displaced Immigrant Population**

Source: Wolde-Selassie Abbute survey /February – March 2001/

**The researcher's main study sites

*The researcher's study sub-sites

@Village abandoned by state-sponsored resettlers and occupied by later immigrant farmers

325

Table 2c: Small Towns' Dweller Population*

No	Present Small Town Kebeles	Emerged Small Towns	Heads of Households			Family Members			Total
			Male	*Fem.*	*Total*	*Male*	*Fem.*	*Total*	
1	*Almu*	*Almu* (Centre of (Admini-stration)	554	150	704	1000	1582	2582	3286
2	*Felege Selam*	*Felege Selam* (L4)	900	200	1100	1165	1600	2765	3865
3	*Addis Alem*	*Addis Alem* (L7)	680	120	800	1400	1640	3040	3840
	Total		2134	470	2604	3565	4822	8387	10991

Source: Wolde-Selassie Abbute survey /February – March 2001/
*The figures include diverse category of population including some of the earlier resettlers and latter voluntary/displaced immigrants among several others.

Table 3a: Ethnic Composition of State-Sponsored Resettler Population

No	Kebele	Villages	Amhara					Kam-baata	Ha-diyya	Oro-mo	Wo-laita	Tigra-way	Agaw (Seqota)	Total
			Wello	Shoa	Gojjam	Gon-dar	Total							
1	**Abbat Beles**	*Abbat Beles*	28	19	86	17	160	-	-	3	-	8	-	171
		L1	160	431	-	-	591	-	-	-	-	-	-	591
		L2	520	-	16	172	708	-	-	-	-	4	-	712
		RDS51	189	-	21	-	210	-	-	-	-	-	-	210
		Total	*897*	*450*	*123*	*199*	*1669*	*-*	*-*	*3*	*-*	*12*	*-*	*1684*
2	L3	L3	-	-	-	-	-	200	793	-	180	-	-	1173
		L4	-	-	-	-	-	40	666	-	60	-	-	766
		Total	*-*	*-*	*-*	*-*	*-*	*140*	*1659*	*-*	*140*	*-*	*-*	*1939*
3	L30	L5	-	-	-	-	-	156	505	-	160	-	-	821
		L6	-	-	-	-	-	418	105	-	-	-	-	523
		L7	-	-	-	-	-	707	-	-	-	-	-	707
		L30	2062	-	-	-	2062	-	-	-	-	-	-	2062
		Total	*2062*	*-*	*-*	*-*	*2062*	*1281*	*610*	*-*	*160*	*-*	*-*	*4113*
4	L23**	L9**	-	-	65	-	65	503	42	-	20	-	-	630
		L10**	-	-	149	-	149	98	354	-	28	-	-	629
		L23**	87	51	82	-	220	-	-	933	-	-	-	1153
		L45**	787	-	43	-	830	-	-	-	-	-	-	830
		Total	*874*	*51*	*339*	*-*	*1264*	*601*	*396*	*933*	*48*	*-*	*-*	*3242*
5	L12 (*Debre Work*)	L11	-	1098	-	-	1098	-	-	-	-	-	-	1098
		L12	51	1188	-	-	1239	-	-	-	-	-	-	1239
		L13	-	462	-	-	462	-	-	-	-	-	-	462
		Total	*51*	*2748*	*-*	*-*	*2799*	*-*	*-*	*-*	*-*	*-*	*-*	*2799*

Ethnic Composition of State-Sponsored Population

No	Kebele	Villages	Amhara					Kam-baata	Ha-diyya	Oro-mo	Wo-laita	Tigra-way	Agaw (Seqota)	Total
			Wello	Shoa	Gojjam	Gondar	Total							
6	L14 (Addis Ze-men)	L14	15	265	-	-	280	-	-	-	-	-	-	280
		L15	-	185	33	-	218	-	-	19	-	-	-	237
		L16	-	805	-	-	805	-	-	-	-	-	-	805
		L130	162	-	-	-	162	-	-	-	-	-	-	162
		Total	**177**	**1255**	**33**	**-**	**1465**	**-**	**-**	**19**	**-**	**-**	**-**	**1484**
7	L21 (Addis Beles)	L20	-	-	-	-	-	223	25	-	-	-	-	248
		L21	-	-	-	-	-	222	94	-	-	-	-	316
		L22	-	-	-	-	-	186	53	-	-	-	-	239
		Total	**-**	**-**	**-**	**-**	**-**	**631**	**172**	**-**	**-**	**-**	**-**	**803**
8	L24	L24	-	-	2565	-	2565	-	-	-	-	-	-	2565
9	L26	L26	-	-	930	-	930	-	-	-	-	-	-	930
10	L28	L28	403	-	22	8	433	-	-	2	-	83	74	592
		L29*	**411**	**-**	**147**	**3**	**561**	**-**	**-**	**18**	**-**	**63**	**125**	**767**
		Total	**814**	**-**	**169**	**11**	**994**	**-**	**-**	**20**	**-**	**146**	**199**	**1359**
11	L134	L131	500	-	260	-	760	-	-	-	-	-	-	760
		L132	260	-	40	-	300	-	-	-	-	-	-	300
		L134*	**600**	**-**	**-**	**-**	**600**	**-**	**-**	**-**	**-**	**-**	**-**	**600**
		Total	**1360**	**-**	**300**	**-**	**1660**	**-**	**-**	**-**	**-**	**-**	**-**	**1660**
12	L17	L17	-	-	-	-	-	382	-	-	-	-	-	382
		R8*	-	-	-	-	-	**270**	-	-	-	-	-	**270**
		R9*	-	-	-	-	-	**342**	**18**	-	-	-	-	**360**
		Total	**-**	**-**	**-**	**-**	**-**	**994**	**18**	**-**	**-**	**-**	**-**	**1012**

Ethnic Composition of State-Sponsored Population

No	Kebele	Villages	Amhara					Kam-baata	Ha-diyya	Oro-mo	Wo-laita	Ti-gra-way	Agaw (Seqota)	Total
			Wello	Shoa	Gojjam	Gondar	Total							
13	R4	R2	-	186	-	-	186	-	-	-	-	-	-	186
		R3	322	377	-	-	699	-	-	56	-	8	-	763
		R4	100	-	-	-	100	-	175	-	-	-	-	275
		R5	54	-	-	-	54	-	152	-	45	-	-	251
		Total	*476*	*563*			*1039*	*-*	*327*	*56*	*45*	*8*	*-*	*1475*
14	R7	R6	80	-	-	-	80	14	228	-	50	-	-	372
		R7	24	497	-	-	521	-	-	217	-	5	-	743
		Total	*104*	*497*			*601*	*14*	*228*	*217*	*50*	*5*	*-*	*1115*
15	RUS51 (Meka-ne Selam)	R46	540	-	-	-	540	-	-	10	-	-	5	555
		R49*	**1045**	-	**10**	-	**1055**	-	-	**10**	-	-	-	**1065**
		RUS50	785	-	-	-	785	-	-	65	-	-	-	850
		RUS51	947	-	-	-	947	-	-	66	-	-	-	1013
		Total	*3317*		*10*		*3327*	*-*	*-*	*151*	*-*	*-*	*5*	*3483*
16	R101	R101	450	-	-	-	450	-	-	-	-	72	78	600
		R127	100	-	-	-	100	-	-	-	-	70	80	250
		Total	*550*				*550*	*-*	*-*	*-*	*-*	*142*	*158*	*850*
17	R104	R104@	-	-	-	-	-	-	-	-	-	-	-	-
		Total	10682	5564	4469	210	20925	3661	3410	1399	443	313	362	30513

Source: Wolde-Selassie Abbute survey (February - March 2001)

**The researcher's main study sites; *The researcher's study sub-sites

@Village abandoned by state-sponsored resettlers and occupied by later migrant farmers

Table 3b: Ethnic Composition of Voluntary/Displaced Immigrant Population

No	Kebele	Villages	Ethnic Composition of Voluntary / Displaced Immigrant Population									Total
			Amhara				Kambaata	Hadiya	Oromo	Ti-graway	Agaw (Gojjam)	
			Wello	Gojjam	Gon-dar	Total						
1	Abbat Beles	Abbat Beles	10	26	2	38	-	-	-	-	-	38
		L1	-	55	-	55	-	-	-	-	-	55
		L2	84	30	179	293	-	-	-	-	-	293
		RDS51	-	5	-	5	-	-	-	-	-	5
		Total	**94**	**116**	**181**	**391**	**-**	**-**	**-**	**-**	**-**	**391**
2	L3	L3	-	20	-	20	-	-	-	-	-	20
		L4	-	66	-	66	-	-	-	-	-	66
		Total	**-**	**86**	**-**	**86**	**-**	**-**	**-**	**-**	**-**	**86**
3	L30	L5	-	121	-	121	20	40	30	-	60	271
		L6	-	80	-	80	-	-	-	-	-	80
		L7	-	110	-	110	-	-	-	-	-	110
		L30	40	-	-	40	-	-	-	-	-	40
		Total	**40**	**311**	**-**	**351**	**20**	**40**	**30**	**-**	**60**	**501**
4	L23**	L9**	-	9	-	9	31	-	-	-	-	40
		L10**	-	40	-	40	7	20	-	-	-	67
		L23**	13	20	-	33	-	-	18	-	-	51
		L45**	26	7	-	33	-	-	-	-	-	33
		Total	**39**	**76**	**-**	**115**	**38**	**20**	**18**	**-**	**-**	**191**

Ethnic Composition of Voluntary / Displaced Immigrant Population

No	Kebele	Villages	Amhara				Kambaata	Hadiy-ya	Oro-mo	Ti-graway	Agaw (Gojjam)	Total
			Wello	Gojjam	Gon-dar	Total						
5	L12 (Debre Work)	L11	-	-	-	-	-	-	-	-	-	-
		L12	-	-	-	-	-	-	-	-	-	-
		L13	-	-	-	-	-	-	-	-	-	-
		Total	-	-	-	-	-	-	-	-	-	-
6	L14 (Addis Zemen)	L14	40	391	50	481				-	-	481
		L15		35		35				-	-	35
		L16		280		280				-	-	280
		L130		195	5	200				-	-	200
		Total	*40*	*901*	*55*	*996*				*-*	*-*	*996*
7	L21 (Addis Beles)	L20	-	138	-	138				-	-	138
		L21	-	157	-	157				-	-	157
		L22	-	139	-	139				-	-	139
		Total	*-*	*434*	*-*	*434*				*-*	*-*	*434*
8	L24	L24	-	17	-	17				-	-	17
9	L26	L26	-	2	-	2				-	-	2
10	L28	L28	40	10	4	54				-	-	54
		L29*	87	22	4	113				12	-	125
		Total	*127*	*32*	*8*	*167*				*12*	*-*	*179*
11	L134	L131	40	80	-	120				-	-	120
		L132	41	55	-	96				-	-	96
		L134*	*48*	*14*	*3*	*65*				*-*	*-*	*65*
		Total	*129*	*149*	*3*	*281*				*-*	*-*	*281*

			Ethnic Composition of Voluntary / Displaced Immigrant Population									
			Amhara				Kambaata	Hadiy-ya	Oro-mo	Ti-graway	Agaw (Gojjam)	Total
No	Kebele	Villages	Wello	Gojjam	Gondar	Total						
12	L17	L17	-	264	-	264	-	-	-	-	-	264
		R8*	-	280	-	280	-	-	-	-	-	280
		R9*	-	315	-	315	-	-	-	-	-	315
		Total	-	859	-	869	-	-	-	-	-	859
13	R4	R2	-	-	-	-	-	-	-	-	-	-
		R3	-	26	8	34	-	-	-	-	-	34
		R4	-	309	-	309	-	-	-	-	-	309
		R5	-	252	-	252	-	-	-	-	-	252
		Total	-	587	8	595	-	-	-	-	-	595
14	R7	R6	-	60	17	77	-	-	-	-	-	77
		R7	4	210	12	226	-	-	-	-	-	226
		Total	4	270	29	303	-	-	-	-	-	303
15	RUS51 (Me-kane Selam)	R46	5	3	-	8	-	-	-	-	-	8
		R49*	18	46	2	66	-	-	-	-	-	66
		RUS50	35	45	-	80	-	-	-	-	-	80
		RUS51	-	-	-	-	-	-	-	-	-	-
		Total	58	94	2	154	-	-	-	-	-	154
16	R101	R101	24	55	45	124	-	-	-	-	-	124
		R127	22	70	-	92	-	-	-	-	-	92
		Total	46	125	45	216	-	-	-	-	-	216
17	R104	R104@	-	1653	-	1653	-	-	-	-	-	1653
Total			577	5712	331	6620	58	60	48	12	60	6858

Source: Wolde-Selassie Abbute survey (February - March 2001); **The researcher's main study sites; *The researcher's study sub-sites

Table 3c: Ethnic Composition of the Small Towns' Dweller Population

No.	Kebele (Small Towns)	Amhara					Kam-baata	Hadi-yya	Oro-mo	Tigra-way	Agaw (Gojjam)	Others	Total
		Wello	Shoa	Gojjam	Gondar	Total							
1	Almu	270	240	1531	505	2546	289	110	20	96	174	51	**3286**
2	Felege Selam	213	186	1550	610	2559	110	309	15	50	800	22	**3865**
3	Addis Alem	550	51	1630	490	2721	216	119	75	73	575	61	**3840**
	Total	*1033*	*477*	*4711*	*1605*	*7826*	*615*	*538*	*110*	*219*	*1549*	*134*	*10991*

Source: Wolde-Selassie Abbute survey (February - March 2001)

333

Table 4a: Religious Composition of State-Sponsored Resettler and Voluntary/Displaced Immigrant Population

No.	Kebele	Villages	Religious Composition of State-Sponsored Resettler and Voluntary/Displaced Immigrant Population									Total Population
			State Sponsored Resettlers					Voluntary / Displaced Migrants				
			Ortho-dox	Islam	Catholic	Pro-testant	Total	Ortho-dox	Islam	Protes-tant	Total	
1	Abbat Beles	Abbat Beles	140	31	-	-	171	26	12	-	38	209
		L1	357	234	-	-	591	20	35	-	55	646
		L2	543	169	-	-	712	263	30	-	293	1005
		RDS51	110	100	-	-	210	5	-	-	5	215
		Total	*1150*	*534*	*-*	*-*	*1684*	*314*	*77*	*-*	*391*	*2075*
2	L3	L3	216	54	400	503	1173	20	-	-	20	1193
		L4	96	76	240	354	766	66	-	-	66	832
		Total	*312*	*130*	*640*	*857*	*1939*	*86*	*-*	*-*	*86*	*2025*
3	L30	L5	60	88	25	648	821	181	-	90	271	1092
		L6	25	75	25	398	523	80	-	-	80	603
		L7	62	16	228	401	707	110	-	-	110	817
		L30	1062	1000	-	-	2062	10	30	-	40	2102
		Total	*1209*	*1179*	*278*	*1447*	*4113*	*381*	*30*	*90*	*501*	*4614*
4	L23**	L9**	74	105	140	311	630	9	-	31	40	670
		L10**	149	70	98	312	629	40	-	27	67	696

No.	Kebele	Villages	State Sponsored Resettlers					Voluntary / Displaced Migrants				Total Population
			Ortho-dox	Islam	Catholic	Pro-testant	Total	Ortho-dox	Islam	Protes-tant	Total	
4	L23**	L23**	220	933	-	-	1153	23	28	-	51	1204
		L45**	494	336	-	-	830	20	13	-	33	863
		Total	*937*	*1444*	*238*	*623*	*3242*	*92*	*41*	*58*	*191*	*3433*
5	L12 (Debre Work)	L11	1071	27			1098	-	-	-	-	1098
		L12	1188	51			1239	-	-	-	-	1239
		L13	422	40			462	-	-	-	-	462
		Total	*2681*	*118*			*2799*	-	-	-	-	*2799*
6	L14 (Addis Zemen)	L14	220	60			280	190	291	-	481	761
		L15	212	25			237	30	5	-	35	272
		L16	805				805	280	-	-	280	1085
		L130	62	100			162	200	-	-	200	362
		Total	*1299*	*185*			*1484*	*700*	*296*	-	*996*	*2480*
7	L21 (Addis Beles)	L20	-	18	72	158	248	138	-	-	138	386
		L21	-	-	-	316	316	157	-	-	157	473
		L22	-	-	-	239	239	139	-	-	139	378
		Total	-	*18*	*72*	*713*	*803*	*434*	-	-	*434*	*1237*
8	L24	*L24*	2565	-			2565	17	-	-	17	2582
9	L26	*L26*	930	-			930	2	-	-	2	932
10	L28	L28	358	234			592	38	16	-	54	646
		*L29**	521	246	-	-	767	99	26	-	125	892
		Total	*879*	*480*	-	-	*1359*	*137*	*42*	-	*179*	*1538*

Religious Composition of State-Sponsored Resettler and Voluntary/Displaced Immigrant Population

No.	Kebele	Villages	State Sponsored Resettlers					Voluntary / Displaced Migrants				Total Population
			Ortho-dox	Islam	Catholic	Protes-tant	Total	Ortho-dox	Islam	Protes-tant	Total	
11	L134	L131	250	510	-	-	760	70	50	-	120	880
		L132	265	35	-	-	300	85	11	-	96	396
		L134*	415	185	-	-	600	40	25	-	65	665
		Total	930	730	-	-	1660	195	86	-	281	1941
12	L17	L17	-	-	-	382	382	264	-	-	264	646
		R8*	10	16	55	189	270	280	-	-	280	550
		R9*	15	15	170	160	360	315	-	-	315	675
		Total	25	31	225	731	1012	859	-	-	859	1871
13	R4	R2	170	16	-	-	186	-	-	-	-	186
		R3	447	316	-	-	763	34	-	-	34	797
		R4	100	-	25	150	275	309	-	-	309	584
		R5	35	25	62	129	251	252	-	-	252	503
		Total	752	357	87	279	1475	595	-	-	595	2070
14	R7	R6	59	62	108	143	372	77	-	-	77	449
		R7	345	398	-	-	743	226	-	-	226	969
		Total	404	460	108	143	1115	303	-	-	303	1418
15	RUS51 (Me-kane Selam)	R46	270	285	-	-	555	3	5	-	8	563
		R49*	241	824	-	-	1065	15	51	-	66	1131
		RUS50	400	450	-	-	850	50	30	-	80	930
		RUS51	513	500	-	-	1013	-	-	-	-	1013
		Total	1424	2059	-	-	3483	68	86	-	154	3637

No.	Kebele	Villages	Religious Composition of State-Sponsored Resettler and Voluntary/Displaced Immigrant Population									Total Population
			State Sponsored Resettlers					Voluntary / Displaced Migrants				
			Ortho-dox	Islam	Catholic	Pro-testant	Total	Ortho-dox	Islam	Protes-tant	Total	
16	R101	R101	490	110	-	-	600	100	24	-	124	724
		R127	185	65	-	-	250	70	22	-	92	342
		Total	675	175	-	-	850	170	46	-	216	1066
17	R104	R104@	-	-	-	-	-	-	1653	-	1653	1653
Total Population			16172	7900	1648	4793	30513	4353	2357	148	6858	37371

Source: Wolde-Selassie Abbute survey (February - March 2001)
**The researcher's main study sites
*The researcher's study sub-sites
@Village abandoned by state-sponsored resettlers and occupied by later immigrant farmers

Table 4b: Religious Composition of Small Towns' Dweller Population

No.	Kebele (Small Towns)	Religious Composition of Small Towns' Dweller Population					Grand Total
		Christians				Muslims	
		Orthodox	Catholic	Protestant	Total		
1	Almu	2187	189	210	2586	700	3286
2	Felege Selam	2709	120	161	2990	875	3865
3	Addis Alem	2500	285	135	2920	920	3840
	Total	7396	594	506	8496	2495	10991

Source: Wolde-Selassie Abbute Survey (February – March 2001)

Table 5: Local Community Institutions

No.	Kebele	Villages	Religious Institutions (Churches & Mosques)					Local Community Institutions#				
			Churches			Mosques	Total	Burial Iddir	Stretcher Iddir	Community Iddir Institutions		Total
			Ortho-dox	Protes-tant	Catholic					Oxen Iddir	Housing Iddir	
1	Abbat Beles	Abbat Beles	1	-	-	1	2	1	1	-	-	2
		L1	1	-	-	1	2	2	5	2	5	14
		L2	1	-	-	1	2	2	7	7	7	23

Local Community Institutions#

No.	Kebele	Villages	Religious Institutions (Churches & Mosques)					Community Iddir Institutions				
			Churches			Mosques	Total	Burial Iddir	Stretcher Iddir	Oxen Iddir	Housing Iddir	Total
			Ortho-dox	Protes-tant	Catholic							
		RDS51	1	-	-	1	2	1	1	1	1	4
		Total	*4*	*-*	*-*	*4*	*8*	*6*	*14*	*10*	*13*	*43*
2	L3	L3	-	1	1	-	2	2	2	1	2	7
		L4	-	1	1	1	3	2	2	1	2	7
		Total	*-*	*2*	*2*	*1*	*5*	*4*	*4*	*2*	*4*	*14*
3	L30	L5	-	1	-	1	2	2	2	1	2	7
		L6	-	1	-	-	1	1	2	2	2	7
		L7	-	1	1	1	3	1	2	2	2	7
		L30	1	-	-	1	2	9	9	9	9	36
		Total	*1*	*3*	*1*	*3*	*8*	*13*	*15*	*14*	*15*	*57*
4	L23**	L9**	-	3	1	1	5	5	10	2	4	21
		L10**	1	3	1	1	6	3	12	3	6	24
		L23**	-	-	-	1	2	4	12	6	7	29
		L45**	1	-	-	1	2	5	12	4	11	32
		Total	*2*	*6*	*2*	*5*	*15*	*17*	*46*	*15*	*28*	*106*
5	L12 (Debre Work)	L11	1	-	-	-	1	2	2	1	2	7
		L12	1	-	-	-	1	2	2	1	2	7
		L13	1	-	-	-	1	1	1	1	1	4
		Total	*3*	*-*	*-*	*-*	*3*	*5*	*5*	*3*	*5*	*18*

No.	Kebele	Villages	Religious Institutions (Churches & Mosques)					Community *Iddir* Institutions				
			Churches			Mosques	Total	Burial *Iddir*	Stretcher *Iddir*	Oxen *Iddir*	Housing *Iddir*	Total
			Ortho-dox	Protes-tant	Catholic							
6	L14 (Addis Zemen)	L14	1	-	-	1	2	2	2	1	1	6
		L15	1	-	-	-	1	1	3	1	1	6
		L16	1	-	-	-	1	2	6	1	1	10
		L130	1	-	-	1	2	1	1	1	1	4
		Total	*4*	*-*	*-*	*2*	*6*	*6*	*12*	*4*	*4*	*26*
7	L21 (Addis Beles)	L20	-	1	1	-	2	1	2	-	2	5
		L21	-	1	-	-	1	1	1	-	1	3
		L22	-	1	-	-	1	1	2	-	2	5
		Total	*-*	*3*	*1*	*-*	*4*	*3*	*5*	*-*	*5*	*13*
8	L24	*L24*	*1*	*-*	*-*	*-*	*1*	*4*	*6*	*5*	*10*	*25*
9	L26	*L26*	*1*	*-*	*-*	*-*	*1*	*1*	*4*	*3*	*6*	*14*
10	L28	L28	1	-	-	1	2	6	12	4	12	34
		*L29**	*1*	*-*	*-*	*1*	*2*	*7*	*10*	*6*	*9*	*32*
		Total	*2*	*-*	*-*	*2*	*4*	*13*	*22*	*10*	*21*	*66*
11	L134	L131	1	-	-	1	2	2	2	2	4	10
		L132	-	-	-	1	1	1	1	1	1	4
		*L134**	*1*	*-*	*-*	*1*	*2*	*2*	*12*	*5*	*5*	*24*
		Total	*2*	*-*	*-*	*3*	*5*	*5*	*15*	*8*	*10*	*38*

No.	Kebele	Villages	Local Community Institutions#										
			Religious Institutions (Churches & Mosques)					Community Iddir Institutions				
			Churches			Mosques	Total	Burial Iddir	Stretcher Iddir	Oxen Iddir	Housing Iddir	Total
			Orthodox	Protestant	Catholic							
12	L17	L17	-	1	-	-	1	2	2	2	2	8
		R8*	-	1	-	1	2	1	1	1	1	4
		R9*	1	-	1	-	2	4	4	4	4	16
		Total	1	2	1	1	5	7	7	7	7	28
13	R4	R2	1	-	-	-	1	1	1	2	1	5
		R3	1	-	-	1	2	2	1	1	1	5
		R4	1	1	-	-	2	1	1	1	1	4
		R5	1	1	1	-	3	1	1	1	1	4
		Total	4	2	1	1	8	5	4	5	4	18
14	R7	R6	1	2	1	1	5	2	2	3	4	11
		R7	1	-	-	1	2	2	2	2	2	8
		Total	2	2	1	2	7	4	4	5	6	19
15	RUS51 (Mekane Selam)	R46	1	-	-	1	2	2	4	4	6	16
		R49*	1	-	-	1	2	2	10	4	6	22
		RUS50	1	-	-	1	2	2	4	3	6	15
		RUS51	1	-	-	1	2	2	6	5	8	21
		Total	4	-	-	4	8	8	24	16	26	74
16	R101	R101	1	-	-	1	2	2	3	4	6	15
		R127	1	-	-	1	2	1	2	1	2	6
		Total	2	-	-	2	4	3	5	5	8	21

341

No.	Kebele	Villages	Local Community Institutions#									
			Religious Institutions (Churches & Mosques)					Community *Iddir* Institutions				
			Churches			Mosques	Total	Burial *Iddir*	Stretcher *Iddir*	Oxen *Iddir*	Housing *Iddir*	Total
			Ortho-dox	Protes-tant	Catholic							
17	R104	R104@	-	-	-	10	10	1	10	10	10	31
18		Almu	1	-	-	1	2	2	-	-	-	2
19		Felege Selam	1	-	-	1	2	2	-	-	-	2
20		Addis Alem	1	-	1	1	2	2	-	-	-	2
	Total		36	20	9	42	107	111	202	122	182	617

Source: Wolde-Selassie Abbute survey (February - March 2001)

**The researcher's main study sites

*The researcher's study sub-sites

@Village abandoned by state-sponsored resettlers and occupied by later immigrant farmers

The roles of different community institutions (especially *iddir*) overlap in several contexts.

Appendix 2. A Brief Questionnaire to Collect Basic Population Data from the *Kebele* and Villages in the Pawe Special *Woreda*

1. Location

1.1 Kebele _____

1.2 Village _____

2. Different Category of Population

Different Categories of Population	Heads of Households			Family Members			Total
	Male	Female	Total	Male	Female	Total	
State-Sponsored Resettlers of the 1980s							
Voluntary & Displaced Immigrant Farmers							
Small Town Dwellers							
Total							

3. State-Sponsored Resettlers

3.1 Ethnic Background

Ethnic Background of Resettlers		Total
Amhara	*Wollo*	
	North Shoa	
	Gojjam	
	Gondar	
	Total	
Kambaata		
Hadiyya		
Oromo		
Wolaita		
Tigre		
Agaw /Seqota/		
Agaw /Gojjam/		
Others		
Total		

3.2 Religious Background

Religious Background of Resettlers		Total
Christian	Orthodox	
	Protestant	
	Catholic	
Muslim		
Total		

4. Voluntary and Displaced Immigrant Farmers

4.1 Ethnic Background

Ethnic Background of Immigrant Farmers		Total
Amhara	*Wollo*	
	North Shoa	
	Gojjam	
	Gondar	
	Total	
Kambaata		
Hadiyya		
Oromo		
Tigre		
Agaw /Gojjam/		
Others		
Total		

4.2 Religious Background

Religious Background of Immigrant Farmers		Total
Christian	Orthodox	
	Protestant	
	Catholic	
Muslim		
Total		

5. Local Community Institutions

5.1 Religious Institutions

Religious Institutions in the *Kebele* and Villages		Total
Churches	Orthodox	
	Protestant	
	Catholic	
Mosques		
Total		

5.2 Community *Iddir* Institutions

Village Community *Iddir*	Total
Burial *iddir*	
Stretcher *iddir*	
Oxen *iddir*	
Housing *iddir*	
Total	

Appendix 3. Ethiopian Calendar and the Gregorian Equivalent

Ethiopian Calendar and the Gregorian Equivalent		
No.	Ethiopian Calendar	Gregorian Equivalent
1	*Meskerem*	September 11- October 10
2	*Tikimt*	October 11 - November 9
3	*Hidar*	November 10 - December 9
4	*Tahsas*	December 10 - January 8
5	*Tir*	January 9 - February 7
6	*Yekatit*	February 8 - March 9
7	*Megabit*	March 10 - April 8
8	*Miyazia*	April 9 - May 8
9	*Ginbot*	May 9 - June 7
10	*Sene*	June 8 - July 7
11	*Hamle*	July 8 - August 6
12	*Nehase*	August 7 - September 5
13	*"Pagumen"*	September 6 - 10 or 11 every leap year

Ethnologie:
Forschung und Wissenschaft

Hartmut Zinser
Mythos des Mutterrechts
Um ein Nachwort ergänzte Neuauflage.
Im Anhang: Rezensionen der 1. Auflage
Was ist das Mutterrecht? In welchen Ländern und in welchen historischen Epochen hat es ein Mutterrecht oder eine Gynäkokratie gegeben, wie sahen oder sehen die gesellschaftlichen Verhältnisse und besonders die Geschlechterbeziehungen unter ihm aus?
Die vorliegende Arbeit bedient sich dennoch nicht der psychoanalytischen Methode in der Darstellung ihres Gegenstandes. Sie wählt die Form des Plädoyers, in dem die Argumente für und wider, auch solche, die sich der Symptomanalyse verdanken, dem Urteil des Lesers ausgesetzt und die Urteilsgründe zusammen mit den Interessen und Bedürfnissen, die in ihr wirksam sind, zur Diskussion gestellt werden.
Bd. 1, 1997, 100 S., 15,90 €, br.,
ISBN 3-8258-2554-X

Günther Schlee
Identities on the Move
Clanship and pastoralism in Northern Kenya (second edition 1994, first published in 1989). This is a title distributed by LIT Verlag. The book was first published by Manchester University Press in 1989. The distributed version is part of the second edition published by GIDEON S. WERE PRESS, Nairobi, Kenya in 1994.
Clans are normally thought of as contained within ethnic groups. In the Horn of Africa the pastoral Rendille, Gabbra, Sakuye and some Somalis of northern Kenya and southern Ethiopia have many clans in common. As a result the clans are not always smaller or less important than the ethnic groups. How such inter-ethnic relationships came about is the subject of this study many go back beyond ethnic divisions to over 400 years ago. The book also examines the uses to which they are put, for instance in managing herds.

Oral history is combined with cultural comparison and the analysis of social structure. The many original texts are themselves of linguistic interest. Blending synchronic and diachronic perspectives, the book synthesises historical ethnology in the Continental tradition with social anthropology. Historically it overturns some established ideas about how the Horn was settled. Anthropologically it shows how relations may exceed the bounds of the ethnic group as the conventional unit of study. It will be of interest to anthropologists, sociologists and social geographers or planners concerned with pastoral development.
Bd. 2, 1994, 288 S., 24,90 €, br.,
ISBN 3-8258-4800-0

Wim van Binsbergen
Intercultural Encounters
African and anthropological lessons towards a philosophy of interculturality
This book brings together fifteen essays investigating aspects of interculturality. Like is author, it operates at the borderline between social anthropology and intercultural philosophy. It seeks to make a contribution to intercultural philosophy, by formulating with great precision and painful honesty the lessons deriving from extensive intercultural experiences as an anthropologist. It culminating section presents an intercultural philosophy revolving on the tenet 'Cultures do not exist'. The kaleidoscopic nature of intercultural experiences is reflected in the diversity of these texts. Many belong to a field that could be described as 'meta-anthropology', others are more clearly philosophical; occasionally they spill over into belles lettres, ancient history, and comparative cultural and religious studies. The ethnographic specifics supporting the arguments are diverse, deriving from various African situations in which the author has conducted participatory field research (Tunisia, Zambia, Botswana, and South Africa).
Bd. 4, 2003, 616 S., 40,90 €, br.,
ISBN 3-8258-6783-8

LIT Verlag Münster – Hamburg – Berlin – Wien – London
Grevener Str./Fresnostr. 2 48159 Münster
Tel.: 0251 – 23 50 91 – Fax: 0251 – 23 19 72
e-Mail: vertrieb@lit-verlag.de – http://www.lit-verlag.de

Göttinger Studien zur Ethnologie

hrsg. vom Institut für Ethnologie
der Universität Göttingen
Redaktion: Prof. Dr. Ulrich Braukämper
und Prof. Dr. Brigitta Hauser-Schäublin

Veronika Fuest
"A job, a shop, and loving business"
Lebensweisen gebildeter Frauen in
Liberia
Bd. 1, 1996, 350 S., 30,90 €, br.,
ISBN 3-8258-2644-9

Klaus Hesse
Staatsdiener, Händler und
Landbesitzer
Die Khatri und der Bazar von Mandi
(Himachal Pradesh, Indien)
Bd. 2, 1996, 358 S., 35,90 €, br.,
ISBN 3-8258-2645-7

Martin Rössler
Der Lohn der Mühe
Kulturelle Dimensionen von 'Wert' und
'Arbeit' im Kontext ökonomischer
Transformation in Süd-Sulawesi,
Indonesien
Bd. 3, 1997, 592 S., 45,90 €, br.,
ISBN 3-8258-3434-4

Renate Kulick-Aldag
Die Göttinger Völkerkunde und der
Nationalsozialismus zwischen 1925
und 1950
Bd. 4, 2000, 136 S., 24,90 €, br.,
ISBN 3-8258-4469-2

Jutta Borchardt
Von Nomaden zu Gemüsebauern
Auf der Suche nach yörük-Identität bei
den Saçıkaralı in der Südwest-Türkei
Bd. 5, 2001, 200 S., 24,90 €, br.,
ISBN 3-8258-4470-6

Holger Kirscht
Ein Dorf in Nordost-Nigeria
Politische und wirtschaftliche
Transformation der bäuerlichen Kanuri-
Gesellschaft
Die Arbeit ist das Ergebnis von rund zwei Jah-
ren intensiver Feldforschung in dem Kanuri-Dorf
Marte und seiner Umgebung im nigerianischen
Tschadbecken. Der Autor hat mit teilnehmen-
der Beobachtung die Lebens- und Arbeitswelt
der Bewohner dieses regenzeitlich teilweise
überfluteten Gebietes untersucht und eine umfas-
sende Dokumentation ihrer landwirtschaftlichen
Kognitionen, Techniken, Erträge sowie ihrer
Konsum- und Vermarktungsstrategien erstellt.
Ethnographisch von besonderem Interesse ist die
detaillierte Beschreibung eines nach den Gestir-
nen ausgerichteten Agrarkalenders. Die in der
Dorfstudie gewonnenen empirischen Daten werden auf einer Makroebene mit der Analyse der
sozio-ökonomischen und politischen Gegebenhei-
ten des Kanuri-Staates Borno verknüpft. Dabei
reicht der historische Untersuchungsrahmen von
den 1990er Jahren ins frühe 19. Jahrhundert
zurück.
Bd. 6, 2001, 360 S., 30,90 €, br.,
ISBN 3-8258-4494-3

Michael Dickhardt
Das Räumliche des Kulturellen
Entwurf zu einer
kulturanthropologischen Raumtheorie
am Beispiel Fiji
Bd. 7, 2001, 328 S., 25,90 €, br.,
ISBN 3-8258-5188-5

Dorothea Deterts
Die Gabe im Netz sozialer
Beziehungen
Zur sozialen Reproduktion der
Kanak in der paicî-Sprachregion
um Koné (Neukaledonien)
Das Phänomen des Gabentausches ist eines
der klassischen Themen der ethnologischen
Forschung im melanesischen Raum. Die Ver-
knüpfung der sozialen, religiösen, politischen und
wirtschaftlichen Bereiche im Gabentausch steht
dabei im Vordergrund. Die vorliegende Studie
untersucht die Bedeutung des Gabentausches für
das soziale Gefüge der Kanak und geht dabei
der Frage von sozialer Reproduktion und sozialer
Transformation nach.
Die Studie beruht auf einer 15-monatigen Feldforschung in der paicî-Sprachregion um Koné, im
Nordwesten der Hauptinsel von Neukaledonien,
das bis vor kurzem ein Übersee-Territorium
Frankreichs war und seit 1999 einen autonomen
Status besitzt. Im Mittelpunkt steht die Analyse
der zeitgenössischen Tauschsysteme in den Le-
benszykluszeremonien der paicî-Kanak und die
Bedeutung der im Gabentausch definierten so-
zialen Beziehungen für die Tradition und für die
Konstruktion einer neuen kulturellen Identität.
Bd. 8, 2002, 336 S., 25,90 €, br.,
ISBN 3-8258-5656-9

LIT Verlag Münster – Hamburg – Berlin – Wien – London
Grevener Str./Fresnostr. 2 48159 Münster
Tel.: 0251 – 23 50 91 – Fax: 0251 – 23 19 72
e-Mail: vertrieb@lit-verlag.de – http://www.lit-verlag.de

Ulrich Braukämper
Islamic History and Culture in Southern Ethiopia
Collected Essays
Studies on Islam in Ethiopia have long been neglected although Islam is the religious confession of almost half of the Ethiopian population. The essays focus on the following topics: *Islamic Principalities in Southeast Ethiopia between the 13th and 16 th Centuries; Notes on the Islamization and the Muslim Shrines of the Ḥarär Plateau; The Sanctuary of Shaikh Ḥusayn and the Oromo-Somali Connections in Bale; The Islamization of the Arsi-Oromo; Medieval Muslim Survivals as a Stimulating Factor in the Re-Islamization of Southeastern Ethiopia.* The essays are based on the study of written records and on field research in southern parts of the country carried out during the first half of the 1970s.
Bd. 9, 2002, 208 S., 20,90 €, br.,
ISBN 3-8258-5671-2

Brigitta Hauser-Schäublin;
Michael Dickhardt (Hg.)
Kulturelle Räume – räumliche Kultur
Zur Neubestimmung des Verhältnisses zweier fundamentaler Kategorien menschlicher Praxis
Das Verhältnis von Raum und Kultur wird zunehmend fragwürdig. Erschienen Kulturen lange Zeit fest in Räumen verankert, so haben Globalisierung und Postmoderne dazu geführt, dass Raum und Kultur selbst in der Alltagserfahrung schon längst nicht mehr eindeutig aufeinander verweisen. Die feste Verbindung einer Kultur mit ihren definierbaren Territorien und Orten löst sich zusehends – ein Phänomen, das oft mit Schlagworten wie Entterritorialisierung oder Entörtlichung benannt wird. Doch wenn Kultur nicht mehr einem Raum zugeordnet werden kann und wenn Räume in ihrer Bedeutung für Kultur vieldeutig werden – wie kann ihr Verhältnis dann sinnvoll bestimmt werden, um die räumliche Dimension des Kulturellen und die kulturelle Dimension des Räumlichen beschreibbar zu machen? Die Autoren und Autorinnen dieses Bandes versuchen vor diesem Hintergrund, aus einer ethnologischen Perspektive das Verhältnis zwischen Raum und Kultur auf der Grundlage

empirischer Studien aus Bali, Neuguinea, Indien, Indonesien und Fiji zu bestimmen. Es zeigt sich dabei, dass Entterritorialisierung und Entörtlichung keineswegs zu einer Enträumlichung des Kulturellen führen: Das Räumliche ist und bleibt fundamental für das Kulturelle, als konkreter Ort genauso wie als formendes Moment menschlicher Praxis. Raum und Kultur sind nach wie vor nur in ihrer wechselseitigen Bezogenheit zu verstehen, auch wenn sie in ihrem Verhältnis zueinander neu bestimmt werden müssen.
Bd. 10, 2003, 280 S., 25,90 €, br.,
ISBN 3-8258-6799-4

Elfriede Hermann; Birgitt Röttger-Rössler (Hg.)
Lebenswege im Spannungsfeld lokaler und globaler Prozesse
Person, Selbst und Emotion in der ethnologischen Biografieforschung
Lebensgeschichten eröffnen einen guten Zugang zu persönlichen Erfahrungen in lokal-global vernetzten Welten. Sie geben Aufschluss darüber, welche Handlungsmöglichkeiten und Handlungsbeschränkungen für Einzelne durch das Ineinandergreifen von globalen und lokalen Prozessen entstehen, welche Wege innerhalb dieses Terrains beschritten werden, und wie diese in der Retrospektive bewertet werden. Biografische und autobiografische Zeugnisse dienen den Autorinnen und Autoren dieses Bandes als Ausgangspunkte für ihre Betrachtungen kulturspezifischer Repräsentationen von Lebenswegen und damit von Person, Selbst und Emotionen inmitten neu entstandener Machtverhältnisse.
Mit Beiträgen von
Birgitt Röttger-Rössler
Wolfgang Kempf
Andrea Lauser
Elfriede Hermann
Anette Schade
Lüder Tietz
Volker Heeschen
Sabine Dedenbach-Salazar Sáenz
Camilo Robayo
Helmut Schindler
Sonja Speeter-Blaudszun
Bd. 11, 2003, 296 S., 29,90 €, br.,
ISBN 3-8258-7049-9

LIT Verlag Münster – Hamburg – Berlin – Wien – London
Grevener Str./Fresnostr. 2 48159 Münster
Tel.: 0251 – 23 50 91 – Fax: 0251 – 23 19 72
e-Mail: vertrieb@lit-verlag.de – http://www.lit-verlag.de